DRUID MAGIC

Bring Your Inner Druid to Life!

Druid Magic offers the adventure of awakening the Druid in you! You can be a Druid rooted in the spiritual tradition of your ancestors. You can be a Druid whose creativity and spiritual strength emerge from deep within. You can be a Druid who knows the sacred power of the rivers, hills, animals, and groves. You can be a Druid who honors sovereignty within yourself, within all beings, and within the land itself. The renaissance is happening now, and Druidry is alive and well!

As magicians, healers, scholars, and bards, the Druids were the wisdom keepers of the ancient Celts. This book combines history, mythology, and hands-on activities to show you how to bring the knowledge of the Druids into your life.

- Learn the art of shapeshifting.
- Discover the meaning of Ogham divination.
- Perform a Druid ritual in your backyard.
- Embark on a mystical journey to the Otherworlds.
- Immerse yourself in the wisdom of the Druids and enter the realm of magic.

About the Authors

Maya Magee Sutton, Ph.D., has taught courses for twenty years at the University of New Mexico, where she originated the Celtic Studies concentration. She teaches Celtic Mythology and Urban Druidry. Dr. Sutton holds Irish and U.S. citizenship.

Nicholas R. Mann is the author of several books on the Celtic tradition, including *The Isle of Avalon* and *The Keltic Power Symbols*. Although a Briton of Scots descent, he chooses to live in the forests of New Mexico.

To Write to the Authors

If you wish to contact the authors or would like more information about this book, please write to the authors in care of Llewellyn Worldwide and we will forward your request. Both the authors and the publisher appreciate hearing from you and learning of your enjoyment of this book and how it has helped you. Llewellyn Worldwide cannot guarantee that every letter written to the authors can be answered, but all will be forwarded. Please write to:

Maya M. Sutton & Nicholas R. Mann
℅ Llewellyn Worldwide
P.O. Box 64383, Dept. K481-2
St. Paul, MN 55164-0383, U.S.A.

Please enclose a self-addressed, stamped envelope for reply, or $1.00 to cover costs. If outside U.S.A., enclose international postal reply coupon.

THE PRACTICE OF CELTIC WISDOM

DRUID MAGIC

MAYA MAGEE SUTTON, PH.D.

AND

NICHOLAS R. MANN

2002
Llewellyn Publications
St. Paul, MN 55164-0383 U.S.A.

SECOND EDITION, Revised
Second Printing, 2002

First Edition, one printing, 2000.

Cover design: William Merlin Cannon
Editing and book design: Tom Lewis
Editing of revised edition: Karen K. Karsten

Library of Congress Cataloging-in-Publication Data

Sutton, Maya Magee, 1938–
    Druid magic : the practice of Celtic wisdom / Maya Magee Sutton and Nicholas.—1st ed.
       p. cm.
    Includes bibliographical references (p.) and index.
    ISBN 1-56718-481-2
    1. Magic, Celtic. 2. Druids and Druidism—Miscellanea. I. Mann, Nicholas R. II. Title.

BF1622.C45 S88 2000
133.4'3'089916—dc21
                                                    99-057358

Llewellyn Publications
A Division of Llewellyn Worldwide, Ltd.
P.O. Box 64383, Dept. K481-2
St. Paul, MN 55164-0383, U.S.A.
http://www.llewellyn.com

 Printed in the United States of America on recycled paper

Contents

Part I—Applying Druid Lore

Part II—From Past to Present

Part III—Advanced Training

Acknowledgments

We are immensely grateful to all the translators who labored so long and hard to make the early Irish and Welsh texts available in English. Without Lady Augusta Gregory, Thomas Kinsella, Jeffrey Gantz, Arthur H. Leahy, Tom P. Cross, Clark H. Slover, Fergus Kelly, Erynn Rowan Laurie, P. L. Henry, Caitlín and John Matthews, Kuno Meyer, Ella Young, Lucy Faraday, Elizabeth Gray, Cecille O'Rahilly, Standish Hayes O'Grady, and all their publishers, we would be unable to present the primary Celtic source material in this book.

We also thank Miranda Green, Peter Berresford Ellis, Peter Harbison, Barry Raftery, Ronald Hutton, and the authors of the many books on Celtic history which provided our factual data; and John O'Donohue and Michael Dames for their fine inspirational works. We are indebted to Ellen Evert Hopman, Searles O'Dubhain, and J. L. Young for help on finer points of translation and detail. Especial thanks go to: Valencia de la Vega, Amy L. Atkins, Catherine Wishart, and Nancy Dye for their suggestions; to the Sandia Mountain Grove for their inspiration and example; and to Philip Carr-Gomm for his valued and continued support.

The authors are grateful to Llewellyn Publications for putting this book out into the world. While acknowledging the contributions of all the people above, we are responsible for the contents of the book, and any shortcomings and errors are our own.

Preface

Three people who will please the Gods: they who love all living beings with all their heart, they who love every beautiful thing with all their strength, and they who seek every knowledge with all their understanding.
—A Triad of Druid Wisdom

Many people today think that hardly anything is known about the spiritual traditions of our ancestors. They think that the knowledge of the Druids is all but lost. But this is not true. The reality is that there is so much information about Druidry, and there are so many new developments in Druidry as a living spirituality, that we need guides to help us follow this ancient but ever-new tradition. This book by Nicholas Mann and Maya Sutton is just such a guide. There are many books now on the history of the Druids—on their philosophy and their spirituality—but there are very few books like this one. This book will take you by the hand and show you in a practical, down-to-earth way how you can walk the Druid path today.

If you feel moved to accept the invitation of this book, a whole new world will open for you—a world of magic and inspiration. The purpose of Nicholas' and Maya's book is to show you how this new world is both ancient and eternally fresh. *Druid Magic* will show you how Druidry can act as a wellspring of spiritual energy and direction. This energy springs from a source rooted in the Timeless, but it is anchored here in this world of Time, in the ancient memories of myth and legend. This book will show you how to use Druid magic today to follow a path of great depth and beauty.

Philip Carr-Gomm, Chief of the Order of Bards, Ovates and Druids
Lewes, Britain
Beltane 1998

Introduction

Do you describe yourself as a Druid? Do you want to know what Druidry means? Do you have Celtic ancestry? If you want to come home to the tradition of your ancestors, this book will guide you into the spiritual path of Druidry. If you want to practice Druid magic, roll up your mystical sleeves, and explore Part I! If you want to know who the Celts and the Druids really were, read Part II for its information. If you want to know the primary tenets of Druidry, you will learn them here. If you want to visit the Celtic Otherworlds and lie in the Streambed of Inspiration, then make the journey on into Part III.

Druid Magic offers the adventure of awakening the Druid in you! You can be a Druid rooted in the spiritual tradition of your ancestors. You can be a Druid with creativity and spiritual strength emerging from deep within. You can be a Druid who knows the sacred power of the rivers, hills, animals, and groves. You can be a Druid who honors sovereignty within yourself, within all beings, and in the land itself. The renaissance is happening now, and Druidry is alive and well!

The path of Druidry emerges as a glimmering strand from the fabric of Celtic culture and civilization. The original Druids were the bards, the storytellers, the ritualists. They were the scholars, teachers, judges, healers, and seers of the ancient Celtic peoples. *Druid* may literally mean "oak wise," from *dru* or *drus*, derivatives from the Indo-European root language, meaning "oak," and *wid*, "to know" or "to see." More likely, it originated from *dru* or *drui*, meaning "firm" and "solid," from which the words "true," "oak," and "tree" also derive.[1] In even earlier times, the name may have applied to any wise man or woman. The shaman, the herbalist, the midwife, the seer, the storyteller, may all have been called the *Dru* (plus suffix), generically meaning a "wise one" or a "truthful one."

After about 500 B.C.E.,[2] however, Druids of a different kind emerged. They organized the knowledge of the Celtic branch of the Native European Tradition so it could be sustained and serve more complex social needs. It is this organizing of Druidry that distinguishes it from shamanism and the school of magical arts later known as witchcraft. Their organization made Druids an easy target for persecution. Picture them as a recognizable group, in distinctive and colorful dress, wielding symbols of authority, teaching select students, and presiding at the center of major rituals. Because Druidry was transmitted mostly by oral tradition, it was effectively destroyed by the Romans and also by its Christian opponents. Apart from such rare inscriptions as the Coligny Calendar, very few traces remain which have come down to us from Druid hands. Greek and Roman Classical writings described them, and Celtic myths and stories were recorded by Christian scribes in the early literature of Ireland and Wales: the voice of Druidry was left to be forgotten.

We therefore have three main sources of evidence for our reconstruction of Druidry: 1) Celtic stories that have survived in folklore and literature, 2) Greek and Roman writings, along with some inscriptions on statues and temples, and 3) material evidence retrieved by archaeology. Each of these sources is partial and has its own difficulties. Firstly, the Celtic stories of Ireland and Wales were in some cases written down centuries after the era they purport to describe. Irish society had gone through major changes during this time, and it is very difficult to extract what may be genuinely Druidic from the texts. Secondly, the Classical writers of Greece and Rome were extremely biased in their views, often writing second- or third-hand accounts. Finally, the archaeological evidence comes to us separated from its context. We often have no idea what a bronze decorative object was for, where it was worn, and what it meant.

You can see, then, why it is very difficult to obtain from historical sources an accurate picture of the Druids. The muddle we inherit leaves us with images of white-bearded old men clutching golden sickles in some dark and bloodstained grove in the middle of the forest!

History is always a one-sided version of the past. History is what people—usually the conquerors with all of their idiosyncracies, biases, and beliefs—chose to record, as seen through the eyes of people today with all of their idiosyncracies, biases, and beliefs about what they choose to remember. There is no such thing as objective history.

It might be advantageous if we rejected outright the word "Druid" because of the preconceptions and strict historical definitions surrounding it, but the word does connect us with a living spiritual tradition. If critics say it is hard to discover and impossible to recreate what is authentic about this tradition, we answer that the value of the Druid Tradition is measured by how it helps us to live our lives now. How is Druidry relevant to us today? Modern Druids do not attempt to recreate the past in historically unobtainable detail. They choose to lie in the stream of a spiritual tradition that, like the Celtic wells of inspiration and plenty, is always pouring forth its abundance. We invite you to enter the stream with us, as *Druid Magic* unfolds.

This book relies on the Celtic myths in the form they have come down to us, and, to a lesser extent, upon the archaeological evidence. The authors believe that these sources give the best opportunity for the ancient Druid tradition to speak for itself. We do not believe, however, that there is any benefit in attempting to remain true only to what Druidry was in the past. Because the authors feel that Druidry is a living tradition, the emphasis in this book is on what we make of Druid wisdom and how we apply it in our lives today.

We cover the three areas of Druid study. These constituted the wisdom of the bards, who offer poetry, myths, and music; of the ovates, who are the seers and magicians; and of the Druids themselves, who are the judges and ritualists.

Druid Magic does not cover every aspect of the Druid tradition. There are other excellent writers and teachers of Celtic lore and Druidry. They, like us, have their area of specialty. Our purpose is to concentrate on the core tenets and magical skills of Druidry, drawing them forth, piece by piece, from the Celtic myths. We examine the implications that arise from them, and illustrate how these principles can be applied. As you learn and apply the knowledge contained in *Druid Magic*, we can't guarantee that you will grow a long white beard! We do know that you will become absorbed in Druidry and become more certain and aware of your role in the Universe.

Notes

1. It is very difficult to know what the Indo-European root words were or meant as they depend upon reconstruction from the languages derived from them. All we can say about the root form *dru-* is that in later languages it appears as the word for "firm," "true," "tree," and "oak." The ending *-id* is even less clear, and possibly originates among Latin authors as simply the plural form of Dru.

2. We use B.C.E., "Before the Common Era" instead of B.C., and C.E., the "Common Era" instead of A.D. This avoids any implicit theism.

A Note on Pronunciation

Dear Readers—

You will see words from the Irish and Welsh languages in this book. As with the majority of European languages, they are descendants of the early Indo-European ancestor tongue. While they are therefore related to English, French, and German, among others, the Celtic languages bear little obvious resemblance to any of the more common European languages, and may look strange.

Their pronunciation can seem stranger still! There are no strict rules for spelling; in fact, a word's spelling changes depending on its place in the syntax of the sentence. While this book does not set out to teach such nuances in the Celtic languages, the authors hope that it will inspire readers to learn more about this rich linguistic tradition.

In *Druid Magic*, words in titles are given exactly as the translators wrote them, so you may notice inconsistencies there. Look in the Guide (page 297) at the end of this book for the commonly accepted spellings and pronunciations of proper names found in Celtic mythology and lore.

Part I

Applying Druid Lore

Welcome! Part I takes you directly into the magical realms of the Druids! You will learn to protect yourself and others, to shapeshift, and to make Druid tools. You will delve into divination, your magus power, sacred sexuality, rituals, and initiation. This first chapter introduces the workings of the Universe that bring about Druid magic. This includes practicing harmony with nature and bringing forth your eternal Self. Dragons, myths, and your own talents are the stuff of magic.

Chapter 1

EXPLORING DRUID MAGIC
(DRAÍOCHT)

It was in ships that the Tuatha Dé Danann, the "Tribe of the Goddess Danu," came. They came from the North, and the clouds and mists that concealed them made it easy for them to land in Ireland at Beltane, the first day of May, unseen and unopposed by the Fir Bolg. From where they came and fought their struggle for poetry, truth, and perfect wisdom, were four great cities: Falias, Gorias, Finias, and rich Murias. It was in these cities that four wise poets and teachers taught the Tuatha Dé Danann their magical skill and occult knowledge. And from these four cities they brought their four greatest treasures: From Falias they brought the Stone of Fál, the Lia Fáil, the Stone of Virtue and of Destiny, which cried out when touched by the rightful king. From Gorias they brought the Spear of Victory, and no battle was ever won against it. From Finias they brought the Sword of Truth, and of those who deserved its stroke none ever recovered. And from Murias they brought the Cauldron of the Dagda, the Cauldron of Plenty, from which no company ever went away unsatisfied.[1]

You are the magician! When you know who you are, where you have come from and why you are here, you can activate your magic. Druid magic works with our eternal Self, the part of us that knows all that there is. Druid magic comes from a true understanding of the powers of the eternal Self, our divine being that incarnates in many lives.

The whole of this book is based on this premise, not on the glamour of slipping through the cracks of time or conjuring something out of nothing. The important thing to keep in mind here—in case you are disappointed and wanted to time-travel and materialize objects—is that the miracle is before us right now! From the eternal Self it is possible to bring about every manifestation in its rightful time and place. As we proceed, you will stay on track if you keep returning to these questions: Who am I? What is my eternal nature? How do I live and what do I bring forth in the world? The popular notion of magic is that it accomplishes things through means that are extra-ordinary, even miraculous. This is a false view of Druid magic. A miracle is, by defin-ition, something that could not happen according to the normal function of the uni-verse or the laws of physics. It must therefore happen according to some supernatural means or by some secret law. In contrast, Druid magic works according to the natur-al means and laws that are available to everyone. It is miraculous in a deeper sense. It accomplishes things according to the ordinary way the universe functions. Druid magic observes nature, dances and works with it, rather than attempting to do things out of the natural order.

This book focuses on developing such skills rather than on making boils erupt on someone's nose! In this book you will not find lists of spells for acquiring wealth, a lover, fame, or friends. Druid magic is for self-growth, for the development of abilities and consciousness. It increases awareness of unity with all life and of power-from-within, to use the term of the priestess and author, Starhawk. This opening chapter presents a variety of practices to demonstrate your own power to yourself.

For the Druid, the universe is the true miracle! The utter sophistication of nature is often beyond our understanding. Its complex structure and interdependencies, its experiments in cellular cooperation and evolving forms are truly marvelous. The life of nature is our life, and we are a part of its great community. If something were to happen outside of the workings of the universe—the common definition of a mira-cle—it would mean that the universe as we know it could no longer exist. The whole space-time continuum would unravel if, say, a single episode of time-travel took place, or a distortion such as matter appearing out of nowhere occurred.

Another way of understanding Druid magic is to picture a situation where you wish to accomplish a certain goal. Say you would like to find a soul partner. It will not do much good to complain that only wretched examples of humanity are out there, nor will it help to rub a lucky charm. You must put forth what you want, in the form of your true self. You develop your spirit, values, and talents so they project your radiant being. You then stay in a positive state of mind, meeting new people or reconnecting with ones you know. They will see you for who you truly are, and will be attracted to you. Your task is to center your eternal Self and follow a natural course of action, rather than waiting for some supernatural or glamourous power to do it for you. The tried and tested pathways of energy are magical in their own way. Have you ever written down an intention, set it aside and forgotten about it, only to find the piece of paper a year later and realize the exact wish had come true? Druid magic will help you enhance such natural, untapped abilities.

As a test of Druid magic, set yourself a goal that is beyond your current ability. State what it is you wish to accomplish—perhaps you want more courage because you need to confront an adversary. Create an altar on which you put items that represent your personal power. Add photos and drawings that have meaning, including one of a heart: remember, "courage" comes from the Latin word *cor*, for heart. Bring in helpful elements of nature, such as fire in the form of sparklers or huge candles. Eat passion-fruit and hazelnuts! For the Celts, hazelnuts embody inspiration and wisdom. Imagine bear cubs within you that you must protect. Set a time and date for the meeting. As the time gets closer, practice a script of what you will say to the adversary. Settle on a symbol you will hold in mind to represent your goal; an example might be clasped hands when an agreement is reached. Talk to your breath and ask it to stand by you under stress. Say lots of prayers. Practice looks of courage in the mirror and register what they feel like inside your face and body. Call on your spirit allies, your mythic ancestors and hero/ines to be with you right through to the end. Remove your expectations as much as you can, and affirm your desired goal. Ask for the greatest good for all concerned. Take with you a small image of your most courageous ally or power animal. Put empowerment symbols in your pockets or wear them if possible, to touch them if you need a burst of energy during the confrontation. When all this personal magic is in place, do it!

We Are the Gifted People

The story that opens this chapter comes from the *Book of Invasions*, which recounts successive takings of Ireland by invaders. Early on, the inhabitants of Ireland were the Tuatha Dé Danann, the Children or Tribe of the Goddess Danu. They were superb at enchantment and all forms of Druid magic. They used these against the Fir Bolg and the Fomorians, and then against the Milesians, Celtic invaders who were said to have sailed to Ireland from northern Spain. The Tuatha Dé Danann were called the *Aes Dana*, the Skilled or Gifted People, and later this name was given to the Druids and poets. These "skilled ones" offered the exceptional gifts they had developed in themselves.

The early Irish and Welsh sources are full of descriptions of Druid magic. The modern Irish dictionary tells us that *draíocht* means both magic and spells. It comes from the root word *draoi,* meaning magician, sorcerer, or Druid. This etymology connects Druids solidly with magic. There are many Druidic stories of transformation and otherworldly power, using magical objects, and casting spells. Here we explore what kind of magic they might have practiced and what we might want to do with it. We no longer know exactly how to perform spells and enchantments the way they are described in Celtic myths, but we have many clues. Overall, the ancient Druids had ways of fending off foes, creating safety for their tribes, and making surroundings sacred for their practices. We have ways of doing these things today.

Awakening Magical Power

You can only perform true magic from the place of the Self. When your true divine Self reigns within your Being the elements, powers, and realms of nature will be accessible to you and in harmony with the whole. When the eternal Self is awake, wisdom, perspective, judgement, inspiration, and skill will be present to accomplish magic. Only then will Druid magic be possible.

How does this translate into practical magic for you? Not hard to tell (as the Celtic myths like to say): Who are you? Why are you here? What do you do well? When you delight a child, how do you do it? When you hunker down with your best friend for true sharing, exactly what do you bring forth from yourself? When you have helped someone to forget physical pain, how did you lift them out of the hurt and create another kind of reality for them? That is Druid magic.

What talents do you have? Do you give excellent advice? Can you make an audience spellbound with your music? Are you a healer? Can you fix things and make things out of spare parts (make something out of nothing)? Do others consider you helpful? Are you genuinely funny? Can you mime and dramatize? These are all magical gifts. What do you enjoy doing? Name a few of the chief skills you have developed in yourself. Such a checklist will help you to discover the warp and woof of your True Self, whence magic comes.

There are many ways to awaken the magical power of the Self. It is up to each one of us to find what works. For one person, meditation is appropriate; for another, a certain body posture brings awareness. Perhaps you need a more dynamic action such as toning until your voice reaches deep, rousing, confident, powerful ranges. Nicholas likes walking in nature, incanting, or concentrating on his Druid's Egg (described later in chapter 3) to bring him to awareness. Maya awakens her powers by sitting in the middle of a specially created altar. Whatever method you use, give it the full and willing cooperation of your whole being. Always remember that you cannot achieve magic if your heart is not in it, if your mind is resisting the material and the body is uncomfortable.

Another way to awaken your magical power is by getting swept away in the Celtic myths. Try to imagine the difference of living in the oral world of the Celts rather than in our written world. Imagine that you take everything in by listening. You remember what you take in because you are emotionally affected. You produce your output by reciting poetry or singing. An oral world follows this cycle of the heart and emotions. Storytellers ranked high in Celtic society because the word had great power. People listened closely to the legends and myths, spellbound with fascination. Listening intently to the myths told by master poets created an effect on the audience akin to spells. You know yourself that a story enters your awareness differently if you listen to it than if you read it. When you hear a story it goes into the right hemisphere of the brain where you create pictures that help you to remember it entirely. Certain parts might strike you deeply and stay with you for a long time. This is the stuff of *draíocht*! On the other hand, when you read a story, it goes into the brain's left hemisphere for comprehending written language. You may have to take notes or reread the story even to partially remember it. This is work, not magic.

So read the Celtic myths aloud. When you receive the mythic message and draw it into yourself, whatever magic it contains transfers directly to you. Celtic stories are divided into categories. The bards told appropriate ones at special events such as a birth, a voyage, or a battle, for good health or fortune, and as teachings during the winter months. From their repertoire of hundreds of tales, they could make an audience weep, gasp, laugh, or ponder, or else color their hearts with other hues. Harpists too had a repertoire of music that could make people cry, sleep, or laugh. We recommend that you draw the myths into yourself and absorb their entrancing powers, absorb their ability to influence the many major events in your life.

Curses (*Mallachtí*)

Because of the potential abuse of satire and curses, we do not advocate their use and we ourselves do not practice them. As with human and animal sacrifice, which was also part of the Celtic Druid world, we do not carry forward all the ancient customs. In the last 2,000 years—fortunately—humanity has arrived at some improvements such as civil rights and humanistic, cooperative management. Still, the old tales mention that Druids used curses unfairly:

> *"An it is for refusing the love of Fear Doirche, the Dark Druid of the Mean of Dea," she said, "I was put in this shape. And through the length of three years … I have lived the life of a wild deer in a far part of Ireland, and I am hunted like a wild deer."* [2]

The word *mallaigh* means to damn someone or something. We do not advocate this, but can give three examples of how cursing was formerly practiced by the Druids. In the British Museum there is a lead fragment found in the Roman layer of London, on which is engraved a curse against a woman. There is no proof that a Druid composed this, but it is from a period when Druids used this type of verbal magic:

> *I curse Tretia Maria and her life and mind and memory and liver and lungs mixed up together, and her words, thoughts and memory, thus may she be unable to speak what things are concealed . . .*

A second example is from the Roman writer Tacitus. He reported that females of the Isle of Anglesey in northwest Wales cursed and threatened invading Roman forces in 60 C.E. when the Romans were battling the Druids throughout Britain. The curses failed and the Druids died. Scholars usually assume that the women were Druidesses, although it is possible they were Celtic women who took part in warfare:

> *On the shore stood the opposing army* [Welsh-Britons] *with its dense array of armed warriors, while between the ranks dashed women in black attire like the Furies, with hair disheveled, waving brands. All round the druids . . . scared our soldiers.* [3]

A third example is the power of satire. Celtic poets used the word for both praise and insult. If a poet's fee was unlawfully withheld or if he was dishonored, he might lampoon the opponent. This could cause blisters to arise on the other person's face, and no doubt the lampoon was repeated as gossip, thus multiplying its harmful effect within the tribe. These powers apparently became so misused that King Aed MacAinmirech and other chieftains of Ireland, meeting in 574 C.E., officially banished all the master poets from the land. They resolved the dispute by imposing stricter regulations on the poets.

The curse is alive and well in modern Ireland: "May the snails devour his corpse and the rains do harm worse, and may the devil sweep the hairy creature soon!" "The devil swallow him sideways." "My curse on you and ruin to you, you lying, thieving rascal." "May you be afflicted with the itch and have no nails to scratch with!" "May the seven terriers of hell sit on the spool of your breast and bark in at your soul-case."[4]

Since we gave the caveat that we do not advocate curses, there is little more to mention except damage from the occasional curse aimed at yourself. The politically correct term at the moment for cursing yourself is "negative self-talk." This takes the form of phrases such as "I'm so stupid! I can't believe I did that!" We don't recommend this, since self-cursing keeps us locked into ruts of abuse and harmful conditioning. On the other hand, positive self-talk—"I feel great for doing that!"—accomplishes amazing things. Perhaps one of the roles of modern Druids is to use modern wisdom to accomplish magic.

By Earth, Sky, and Sea

Let us examine the Irish story *Cath Maige Tuired*, the "Battle of Moy Tura," from the *Book of Invasions*, to understand how the Celts perceived magic. In this scene the Tuatha Dé Danann are beset by the Fomorians, and Lugh of the Long Arm has come to help them. Lugh calls an assembly of the Tuatha Dé Danann. He asks each profession how they will help to defeat the Fomorians and each answers with a different magical practice.

> *Lugh called together all the Tuatha Dé Danann to make plans for battle. He asked the Magicians what they could do to help them.*
>
> *"This is what we can do," they said. "The twelve chief mountains of Ireland will fight for you . . . and will roll their tops down upon the Fomor."*

Then Lugh asked the Cup-Bearers what help they could give.

"We will bring the twelve chief lochs of Ireland before the Fomor, and no mat-ter how great their thirst they will find no water in them. But the men of the Tuatha Dé Danann will find drink in them if they were to fight for seven years."

Then Lugh asked what the Druids would do to help them.

"We will rain three showers of fire upon the Fomor," they said. "We will take from them two-thirds of their bravery, their skill at arms and their strength, and the sickness of not passing urine will be upon their bodies. But every breath of the Tuatha Dé Danann will increase their bravery and strength and skill at arms, and even if they are in battle for seven years they will never become sick or weary."

Then Lugh asked the three Battle Goddesses what they would do to help.

"It is easy to say that," they said. "We will put an enchantment on the trees and the stones and sods of the earth, and they will rise up and be an armed host against the Fomor and put them to the rout."

Then Lugh asked what the Poets would do to help them.

"Not hard to answer," they said. "We will stand on a hill top at sunrise, with our backs to a thorn tree and a stone and a thorn in our hands, and make a satire that will put such shame on them they will not be able to stand against fighting men."

Then Lugh asked what the Smiths would do to help.

"Even if the men of Ireland fight for seven years, every sword or spear that is broken will have a new one put in its place. And no spear made by us will miss its mark," they said, "and that is more than the smiths of the Fomor can do."

Then Lugh asked what the Physicians would do to help them.

"Every man that is wounded," they said, "unless his marrow is cut through or his head struck off, we will make whole again on the morrow."

In this way Lugh asked every craftsman and poet and Druid and man and woman of the Tuatha Dé Danann in turn what they could do, so that each one felt within them the spirit of a noble king or of a queen or of a great lord.[5]

This story demonstrates that magic comes from the Self. Each person is skilled in a different way, and to accomplish *draíocht* the intention must come from personal truth. The techniques for doing this vary, but the method of the poets given above is an excellent example: "We will stand on a hill top at sunrise, with our backs to a thorn tree and a stone and a thorn in our hands." The story gives us a full set of spatial and temporal coordinates. The hill establishes a central and prominent place, and sunrise establishes a critical time. The thorn tree establishes position; the stone and thorn establish posture and are uncomfortable enough to keep one's mind on task! All these generate the kind of centering and intention that is necessary to awaken the eternal Self and for the spell to work.

Each group of the Tuatha answers from the place of their skill. Although the replies sound like boasts, what Lugh is doing is bringing each individual to the center of her or his true nature. Lugh is not commanding what each person should do. He is allowing the deep eternal Self of each individual to rise to the occasion. He is encouraging those present to be all of what and who they are, in harmony with everyone else. This is magic and these are true spells. With this power, the army of the Tuatha Dé Danann can accomplish anything—even what they are claiming! The myth says that each one felt like a noble spirit because Lugh inspired their full magical power to arise from within.

The symbolic associations of all the magical acts described in the story above can be distilled down to three things: earth, sky, and sea. Most Druid magical acts braid together these three powers. The three-armed or three-legged spiral of the Celts known as the *triskele* shows earth, sky, and sea in union. Conceive each one as a dragon: a Dragon of Earth, a Dragon of Sky, and a Dragon of Sea. The Magicians, Cupbearers, and Druids of the story promise that they will harness the power of their dragons in the forthcoming battle. The Dragon of Earth will fall upon the Fomor, the Dragon of Sea will rise up in the rivers and lochs, and the Dragon of Sky will rain fire. Visualizing the earth, waters, and sky as dragons is enormously useful in magical work. It will enable you to bring in the exact amount of each that you need. After a while of working with the dragons, you will quickly feel their different powers. Even within one energy source, such as the earth dragon, it becomes possible to distinguish and introduce the subtle qualities of the head or eye, as opposed to the tail, the belly, or the heart.

The Heron Pose

When the time comes for battle, the Tuatha Dé Danann hold Lugh back for fear that he might be killed. When he enters the battle, Lugh assumes a magical posture and chants a spell.

> *At this point, the Tuatha Dé Danann rose up, and the Battle Goddesses, Badb, Macha, and the Morrigan, stood among them. Lugh broke from the men holding him from battle and led the host. He sang a song of courage as they advanced, and he chanted a spell as he went around the army on one foot, with one eye closed.*[6]

Let us look at the posture Lugh assumes in the story. It seems that Druids assumed the pose of standing on one foot and holding a hand over one eye when performing magic. We call it the Heron Pose, and its primary purpose is to concentrate attention on a desired end. It is a technique for gathering up the powers of the Self and directing them in a single-minded way.

In the Celtic folk tradition there is a character depicted with one leg and one eye. He is called the Fynoderee on the Isle of Man, and the Gruagach in Scotland. An enormously powerful being, he is a resource of natural energy who devotes himself to tasks with single-minded enthusiasm. The Fynoderee will bring in every creature from the field if asked to gather the sheep, or cut the corn stalks to below ground level if asked to harvest. This relates directly to the kind of energy brought to bear when assuming the Heron Pose, a stance which draws on the powers of the creatures of the natural world. The heron is an excellent example of patience, stealth, concentration, and directed action as it moves one leg at a time through the water, hunting for food.

In Argyll, Scotland, there is a craggy hilltop known as Dunadd in the center of a fertile plain. You can see the remains of a Celtic fortress there, and the site is famous for being the coronation place of the Dalriadan Scots. On the summit of the hill is a stone with a single footprint carved into it. The legend surrounding coronation says that the king would stand on one leg in the footprint, with one eye closed while reciting his oaths of office. With this legend, we are drawing close to the essence of the magical Heron Pose. In the story of Moy Tura, Lugh must center himself in order to win the battle. Parallel to this situation, the king had to call on his own sovereign powers through that special pose in order to assume sovereignty at Dunadd. For the powers of nature to support a goal, the individual needs to call on the power of the eternal

Self. The Heron Pose quickly brings a person back to center and focuses sovereign power with great energy on the task at hand.

We describe the use of the Heron Pose for establishing order in the Lughnasadh ceremony in chapter 7. Lugh used it to instill order among his people in their struggle with the Fomorians. The Fomor represent the chaotic, fluid, visceral parts of ourselves. They also represent the wild aspects of earth and water, which require discipline and regulation so as not to let them get out of hand. Using the Heron Pose is a swift and effective means of coming to center, to balance. We recommend its use whenever you feel the need to accomplish this, especially in crisis.

The Heron Pose should be performed in a quiet place where you will not be distracted. Get a good balance on one leg and then wrap the free foot around it. Bring one hand up over an eye, and place the other hand underneath the elbow to support the arm. Intuit which leg you need to stand on and which eye you need to cover. Nicholas covers his left eye and looks inward with the right eye to access the rational abilities of the left side of the brain (you'll recall that the wiring switches over in the human brain: the left side of the body is controlled by the right side of the brain, while the left brain controls the right side of the body). He covers his right eye and gazes with the left one to access the intuitive abilities of the right side of the brain. Stand only as long as is comfortable. The pose works very quickly.

The second part of this practice is for you to focus and apply your intention and power. Assume the pose, come to balance and center, and concentrate on the task at hand. Bring all the powers of attention and single-mindedness to the subject. Like the heron, be absolutely still and focused. If you feel concentration slipping, focus on your breath and follow its rising and falling. It is a good idea to focus on breathing anyway as a source of the energy that you are bringing to the task. All at once, release the pose and send your intention and energy flashing outwards to achieve the goal. If there is a task you can do immediately, expend your energy on it quickly and vigorously.

The Harmony of *Draíocht*

The whole of the *Second Battle of Moy Tura* describes establishing order throughout the world. The orderly progression and seasons of the solar year triumph over the chaotic forces of the Fomor. Here is another part of the story:

> *Lugh and his companions then came upon Bres who had brought the armies*
> *of the Fomor to Ireland. Bres asked to be spared in exchange for making the*

cows of Ireland always give milk. But Lugh would not accept this as Bres had no power over their calves. So Bres offered a harvest of grain every quarter. But the Druid Maeltine of the Great Judgements said: "It has suited us that the spring is for sowing, the summer for strengthening, the autumn for harvesting, and the winter for consuming the grain."[5]

The point being made is that order means a natural cycle of things. Lugh will not accept a harvest every quarter from Bres. As the Druid Maeltine tells us, only the autumn is for harvesting, while the other quarters serve other roles in the cycle of the year. This is wise. Magic is not about accomplishing the impossible or expecting miracles. Magic is the alignment of the Self with the harmony of the cosmos. This is a fundamental principle of *draíocht*.

Activities

Definitions. We usually use words to think with. When starting a new field of study, it is important to give our brain clear words to use for building up concepts, so that we understand everything from the first moment on. If we practiced this perfectly, each of us would be able to understand nuclear engineering, since concepts aren't confusing when we know what every word means. A great place to start studying is by defining key terms. Nobody else knows better than you what a word means.

- Define "magic" in your own words.
- Define "Druid magic" in your own words.

Emphasize the definitions in any way you wish and hang them up in plain view. As time goes on, you'll elaborate and clarify these definitions. Your brain will be glad you are keeping up to date on what you mean by Druid magic, since everything else you do depends on these building blocks.

Mind Mapping. There is a right-brain way of organizing, called "mind mapping." This technique allows you to brainstorm, to activate the creative right hemisphere of your brain before analyzing and critiquing with the left hemisphere.

Take a blank piece of paper. In the center print in block letters the word MAGIC, enclosed in a rectangle. Around it, write down all the words and images you associate with "Magic," by drawing a line out from the rectangle a short way and writing a word at the end of each line. On a separate piece of paper, do the same for DRUID MAGIC.

When your ideas are written, your left brain can take over and organize what you wrote. Using color codes or different kinds of borders around related words, start to connect the dots, so to speak. Connect words that came from your mind, then those from your heart, from your body, from ancient memories, from reading. Or connect words into groups based on known facts, speculation, imagination, or any other patterns. Which inner part of you produced the most ideas? What does this tell you about yourself and your reasons for pursuing Druidry?

Moy Tura Skills. The story of the Battle of Moy Tura names many professions among the Tuatha Dé Danann: magician, cup-bearer, Druid, poet, battle goddess, blacksmith, physician. On a piece of paper, name your own profession(s) and skills. Go beyond your profession's "job description" and think about the magical powers of the Dé Dananns in that story. How could your job or your profession be advertised in a magical newspaper's classified ads? Write the advertisement that would ask for the magical properties of your craft.

The Poet's Spell. "We will stand on a hilltop at sunrise, with our backs to a thorn tree and a stone and a thorn in our hands . . ." Go to a hilltop as the poets of the Tuatha Dé Danann describe, taking appropriate objects with you, stand with your back to a chosen tree, and declare a spell that you are working on. Form the spell into a poem.

The Heron Pose. Practice the Heron Pose described in this chapter. You never know when you will need it!

Earth, Sky, and Sea. Incorporate the braiding together of these three elements into your magical practice. See them as dragons and/or as a *triskele* (triple spiral). Acquire a *triskele* or braid together your hair or some other material with this awareness in mind.

Notes

1. From *Cath Maige Tuired*, the "Battle of Moy Tura," recension based upon the translations of Elizabeth A. Gray (1983), Lady Gregory (1904), and R. A. S. MacAlister (1938).

2. Lady Augusta Gregory, *Gods and Fighting Men*, p. 150.

3. Tacitus, *Annales* XIII.30.

4. http://www.ncf.carleton.ca/-bj333/HomePage.curses.html

5. These stories of the Tuatha Dé Danann belong to the *Mythological Cycle* of Irish literature. The legends of their arrival in Ireland and battles with the Fir Bolg and the Fomorians come from the *Leabhar Gabála Érenn*, the "Book of the Taking of Ireland," usually known as the "Book of Invasions." These stories must belong chronologically to the earliest period of Celtic legend, despite being written down at a fairly late date, circa fourteenth century. The recension from the Irish in this and the following extracts draw on Lady Augusta Gregory (1904), Elizabeth A. Gray (1983), R. A. S. MacAlister (1938–1956), and T. P. Cross and C. H. Slover (1936).

6. Op. cit., note 5.

Chapter 2

PROTECTING, LOCATING, AND SHAPESHIFTING

Then the magical sweet-mouthed harpers of Cáin Bile came out from the red cataract at Es Ruaid, to charm the host [army]. But the people thought that these were spies from Ulster among them, and they gave chase after them until they ran in the shape of deer far ahead of them to the north among the stones at Liac Mór, they being Druids of great knowledge.[1]

In this chapter we will demystify magic and show some of its major uses. Druid magic involves protecting people, places and things, locating lost items, practicing illusion, and shifting shape in wonderful ways.

We define magic as actions, thoughts, intentions, and energies that cause transformation or change through a knowledge of all aspects of nature. Starhawk says that the "skills of magic are the techniques of moving and shaping energy."[2] Druids were trained to use normal abilities that we all have access to. It makes sense that humans all over the world, across the mists of time, have used magic because it is such a powerful way to change ourselves, and to connect with all there is!

The deepest change that comes from magic is often in the person's own perceptions, in consciousness, in her or his development as a fully expanded being. The quest to understand Life in a greater way, to know the primal order, and to connect with the

Source is often the impetus for walking a spiritual path. The Wiccan priestess Amber K says that a superb way to know that we are part of all things is through magic, so "we can experience existence from the perspective of other parts."[3] You will have these experiences directly because of the Druid emphasis on getting inside all other existences such as the tree and animal realms, and journeying to the Otherworlds. Ethics form one of the central components of Druidry, so we will explore ethical questions from a Druidic point of view throughout this book. For modern Druids, magic is always used for positive purposes that harm no one. Whenever you choose to use the powers of the eternal Self for magic, wish for an outcome that is beneficial for all concerned. As you practice Druid magic, the connection between power and responsibility increases. The more power and wisdom you accrue, the more you become responsible for the spheres around you. This responsibility is especially great when you are involved in magic.

On the other hand, magical moments occur for all of us that are very light and serendipitous. A few years ago Maya and her sister were on a late-night flight with a long layover in Los Angeles. They got off and back on the plane through the jetway door several times. As they once more returned to board through the closed door—this time with sandwiches for the crew—one of the waiting passengers asked: "I've seen you two getting on and off this plane. How do you do it? Every time I try that door it's locked, and we're told no one can reboard till later." Maya looked at him and said, "You're not Irish, are you?" He shook his head no. "That explains it then," she said, going down the jetway again.

We are sure our readers have experienced times when the veil between different realities parts. At these times you pass easily between the worlds, or you can stretch time beyond human belief. Maybe you take a trip that unfolds like a wonderful fable, or you encounter a friend coincidentally in Dublin, or you can't believe your luck or the incredible timing of something. Our purpose here is to demystify magic so it becomes as believable as the recurrence of the sunrise! Let us examine some Druidic magical practices.

Protecting with Wards

Take a look at these words and see what they have in common: reward, guardian, warden, steward, warn, wardrobe, garrison, warrant, guarantee, wary, and beware. They all come from the Old English root "ward," that means to guard, protect, or watch out for. "Setting the wards" is a magical technique for guarding and protecting an area or a person. Maya discovered the concept in a novel about Druids; this powerful protection has been successful for her countless times over the years, and can be learned by all.[4]

We know that the Druids protected places from unwanted attention. The Roman poet Lucan wrote of a grove never violated over the ages, which the people did not use for worship but left fallow for the gods. This inspired Maya to write of an ancient Druid ritual: "Small bone-fires, set in the four directions, ward against outsiders entering the holy place. Roman soldiers do not know of this grove in the northern forest."[5] An Irish legend from the Fenian cycle tells us that the "Dark Druid" changed Fionn's wife Sadbh into a deer and hid her in a valley that all the troops of the Fianna never found in years of searching.

We also know that the Druids protected people by making them invisible to unwanted eyes. The *Exile of the Sons of Usnach* tells us that Deirdre was exquisitely beautiful when she was born and that she was reared apart from the rest of the world, under the care of Leborcham, a female Druid. No one could see or hear her, or even locate their house with its roof of magical sod.

Guarding people and places is within our ability today, and setting the wards is one way to do it. This method is based on the shape of a square or rectangle, in contrast to the circle used in other pagan work. Picture a square or rectangle fitting outside the area or person to be protected. You might wish to set the wards around the bed of a sleeping child before the babysitter comes, or around your house as you leave on vacation. You can set them around your car whenever you park it, or around yourself, your family, and your possessions when traveling. Until you perfect the practice, it is preferable to be physically present where you want the wards set. Later on you can do it from a distance.

Let's go through the procedure. It is all done by envisioning and waiting to receive a protective image. Stand outside the envisioned square and select one corner to start the protecting. Maya usually begins at the front left corner. You will be designating the corners as black–white–black–white. Call the first corner "black" and allow the polarity of blackness to be there. With strong intention, start some energy at that corner in order to ward off anything unwanted. Turn toward the next corner (you may not be able to see it in actuality) and call it "white." Move your intention and the protective energy around to that corner. Continue: the third corner is black and the fourth is white. Move the protection all the way back to the starting point. Two corners opposite each other will now be black, and the other two opposite each other are white.

They will be holding a dynamic guardian tension among them. You have set the perimeter and called in the balance of light and dark to work with you. Complete safety, however, requires three-dimensional protection, moving into the spheres of Above and Below. Envision the protected area extending down into the earth and up into the sky.

The next part of setting the wards requires you to shift from sending out energy to receiving an image. Stand there and concentrate on the space or person you are protecting. Let an image come to you that arises naturally. It will be the correct one. You won't have to make an effort. You will simply be the conduit for the already existing spirit of place or the guardian of the person. Let that image emerge and move until it covers the entire space, above, below, and all around. The power that has chosen to be the guardian has volunteered and knows what to do. In your mind, see and say clearly what the protective image is. You can leave now, in total confidence that the wards are set and the space or person is protected. Reset the wards if anything changes, such as a child going to a new school, getting the car back from the mechanic, or building an addition on your house.

Some examples from Maya's experience should clarify how this magic works:

> During a full moon ritual I set the wards on those of us doing the magic, and the image of an old-fashioned wooden sailing ship patrolled our circle, complete with pirates! As far as doing this around a place, my friend Amanda asked me to protect her empty house until it sold. I set the wards tightly around the yard and house, the ground below, the trees and sky above. No burglars or even bird droppings would get in there. Neither, however, could the realtor get in to show the house. She drove past the address and had to backtrack, then couldn't get the gate open, climbed over and then the key wouldn't work. How could she sell the house this way? Oops. I went and opened a path, but only for Amanda, the realtor, and her clients.
>
> In Britain I set the wards on a place where I was house-sitting and got the image of parapets and high, crenelated walls with a huge black panther prowling along the top. When the owner returned I told her of this and she said, "Oh, you saw the big black cat, did you?" It was indeed the spirit of the place and had been her protector for years. In contrast, our friend Brennan asked me to protect his family after the third break-in of the their house, when his daughter awoke at night to find someone trying to strangle her. I worked

for a long time but the wards would not set. Realizing the house could not be protected as it was, I envisioned it rising fifteen feet in the air and then a weak effect of guarding went into place. The family moved soon afterwards and the landlady tried to rent it but found she needed to do massive repairs. As workers ripped up the floors, they found two pits under the house, large enough to hold people standing upright. The house was geopathic.

It's also a good idea to protect people, animals, and cars. Set the wards on young people before they go to school. Protect your animal companion before you take it to the veterinarian. When you park in a questionable place that might result in vandalism or a meter maid visit, set the wards on the car. My favorite image is to make my car a sheriff's vehicle (no ticket, no vandalism). Occasionally the picture is so strong that I can read the official-looking decal and lettering on the side of the car.

The Lost Is Found

A fascinating type of magic is finding lost items. If something is yours, don't worry: it will remain yours. Set the wards on the missing item from a distance. Once you physically track it down it will be there, because it is rare that someone else can keep something of yours once you have protected it magically. We will now look more closely at locating things the Druid way.

The Druids and all the Celts used their heads. They revered the mind, words, and inspired thinking. Borrowing from this, the key to finding things is not to search! Turning your house upside down is a primitive method compared to the tools we have. Find things with your mind, not your body. Don't search. Instead, recall or remember. Backtrack in your mind. Open up freely to getting a picture of where the object is. Think back to when you last had it, where you were, what you were doing and with whom, why you had the object with you (keys, wallet, jewelry), what you were wearing. Picture it in detail. Ask yourself to find it. Ask, "What did I do with it? Where is it?" The answer will pop into your head and you'll go straight there and find the lost possession.

This magical way to find lost items builds on ordinary memory but contacts a different part of our brain's equipment. It is based on knowingness—trusting that we have huge abilities within, even though we are not accustomed to using them. Some sense within us knows more than we consciously realize. For example, the hypothalamus, a gland located deep within the brain, knows the correct answer on multiple-choice tests: it gives off a tiny electric twiggle of recognition for the right answer, but we often override that sign. Druids and bards went through rigorous training to bring such places in the mind to consciousness.

If something keeps telling you that a lost object is in a certain place, even though you have looked there three times already, go to that spot, put out your hand and the object will be within reach. It is uncanny, and you might swear someone put it there since you looked last, but the difference is you are now looking with your mind open instead of shut. If something is precious to you, it is especially likely that you will find it because it cannot belong to anyone else. As with a lost dog or cat, what is yours will return. If it does not, ask yourself if it was time to let go of what it represented and if someone else now needs it.

Here are some examples of Maya's practice with this kind of "magic":

> *At a business lunch with a woman I had just met, I commented on her ear-rings. A sad look passed across her face and she said she had lost her favorite ones that her son had made, a beautiful pair of great sentimental value, irre-trievably gone months ago. An image came to me. I asked her if she had a long dark skirt, navy blue or black, soft, velvet perhaps, with a pocket . . . .*
>
> *I got no further. She jumped up, startling people in the restaurant. She said, "That's where they are! I forgot I borrowed Suzanne's evening skirt. They're in the pocket of her velvet skirt!"*
>
> *A friend named Noreen phoned to ask if she had left her wallet at our house. I quickly cast around with my visual mind but didn't sense it in the house. I cast out further and said, "Did you look on the floor in the back seat of your car? I think it's there." It was.*

You will get the idea that one does not try to find missing items: *they know where they are.* Simply send out a request to hear from them in some way, or to be able to visualize their surroundings. Once you pick up on the incoming message, the object is as good as found.

Illusion

Druid magic makes heavy use of illusion. As you get to know the Celtic myths thoroughly, you will notice that such illusion is often created with the help of a mantle. Mantle or cloak in Irish is the word *brat*, and a smokescreen is *brat deataigh*. Notice how "cloak" in English as a verb means to hide or conceal, as does "mantle" when used as a verb. We are onto something here, and as we dig deeper it gets more exciting: mantle in ornithology means the wings, shoulder feathers, and back of a bird. In all your studies, when have you come across the use of a cloak or mask of bird feathers to conceal someone? Exactly! That is the garb of shamans, throughout the world.

Mog Roith, the great blind Druid, calls for his bull's hide and bird headdress with wings in order to rise into the air and view the battle he is directing. His Munster warriors are victorious because of the magical Sight this Druid garb affords him. Aonghus Óg is the son of the Dagda and the goddess Boann who gave her name to the river Boyne. Aonghus lives at Brú na Boinne, "magical dwelling place by the Boyne" or Newgrange today. He loves and protects the young warrior Diarmuid, who is his foster son. Diarmuid has run off with the goddess Grania, betrothed to the chief of the Fianna. Each time the troops of the Fianna corner Diarmuid and Grania, Aonghus Óg arrives out of nowhere, covers Grania in his mantle, and takes her away to safety. We realize now that he created the illusion of coming out of nowhere because he was cloaked like a bird in the sky. He was able to "see" that Diarmuid and Grania were in trouble because he had journeyed in his mantle to find them.

Maya and Nicholas have a number of fabulously colored and exotically designed bird masks from Mardi Gras that they use for ritual. Maya made a mantle when she self-initiated as a Druid. It is a long circular cape and hood in fiery red and gold brocade with a dramatic appearance; in a former incarnation the fabric was heavy drapery. For our Druid wedding as King and Queen of Faerie, Maya wore wings on the Celtic crown we created, and an other-worldly lacy gown. Nicholas wore a flowing green cloak we fashioned with gold trim and gold Celtic spirals across the back. Many of the guests donned wings over their ritual outfits and danced through the circle with scarves. Banners were flying, a Celtic harpist played, wands were waving, and there were flowers everywhere. An eight-year-old guest whispered: "This is fairy land!" The illusion had been made real.

Shapeshifting (*Fith-Fath*)

Fith-fath (fee-fa) is a Scots Gaelic term meaning an incantation to change shape and become invisible. *Fith* might come from the word for deer in Irish (*fia*) or the word for vision or dream (*fís*).[6] There are numerous Celtic stories of people being changed into deer. For example, Sadbh, the wife of Fionn mac Cumhail, had been changed into a deer for refusing the advances of the Dark Druid of Dea. Fionn first saw Sadbh as a fawn who followed him home and then turned into a beautiful woman. They married and she became pregnant. When Fionn was away fighting invaders, the Dark Druid enticed Sadbh out of the safe keeping of Fionn's dun by enchantment: he appeared as a shadowy form of Fionn himself. He struck her with his hazel rod and she returned to the shape of a fawn. She gave birth to Fionn's son and raised him in the forest for seven years until Fionn found him and named him Oisín ("little deer").

No, we can't teach you how to become a deer, a salmon, a wolf, or an eagle in this chapter! Though such transformations into animal shapes are common in the Celtic myths, they are the stuff of fable. We are able, however, to share with you numerous ways of shapeshifting that are Druidic, magical and far more usable. When used as a charm, for example, *fith-fath* can change one's guise or make a person invisible. This has obvious advantages of protection.

We will look at six magical ways of shapeshifting in the remainder of this chapter. If you feel disappointed just now because we are not claiming to be able to turn you into a dragon or make you invisible by saying mysterious words, please read on! What you will find are practical processes you can actually perform. We shapeshift for protection, for exploration, for understanding from the perspective of all existences, and for tapping into the creative energy of the universe.

Welsh Mythic Shapes

Many of the tales of shapeshifting come from Welsh sources. Igraine, the mother of the future King Arthur, was tricked into making love with the warrior chief, Uther Pendragon. Merlin changed the warlord into the form of her legal husband, allowing him to enter her castle as if he was the resident lord. Merlin himself, according to the author T. H. White, trained young Arthur to experience the virtues of the badger, hawk, and bird by changing the boy into those forms.

Morgan Le Fay, sister to King Arthur, was an herbal healer and probably a banshee; *bean-sídhe* is Irish for "fairy woman." The earliest mention of her is as Morgen, leader of eight other women who breathed on the cauldron of rebirth in the Welsh Otherworld called Annwn. She is one of many mythic characters who changed into birds, creatures which may represent sky deities and the easy movement between the disparate worlds. More than 800 years ago, Geoffrey of Monmouth wrote: "Her name is Morgen, and she . . . knows the art of changing her shape, of flying through the air, like Daedelus, on strange wings."[7]

Her counterpart in Ireland is called the Morrigán, "phantom queen." This Goddess is one of the most powerful in all the Celtic myths. In the *Táin*, her advances toward the hero Cuchulainn are rejected and in a rage she turns herself into an eel, heifer, and wolf in order to entrap him; in each guise she is wounded. Later she presents herself as an ugly old woman and tricks him into healing her. Her most common guise is that of raven or crow, the prophet of war who does no killing but is the onlooker at battles, the devourer of carrion. The Morrigán enters all the Druid existences of sea, earth, and sky. She changes into a water animal and two land animals, but is most commonly the raven of the sky.

In our Grove, one member claims the raven as his power animal. As a dress rehearsal for writing this chapter, we all shapeshifted him into a raven and journeyed on the wings of magic with him.

The best example of animals representing the four elements of earth-air-fire-water, comes from the story of Ceridwen, the Welsh deity often seen as a hag or sacred wise woman. She was keeper of the Cauldron of Inspiration, the greatest gift a Celtic bard could achieve. When the village boy Gwion stirred the cauldron, he accidentally splashed his thumb from the brew and cooled it in his mouth, instantly receiving the brilliance of all the ages. He fled from Ceridwen in earth form as a hare but she shapeshifted into a greyhound and outran him. He changed into a fish and she into an otter as they explored the water element. You can see how she is teaching him about "all existences" in the Druidic manner. Next he became a bird, but she became a falcon and they swirled through the air. Finally he became a kernel of grain and she the earth-bound hen who ate it, putting him into her womb—her cauldron—the element of fire.[8]

As far as applying these teachings, keep in mind that *fith-fath* means a guise or appearance. When you learn to shapeshift, the purpose is to become *like* something else, so like it that you almost *are* it. From these Welsh myths, you get the idea to work with the animals that you feel closest to. Examine your interests, hobbies, recreation, and personality tendencies. Also refresh yourself on your zodiac sign. All these will point to whether you want to work with animals of sea, sky, or earth. Once you have selected the best element for you, think deeply about specific animals. Visualize them, visit animal refuges, wildlife sanctuaries, aquariums, and the like. Hike in a wilderness and sleep out to see who comes to visit you. You might already have a burning attachment to manatees or falcons, feral cats, or pot-bellied pigs. Make representations of your chosen animal to help you shift into that reality. These separate realities all exist simultaneously and it is up to us to find the veil or crack between the worlds.

When you have found your animal presence, perhaps through the quality of an element or lucid imagery, be ready to slip across realities and into its form at any time. Remember, this form is an ageless presence: it may have been on the earth far longer than humans, and its intelligence is of the primal order of the world. Birds know their migration trails and when to use them. Cetaceans and fish follow the currents and rivers formed when the earth was young. The herding animals not only know the plants and terrain but helped form them by their actions long before the first humans appeared on the scene. Entering the form of an animal places you within a primal order where nothing is fixed and transformation becomes possible. It puts energy at your disposal for creativity and action.

Tattoos of the Picts

Besides the Welsh, the other major Celtic group on the isle of Britain are the Scots, and they too have stories of shapeshifting. A race or tribe in Scotland that paralleled or may even have predated the Celts was the Picts, who possibly practiced a manifest form of altering themselves—tattoos (this people's name comes from Latin *Picti*, "the painted ones"). They covered not only their faces but their bodies with blue woad paintings of beasts, birds, fish, and enigmatic geometric designs. They took on the powers of living animals animated by the muscles of the Picts' own bodies. Some of their designs are known to us through the Pictish Symbol Stones, symbols which are unique to the Celtic world. They paved the way for the spiral interweave and zoomorphic designs of the Celtic Christian era.

The Celtic linguist Caitlín Matthews postulates that the name the Picts used for themselves, *Cruitneach*, comes from the word for shape or appearance.[9] The Picts coexisted with the Indo-European Celts in Britain for over 1,000 years, and doubtless the older group taught the Celts in that time the significance of tattoos and also of shape-changing into battle frenzy. Tales of blue-painted Druids and warriors probably evolved from this source.

To apply this information, you will need to research the sacred meaning of tattoos. While the Picts left no decipherable information, apart from the Symbol Stones, and the Druids hardly more than that, other tribes exist which practice marking the body in concert with spirit. Learn about other groups that use tattoos ritually, such as the Maori of New Zealand: talk with some Maori women and men who still build up these images on their bodies by rites of passage. The shapeshifting they experience is both spiritual (which they may not be at liberty to discuss) and physical, which is in the symbolism of the tattoos. After some deliberation, select a temporary tattoo that fits your Druidic practice, and apply it to your body. If the pattern is right for you on many levels, you may decide to make it permanent. One of our friends, a Celtic artist, has nearly completed the process of having her own drawings of animals tattooed around her body in a large spiral.

Animal Shapes

For students of Druidry, we recommend connecting intimately with your power animal. Pray with it, study its appearance and habits, learn its magical qualities and abilities, receive its teachings. Shapeshifting requires work, devotion, practice, and intention. Eventually during meditation, dreams, or trance work, you can be taken inside the essence of your power animal. In this enchanted way you can move as it moves, see as it sees, know what it knows.

Our European ancestors from the last Ice Age knew about shapeshifting through the magic of animals, and depicted this in the painted caves of France and Spain. These spirit-workers were ancient precursors of the Druids. How exquisite are the paintings and bas-relief sculptures in the caves! You owe yourself a trip to these places, to connect with the origins of your people, the origins of your art and creativity, of your magic. Scientists are still debating what the paintings meant to the people of the time. Do they depict hunting magic, fertility magic, initiation rites, hallucinatory images?[10] If you merge those paintings with what you know of Celtic shapeshifting, you will have a useable base for understanding how to shapeshift through animals. Let the art filter through your layers of consciousness, and emerge in your connection with a totem animal.

In the old myths, Druids changed into animal shapes. Tuan mac Carill lived for 300 years in each form as a stag, a boar, a hawk, a salmon, and as a man. The great Druid Mog Roith is enlisted to help the people of Munster to repel the invasion of Cormac mac Airt and his army. Mog Roith calls up an "army" of magical cows, bulls, ants, and boars. To counter this onslaught, Cormac's three Druidesses change into sheep with the unlikely traits of being as swift as swallows and as agile as weasels. The story goes on and on, with the Druids of both sides pitted against each other. The centuries-old training of Mog Roith outwits the enemy. He puts on a bull's hide and a speckled bird headdress so he can rise into the air and shamanically see the opposition in action, although he was blind in his physical body.

A type of spirit called *púca* manifests itself mischievously in animal forms in later Celtic legends. Its name is probably a term imported with the Norse invaders, and is the root of the name "Puck" in English, best known from Shakespeare's *A Midsummer Night's Dream*. Jung may have had this in mind when he described our shadow side, building on Freud's earlier conception of the id. The Celts knew how to work with the dark side, a topic Nicholas explores in his recent book, *The Dark God*.[11]

Use your *púca* dramatically and effectively as a spirit guide. If you've ever had an apparition that frightened you, perhaps it was your *púca* emerging with a valuable message. What a wonderful opportunity this being gives us to bring forth our wild side and our passions, weaknesses, urges, and creativity.[12] Use this internal rebel, this adventurer, to break out of patterns that no longer serve you. Be conscious about this, be deliberate, be careful. Express the wild side purposely, perhaps through ritual. It is best to name what you are bringing through, associate it with an animal if possible, and costume yourself powerfully. Prepare to write down any inspiration that comes.

Threshold guardians are another form of shapeshifter. You will recall these from fairy tales—the giants, misshapen figures, animal-like humans, magical but scary shepherds. Alice encounters them in Wonderland, Odysseus in the islands of the Cyclopes. In the *Mabinogion*, Pwyll, Prince of Dyfed in Wales, encounters the Underworld god Arawn after he has killed a magical deer. To atone, he changes places with Arawn for a year. This exchange of power is tremendously important. Once a guardian reveals its secret, the guardianship changes hands.

Let us apply this to ourselves. Once we claim the secret treasures guarded within us, we must take responsibility for how they manifest because we become their guardians. If you uncover inner courage, for example, you might feel like a lioness or a bear, rearing up every time you need to be courageous. We need to be able to shapeshift into whatever guards our threshold, our entry to inspiration, skill, courage, full sexuality. These forms are the dragons that guard our inner treasures: we must become those dragons in order to get our treasures. Great spirituality surrounds this quest . . . great fear usually stands in the way . . . great outcomes lie ahead.

If you are wondering how to contact your dragons, use whatever methods fit you best. Do you visualize easily, with sharp clarity? Do you meditate frequently? Is shamanic journeying within your skills? Are you artistic, and can you paint or sculpt your dragons in order to contact them face to face? Let them know you are coming and that you no longer fear their countenance. Journey on the back of the power of your Self. Maya created a ritual of reclaiming her powers from an immense dragon, after her parents died. Friends in a magical circle stripped away the parts of Self she had lost in her family of origin, and placed them under the dragon's canopy. She reclaimed them one by one, and the friends attached ribbons and scarves to her as she named her powers. The dragon was depleted, shook, and revealed itself as nothing more than projected fears and lost threads of wholeness. The effect was convincing for those present, life-changing for Maya.

Talking with Nature

Michael Roads lives in Australia. He must be quite like the Druids of old in his ability to speak *directly* with rivers, rocks, and trees. When it first began happening to him, he didn't believe it, but the nature elements around his farm provided him information so that he could write a book about them. He balked. One day, seated beside his favorite river, he heard:

> *Do as the dragon did. Let go and fall into the river. Let the river of life sweep you beyond all aid from old and worn concepts. I will support you. Trust me. As you swim from an old consciousness, blind to higher realities beyond your physical world, trust that I will guide you with care and love into a new stream of consciousness.*[13]

He trusted, and the book *Talking with Nature* is the collaborative result. Be assured that you also can talk with nature. To do it, you will need to shapeshift. Drop any façade of being outside, superior or separate from nature, and acquire the guise of the part of nature you want to communicate with. Lie in the stream, sleep in the tree, go and sit among the Rock People and say what is in your heart. Make your thoughts as big as mountains, your limbs as accepting as trees, your cells as old as rocks.

We have another friend from Australia who is a water spirit. He has surfed almost as many hours as he has slept! One day hiking around Dartmoor in southwest Britain we came to a stream of clear deep water high in the hills. Our friend slipped out of his clothes, into the water, and began a long undulating glide below the surface. When he emerged he told us of meeting ancestral spirits in the stream, the guardians of the moors. We photographed him from above and later, when others saw that photo they asked, "Is that a dolphin, or a salmon, or a water serpent?" Our friend has done his work over many years to earn his shapeshifting powers as a water animal. If you resonate with the sea, if you feel the tide as the breath of the ocean, you are a water spirit.

Druids today do not try to order nature around, nor do they practice weather witchcraft on a cloudy day to make winds come up and the sun appear. It works much better to shift to the reality of the part of nature that is your concern, and ask for some action that is congruent with the natural cycle. If you do not want rain on your parade, go to the rain clouds and ask where else they are willing to go. Of course, you don't want ants on your back porch where your toddler plays. You can go to the ants, let them know the situation and see where else they are willing to go. If you want a garden worthy of Findhorn, go to the seeds, ask where to plant them and how to nurture them, ask the elementals to bring their energy, and begin gardening.

Masks, Guises, and Costumes

We have all seen people in masks and costumes, whether it is children at Halloween, adults at Mardi Gras, or shalakos at Zuni ceremonies. The mask is as old as art and religion, and is found in traces of all cultures. You have seen photographs of people undergoing initiation in masks and native dress, and may wonder why they don this attire. The significance of masks is to endow the wearer with awe-inspiring powers. We are to gain the *essence* of what the mask represents by wearing it. Dancers and musicians in ancient Greece and Rome wore masks as interpreters of the divine sound of music. Masks found by archaeologists seem to depict rituals and mythological scenes. Images of myth reflect our own spiritual powers: by wearing masks we evoke mythic powers in our lives. Disguising oneself at Samhain is wise so that wandering spirits—which can easily cross over to the human realm at that time—will think we are as dead as they are.

To practice this form of shapeshifting, make some masks! Make them frequently, especially in groups of like-minded people who want them for ritual purpose. Gather many sorts of materials, both two- and three-dimensional, made of paper, wood, fabric, leather or yarn, glittery and colorful, strong and sheer. Lay out newspaper, set out materials, and let your imagination guide you. Plan something for each cross-quarter day. At Beltane on May 1, for example, have someone dress as the Green Man completely covered in leaves so he can anonymously pursue those present and stir them up to frivolity.

Maya has conducted workshops where participants made masks, and were always excited and lively at first. Then, as the spiritual essence moved through each participant, quiet reigned: the group had left the social level of consciousness and was now experiencing the workshop on the magical level. For Maya's university courses on women's rituals and Celtic goddesses, students make masks. Outstanding, fearsome, breathtaking, wrenching, exquisite products come from that merging of creativity, myth, and spirit. You won't believe the power of masks until you try making some.

Regarding costumes, we recommend that you consult your inner wisdom each time you need to wear one. Take your time, plan ahead, write out some ideas, wait to see what comes forward as the best idea. For Maya's fiftieth birthday, she asked everyone to come dressed as "any lifetime, past, present, or future," and she herself chose to come as an Afghani warrior of a century ago. Dark make-up, turban, shirt, weskit, pantaloons, boots, and authentic weapons transformed her into a Middle Eastern male. She wore no mask at all. So complete was the shapeshifting that she stood next to friends and one asked her, "Is Maya here yet? I don't see her."

Teleportation

It is difficult to reconstruct the dual and triple layers of meaning that shapeshifting once had. One layer probably involved shifting where a Druid was located bodily. We know from the myths that Druids used teleportation, the act of moving oneself quickly over a distance. Deirdre of the Black Mountain, the female messenger of Fionn mac Cumhail, moved so swiftly that it is impossible to tell from the myths whether she was flying or merely running. We can create aspects of this ability by using the same powers and attunements that probably instructed the Druids of 2,000 years ago.

Celtic Druids seem to have kept special locations activated where they went to do magic, and we don't mean to make this sound like Clark Kent's phone booth where he turned into Superman! As is true today, Druid power accumulated in selected spots where they concentrated their rituals. They could quickly recontact their accumulated deep intentions at the special place. They probably could shift shape at will almost immediately, and leave that place by air, water, or land. They could transfer into shapes that held special symbolic meaning for them. The best form sometimes is no shape at all, instead becoming the wind or time or space itself. Deirdre traveled "like the wind over bare mountain tops."

Driving on a trip through Brittany, Maya once "lost" fifty miles according to her brand new map. She came to a junction and saw a very new road without signposts stretching ahead, while the old road curved right. As happens when magic is afoot, a man was standing there, in the middle of a mist. He assured her that the new road went where she wanted to go, though her map showed nothing of the kind. He called the road by a word Maya had never heard before but later she learned it meant "fairy path"! She drove on it, never saw a single sign or another vehicle and arrived at her destination an hour sooner than was possible.

How can you apply teleportation to your training as a Druid without making it into a parlor trick? The answer is to go to the essence of magic. We define this as actions, thoughts, intention, and energy that bring about transformation or change through a knowledge of all aspects of nature, including parts we do not fully understand. The deepest change from using magic might well be in the person's own perceptions, in consciousness. Teleportation requires just such a change in perception and consciousness. First, you need to "intend" to be elsewhere. Then you envision getting there despite any rational voice that says this is impossible. Apply your ability to sense when something magical is happening and go with it, if you choose. Activate a place where your meditations and visions make it easier to pass without physical restrictions. As with everything in Druidry, you must practice.

An example of practice would be to teleport yourself to the bedside of a loved one who is sick or dying. Set your intention to go there. Free yourself from mental and physical bonds to where you are at the moment. Be willing to be at that bedside. Go there. You can make your presence felt physically, to the point that others will later tell you they saw you. Another example of using teleportation is when you need to move yourself out of danger. If you are about to be trapped in a building or car or dangerous situation, you can leap out of it. You will suddenly find yourself physically outside of harm's way, as an onlooker rather than a victim. Keep in mind the myth of Diarmuid and Grania, when the god Aonghus Óg arrived through the sky in his mantle and removed Grania from danger; teleportation can benefit you in much the same way.

Activities

Magic. Leave your definition of "magic" (from chapter 1) as a work in progress for the time being. Could someone else comprehend it or do magic based on your definition? Write out exactly how you will use magic: for self-gain? Against others? For beneficial ends only? To heal? To learn?

Setting the Wards. Set the wards on a person or thing. Write what image comes as the protecting force. Do this at least once a week for practice.

The Lost is Found. Find a lost item, something that is unmistakably yours! Call to it and listen for its voice. The item knows where it is. Intend to retrieve it. Imagine what you will do with it when it returns. Locate it in your mind and go put your hand on it.

The Cloak of Illusion. Paint or make a mantle or headdress to alter your presence. In what setting do you blend so well that you seem invisible? What colors alter your perceptions and appearance? Use those clues to make your magical garb.

Talking With Nature. Talk with nature at least once a week. Select a rock where you'd like to spend some time, sit on it, and wait. Rocks have existed since the beginning of the world. They have seen and heard everything. They speak almost as slowly as they move. They have something to teach you about patience, reliability, and age-old wisdom. Next week, learn from a tree, which knows about community and connecting roots but not much about moving. Then make friends with water, which knows a lot about moving, and on to other forms of nature that are waiting to talk.

Masks and Costumes. Masks and costumes are great fun! They are also powerful. Do make some. For those who don't sew, fasten your costumes with hot glue. Halloween patterns at a fabric store will get you started. Create a ritual outfit in honor of your totem animal or help someone create a magical cloak.

Notes

1. From *The Tain*, in Miranda Green, *The World of Druids*, p. 127.

2. Starhawk, *Truth or Dare*, 1990, p. 124.

3. Amber K, *True Magick*, pp. 4–6.

4. The term is commonly used by a wide range of modern practitioners of magic. Katherine Kurtz' *Deryni* books have introduced the phrase and concept to an even broader audience.

5. Nicholas R. Mann and Marcia Sutton, *Giants of Gaia*, p. 147.

6. *Foclóir Gaeilge-Béarla*, compiled by Niall Ó Dónaill. An Gúm, 1992.

7. Geoffrey of Monmouth, *Vita Merlini*, translated by J. J. Parry.

8. Gwdihŵ, *Ceridwen's Cauldron*, Oriel Cambria, 1997, p. 80.

9. Caitlín and John Matthews, *The Encyclopaedia of Celtic Wisdom*, pp. 157–8.

10. Paul G. Bahn and Jean Vertut, *Journey through the Ice Age.*

11. Nicholas R. Mann, *The Dark God.*

12. Tadhg MacCrossan, *The Sacred Cauldron*, p. 106.

13. Michael J. Roads, *Talking with Nature.*

Chapter 3

CREATING DRUID MAGICAL TOOLS

Math, Lord of Gwynedd, met his nephews after three years of making them live as a deer, boar, and wolf. He struck the two with his wand so that they recovered their own forms.[1]

This chapter contains practical ideas for making and acquiring tools to practice Druidry. It describes magical items from Celtic myth and the four talismans of the Tuatha Dé Danann.

The Druid Wand

The wand is a magical tool that is very personal, and no one but the owner should use or touch it. It is most often used to focus intent and direct any power you wish to send, although you can use it for any purpose. A wand can help you to set wards, for example. Saying that others should not touch the wand does not imply that the magic resides in the tool. The magic comes from you and the Universe. The tool is merely the conduit, while you are the conductor, orchestrating the power and outcome. In general, it is convenient to have external tools, but the aim of Druid Magic is to draw forth your powers from within.

The ideal Druid Wand is not an easy item to obtain. You yourself should find it, not cut it from a living tree. The most difficult part is to find such a branch or stick with a spiral formed on it by the action of a creeping vine such as a honeysuckle. An old Druid in Britain told Nicholas that a wand formed in this way by the natural action of a vine is called a "dragon." If the wood is ash, then it is an ash dragon. If it is hazel, then it is a hazel dragon. If it is oak, then it is an oak dragon, but an oak dragon is extremely rare.

This search for the ultimate wand may take many years. Meanwhile you can obtain a wand other than a dragon from any kind of wood, as long as you obtain in an honorable way. You should make it from the wood of a tree that speaks to you in some way. You might choose to increase and define the quality of your wand by carving Oghams onto it. Druids of old favored yew or hazel for ogham inscriptions, but other kinds of wood are fine, and apple prunings, for example, are ideal. The wand can be · any size.

Nicholas prefers a wand that comes as a gift from a special place. The qualities of the tree and the place imbue the wand with power. He found his ash dragon in a forest in the county of Devon over a dozen years ago. A passing farm vehicle had struck the tree, and the spiral wand was dangling at eye level when he came by. He made an offering to the rest of the tree, which was doing fine, and trimmed the ends of the broken branch and the wand with his pocket knife. The honeysuckle that created the spiral is wrapped around the ash to this day, due to the periodic oiling the wand receives. He uses it to protect a circle, to send energy out after raising a cone of power, and to direct healing energy, among other things.

Maya has lived in the desert of the American Southwest for decades, where neither vines nor dragon wands are likely to be found, so she waits for special wood. A large piece that fell from a sycamore tree where she lives became the wand for her self-initiation as a newly minted Druid several years ago. She affixed symbols for earth, sea, and sky, for life, death and rebirth, sun and moon, and a symbol from every country in which she had performed ritual, including Mongolia. The wand became immediately powerful. She uses it now for protection and for the most serious intentions in ritual. She made another wand during a full moon with wood from a mulberry tree on the property. The fairies had a hand in this, and it became wound with sparkles, leaves, bells, and a spiralling snake. She keeps it by the computer and waves it vigorously to draw inspiration to her!

One of the most famous of all Druid Wands is the Silver Branch. This shining branch, usually decorated with silver apple leaves and blossoms, appears when a journey to the Otherworlds is about to take place. You can use a Silver Branch in your Druid practice for protection whenever you feel that the Land of the Living or the Fairy World is drawing close. The ancient Druids used a similar wand, decorated with little bells, to quiet an assembly. One touch of the wand of Math revealed the truth, but he also used it to change his nephews into a variety of creatures and then back into human form, as the quote opening this chapter shows. This ability to effect transformations is probably the power most frequently ascribed to the Druid Wand.

The Druid Rod

The Druid Rod is closely related to the wand, and may double as the same thing. It is practical as well as magical. The rod is always measured to a precise length, and its main uses are for protection and laying-out of space. The original tool for laying out space was a staff planted in the ground, technically known as a gnomon, and the shadow it cast was carefully observed. This practice is capable of defining a center and the six principal directions: above and below, north, south, east, and west. Though simple in concept, setting the sacred center and the directions is an ancient and profound rite. You might set aside a day of retreat to connect with the sun and earth when you enact this rite with your Druid Rod.

Place the rod upright in the ground. This defines the vertical axis, locating and defining the center. Draw a circle around the center at the same distance away as the length, or multiples of length, of the rod. Two rods may be of value here. At some point in the course of the morning, the tip of the vertical rod's shadow will cross the circle. It will repeat this at some point in the afternoon. The line between the two points where the shadow crosses the circle will be an exact east-west line, and a line drawn at 90° to this is the north-south meridian. Establish the right-angles involved by using a Druid's Cord. The vertical rod, as *axis mundi*, also represents the World Tree. You have connected with the center of Celtic cosmology.

The Long Man of Wilmington is a figure almost 300 feet tall, cut into the South Downs in Sussex, England, by the simple act of removing the turf to expose the white chalk of the hillside underneath. The Long Man carries upright staffs in either hand. The date he was first made is disputed, but it could be Celtic. He is usually interpreted as a surveyor. A person with rods in hand must have been known early in history, as two rods provide the simple yet effective means of laying-out space for construction. The rods measure distances and straight lines of sight. We can imagine such a surveyor laying-out the linear avenues, popularly interpreted as ceremonial or chariot ways, at Tara and Rath Cruachan. We know that many of the straight roads of Britain, previously interpreted as Roman, were constructed earlier in the Celtic Iron

Age. These must have employed a person with two staffs, who was probably known as a Druid!

As far as the length of the Druid Rod is concerned, we recommend 6 or 3 feet. The foot is an accurate, ancient measure and priority ought to be given to it. Some have proposed units of measure such as the Egyptian, Roman, or Greek cubit, but these measures are all related to the English foot, yard, furlong, and mile, and all originate in geodesic distances. The term "geodesic" means the ratios and units of measure found in terrestrial proportions. We do not know how ancient people deduced the radius and circumference of the earth, but their calculations have proved far more accurate than the relatively recently introduced metric system. The metric system claimed to employ units that were fractions of the earth's circumference, but these were miscalculated. Others have suggested using the megalithic yard, 2.72 feet or multiples thereof, but this measure proposed by Alexander Thom relates to sites that were built before the Druids. This is a complex subject, and readers should consult the references listed at the end of this chapter if they want to pursue ancient measurement systems further.[2]

The rod can also be a staff, such as the scepter of power used by kings and religious leaders. You may decide to create a staff similar to a walking stick, and carve it with symbols or Oghams. Do some research and select early Celtic symbols. The later knotwork, so popular now in the Celtic renaissance, came from the post-Druidic Christian period. Knotwork on Pictish symbol stones is the exception, as some of this is pre-Christian.

In Celtic times, the *bunsach comairce* was a rod of safe conduct given by a Druid *file*, allowing the bearer the privilege of traveling freely across borders. As the wand or Silver Branch gives protection and safety to the traveler to Otherworlds, so the *bunsach comairce* provides safety to the traveler in this world. On the other hand, a rod made of poplar or aspen, known as the *fé*, guaranteed danger and bad luck, as, according to *Cormac's Glossary*, it was used to measure bodies and their graves.

The Druid Cord

A British Druid of the mathematical persuasion gave Nicholas something that he called a Druid Cord. It is a flexible string of a quality that does not stretch, divided into twelve sections of equal length through colored markings and knots; it is about a yard long. If you decide to make such a cord, it can be any length. When held as a triangle, with sides of three, four and five sections, the cord creates an exact right angle. This is an extremely quick and efficient way of creating a right angle without involving any mathematics. The Druid Cord also provides a way of measuring the circumference of cylinders such as tree trunks if one is selecting similarly sized ones to be pillars in a temple or home. The Druid Cord acts as a collapsible, pocket tape measure!

As you probably know, Wiccans measure themselves from head to toe with a cord prior to their initiation to the first degree, and thereafter wear that cord about the hips. They revived this practice from the Burning Times, to counteract that dreadful era when such a measured cord was misused by Inquisitors who said anyone they could find of its exact height was a witch. Other examples of a special cord with knots or beads at intervals come to mind, such as the Catholic rosary, Tibetan prayer beads, as well as Christian monks' and nuns' waist cords. If the Druids once used such a cord, then no doubt it possessed symbolic meanings that will only return to us with usage.

The Druid Egg

Pliny the Elder, a Roman scientific writer, mentions the Druid Egg in his *Historia Naturalis* ("Natural History," XXIX.52). He said it was a small talisman called a "serpent's egg" that gave an unfair advantage to a Gallic Vocontian chief who carried one during a legal battle. Pliny wrote that the Druid Egg was the size of a small apple with a pocked shell made of something like cartilage. This description has led people to speculate about that Druid Egg. Pliny's improbable conclusion was that it was made of secretions of entwined snakes. Recently Stuart Piggot suggested it was fused whelk (scallop) shells from the shores of northern Europe.

For our purposes, the Druid Egg is a smooth round, oval or, yes, egg-shaped stone that can conveniently fit in a pocket. It may be of any mineral including glass, and of any color. Keep your eyes and ears open until you find a stone that signals to you. Use the egg for developing single-mindedness. Stones are good at waiting, at not leaping into the future, so they can help you to stay in the present. Hold your egg up and study it whenever you wish to concentrate. Focus your gaze on the egg until distractions die away. You will be centered and ready to concentrate on the matter at hand. No doubt it was this ability that gave the Vocontian chief an advantage in the law courts of Rome!

Study your Druid Egg in order to rediscover some of the important meanings associated with this object. We recommend carrying your Druid Egg into court during any dispute, as well as holding it anytime you must make a just decision by yourself.

Any kind of egg is also a fertility symbol. In ancient times the egg appeared in the company of goddesses and serpents. It contained treasure, new life, the possibility of eternal rebirth. Sometimes a serpent was wrapped around the egg. The Celts carved serpents on phallic stones; one found in Cumberland, Britain, has an egg emerging from its mouth.

The Druid Sickle

Pliny also describes the cutting of mistletoe as the central Druid rite: "The Druids . . . hold nothing more sacred than the mistletoe and the tree on which it is growing, provided it is an oak." He goes on to say that Druids cut the mistletoe with a "golden sickle" and catch it in a white cloth.[3] Pliny was hostile to the Druids, and we should discard most of what he says. Mistletoe, for example, did not enter Ireland until fairly recently. Nicholas, in all his years of working with trees and looking for mistletoe, has never found it growing on an oak in Britain! Nevertheless the passage does have some value. Mistletoe has curative powers and some symbolic ones, but it is hard to know what these were to the Druids. Cutting the mistletoe may have represented garnering the power of the oak. The rich, sticky, semen-like juice of its berries may have represented powers of fertility. They would have cut it with great care to preserve these qualities.

Since Celtic Druids worked with trees as well as with plants and herbs, they probably had special sickles or pruning hooks. They may have used gold on sickles for gathering healing plants since it is a highly prized, noncontaminating metal. The edge would need to be supplemented by something that would cut, such as bronze. Possibly their sickles were only gold-plated or polished to the color of gold. The shape of the pruning hook echoes that of the crescent moon. It also echoes the shape of the lunulae worn on the necks of important people in the Bronze Age. Some of these lunulae, of gold and bronze, may have survived into the Celtic era, and may have been perceived as highly magical objects.

The sickle is an ancient tool for harvesting the bounty of the earth, and we recommend that you obtain one. As you work with it, see what the shape signifies to you. The sickle we use in our present ceremonies is of bronze, and we obtained it from a store in Glastonbury, Britain. We use it to bless the grain it might have cut, that is baked into our sacramental bread or ritual communion. Some vintners in California use a small hook for pruning grape vines that is ideal for Druid purposes. You may know a blacksmith, jeweler, or other craftsperson who can fabricate this tool for you.

The metal, your hand shape, and intended uses will inform you of the design you need. If you are a metal-worker who can fashion your own sickle, so much the better!

The Druid Robe

In popular imagination, Druids wore hooded, long, white robes. The original robe was probably much closer to the dress or apron worn by shamans and blacksmiths. The main purpose is to protect the wearer from harm of any kind—whether physical or psychic in nature. To do this effectively the robe must be thick, strong, and environmentally neutral. Wool and leather are ideal. Druids probably wore something like this in general practice, but to perform particular work the robe might have been of special quality. The Druid of the *Tarbhfeis*, the "Bull Feast," for example, lay wrapped in the hide of a bull in order to perform divination. The sources also mention a cloak of feathers.

Brigit wrapped her mantle of protection around people, houses, animals, and the very hearth-fire itself that represented the vitality of life: you know how important fire is if you've ever experienced the damp cold of Ireland! Her mantle's protection spiritually encircled all that was important to the Celts in the physical world. Today you will find Gaels who pray for St. Brigit to protect the sanctuary circle of hearth, family, and flock, the above and the below, perhaps without realizing how ancient their prayer is.

The Druid mantle must have been steeped in significance then, just as the Scottish plaid is today. Each clan has its plaid with a distinctive checked pattern or tartan. To anyone who has not experienced this, the wearing of the clan tartan is not just a means of dress for the Gael. It is an emotionally and symbolically laden object enwrapping the wearer in the clan, the lineage, the ancestors, the whole way of life of their tradition. Women wove the original plaids at home from wool shorn from sheep raised on the tribal lands. They collected the dyes for the colors of the tartan from local plants. The patterns of the tartan represent certain qualities of the clan: the sea, the mountain, the river, and the arrangement of social and political affiliations. Putting on the tartan wrapped wearers in every element of their life, shielded them from harm, stated who they were, where they had come from, and indeed where lay their destiny—for no self-respecting Highlander today is buried without his or her plaid.

As far as we know, not a single example of ancient plaid exists from the time of the Celts, due to the dampness of the climate. We do know that cloaks of wool from the northern Celtic lands were highly prized in Rome, and that Roman writers commented on the checked patterns and bright colors of Celtic dress. We also know that, according to ancient Brehon Law, the *Ard Rígh* (the High King) could wear seven colors; Druids, lords, and poets six colors; a provincial chief five colors; a wealthy landowner four colors; a warrior three colors; a peasant two colors; and a slave one color. These prescriptions surely must refer to the plaid.[4] There is every reason to think that the plaid with its tartan designs originated in ancient times and carried the same wealth of meaning for the Celts as it does today.

It is vital, therefore, when considering wearing a mantle for Druid work and inspiration that it carry this kind of meaning. It will not do to wrap oneself in a cloth or leather of any origin. Try to obtain, for example, raw wool or leather from the source. Otherwise you can make the mantle from woven fabric or tanned leather. Additionally, we recommend wearing the robe only for sacred purposes. Dedicate it under auspicious circumstances, allow no one but yourself to wear it, and store it in a safe and protected place. If you are thinking of obtaining a hide for purposes of divination, you are under even tighter restrictions. In the United States, a hide obtained from a bow hunter of an elk, deer, or caribou would be appropriate. If you obtain a hide in other ways, you can consecrate it with an aura of respect and power.

The Crane Bag

The Crane Bag is one of the most fascinating magical tools that present-day Druids will ever have to work with. Celtic mythology says that the Crane Bag was in the possession of the family of Fionn mac Cumhail. They lost it, and when Fionn won it back, it assisted him in his knowledge of poetry and wisdom. We write "assisted," as Fionn had other means of tapping into this knowledge, including putting the tip of his thumb into his mouth and touching a certain tooth. He had also eaten of the Salmon of Wisdom. The God of the Sea, Manannán, appears to have made the original Crane Bag, and it contained certain treasures:

> *Of crane-skin it was made, skin that was at one time the skin of Aoife, the beautiful lover of Ilbrec, son of Manannán, who was put into the shape of a crane because of jealousy. It was once kept in the house of Manannán, and these are the treasures that were kept within it: Manannán's shirt and knife, the belt and hook of the smith* [god] *Goibniu, the shears of the King of Alban*

[Scotland], *the helmet of the King of Lochlann* [Norway], *a belt of the skin of a great whale, and the bones of Asal's pig brought to Ireland by the three sons of Tuireann. All these treasures would be in the bag when the tide was full, but at the ebbing of the tide the bag would be empty. The crane-bag went from Manannán to Lugh of the Long Arm, son of Eithlinn, and then to Cumhail, husband to Murna, who some say was Ethlinn's daughter, and thence to Fionn.*[5]

This passage is not very clear and suggests the contents of the bag were a secret, as are the contents of Native American medicine bags. The Crane Bag seems to be the Irish version of the Grail. It appears and disappears (the ebb tide), shifts guardianship (four times), and shifts worlds (sea to land; god to hero). Just as the sun finds hidden crevices on the mountain at every sunrise, so you can find meanings of the Crane Bag that will illuminate your inner Self.

The crane is a bird associated with letters and the alphabet, so this might be a clue to the source of poetic wisdom the bag contains. The crane is also associated with death, rebirth, and the labyrinthine path between the worlds—a further clue to the bag's contents. The sea symbology is strong. Manannán is a sea god and psychopomp, while Ethlinn was the daughter of Balor, a Fomorian sea giant. In addition, the contents of the bag ebb and flow with the tides, giving a lunar connection.

Another type of bag appears in the Welsh myth of the wise old dark goddess, Ceridwen, and the famous bard Taliesin. This story is given in chapter 19. Ceridwen had the child Taliesin sown into a leather bag and thrown into the ocean. He lay there for many cycles of the sun and moon, until caught on a fishing weir. There is reason to believe Taliesin not only received the power of poetic inspiration from the three drops of Ceridwen's cauldron, but was also taught the secrets of sky and sea while floating in the bag. The old Irish fishing boats or curraghs (known in Welsh as a coracle) are skin-covered, which is perhaps a remnant of this mythic container.

We suggest that, as a student of Druidry, you pursue the subject of the Crane Bag very carefully. When you feel that you understand what it is made for, and what it contains, then you are ready to make one. We feel you should undertake this secretly, and never divulge the contents to anyone else. The Crane Bag is among the most personal objects that a Druid can possess. Quite probably, one's Crane Bag should accompany the Druid to the grave.

The Four Talismans of the Tuatha Dé Danann

Among the magical tools of the Druids is a special category of objects from the foundation myth of the Tuatha Dé Danann. These were talismans, a wonderful word for consecrated objects marked with magical signs and conferring supernatural powers. The myth discussed in chapter 1 says that the Tuatha Dé Danann came to Ireland from four great cities, each one of which possessed a great treasure. From Falias they brought the Stone of Fál, the *Lia Fáil*, the Stone of Virtue and of Destiny, which cried out when touched by the rightful king. From Gorias they brought the Spear of Victory, which is likely to be the spear Lugh used to kill Balor and defeat the Fomorians, and with which no battle was ever lost. From Finias they brought the Sword of Truth, wielded by their king at that time, Nuada, and of those who deserved its stroke none ever recovered. From Murias they brought the fourth treasure, the Cauldron of Plenty, and when the Dagda offered this cauldron, no company ever went away from it unsatisfied.

The myth also says that in Falias that lay to the north of their land, their teacher was Morias, the "Great Wisdom"; in shining Gorias their teacher was Urias, the "Way of the Noble Nature." In the city of Finias their teacher was the fair-headed poet Arias, of the "Great Ocean"; and in Murias their teacher was Senias of the "High Air." It was from these four poets that the Tuatha Dé learned *amainsechta* and *amaidechta*, their "magical skill" and "occult knowledge."

From this myth it is possible to arrive at a complete set of elements, powers, and qualities associated with each talisman:

Talisman	City	Teacher	Element	Qualities
Stone	Falias	Morias	Earth	sovereignty, wisdom, virtue, destiny
Cauldron	Murias	Senias	Water	wealth, abundance
Spear	Gorias	Urias	Fire	victory, the path or the way
Sword	Finias	Arias	Air	truth, discrimination

Some writers have even derived the four directions or compass points from this myth. However, it is likely that this order and these qualities were added at a later date to the text to make it more poetic, and it is difficult to know which tradition is authentic. This would not matter—the text probably inspired the redactors—were it not for the fact that we never find such correspondences used again. According to other Druidic sources, there are only three elements: the Sky, ruled by the Sun and Fire; the Sea, ruled by the Moon and Water; and the Land, ruled by the Earth. The only equivalents of the directions are the four winds: the North, South, East, and West Winds. The four talismans of the Tuatha Dé Danann therefore stand in a category apart, and it is difficult to fit them into magical traditions to which many modern people are accustomed.

Having said that, each talisman does repay serious study. When examined in the context of the Celtic worldview, it is clear that each one has enormous meaning. Throughout this book, the spear, the sword, the stone, and the cauldron are mentioned repeatedly. We urge the reader to study the stories featuring such objects, to gain an understanding of them. In the meantime, we will offer a magical cycle for you to think about. The following way of using the talismans and their correspondences arises from the authors' understanding. The cycle may be as short as a breath and a thought, or as long as a day, a year, or even a lifetime.

> **The Stone** is the root, the earth, the chthonic source of life. It is midnight, darkness, and the Winter Solstice. It is the connection to the ancestors; the moment of conception and of death.
>
> **The Cauldron** is the process of birth, of growth, of emergence into the light. It is dawn, Imbolc, and the Spring Equinox. It nurtures, provides, actualizes the root energy of the source.
>
> **The Spear** is the creative outpouring of the mature individual. It is noon, light, the Summer Solstice, the peak of abundance, the crown of the head, the realization of art.
>
> **The Sword** is the subtle power of discrimination. It is evening, the Autumn Equinox, the time of harvest and cutting away. It starts the return to source.

This is only a summary of the qualities associated with each talisman in this method of working. As you visualize and work with this cycle, you will come upon more ways in which the talismans can be extremely powerful. Try using the cycle to aid your creative process. Begin with the stone when you are conceiving a creative project, move on to the cauldron when ideas start to pour forth, work with the spear at the time of manifestation, and with the sword when completing. You can use this cycle to focus and direct sexual energy, as explained in chapter 6. We think you will find that transformation as well as creativity will come more easily, since the process operates in harmony with the naturally occurring patterns of the world.

Let us say you obtain a suitable stone, cauldron, spear, and sword, and you like to work with an altar or sacred space. We recommend that the stone be the prominent or ruling feature in that space from Samhain to Imbolc, the cauldron from Imbolc to Beltane, the Spear from Beltane to Lughnasadh, and the sword from Lughnasadh to Samhain.

In our wedding ceremony we used the four talismans in a wonderful and powerful way. We asked four friends to call the quarters (also known as the directions). They all happened to be familiar with Wiccan ways of working sacred space, and we asked them to add the four talismans as a Druidic influence. They called in the sword in the East, the spear in the South, the cauldron in the West, and the stone in the North. Each person performed a beautiful evocation of the qualities of each talisman that magically set the sacred space. When all the quarters, and the Above, Below, and Center, were called, our friends carried the four talismans to the center. They placed an exquisite sword, spear, cauldron, and stone on the altar, which we did not know were going to be wedding gifts for us! We treasure these objects to this day, and are certain from this experience that there are many more ways of working with the four talismans of the Tuatha Dé Danann than are mentioned here.

Activities

Tools of the trade. It seems that Druids made their own magical tools. So can you, with your imagination and perhaps with the help of a friend. You can set yourself the goal of creating a magical tool every three months. To get started, pick one of the following and carefully produce an excellent object for ritual use. Imagine that you have been apprenticing and this will be your "master" piece.

- A robe of your own design.
- A sickle.

- A wand or Silver Branch.

- A rod.

- Jewelry.

- A cord and belt.

- A Druid Egg.

- Something made from a tree you are working with.

- A blank book for recording poems, songs, stories, and rituals which you create.

- A musical instrument.

- A weaving.

- An altar cloth.

- A Crane Bag.

- A set of Ogham sticks.

- Objects that represent the earth, sea, and sky.

Talismans. Take your time, set your intention, and make or obtain the four talismans. They may come to you in any order until you have a Stone of Destiny, a Spear of Victory, a Sword of Truth, and a Cauldron of Abundance. This latter can be anything from the traditional witch's cauldron to a *quaich*—a broad two-handled cup offered full of whiskey in Scotland as a token of friendship and hospitality.

Notes

1. *The Mabinogion*, translated by Jeffrey Gantz, p. 106.

2. Alexander Thom, *Megalithic Sites in Britain*; John Michell, *The Dimensions of Paradise*.

3. Pliny, *Naturalis Historia* XVI.249.

4. Based on ancient and modern sources, Searles O'Dubhan suggests these colors for the different levels of Irish society: *Ard Ríph*—purple, white, black, blue, red, green, and yellow (the colors of the Royal Stewart Tartan.); Druids, Churchmen, Lords, Poets—white, black, blue, red, green, and yellow; Provincial Chiefs—black, blue, red, green, and yellow; a Bruiden or Wealthy Landowner—blue, red, green, and yellow; a Warrior—red, green, and yellow; a Peasant—green and yellow; and a Slave—yellow. O'Dubhan maintains a website at http://www.summerlands.org

5. Translation from Lady Gregory (1904).

Chapter 4

Developing Yourself As a Seer

The Druid took four wands of yew and upon them he wrote Oghams, and by his keys of poetic wisdom and through his Ogham he divined that Etain was in Bri Leith with Midhir.[1]

This chapter takes us into divination, or nonordinary ways of knowing. Ogham utilizes tools, whereas Second Sight and augury do not. As with seers in Celtic times, divination today pertains more to knowing the hidden present than to knowing the future.

Druid Methods of Divination

As well as being historians with knowledge of the past, Druids today seek knowledge of the unknown in the present and the future. In reading the Celtic myths you will notice, surprisingly, that ancient Druids looked into the present more often than they prophesied about the future. The quotation that begins this chapter is an example. The Druid found the missing Etain within the Fairy Mound of Bri Leith but he did not predict whether she would leave it. When Druids predicted outcomes, their predictions were based on the best available knowledge, personal intuition, and the most appropriate behavior to be done. One thing is different. Druids in the Celtic era needed long training in the laws of probability and patterns of nature in order to prognosticate about outcomes and weather, whereas we use computer models and meteorological satellites to know those things today.

Prophecy creates behavior. Celtic sources record that the fate of many a venture depended upon divination by Druids. Imagine living when people did nothing of significance if the Druid pronounced a day or a time unfavorable. The longest surviving text from Celtic Gaul, known as the Coligny Calendar, is an inscription on bronze that defines favorable and unfavorable days for a period of sixty-four months. As astronomers, the Druids looked to the heavens in the manner of modern astrologers to determine these auspicious times, as well as reading entrails and other omens that we prefer to omit here!

True magic, like true love, takes time to unfold inside you. Magic comes only as a result of extensive training, as you have already divined from previous chapters. This chapter is about training yourself to be a seer. Divination that calls on poetry and song is covered in chapter 19.

Divining with Ogham

The extract quoted above tells us that when the king, Eochaid, needed to find Etain, his Druid wrote Ogham letters on four wands of yew and from them divined where she was. When Druids used Ogham for divination purposes, the sources always say they were written on wood. The key to working with Ogham for divination purposes is understanding the trees from which the letters came. Please look ahead to chapter 17 concerning the Celtic Tree Alphabet, and study the Ogham letters and trees there.

Once you can create a set of Ogham inscriptions in the manner described in chapter 17, you will be well on the way to understanding their meaning and use. You will only understand the set of correspondences surrounding each Ogham when you take the time to tune in to the spirit of the tree for which each letter is named. The Ogham of birch, for example, might inspire you with the feeling of being in the midst of a grove of silvery barked trees, with their delicate leaves rustling overhead, in a fresh, light-filled and lively atmosphere. If you are also aware of the kinds of minerals that birch grows in, and the birds and creatures, fungi and plants that birch is host to, so much the better. It is this total context where the spirit of birch thrives that makes it possible for you to gain a glimpse of the deeper spirit presences within the tree. We say in our Druid Grove that it takes a year to really understand a tree, so to become familiar with the twenty trees of the Ogham system will take twenty years!

Remember, Ogham is a magical system. It relies on your ability to allow the marvelous presence of the trees to come into you. The trees themselves will suggest the answer you are looking for, according to the way their Oghams fall in relationship to each other. But as in all divination systems, the answer they give will only be as incisive as the question you ask and the system you develop for asking. It is also up to you to constantly develop your knowledge of trees and their correspondences in the natural world. The best equipment available for becoming an expert in Ogham interpretation is quite likely a pair of binoculars, a stout pair of boots, and a set of good books on bird, tree, plant, and fungus identification!

Keep in mind that you must begin somewhere in your practice of divination, because you can't be an expert without first becoming a beginner. Make a set of Oghams carved or painted on a kind of wood that you are comfortable and familiar with. We recommend the following methods of Ogham divination. (A further method is given as an Activity at the end of this chapter).

A General Reading. Take out your set of Oghams from its safe place and prepare an appropriate space in which to work. Shuffle the Ogham sprigs and ask about the influences of the present moment. Remove a sprig at random. It doesn't matter if the Ogham comes out upside down: since there is no reversal of meaning in Ogham, just turn it around. To read the Ogham requires tuning into the spirit of its tree and inviting the message that is there to emerge. Leave this Ogham out for a while so you can dwell on its meaning over a period of time.

Answering a Specific Question. Decide on a question for divination. Follow the steps described above, but this time take out several Ogham sprigs, one after the other. Keep your question in mind. Lay the Oghams out in a sequence. In the old days they were read from the bottom up, but they are easier to read running left to right. You may like to predetermine how many you will draw beforehand, or you can stop when you intuit that you have drawn enough. Read what the Oghams say. We assume that you will ask them to spell out words in English, but sometimes we find the words are obstinately Irish, complete with the Ogham tradition of dropping vowels! If an Ogham is unclear, draw another and lay it beside the first.

A Specific Reading. Predetermine a pattern or structure for laying out the Oghams. It may be similar to the layout of Tarot cards. Slowly remove one sprig after another and lay them out in that pattern. The first Ogham may refer to the topic you have named, the next to the past, the next to the present, and the next to the future, and so on. Look at the pattern before you and build up a sense of interpretation. The interpretation works on two levels: the first is from the letters themselves—is there a literal message? Or, second, is the message coming from the symbolic meaning of the trees?

Ogham *Draíocht*. As an exercise in Druid magic, take your Ogham set (or a Celtic divination set such as the *Druid Animal Oracle* or the *Celtic Shaman's Deck*) and spread the entire set of sprigs, cards, or stones out in an even circle. Do nothing except contemplate the many aspects of life the set represents. The set reflects your many choices on the Wheel or the Tree of Life. You are at the center, and can go in any direction because there are so many choices and possibilities. Throughout this process, you will choose to remain at the center.

From this center, contemplate the things you would like to achieve. There is no limitation on them, nor on the means of accomplishing them. From the center, everything is present and everything is possible. Now select an Ogham that represents some aspect of your life, or something that you would really like. From the perspective of the center, think and feel about this thing. How can you improve it? What are you willing to do to get it? Bring all the powers of your Self to bear upon this subject. If you decide this is not what you really want, select another Ogham.

When you are absolutely certain that you have found something you would like to put energy into, place the Ogham representing that thing at the center. You may say something over it such as: "I dedicate my Self to this end." What tools are available to help you achieve it? What are you willing to do to accomplish this objective? You may find that some notions you were holding about the subject are self-defeating or even unethical. Search for a course of action that will accomplish the objective in a manner that satisfies your eternal Self.

When you have found the right course of action, make a statement about it. The statement might sound like this: "I swear by Earth, by Sky, and by Sea, that I am willing to devote myself, body, mind and spirit, to the practice of . . . " (my craft, my art). "From the place of my eternal Self I dedicate myself to the cause of . . ." "I will use all the powers of my Druid magic to accomplish the goal of . . ." "By the power of the Ogham (name it here) I swear to pursue this Truth . . ." These words put you in league with the Celtic wordsmiths and Ogham magicians.

Prophecy and Second Sight

It was the Druid Ovates who were the clairvoyants, seers, prophets, and diviners in Celtic times. As you read the original sources, you will find that Ovates usually divined things happening in the present, or determined if the present was auspicious for a major activity such as ritual or battle. You will also notice that the Ovates performed divination to know about things at a distance. Telling the present from afar was therefore a strong point of Druid diviners.

We will not attempt to review all the means of divination, such as precognitive dreams, astrology, trance songs, and divining patterns from bird flight, although chapter 19 does deal with some classic Druid techniques of divination through poetic inspiration. We won't try to prove that present-day Druids can do all that Celtic Druids did: communicate with spirits and the dead, reveal the past, remove spells, cure fairy strokes, and bring people back from Fairyland![2] We will concentrate on two methods of knowing the present: Second Sight and augury. Second Sight often happens spontaneously, without bidding, whereas augury is formal and requires training, perhaps even trance or ritual.

Second Sight or The Sight are terms that refer to the ability to see what is not in front of your eyes. A good explanation is that people with this ability have one eye in this world and one in the Otherworlds.[3] They can see visible and invisible reality at one time.[4] Another explanation is that there are two races in Ireland: the visible Celtic race and the invisible Tuatha Dé Danann who once dwelt on the land and then became the Fairy Folk, the *Sídhe* of Irish mythology. People with Second Sight can communicate with both races.

The closest that science can come to an explanation for Second Sight has to do with dimensions and planes of existence. Nature seems to have a kind of memory that retains impressions of physical actions—"morphogenetic fields" is the current term for this phenomenon. Seers can observe nature's "mental records" like pictures projected on a planetary movie screen. They can temporarily function in the consciousness of that extraordinary plane and perceive as clearly as we all do in ordinary reality.

Second Sight occurs when someone suddenly "sees" what is happening in the present with people who are at a distance, or can "see" what will happen in the near future. Many people in Celtic lands to this day have Second Sight. Some are indeed thought to be able to see and talk with the Fairy People. It may be that everyone has this ability, but as with so many other senses and magical workings, we become convinced that we cannot do it. Posh and bother! You too can see with Second Sight! You need to validate your experience when it happens, remaining open to this nonordinary ability so that it returns more often.

Here is what we suggest. Affirm to yourself that you have had experiences with Second Sight, and that you are open to having more. Recall the circumstances when you felt this happening: maybe it was at night, you were feeling empathetic and aware of a problem in the family, you glanced away and saw a vision of the family member in question. You had a premonition that something was about to happen, and it did— although you might not have believed enough in your ability to act on the premonition at the time. When similar feelings recur, be ready for The Sight next time. Talk with family and friends to see if anyone else has this gift. Treat it like a shy animal, letting it approach a little closer each time until you are as much of a ready conduit as you would like to be.

Please refer to the section in chapter 2 called "The Lost is Found" for details on locating missing people or items. We mention it here because it connects with Second Sight. When Maya finds lost things, she uses The Sight, a longstanding tradition of the Irish people. "Seeing" in this unfocused way tells her whether something is in a certain place without rummaging frantically for it, and if she cannot "see" in that place, it tells her the object's actual whereabouts.

Recently, a young friend was distraught over losing her airline tickets and jumped to thinking they had been stolen out of her suitcase. Using Second Sight, Maya could see them in a flat space. In your own practicing, when you get to this point, stay open and unfocused. Allow thoughts, words, and images to keep on coming. At this point, Maya found herself saying aloud that packing papers separately from clothes safeguards them. The friend insisted she had thrown everything in the bag together. Maya asked to look at her luggage. There, at the bottom of one side was a small, flat pocket that indeed held the tickets. Using The Sight, all you have to do is translate what you "see" into the most likely real location. For something lost while traveling, look in the luggage.

You have probably heard many tales of someone who knows when a loved one is in trouble or injured, even if the other person is thousands of miles away. Druids of old could perceive happenings at a distance, and so can you! If you think back, you will probably recall several instances when you "knew" something was about to happen. Although Second Sight often happens unpredictably, you can also request a sighting.

When Maya was teaching in Mongolia and out of touch with the rest of the world, she became concerned about her dogs, who had been left in the care of a housesitter. Second

Sight told her the dogs were fine, but worry set in. Without realizing it, in the past Maya had always confirmed Second Sight findings by checking the outcome. Not only was there no e-mail or fax in Mongolia, there was no postal or telephone service, and of course no other Druids! This time no checking was possible. Though that area is where shamans originated, she did not know any, so she asked for a reading with ritual stones from a Mongolian woman. The reading confirmed the dogs' health but showed that the one Maya had rescued was fretful. The lesson is to trust your own ability and even delay checking on results so you rely on The Sight rather than the phone.

You should know that people with Second Sight can see the "good people" from the Fairy Realm. Such a vision may come about in a "rapture, transport, a sort of death," or in a type of ecstasy.[5] This has happened twice when Maya has been lying in bed awake, completely without warning. Both times a strange feeling came over her— insistent sensations of something happening. Her body felt fixed to the spot while other parts of her were light and ready to go with the experience. In the first rapture, she saw indescribably vivid colors swirling, forming and reforming shapes that were recognizable for an instant and then dissolved. The message was that absolutely everything is in flux whether we normally see it that way or not.

The second rapture occurred in Glendalough, Ireland, a place of mysterious happenings and the site of Nicholas's spontaneous initiation with the Horned God. This time Maya went on an actual journey to the land of Fairy. She felt taken over by bodily sensations and forces that altered her reality. A beetle led her to the edge of a boulder and she peered down through a crack. Suddenly, like Alice in Wonderland, she was small enough to slip through the crack and enter the Otherworld with her beetle guide. Into a lovely parallel world she went, where groups of small beings were working at crafts, having dinner, walking in the forest. No one remarked on Maya's presence, even though she stayed for a long time. The message in this experience was that only size and perception prevent us from entering other realms, experiencing them as directly and certainly as knowing what we ate for breakfast.

After having these experiences, Maya read the 1906 testimony of an eighty-six-year-old Irish woman who said that she had often seen the good people or fairies while in her bed. She thought they lived in the rocks throughout the nearby mountains.[6] That certainly agrees with Maya's experience!

Augury

Queen Maeve encounters the Druidess Fedelm before engaging Cuchulain in the epic battles of the *Táin*, and the young prophet proclaims: "I see crimson, I see red." Maeve in her usual imperious way rejects this prophecy of death for her army, but the seer persists. Seeing blood, the color red, the Washer Woman at the Ford with your own garment dripping in blood, or hearing weapons shriek aloud are bad omens, and we sincerely hope you do not see them in daylight or in your dreams! Augury is divination or foretelling by observing signs and omens. This form of prophecy was common in Celtic times. Getting results required training and preparation.

Certain animals presaged danger or death, the most notable being the ravens who surrounded the dark goddess the Morrigán. Maya's mother was brought up by an Irish-born aunt who lived by the old superstitions and cursed in Irish (the native language of Ireland is now called Irish, since Gaelic took on a pejorative meaning under English rule). Old Aunt Maggie could predict deaths by reading the behavior of dogs and horses. Since we know that animals can presage earthquakes, it is just as likely that they can presage human death. Most of us have not learned to comprehend these messages from animals.

Let's look at augury using the hands and face to create a force-field of divination. In both pagan and Christian times, Brigit was connected with augury. She may have been an Ovate. The pagan goddess Brigit ensured fertility and abundance in humans and animals, while the Christian St. Brigit was the patron of fertile, pregnant women. In Celtic Christian lore, Brigit was a close friend of Mary and was midwife at the birth of Jesus. This makes her the foster-mother of Jesus, a tradition that is one of the central links between the pagan and Christian Celtic worlds.

The augury of Brigit is reported in a story in *Carmina Gadelica*. The boy Jesus made his first public appearance in the temple and was thronged by incredulous adults. Mary lost contact with him and reportedly appealed to Brigit to find him. Brigit cupped her hands over her eyes to form a cone or tube. Looking down this magical passage, she had a vision of Jesus by the well of the temple, which is where Mary found him.[7] Not surprisingly, pagan Brigit was associated with sacred springs and wells, while throughout Ireland and Scotland today, miraculous wells are attributed to the Christian Brigit. Chapter 5 reaches deeper into the mysteries of Brigit.

Several cultures use the placing of hands over the face for healing and for augury.[8] There are references, in *Cormac's Glossary*, to Druid poets placing their palms over their cheeks and awaiting a desired answer.[8] Think of it: putting the hands over the face is an inborn human reaction to strong emotions such as surprise, pain, embarrassment, or hearing bad news. Now you can use it purposefully. If you want to visualize things or people at a distance or in the future, get yourself quiet and centered. Place your palms or encircled hands over your eyes and unfocus your vision. Gaze into the dark and wait.[9] Whatever impressions come to you are the answer; they may be a combination of seeing with your eyes and your other powers.

Druidic training in augury demanded much discipline and preparation. Celtic augurers followed certain conditions. They fasted, dressed in a certain way, and kept their feet bare. After praying and meditating upon the chosen matter, they chanted and walked in certain patterns, most likely at sunrise. You may modify these conditions but should still expect to put out some effort and preparation, at least if you wish to obtain good results.

Activities

The Ogham Cast. First put down a square or circular cloth: as this will help establish the frame in which to read the sprigs. If you wish, lay out your cloth according to the directions of sacred space: the four cardinal directions, plus above and below, and visualize the World Tree standing in the center of your sacred ground. Take your whole set of Oghams, cast them onto the cloth and see how they lie. Some will fall outside the bounds of the space, others will be invisible, others may point directly at you or at another person present. Any Ogham that falls outside the bounds may or may not be significant, depending on your method and the circumstances, which are up to you to intuit. In our experience, any Oghams that create a readable sequence or a figure such as a cross, a square, an arrow, or even another Ogham are important, while large groups tend not to be significant. Interpret the Oghams according to the framework you decide on. It is up to you to develop an interpretative system that allows you to get inside the space the fallen Oghams create, and divine from there. You may wish to spell out words from the letters or follow the symbolic and divinatory meaning of the trees.

The Seeing Cone. Use the "seeing cone" of Brigit to locate people or things missing at the present time. Curl your hands over your eyes; open or shut eyes make no difference. Look down the passage into the dark. Ask for the vision you want, and wait. Trust what you see. You can ask that a missing person get in touch with you or that a missing thing come in touch with your hand.

Second Sight. To develop Second Sight, give yourself a month of uncritical openness and awareness of your already-existing ability to know what is going on in other realms or in other places. The only guideline is that you must say *aloud*, or write down with date and time, anything you sense or "see," along with a short description of your sensations. At the end of the month, take note of how accurate you were and note the pattern of sensations that cues you to a Second Sight occasion.

Geomancy or Earth Divination. Go to a sacred site. Ask permission from the guardians and the spirits of place to work there, and make sure you are centered. Then conduct a search with your divination skills for subtle energies. Use augury, watch the patterns of animals, envision with the "seeing cone," or employ techniques such as Setting the Wards described in chapter 2 to see what images come.

We think that a whole system of earth divination is possible for the Druid Seer. The Druidic system of earth divination is oriented to the holistic qualities of a place as created by nature and not to human-made systems. The Druids built very few sacred sites, and went to places already made powerful by nature rather than by the hands of human beings. Ley lines and geometrical figures, characteristic of most contemporary earth divination, are not natural phenomena: they are part of human-made constructs, often imposed upon random natural landscapes. The energies that Druids pursue are more complex, cyclical, and dynamic, demonstrating the chaotic patterns of nature, rather than fixed and often simple mental constructs. Examine the curvilinear, asymmetrical artwork of the Celts, especially that of the La Tène era. This should confirm for you that the subtle energies worked by Druids at sacred sites were always in flux.

Brigit the Guidance Counselor. Take this opportunity to consult Brigit as your guidance counselor. Cup your hands over your face and ask an augury question about your career (a word that means "path, road") or vocation (a "calling"). What do you see and what do you hear?

Notes

1. *Tochmarc Etáine*, recension based on Lady Gregory (1904), A. H. Leahy (1905), and Jeffrey Gantz (1981).

2. W. Y. Evans-Wentz, *The Fairy-Faith in Celtic Countries*, pp. 264–5.

3. Erryn Rowan Laurie, "Turned by Joy or Sorrow" section of *The Cauldron of Poesy*, 1997.

4. Judith Orloff, M.D. *Second Sight*, 1997.

5. Evans-Wentz, p. 91.

6. Ibid., p. 77.

7. Carmichael, *Carmina Gadelica*.

8. Regarding augury, the Chinese suggest "palming" the eyes to quickly leave physical reality. Regarding healing, they suggest using the fingers on acupressure points around the cheeks and eyes for tension release.

9. Nora K. Chadwick, *Scottish Gaelic Studies*, 1935.

10. When Maya was teaching in Mongolia, a female seer taught her a very similar technique.

Chapter 5

BECOMING A DRUID MAGUS

And you, O knowledgeable boy, whose son are you?

I am the son of poetry,
Poetry, son of reflection,
Reflection, son of meditation,
Meditation, son of lore,
Lore, son of research,
Research, son of great knowledge,
Great knowledge, son of intelligence,
Intelligence, son of understanding,
Understanding, son of wisdom,
Wisdom, son of the three gods of Dana.[1]

In this chapter you will work with the cauldron of wisdom and inspiration, among the other gifts of the goddess Brigit. You will see how to incorporate Brehon Law into your life in making wise judgements. You will learn the importance of genealogy in preserving the ancestral wisdom of your people. You will become a Druidic "Ph.D." and create a personal mission statement, revealing to yourself how to present your wisdom to the world.

Being a magus or wise person has been the profession of Druids for thousands of years. For all we know, the three Magi might have been Druids! Magus comes from an Old Persian word for sorcerer, the same root which gives us the word magic. In your practice of Druidry, you will be developing your wisdom, thereby becoming a magus. May the goddess Brigit be your guide.

Brigit of Wisdom, Healing, and Livelihood

Brigit is a powerful feminine figure to study, as old a divinity as you will find in Celtic mythology. She is the daughter of the Dagda, one of the great father-heroes of the Tuatha Dé Danann. Later, she was one of the few deities known all over Europe: Brigantia in Britain, Bride in Scotland, Birgitta in Scandinavia, and in Gaul the Romans called her Minerva. Still later, the Irish so revered her that the Christians made her St. Brigit, patroness of Ireland, rivalling St. Patrick in importance. If St. Brigit the Christian abbess ever truly lived, it is likely she was a generic female spiritual leader of the Abbey at Kildare. Subsequent abbesses took "Brigit" as a title, not as a personal name. Likewise in earlier Neolithic and Celtic times, her name, translated as "The High One," may have been interchangeable with "goddess" in that she was *the* Goddess for a long time.

No major myth exists which features Brigit, though she is mentioned several times. We study Brigit because of the continuity of her presence throughout history—devotion to her has never died out. This long-standing presence validates that her gifts of inspiration, healing, and craft or livelihood are necessary for humanity: they make us whole. We also study her because the historical Brigit, reportedly born in 450 C.E., was the daughter of a noble Druid father, Dubhthach, and a slave mother, Broicseth. Lineage that straddles such extremes usually connotes the birth of an unusual being. As an infant, before she could speak, Brigit made a prophecy that a Druid interpreted. She proclaimed herself as goddess of sovereignty over the land, by prophesying that the land would later belong to her. We can become sovereign over ourselves by incorporating the physical, mental, and spiritual attributes that she represents. Let us look further to see why Brigit's gifts are so powerful and lasting.

Brigit's Gifts from Sea, Earth, and Sky

You will often read that Brigit is the patron of healing, smithcraft, and of poetic inspiration. She brings these attributes out in us, rather than instilling them in us. As Druids, we translate those gifts as being from the sea, earth, and sky:

> **From the sea: the knowledge of healing waters**. Water was a prime element in the pre-Celtic and Celtic traditions. There are hundreds, perhaps thousands, of healing wells dedicated to Brigit still in use in Ireland and Scotland. They are places of pilgrimage and prayer, fountainheads of heal-

ing for body and spirit. We have bathed ailing body parts in Brigit's springs, and brought the water home for use in rituals.

From the earth: the blacksmith's knowledge of metallurgy. The extraction of metal from ore and the use of fire to shape metal were arts taught by a smith deity. Although this was originally a member of the race of the *Sídhe*—Goibhniu in Ireland and Govannon in Wales—in most Celtic cultures this later became Brigit. Blacksmiths had a special magical status and primacy in Celtic communities; they were fed first at feasts after the king or chieftain. Blacksmithing is still called "King of the Crafts."

What does this mean to us today? As goddess of smithcraft, she helps us to magically change our dreams into reality. It means that Brigit is the patroness of our livelihood, our mental fire, the forge of our being. The forge of the blacksmith was in actuality the fire for the whole community, and its flames were never allowed to go out. Likewise, Brigit is patroness of the hearth fire, which must never go out in the home. Brigit is the guardian of our crafts, skills, and work.

She and all smiths are associated with alchemy—changing something into something else, usually by using fire. Women do this in gestating and breast-feeding babies and in the traditional crafts of baking bread, weaving, and pottery. "Craft" is a synonym for wisecraft, making Brigit patron of Druids, prophets, enchantresses, priestesses, and all women and men who practice sacred power responsibly. Shamans are alchemists who can change from this world to the Otherworlds and back again, bringing with them a message, a piece of lost soul, or healing. Geoffrey Ashe, in *Dawn Behind the Dawn*, postulates that the original shamans in Siberia were women, and male blacksmiths made magical gear for them. A Yakut Siberian proverb says: "Smiths and shamans are from the same nest."[2]

From the sky: cosmic inspiration. Brigit is patroness of poetry in the sense of helping us bring forth our sacred, inspired wisdom. The Celts perfected this flow and had names for people who could do it. In Welsh an "Inspired One" was called *awenydd*, while in Irish the term *file* refers to a "Vision Poet." Brigit helps us on the sacred Celtic journey we are taking in order to recover traditional lore and ancestral wisdom. It is a journey to validate each of us in our creativity, imagination, and spiritual path. This gift from Brigit helps us to solve problems and to nourish spiritual waste-lands. She is the Celtic muse. You will learn to lie in the streambed of her inspiration when you accomplish the activities in chapter 19.

The Mythic Cauldrons

For a long time we wondered how Brigit's three aspects of healing, craft, and inspiration fit together. Healing seemed to pertain to the physical, smithcraft to earning a living with our wits, and poetic wisdom to being in-spirited. We realized that Brigit's three gifts fit the body-mind-spirit domains which together (adding emotions) make up the whole human being: her gifts cover every aspect of being human. It is up to us to learn how to carry out her attributes in our lives in order to reach fullness. Brigid represents fullness or holism. When her attributes are actualized in our lives, they bring about a total, integrated, complete, and sacred way of living. After much study, we discovered that Brigit's gifts are at the center of Celtic and Druidic magic because they are the outpouring of the mythic cauldrons, the very fire of life!

It becomes apparent why Brigit is Goddess of All when her three aspects are connected with the three cauldrons mentioned in Celtic myths. Brigit is patroness of a power within each of the three cauldrons. She can help you in body, mind, and spirit. She is said to be the daughter of the Dagda, from whose cauldron no one went away unsatisfied. To us, she is the Irish version of the amazing Ceridwen, the Welsh keeper of the cauldron containing all the wisdom of the ancients. That cauldron of wisdom causes shape-changing and therefore rebirth in all who imbibed its contents, which relates to Bran's cauldron of regeneration.

Take some time now to contemplate what this table of aspects means in your life. Are you complete? Do you concentrate on your work to the detriment of your body

Cauldron	Gift	Brigit's Aspect	Human Aspect
Bran	rebirth = physical restoration	healing, medicines, herbs	body
Dagda	plenty = livelihood, vocation	smithcraft, work	mind
Ceridwen	wisdom = sacred inspiration, or *awen*	bardic poetry	spirit

and spirit? Are you introverted to the point of neglecting to relate to others through your talents and spiritual practice? Do you feel in balance? This is the opportunity to look at yourself with awesome truthfulness. This is the opportunity to allow Brigit to bring her power of the ages into your life.

The Cauldrons of Poesy

The three cauldrons most mentioned in Celtic mythology—Bran's for physical regeneration, the Dagda's for plenty, and Ceridwen's for inspiration—match perfectly with three described in the old Irish text the *Cauldrons of Poesy*. The text says the Cauldrons of Poesy are inside us, and act on us in mysterious ways. They are, first, the cauldron of physical warming or incubation. Within this cauldron you heat and brew your health. You can see that this refers to the physical domain and equates to Brigit's healing aspect and to Bran's cauldron of physical regeneration. Second, there is a cauldron concerning your course of action or achievement. Here our emotions and talents are on fire. This refers to the mental-emotional domain. It also equates to Brigit's smithcraft aspect, helping us with whatever craft is our mental talent for earning a living. Third is the cauldron of wisdom. This holds all of our innate abilities and potentials that we can develop to their fullest intensity. The idea of self-actualization lies within this last cauldron's attributes.

Inspiration and wisdom are two of the words most frequently used in Celtic lore. Let us look deeper into the cauldron of wisdom. In the old days, Druids expected the Irish people to exceed limitations of birth and magnify their gifts and artistry. In poetic terms, these are the liquid fires of creativity that come from drinking at the well of wisdom. This cauldron unleashes the speech of your soul. Have you experienced an enlightened time when passionate creativity filled you? Have you felt the magic from releasing it, and becoming further filled? If so, you have experienced the cauldron of wisdom, the fire in the head.

You can see in the table below how the triple attributes of Brigit relating to our body-mind-spirit also equate to the internal Cauldrons of Poesy. Physical incubation is the same as healing. One's livelihood or craft is the same as one's course of action. Inspiration is the same as wisdom.

Note an extremely important symbol: all these aspects relate to fire. Since we derive Brigit's attributes, the Bran-Dagda-Ceridwen cauldrons, and the Cauldrons of Poesy from mythic (or at least very old) sources, we should think of the symbol of fire mythically. That puts us in the realm of alchemy and alchemical transformation, which is the work of fire. You may recall that alchemists used an alembic or cauldron in which they distilled and purified substances, and this equates to the incubation and physical regeneration referred to above. When you study cauldrons in Celtic and Druidic work, take yourself out of the literal realm and put yourself in the realm of transformation. As you work with these cauldrons, be ready to experience profound changes.

Let us look again at Brigit's gifts, from the viewpoint of alchemical fire. The first two columns refer to the cauldrons that are central to working with Celtic and Druidic teachings. The final column refers to the types of transformative fire which Brigit ignites in us.[3]

Mythic Cauldrons	Poesy Cauldrons	Fires of Life
Bran—regeneration	Physical Incubation	Healthy body/ personal hearth
Dagda—bounty	Course of Motion/ Achievement	Smith's forge/ community fire
Ceridwen—inspiration	Wisdom	Eternal soul/ cosmic purpose

Let's take one of these as an example of how to apply this wisdom in actuality. Have you ever let your hearth fire—that is your "heart fire"—go out? Maya describes this experience in her own life:

I let my hearth fire go out several years before I ended a long marriage that had died in still waters in the 80s. I let the fire go out inside me and in the house. When he left and took what was his, very few possessions remained and little of me. I had been living without manifesting my being, my heart fire. So I meditated in the empty house until I found my home Self. Slowly I furnished my home and refurbished my inner Self. I called on Brigit, the Hearth Goddess, to help me do this and she has been by my side ever since. Nicholas and I married in the 90s. When we bought our first house together, we spent the first day in ritual and prayer, dedicating the land to the directions and spirits of place, and especially dedicating the hearth to Brigit.

In like manner with community and cosmic fires, we as Druids have a responsibility to put forth our talents in ways that keep those fires burning and in ways that benefit others.

The Wise Judge

Brehon Law was an ancient code of the Celts, superior in concept to Graeco-Roman law because of its fairness to both sexes and all classes of people, and its protection of the weak against oppression. As a model for our behavior, it has many virtues. Certain Druids were trained as Brehon judges. Based on laws of justice, they planned the course of action for chieftains and kings. They had the power to stand between two opponents and stop their fighting; even more astoundingly, they could stand between two armies and stop war! This tells us that they were mediators, strategists, and ambassadors who negotiated treaties.[4]

Celtic law was based on the principle of restorative justice. The goal of Brehon Law was the restoration of balance. Compensation rather than punishment was the premise. The current practice of having law offenders provide community service fits the idea of restorative justice. Brehon Law required Celts to face up to any wrongdoing, set it straight, and get on a good footing again so that each party was satisfied—quite an issue in those bloodthirsty days! Revenge killings were part of the law, with boundaries set as to how many others could be killed. The Irish loved equal justice even when the outcome went against themselves, because on balance, the law protected and benefited everyone.[5]

Julius Caesar wrote detailed observations of Celtic society in Gaul, including this:

> *Throughout Gaul there are two classes of men of some dignity and importance . . . One of the two classes is that of the Druids, the other that of the knights. The Druids are concerned with the worship of the gods, look after public and private sacrifice, and expound religious matters. A large number of young men flock to them for training and they are held in high honor by the people. They have the right to decide nearly all public and private disputes; and they also pass judgment and decide compensations and penalties in criminal and murder cases and in disputes concerning legacies and boundaries. When a private person or a tribe disobeys their ruling they ban them from attending at sacrifices. This is their harshest penalty.[6]*

We are certainly not advocating that you ostracize people from attending human and animal sacrifices! Rather, we are advocating that all of us learn to make decisions based on agreements concerning behavior and social justice. We advocate learning how to decide just outcomes of disputes. We advocate knowing our personal boundaries, having standards for our public behavior, living up to our standards in private, and carrying out meaningful rituals. These are modern applications of the Druidic practices mentioned in the passage above.

A more public application would be if you learned arbitration or mediation techniques and offered them to the community. You could become an advocate (a term from Latin meaning "speaking to," in Scottish and French it has come to mean "lawyer"), one who argues for a cause, one who supports or defends others such as organic growers, children, or animals. Similarly, an ombudsman is one who investigates citizens' complaints against bureaucracy.

Brehon Law was based on ethical values. These were standards agreed on by individuals and groups in Celtic society. That gives us the building block: we modern Druids must all stand upon our values. Take some time now to ponder and write down exactly what values you live by. What are the three or four most important standards you have? Which are "social" or politically correct or proper but do not come from your essence? Which would you die for?

Now test yourself in areas where you still need to develop wisdom. Which individuals and groups strain your ability to be fair? To whom do you have flashes of being cruel? When you make a snap decision, do you later regret it? Do you have an addiction that clouds your judgement? Do you have any double standards, applying one set to yourself and to those you like, another set to those who are different from you, including other races and the opposite sex?

The word Druid means knower of trees or, more generally, it means "wise person." A key place where we require wisdom in our lives is in making decisions and judgements. You have a wise judge inside you. The best guide is to judge your actions and make decisions based on your inner Truth. You are the self-elected chieftain, the royal leader of your mind and spirit, of your whole life! With study and practice in Druidic ways, you can develop this innate ability and apply it in situations requiring just decisions. Think of an event such as an auto accident, a conflict, or lawsuit when something went against you and you still carry a grudge or the desire for revenge. Now turn that situation around and think of yourself not as the winner or loser but as a Brehon judge. Rewrite the script of that incident until you can feel "equal and indifferent justice." When you reach this plane of justice, you may be moved to contact the other party and rectify things further.

Wisdom-Keeper of Your Ancestors

Celtic myths were the cinema of the past, and the songs sang of glorious ancestors! The Irish *filidh* or *filí* (alternative plural spellings of *file)* were Druids who studied for twelve years to learn the lore and genealogies they were sworn to preserve. Some sources call them "seer-poets" because they could predict the future as well as recite the past.[7] The Celts had no interest in preserving history as we study it today: disembodied facts, dates, and battles. Rather, they learned honor and behaviors from the past by means of stories, songs and poems, recitations and lists of ancestors. Theirs was a heroic society, with heroes and heroines embedded in their cosmology of sacred places, deities, and supernatural powers. The epics carried the grandeur of the lineage and reenacted famous battles.

The Celts did not study geography as we do: trade routes, mountain ranges, and political divisions. Instead, place names and legends kept alive the "geomythics" of the people. For the Celts, as for the Neolithic people who preceded them in Europe, water, stone, and tree were sacred. The legends of the land were anchored to springs, wells, and rivers. The Neolithic mounds, dolmens, and stone circles often figure in the stories. The waters and ancient sites were the dwelling places of mythologized ancestors. Places were named for natural features such as the rocks of the Giants' Causeway off Northern Ireland. The Bards named stories for their location, such as the *Táin Bó Cuailgne*, the "Cattle Raid of Cooley," (now the Carlingford Peninsula near Dundalk). Celtic children learned geography from these tales. Characters in the stories were named for their traits, such as Bricriu of the Poisoned Tongue who always stirred contention in any gathering.

With this background in the Celtic way of preserving the past, let us consider becoming *filí* ourselves. To a degree, we as Druids have a *responsibility* to be the wisdom-keepers of our ancestors. Enormous amounts of human energy, hope, plans, desires, and hardship went into producing you from the bedrock of your forebears. Being part of the Celtic renaissance makes you a wisdom-keeper when you bring forth the music, art, and lore of the Celts. Being a Druid makes you a keeper of the Druid tradition, and being the wisdom-keeper of your own family history is the most specific sort of all.

Some people are naturals at genealogy, the record of your genes over the generations. They delve into family background and are caught up in generational frenzy! They spend hours in archives with microfiche, writing to government record offices, looking at family albums, letters, and files. They compile charts and display them at family gatherings, but usually only one or two people are caught up in this search while the others consider it show and tell.

We recommend that you do some genealogical searching two or three times during the next year and see what happens. You may be fascinated by what you find, or you may come to a dead end and give up. Maya and a cousin are the only ones in their family with any interest at all, and it grows with each discovery and visit to the birthplace of an antecedent. Nicholas had a breakthrough when a paternal cousin unearthed important family documents. He hit the jackpot when a maternal cousin turned out to be president of a Scottish genealogical society, complete with a portrait of almost every ancestor back to the 1700s!

See if you can unearth the exact place-names where your great-grandparents were born. Translate the names and find out what they refer to. Ask older relatives for nicknames of people in generations before them and see what traits they name—perhaps there is a Poisoned Tongue or White Swan Neck among your relatives. Record on tape or paper all the stories, poems, and legends that your family elders can remember. Did any relatives take part in an uprising, war, or migration? Find out where, when, and how they fared. There are mountains of books on how to conduct genealogical searches. Start with living generations and work backwards. Don't wait, or someone with irretrievable information may pass away. When you have a rough idea of family branches, chart everything on a genogram. This is a long paper that lists the last few generations, especially noting unusual traits. These can be physical distinctions such as nose shape, height, six fingers on one hand, or any other distinguishing features. They can be chronic illnesses such as diabetes or weakening characteristics such as respiratory illness. They can be causes of death. The traits can be mental and emotional, such as depression, or can be combined with physical susceptibility, such as alcoholism or other addictions. You can note adventurers who move to another continent and those who stay put for generations. Soon you will be able to glean where some of your traits come from, and that is important and exciting information.

If you do not like your family of origin or are adopted (and can tell by your looks that you are Celtic), you can start at the other end of time and work forwards. Start researching the pre-Celts and Celts in general, in areas of Europe that interest you the most. Go and visit lots of places until you focus in on your greatest interests. We offer suggestions for visiting the homelands in chapter 14. Start reading all you can about those ancient people. It becomes more vivid when you realize they are people whose

DNA you probably carry. The reality that DNA is passed live from generation to generation, that your navel was connected to your mother's and her mother's as far back as your mind can imagine, gives excitement to the study of your genetic line. We urge you to jump into this study at whatever point you choose—ancient or modern—and get caught up in the bloodlines that created you.

Becoming a Ph.D. (aka Practicing Holistic Druid)

At this point in the chapter, we are moving along a path which leads to transforming ourselves into Magi. We have gleaned much from Brigit's gifts and the cauldrons of mythology. We can learn the wisdom of the Brehon judges. We can carry forward the knowledge of our ancestors. All of this now comes to a focal point: you! Each individual Druid has a responsibility to be the fullest True Self possible.

What special skills do you have, that friends call on when in need? What unexplainable gifts do you have? What have you learned to do exceptionally well? What wisdom can you share with the world? As Druids we have the responsibility of putting our skills out into the world to keep the forge fire glowing. Sometimes we are not sure of what to do. Now is your chance to become a Ph.D., or Practicing Holistic Druid.

The following process can determine two things: (1) Why are you here on this planet? (2) What is your course of study as you fully become a Druid? The art of Druid magic and alchemical transformations will probably reveal themselves in your answers. This procedure helps you to integrate your body-mind-spirit development and to know your life's purpose. Take each step and ponder it for as long as you like before moving on to the next. We have shared this process with many people, to good effect. We want to alert you that some people, at the end of this process, have jumped up and sped away to get started on the rest of their life! Here are the questions to turn you into a Ph.D.

What do you want? List all that you want. Take a look at these areas: spiritual, emotional, material, professional, cognitive, social, financial, physical, and more. Jump in and commit for now. Write down whatever comes to mind, in any order. You can look for patterns later.

What is not finished, and with whom? (parents, past partners, coworkers, children)

Learning list. What kinds of books do you read most often? What do you want to learn? What do you want to master? Write as fast and much as you can, and organize it later. Your answers might range from computers and outer space to inventing wordless communication.

What do you want to produce or put out into the world? This might be a physical product, an art form, a service, or a form of energy.

Who can help with the above four areas?

What are your abilities? These might be natural talents or learned skills.

What resources do you have? What resources do you still need?

What do you enjoy doing so much that you are unaware of time passing?

What is your learning style? How do you prefer to go about a goal? Examples are to dream, visualize, think, write, join a group, talk, plan, do body work, create a timeline, pray.

Who are you, really?

Write a Personal Mission Statement. This is your affirmation of Self, your guiding light. It reminds you who you are, keeps you centered and aware of your path. Your focus on Druidry will probably bear some fruit and show up in your Mission Statement.

Some Mission Statements that people have written after this process are:

- I am a writer who tells the truth about my people (this person is finishing a novel about her biracial upbringing).

- I am a strong, pagan, independent woman, a Druid, and teacher of the new/ancient ways. (This is Maya's, who teaches Celtic Mythology and is writing a Celtic novel).

- I am an ambassador of the Goddess Aphrodite, for health and beauty (her book of goddess beauty is being published).

- I am a healer with a long journey ahead of me (a nineteen-year-old heading for medical school).

- I am an intuitive organizer who expertly connects others to the people and things they need, also helping with their positive self-development (a counselor who is a phenomenal resource person).

We are almost there. What remains is to write your curriculum, the course of study that will lead from here and now to where your Mission Statement points. Maya's has evolved into three interrelated strands: historical, spiritual, and magical. Her study of prehistory and history includes Paleolithic and Neolithic eras, shifts of consciousness, imagery, people of power, and sacred sites. Her study of spirituality includes the Celtic goddesses and gods, the Dark Goddess and Dark God, relationship as a spiritual practice, work as a spiritual practice, initiation and rites of passage. Her study of magic includes various magical paths, practices, tools, the elements, Druidic and Fairy lore. By interweaving these strands, many years of study and productivity have appeared. You too will see the map of your studies if you take a few hours under inspired conditions to write down what your Mission Statement is urging you to do.

May you activate your Druid power, may you speak your purpose in this life, and may your path open before you!

Activities

Relighting your Hearth Fire. If you ever let your hearth fire go out, rescript that time and relight that fire. If your hearth fire, your personal well-being, is at a low point right now, mind-map some ideas for warming it, for incubating better health. Then select one of those ideas and implement it not out of "will power" (which might be lacking) but as a practicing Druid whose sacred duty is to bring your flame to the world.

Cauldron of Physical Renewal. How will you incorporate the cauldron of physical regeneration into your body? What ails you? What are you doing to heal yourself? If you could renew one thing physically, in Brigit's healing well, what would it be? Bless some water, or use water from a holy well, and put it on your ailing body part. Pray with Brigit to restore you physically. Now go beyond "absence of illness" all the way to wellness. What are you doing to reach optimal physical well-being? Bring the power of Brigit into your body and live with her holy water and fire inside you.

Cauldron of Livelihood. How will you incorporate the cauldron of livelihood into your life? How does your work or craft align with your True Self, your eternal soul? How can you practice spirit at work? Think about your ideal work situation. This cauldron represents the fire of the blacksmith, the fire of the forge that serves the whole community. How does your livelihood serve others? If it does not, think about changing what you produce with your mind and hands so that your creative fire contributes to the community at large.

Cauldron of Inspiration. How will you incorporate the cauldron of fertile imagination or spiritual fire into your life? How could Brigit inspire you, light the fire of your soul with *awen*? What part does spirituality have in your overall reasons for being? Name three areas in which you are presently self-actualizing—reaching the outer limits of your potential. What is *your* form of sacred poetry that your inner fire urges you to bring forth?

Be a Druid Activist! Read Starhawk's poem about Brigit— "Litany of the Holy Well and the Sacred Flame"—in *Truth or Dare*, pages 289–95. Create a ritual with fire and water as the central elements. Set an intention, perhaps for political outcomes on the local or global level, such as Starhawk does. Allow yourself to be visible in the community as a Druid and watch for openings to do more.

Brehon Justice. Within the next week, resolve a conflict by restoring justice and avoiding punitive measures.

Festival of Tara Code. Instead of New Year's Resolutions, write your ethical code and live by it. Every three years, as was done at the Festival of Tara, revise your code to come more in line with your Druidic practice of justice, arbitration, and decision making.

The Ancestors. In your mind's eye, see your two parents. See them clearly before you. Do not accept or reject any aspect of them, just see them as your two genealogical parents. Now see their parents, your four grandparents, behind them. Picture them clearly, without acceptance or rejection. Now see their parents, your eight great-grandparents, behind them. Slowly picture the lineage or tribe of which you are a part. See the web of lineage that connects you to so many people. Now select an ancestor who seems particularly promising. It might be a great-grandmother or a great-uncle who has a quality that you find attractive. Picture their parents behind them, intuiting which parent also possesses this attractive quality. Hold an image of the ancestor that carries a quality or power that you are drawn to.

At some point on this trail, you are drawn to an ancestor or ancestors who loom much larger than life. They may have a greater stature or numinosity than their descendants. They are the source of the quality you are pursuing. Approach one of these great ancestors. See the details around this being. Observe, without acceptance or rejection, their epoch, their dress, their visage, their aura, and anything they might be holding or doing. What qualities have they enshrined in your lineage? If you like, you can absorb some of these qualities into your life. You may return to this ancestor again and again for the wisdom permanently planted in your genetic inheritance.

Your Mythic Origins. Write a story about your earliest ancestors. You do not need facts. Through meditation, art, dreams, drama, writing, or other form, derive a satisfying glimpse of your mythic origins, which need not be human. Are there any Druids in your ancestral story?

Notes

1. From Nede mac Adne's mystical ancestry in the *Colloquy of the Two Sages*; quoted in Caitlín and John Matthews, *Encyclopaedia*, p. 235.

2. Geoffrey Ashe, *Dawn Behind the Dawn*, p. 166.

3. Based on translation of the *Cauldron of Poesy*, by Erynn Rowan Laurie (1997).

4. Berresford Ellis, *The Druids*, pp. 190–4.

5. Ibid., p. 196.

6. Caesar, *Bellum Gallicum* VI.

7. Miranda Green, *Exploring the World of the Druids*, p. 15.

Chapter 6

LIVING YOUR SACRED SEXUALITY

"Tell me, Diarmuid O'Duibne," she said, "why does the heron cry?"

"O Grania, princess of Tara, woman who never took a step right," said Diarmuid; "the heron cries because it is frozen to the rocks. Here am I with you, Grania, you, who are more beautiful than a tree in blossom, and I am frozen out and banished from my people. I am like a wild creature that is astray, far from home, hunted by those who were once my kin. Here I am with you, Grania of the beautiful hair, and your love is like the cold mist that rises and departs at the break of day."

"O Diarmuid," said Grania, "my heart falls down whenever you come near. Each day is the whole of my life when you are beside me . . . Do not leave me; with my love for you growing like the leaves on the tree in the kind long heat of the day."

"You are a woman too fond of fine words," said Diarmuid. "When I did take you with me, you struck at me for the sake of a man of the Fomor."

Grania was silent. They walked on for a while until they came to a place where they could drink and rest.

"Would you like to eat now?" said Grania.

"Yes, I would eat now," said Diarmuid.

"Then give me a knife so I can cut this bread and meat," she said.

"Look for the knife in the sheaf where you put it," said Diarmuid.

Grania looked and saw that the knife was still in his thigh where she had struck it. She was horrified and ashamed; and because he would not draw it

out, she had to draw it out herself and the wound was dressed with her tears
and lamentations.

They returned to the cave, and spent the night there. On the next day when
they departed, Diarmuid did not leave a loaf of unbroken bread as a token that
he had kept his promise to Fionn. It was a broken loaf that he left behind him.[1]

Starting from an ideal of sacred sexuality that involves the whole being—body, mind, emotions, and spirit—we will trace a progression of skills, practices, and effects of Celtic sexuality in this chapter. We support each portion with relevant episodes from Celtic myth. Using our theme of stitching together known pieces of the material, this chapter shows you the most plausible "whole cloth" of Celtic sexual practice, whether it be verbal, sensual, erotic, or ecstatic.

Because the Celts were lusty and energetic, it is almost certain the original myths brimmed with sexual scenes. Many of these were deleted centuries later by scribes who were celibate Christian monks. Instead of the impossible task of trying to suppress sexuality with celibacy in order to achieve spiritual states, the Celts merged the two into sacred sexuality. Celtic stories of love and consummation between partners are frequent enough to piece together a pattern ranging from first glimpse to dual ecstasy.

The Celts did not lack for variety, raciness, and the exotic in their love lives. The icy queen Arianrhod proclaimed that she'd not had sex with any man. Nevertheless, she did mate with the sea-god Manannán and with her brother the sorcerer Gwydion, though she disowned the divine offspring from those matings. In the same story, her son Lleu Llaw Gyffes, the Welsh version of the sun god Lugh, took a magically conjured wife Blodeuwedd, who was made of flowers. Her innocent-sounding origins hardly warn us that she later betrays and kills Lleu when she finds a lover she prefers to her husband.

Maeve, queen of the Irish province of Connacht, had multiple partners. She gave the "friendship of her thighs" and that of her daughter's as political favors. She claimed to always have "a lover waiting in the shadow of another." Cuchulainn also had multiple partners. This did not cause jealousy in his wife Emer, until he had an affair with Fand, a woman of the Fairy World with whom Emer felt she could not compete.

The stories that come down to us focus on love between heterosexuals. This certainly does not preclude homosexuality in Celtic society. Aristotle mentions that the Celts openly demonstrated love between men, but the surviving stories give no details. About all we know is that men admired each other physically. In the stories of

Cuchulainn, he and his foster brother Ferdiad grow up sharing everything: they exchange kisses and, after their battles, put herbs and oils on each other's beaten and sore bodies.

We will look at four key approaches to Celtic lovemaking in this chapter. They constitute the verbal, sensual, erotic, and ecstatic aspects of sexuality. You will see some similarities to practices from other cultures and no doubt to your own practices. The combination of these four keys is what makes Celtic sexuality special and sacred. Before we begin, let us glance briefly at the part of the Brehon Laws dealing with marriage and offspring.

Brehon Equality of the Sexes

The Brehon Laws recognized ten degrees of marriage. It seems the main purpose of the marriage laws was to give legal status to offspring. Women and men were treated equally under the law, although Celtic society was rooted in a hierarchy of social classes. Marriage of the first degree was between equals in status and wealth, and therefore the *eric* or honor-price of the woman and the man was the same. Marriage of the first degree was the most desirable and ideal form. The myths describe some male-female encounters where the characters are discovering whether they qualify for a first-degree marriage. The exchange of riddles between Emer and Cuchulainn, quoted in the next section, establishes their equality. Emer is unwilling to accept anything other than marriage of the first degree, although she knows that her father will not accept Cuchulainn at all.

The Celtic sources, to us, show that the role of the man in a marriage of equals is to learn to contain and direct his sexual energy. The role of the woman is to learn to direct and administer not only her sexual energy but his as well. These parallel roles appear over and over in the ancient stories. The woman embodied the hearth, the home, the rath, the *dún*, the land. Her body was connected to the source, the womb, and to sovereignty. It was the custom for the woman to be identified with the estate. Such great places as Tara, Emain Macha, and Dún Ailinne were all named after women. Celtic women were the administrators, whereas men were the defenders and workers.

While the women learned what it meant to embody the power of place, a task of initiation for young men was to undertake a *táin* or cattle raid. This was an attack on the estate of an older man, a father in most cases, who had to defend his cattle. By doing this the older man proved his value to his wife and, most importantly, prevented the attempt to carry off their daughter. In a *táin*, the young man had to prove himself worthy of a young woman. If his youthful and wildly sexual energy resulted in a fiasco, then the result was not so much loss of life as it was loss of face. If he could prove himself honorable and brave in his actions, then he could contain and direct his energy, and thus qualify as a suitor.

The Verbal

You know that the head, as the repository of mind, mouth, and words, was the "organ" crucial to Celtic creativity. We would expect, then, to find verbal interaction high in sexual importance and it is. In Druidic lovemaking, you do not need to worry about your partner saying "Don't talk!" For the talk is not chatter: it is aimed at heightening the attraction and connecting the head with the genitals. Here are some examples for you to practice.

Use words to express to your lover what you saw at the very first glimpse, the first moment you laid eyes on each other. Grania, daughter of the king of Tara, asked her father's Druid to tell her about all the men at the banquet that was supposed to be celebrating her wedding. But earlier, she had seen the "love spot"on the forehead of Diarmuid, which caused her to fall in love with him. Perhaps this was an early example of pheromones at work! Tell your lover what the "love spot"was: the characteristic or quality that caused you to fall in love with this person, his or her enticement. At a public gathering, honor your partner by look and glance across a room, and then when you are together, say what that look meant.

Celtic women and men looked at each other openly and asked for what they wanted. In the tragic love story, the *Exile of the Sons of Usnach*, Noisiu and Deirdre size each other up:

> *"That is a fine young heifer going by."*
>
> *"A fine young heifer it is," said Deirdre. "They grow this way where there are no bulls."*
>
> *"You have a bull of your own," he said, "the King of Ulster."*
>
> *"If I could choose," she said, "I would take a younger bull like you."*
>
> *"That can never be," he said, "for I fear the prophecy of Cathbad."*
>
> *"Are you refusing me?"*
>
> *"Yes, I must."*
>
> *Then Deirdre rushed at him, and seized him by his two ears. "Two ears of mockery and shame on you if you reject me!"*

"Let go of me, woman!"

"You have no choice," she said, and he was bound to her through her words.[2]

Tell your lover frequently what you are seeing in the other's face, body, and soul, so you mirror what it would be like to be outside oneself looking in. Honor each other with heartfelt compliments.

Queen Maeve and her husband Ailill would conduct pillow talk. At first they voiced each other's likeable traits: He was generous, brave and free of jealousy, and she was a fitting wife for him who was a king's son. However, their pillow talk eventually degenerated into rivaling each other in possessions, and we do not recommend you use that as a model!

You could test each other's mental agility with puns, riddles, and references, as Emer and Cuchulainn did when courting. Later in your relationship, use private language, innuendoes, or certain love words that only the two of you understand.

Emer lifted her lovely face when she heard Cuchulainn come up. "May your path be smooth before you," she said.

"May your eyes see only good," Cuchulainn replied.

"Which way did you come?"

"From the cover of the sea, over the secret of the Tuatha Dé Danann, the foam of the horses of Emain, over the Morrigan's garden and the Great Sow's back, between the God and his Druid, and the Marrow of the Woman, to the Remnants of the Great Feast and the Gardens of Lugh," Cuchulainn said. "And how do you account for yourself?"

"Not hard to answer," replied Emer. "For what should a maiden be but a Tara of the hills, a watcher that sees no one, an eel in the water, a rush out of reach, a flame of hospitality, a road that cannot be entered? And what should a maiden have but a following of champions to protect her?"

. . . As Cuchulainn and Emer spoke he caught sight of her breasts over the top of her dress. "I see a sweet country,"he said, "a fair plain with noble hills."

"No one comes to this country until they have done three times the feat of the salmon carrying twice their weight in gold. No one comes here until they have struck down three groups of nine men with a single stroke, leaving the middle man of each group unharmed."

"Everything you have asked for," said Cuchulainn, "will be done."[3]

Their ability to inspire oral creativity in each other shows that Emer and Cuchulainn are equal, and on the way to a union with their whole being, not just the sexual organs. The Druidic emphasis on verbal skills means that you enter sexual union through the mind as well as the body. A couple must be equal in partnership, and able to communicate, establish goals, direct themselves, and so bring their whole being to the relationship. Their sexual energy is not separate from their being, but they must first learn to direct it internally.

The use of language in lovemaking can tap into the deepest potential of a human being. Talk during sex may resolve one of women's greatest laments about men—lack of communication. Love talk is a means of awakening every faculty, intensifying passion and concentration, allowing the expression of emotions and of the sacred. These in turn allow the visionary power of the Self to emerge in sex and in other creative acts.

You could create an evening of questions, where you alternate asking five or so pre-arranged questions about deeper aspects of life and thought. An example would be, "How would you describe me to a wonderful old friend you haven't seen for ten years? What images would you use?" Or "When you wake up in the middle of the night, what comforts you so you can go back to sleep?" Following on from this, you could have an evening where you sit across an altar from each other near your sacred bed. Reveal yourself in words, being open with your emotions, admitting frailties, revealing inner parts of your core self, telling secrets that no one else except your lover knows. You could meditate together and speak aloud whatever comes to you.

Find some love poems and read them to each other. Better yet, compose your own poetry as a gift to your lover. Then you can create a special romantic occasion and present your poetic offering. The poems can describe the beauty of your partner's naked body, with metaphors of a burgeoning plant or a river between hills! You can tell your lover in detail what you will do next while making love. In poetry, let your lover know how to pleasure you, using highly descriptive words and images.

Celtic women were queens of their rath or homestead. As you know, the concept of queen or king in a myth refers to the sacred in the human, a reference to our highest Self. So tales that involve finding one's way into the rath tell us that Celtic women directed their pleasuring and retained their sovereignty in lovemaking. Find or create scenarios where you each enact a part and carry it out fully to the end of the scene. In the scenario, you have to do what the other says. You could do shapeshifting, playing several aspects or characters from a mythic tale one after the other. These are some ways to enjoy being a verbal Celt!

The Sensual

Think of your five senses first and then we will go beyond them. How could you include the sense of taste in lovemaking? The Celts excelled at feasting, fighting, and . . . lovemaking. They probably wrapped all three together at times. Feasting can be the prelude or conclusion to your lovemaking. Remember the classic eating scene in the film *Tom Jones*, where the couple's eyes make love to each other while their mouths savor and sensualize the food? Prepare food that is delectable, gorgeous to look at, and otherwise wonderfully adaptable to tasting your lover. Eat the food yourself and feed it to each other. Establish a rhythm between you that increases in pulsation as the arousal level increases. Apply food such as honey to the skin and taste it there. You can make your own edible potions from herbs, and you might try some Druid magic by concocting love potions.

Closely connected with taste is the sense of smell. Be lavish with this sensual avenue! Light up some incense noted for having an aphrodisiac effect. Create a "dream pouch" in which you gather dried herbs that are very pleasing in aroma to both of you, wrap them in a wonderful piece of fabric tied around the top, and place it under the pillow. Select oils with fragrances you both enjoy, place them in decorated bottles of your own making, and have them handy to rub on the body. Celtic myths record the use of both herbs and oils for healing and honoring the body. A subtle way of connecting through smell is to stand close, naked but not touching, with eyes closed and sense the other by breathing together. Slowly move closer until you can detect your lover's familiar smell.

Do you use the sense of hearing in lovemaking? As you can imagine, Druid bards were magical musicians and poets. We don't all have musical talent, but some instruments are easy for anyone to play. Get yourself a flute, recorder, or ocarina made of wood or clay—something natural that might have been available in Celtic times. Learn to play some pleasant tones on it. They can be repetitive at first and you can branch out from there. While you play, your partner can intone with the voice, varying the sounds so that they weave with the tones you are making with the musical instrument. This is musical lovemaking, where you can actually *hear* yourselves coming together. If you know someone who plays an instrument or sings beautifully, arrange to record that music and play it back during your lovemaking. If you yourself have a talent, so much the better!

Music transports us out of the ordinary. It can soothe or arouse us. Celtic bards had to learn four categories of songs: those that could make people relax or play, cry, sleep, or feel romantic. In a time before history, it may be that society was literally *conducted* into behaving honorably by official musicians, who could create a mood among the tribe or village by playing in defined and powerful ways. The counterpart to creating attractive sounds for sacred sexuality is to remove any unpleasant or unwanted sounds in your environment.

For humans, the sense of sight often overpowers the others. We left it for last (the sense of touch is covered in the following section) so you could get a good grounding in the other senses and give them equal importance to vision in sexuality. Onward to what the eyes drink in! Together you can build up a collection of beautiful erotic art. Your erotic collection can be pictures from advertisements, photocopies from art books, or from other sources. Slowly look at the pictures together, murmuring what turns you on and what does not, as a way of giving subtle suggestions to your partner. Advance the use of erotic art by drawing some pictures specifically for each other; you might practice first so that your drawing skill increases.

The Celts were almost obsessed with wearing beautiful clothes and doing up their hair. Descriptions of scarlet cloaks with gold clasps and hair stiffened with lime (perhaps not today's style) abound in the myths. Taking this cue, have a collection of "play clothes" such as scarves, robes, feathers, kimonos, and sarongs, see-through items, very light and very dark items, fabrics of differing consistency such as silk and leather. As the mood arises, dress yourself or dress each other in wonderful ways. The more you do this, the more inventive and less conservative you will become!

Bring glamorous and magical aspects into your lovemaking. Create illusions with fabric, shadows, and disguises. On occasion, wear masks all the way through the act of love. The Picts in particular used body tattoos, but so did the Druids in certain traditions. Try applying temporary tattoos on each other where they would not be visible when clothed. Enhance your features with exotic makeup, as the Celts frequently described the lips as red as berries, hair black like a raven. Another suggestion is body painting. Ask your partner what pictures or images she or he desires, and then apply them as well as possible. The entire naked body can become a phallic tree, a garden of pleasures, a spiral or labyrinth to be threaded until the sacred center is attained.

Robing and disrobing can become central parts to your lovemaking. The outdated idea of removing your own clothes in a half-darkened space and letting them drop to the floor has no art, no sensuality in it. Instead, set the stage by using an array of candles, firelight, or cleverly muted lighting. Play off against this lighting by moving in front of it to put yourself in silhouette and around it to make shadows. Dance and move sensuously in the process of disrobing, so your lover's eyes can feast on individually presented parts of your body, and delay gratification until seeing the rest. Stay in poses where you intend to arouse, so that your partner can take in the lines of your figure and make a mental imprint of them.

The bed or nest for sacred sexuality can itself be a feast for the eyes. Drape it, cover it, put a canopy over it, light it, surround it with things of tempting beauty. Piles of pillows and cushions make a wonderful setting: they are inviting by look and changeable by design. Add attractive, stunning, sensual items all around your sacred bed. You can't overdo colors and attractiveness! In every direction, wherever your eyes look while making love, create views that will enhance what you are doing.

Beyond the commonly accepted five senses, think about other pathways of input and output that you recognize in your body. The sensation of flowing movement and lightened gravity when we are in water is easily introduced to sexuality. Being together naked with your lover in a large tub, spa, pool, or natural body of water is a high experience. In hot and humid weather, the slippery suction of skin against skin creates a sensation that is arousing. Try sensing your partner in ways of perceiving that are more subtle then physical. Close your eyes, run your hands near your partner's body an inch or two away from the skin and absorb the messages from the other's energy field. Or while breathing rhythmically together and with the other's agreement, enter the mental sphere of your partner and absorb the images and thoughts going on there.

The Erotic

What an arena for the play of lovers exists in erotica! Currently, we in Western society are so inundated by forms of sex with lascivious, aggressive, and abusive intentions that we often miss the wonderful opportunities of the erotic, a word originating from the Greek word for love, *eros*. Erotic writing, art, and skills arise first from love and then from the intention of arousing each other sexually. Erotic acts occur before sexual intercourse and are so pleasurable that you might find at times that they replace the sexual act itself. When you are feeling amorous, that is erotic. When you love and want to express it sexually, that is feeling erotic. Desire is the key to the erotic. Touch is the pathway. Quite possibly, the Western frenzy for sex is actually "a search for the satisfaction of the need for contact."[4] Operating from the idea that no human has ever been touched enough lovingly, we invite you to change that with your partner!

Have your lover massage every part of your body with warm fragrant oil. The slow circular motions of your partner's hands will give you plenty of time to absorb the love, desire, and sexual expression your body is relishing. As you breathe rhythmically and massage each other, let passion take over. Then stop before cresting, calm down, and keep going with no purpose to accomplish. Let the lovemaking end naturally. One of our favorite sayings is that bodies always know what to do.

Sometimes your body will want to be active, on center stage. Select sensuous music and dance! Dressed in ways that suggest more to come, you can move in serpentine patterns, gaining speed until you whirl like a dervish. You weave in and out of your partner's reach, touching the other, being touched, hungering for more but not hurrying for it.

We also suggest borrowing animal traits. The Celts were intensely familiar with the animals of their surroundings and could imitate their calls, movements, and behaviors. You might try the same. You could prowl, crouch, leap, burrow, curl, prance, jump, graze, and twirl. You could enfold, nuzzle, soar, nest, nibble, and sniff. You could growl, squeeze, gallop, climb, snort, rub, play, toss, buck, paw, and roll over! In fact, rolling over and over each other is a playful and exciting thing to do because it tells your bodies to go on and do what they know so well.

The Ecstatic

Ecstasy! If you've been there you can hardly describe it, and describing it won't help anyone to achieve it. Ecstasy is spiritual orgasm. A physical orgasm might take seven minutes to arrive and seven seconds to dissipate. What you feel is heightened bodily sensation, usually localized around the genitalia. By contrast, a spiritual orgasm might take several years or at least months of training to experience for the first time. What you feel is your whole being breaking through the ordinary into the extraordinary. It feels like soaring into the universe. Your consciousness increases to include unusual awareness. You feel union and connection with your partner and everything that is, instead of splitting off from everything for a few moments. Ecstatic union might take place during several hours of lovemaking and the state of being might last for several days. You can reverse that popular saying to be: One reason sex is better than chocolate is that you can make sex last as long as you want it to!

If ecstasy can be defined, it means being transported to an exalted and intense state beyond normal. This is a sexual trance state that comes by concentrating on heightened sensory, emotional, and spiritual experiences. One remains conscious but sets rational thought aside while focusing on blissful, extreme experiences in the present.

People often have sex to relieve their sexual needs and to feel good for a short while. Any number of partners can provide this. Sex doesn't require love, commitment, attention, or caring about the other, although we might wish for those conditions. Ecstasy, on the other hand, requires knowing and loving ourselves and then knowing and loving one's partner. You need to grow into ecstasy with the same love partner, because you interact intimately along the way. On the physical level, you need to have an agreement that neither of you will release in orgasm at the typical moment. You will ride the wave of sexual arousal up to a peak and then let it subside. During this, you will be connected in spirit. Your thoughts concentrate on spiritual union with your lover. Your eyes look into the soul-door of your partner. Your body yearns for ecstatic union. Instead of succumbing to the urge for orgasm, you by-pass that pressure relief valve by reducing the arousal and staying connected. You honor your partner if the other says or indicates a need to lessen the intensity for a while. You know for certain that exploding the pressure will take you only as far as physical orgasm, and that is not your intention now. Staying under the ceiling of climax creates a state within you that far exceeds the physical geyser.

Within one to three days of making love in this way, your soul will spontaneously pour beyond any sensations you have ever experienced from sex before. Your spirits will burst out of any physical bounds. You might feel the two of you are ascending to cosmic heights. You might feel that your body cannot contain these sensations and you need to leave it. You might sail into realms depicted in the Celtic myths and realize they are not fables but actual states of existence.

The quote that opens this chapter reveals how Diarmuid and Grania grow from being in love to being ecstatic lovers. Like most couples today, they must learn to resolve their differences, speak what is on their mind, and accept full responsibility for their actions. After a long time of abstaining, they learn to direct their sexual energy. When they have matured and are acting from their true selves, they achieve ecstatic union. The story goes on to show Diarmuid and Grania at the top of the magical quicken tree. This provides a superb example of how the Celts would elevate sacred spirituality to the top of the Tree of Life; contrast this with Christian myth, where sexuality leads to expulsion from the Tree of Life.

The Beheading Game

Men can benefit enormously from studying the close connection between language and sexuality—between the head and the sexual organs—in order to achieve ecstasy. The Celtic tradition sees language as the supreme ability of consciousness. Since the brain and head are connected through the spinal column to the penis, communication during sex can raise consciousness to the highest of levels. The oral and genital areas are mediated by the common fluid of the spinal column.[5]

The cup or cauldron as the symbol of feminine sexual power is matched in the Celtic tradition by the head, as well as by obvious symbols of masculine power such as a sword or spear. The Celts kept the heads of heroes and kings as symbols of their power. The head of Bran was said to speak for almost a hundred years after it was separated from its body. True champions learned to direct the fire of sexual power through their being to emerge as the "hero light" or "hero halo" above the head. Just before a decisive battle, the *Táin* says of Cuchulainn: "So strong and bright was the halo of the hero that it was no longer his appearance he had on him, but the appearance of a god."[6]

The ability of men to direct their sexual energy in this way is tested in the classic Celtic story of the beheading game. In the *Championship of Ulster*, Cuchulainn, Laeghaire, and Conall Cernach compete to demonstrate their abilities. The head manifests the qualities of the Self as truth, honor, poetry, and judgement. These are tested in the ultimate challenge put to the heroes by the giant, Curoi mac Daire, Lord of the Animals. He is the shaggy, leaf-clad precursor of the Green Man, who also appears in forms such as Robin Hood or the Wild Herdsman.

> "Here is this axe," he said, "and the man who uses it to cut off my head today *must return tomorrow for me to cut off his head. As it is the men of Ulster who have the reputation above all others for strength, valor and greatness, for dignity, truth and for generosity, let one of you make this bargain with me and* keep to his word. (our emphasis) *Whoever offers to cut off my head tonight, I cut off his head tomorrow night.*"[7]

The game tests the true inner power of the men. Will they betray their word and in trying to keep their head, in fact, lose it? Laeghaire and Conall refuse to lay their heads on the block and thus break their word. They lack a nobility of the Self. They cannot put their heads down in readiness for the reciprocal blow because they have not channeled their sexuality to reside as fire in the head. Cuchulainn can lay his head on the block because he does possess this power. Curoi brings down his axe beside Cuchulainn's head and proclaims him the true champion of Ulster.

A man following the Celtic path can practice this lesson by *keeping to his word* in sexual relationships. This means dancing, singing, praising with the whole being. It also means not promising anything you cannot keep, and, if promising anything, keeping to it. It means bringing the whole of the self into lovemaking. It means staying conscious, focusing desire and sexual arousal through all the human faculties. You may have learned to focus intensely like this through training in tai chi, karate, meditation, hunting, or other practices.

Sex provides a magnificent opportunity for the awakening of the fire in the head. Agree with your partner to abstain from actual intercourse and orgasm, instead allowing other sexual activity to flow. This may be simply flirting, or it may be holding each other. Explore the immense range of sexuality in the tantric tradition. Keep to this agreement. Over a few days, especially if there is an intense attraction, a huge amount of energy will build up. Use this energy to go to sacred places inside yourself or outside, or both.

A powerful image for making this internal journey is a white animal, such as a bull, stag, or horse. The white animal symbolizes white semen and the spinal fluid, making the passage of energy from the genitals through the spine to the crown of the head. Follow this image in your mind's eye during your lovemaking. A lucid journey will come that will take you through the inner world. Allow whatever images come to be your guide, but direct the sexual energy inwards. Remain true to your word, to your commitments. Stay in the present. Then the sexual energy will activate centers in the head. You may experience horns, or you may experience one of the Celtic "gods." You may experience the power animals or other mythic imagery from the Celtic tradition. Whatever the case, after such a sexual experience you will likely have a tremendous outpouring of creative energy. You might compose some music, poetry, or express yourself in other artistic forms.

Sacred Sexuality

By reading Celtic myths we learn that sexual energy is an extremely powerful force that we can direct into many forms of creativity, not just for procreation. The Druids were not celibate: Sencha had many children; Cathbad was the father of Dechtiré, the mother of Cuchulainn. These Druids combined the spiritual and the sexual. Let us be among those who embrace the sexual within the spiritual.

Spirit shows itself in every domain. Since we have bodies, spirit can display itself physically. Think of the exhilaration after a hard, sweaty run, for example, when your whole being was poured into achieving a personal best. Sexual expression is one of the body's favorite ways of showing spiritual energy. Too often we use sex for power over another, but in its sacred form it is our higher power flowing forth, fulfilling ourselves and our partner. The surge of life force that is carried on sexual waves connects us with all the life forces in the universe: in ecstatic moments, we feel union with all that is! In sex, we feel we can overcome past limitations and soar to completion!

Through sexuality it is possible to feel the life force circulating around and over the body and between you and your partner. Union occurs when there is interaction on deep levels of body-mind-spirit awareness. Partners can help each other do this through communication, movement. and visualization. Dancing, singing, and visualizing the flow between you and your partner's body is a fine way to exchange love energy.

Sexuality is one of the most easily available means at our disposal for entering into the inner realms and tapping and directing our sources of inner power. When we direct this creativity through dance, verbal communication, and in-turned sexual energy, the potential for transformation becomes enormous. An extremely valuable way of working a path into the inner realm is through myth. The characters in our mythic tradition are the archetypes within ourselves—the giant figures of the past abiding in our subconscious. Through recounting a Celtic myth in lovemaking, each partner assumes personally meaningful roles, and the archetypes come to life. We can direct them at the same time as they direct us. Certain mythical themes will speak more strongly to us than others, depending on their relevance in the immediate situations of our lives.

We recommend living your relationship as a spiritual path. This is a major leap toward sacred sexuality. As part of your spiritual work in this lifetime, you and your partner can truly live and grow together. In addition to the undeniable benefits of sharing companionship, you can share your own spiritual growth. Within a sacred relationship, you express true feelings. Conflict is accepted. The two of you work through conflict by remaining on the same side and finding a solution that keeps your spiritual goals intact, while preserving your individual self-esteem.

You can share the dance with a lover, the dance you make as an immortal being of spirit in the world. Your lover can be a teacher showing your spirit how to live in the physical realm. Your lover's body provides a form for your body to dance with, in the same way as the infinite provides the arena for your spirit. Through sexual love, the Self learns spiritual love.

It is said by some that our spirits have chosen a mate through many lifetimes and many worlds. There is some indication of this in Celtic mythology, for example, when Emer chooses to die with Cuchulainn. While we can't know for sure, it seems to us that over many lives there will be many lovers who teach us many things. When you meet a mate and you are in love with that person, it triggers feelings of forever. Yet the "forever" is within us, in the love of our eternal Self with life in this world and the next.

Relating to each other in a sacred way brings about other changes. Instead of seeking in one other the fulfillment of all your desires, you understand that your fulfillment comes from the sacred. It has the face of your lover upon it. The other knows who you truly are as an eternal being. All of your being, even the less-than-beautiful parts, are accepted. You know that as you grow old together, your lover will manifest all the stages of life: maiden, woman, mother, and crone; youth, man, father, and sage. The two of you, as eternal beings dancing through the stages of nature in this life, are greater than the problems that may beset you. Your sexual union expresses the union of your self with nature and, ultimately, the union of your eternal Self with the infinite.

Sacred sexuality means that our bodies are inspirited. Sacred lovers attain a plane of ecstasy through their physical bodies. We wish you many hours, days, and years of this supreme enjoyment!

Activities

Sensuality. For each of the five senses, add one or two ideas of your own to those given in this chapter, in order to create more *sensual* lovemaking.

A Celtic Festival of Art. Create a romantic Celtic weekend for honoring the mind. Plan the clothing, food, indoor decor or outdoor setting, and Celtic ways to appeal to the five senses. Concentrate on intellectual challenges and interplay, such as enticing each other with poetry and art. Write a love poem based on the way the

Celts honored words, the head, and physical appearance. Write an article describing your weekend and submit it to a Celtic publication.

The Skilled Lover. What training do you need to be a skilled lover? The Celts practiced skills in conversation, dance, ceremony, massage, music, costumes, and grooming, among others. What training do you need to reach ecstatic sexuality? How will you go about that?

The Inner Cycle. Circulating the internal energies of the body, described in the section the "Four Talismans" in chapter 3, can be done in one breath, in a meditation, or as a year-long ritual reenactment. This cycle attunes us to the rhythm that is deeply imbedded in our body-mind-spirit processes. Here is a visualization to help circulate the internal energies in your sacred sexuality.

> *See the stone (earth) at midwinter as the source of power and the seat of sovereignty—the beginning of the inbreath—located at the genitals. Picture the cauldron (water) at the Spring Equinox blending the different currents of energy arising from the source in the trunk of the body—the middle of the inbreath. Direct them to the spear (fire) at Summer Solstice, the head,—the place of the highest manifestation of sovereign power—and the end of the inbreath. Release and disperse the powers, as if at Autumn Equinox and Samhain. Pass them over the surface of the body, the skin, with the outbreath. See them transmute by the sword (air), die to themselves, and come back into the psyche as renewable resources at the Winter Solstice—the genitals, and the end of the outbreath.*

As you can tell, although ejaculation is not the goal, neither should a man avoid it when it comes. Precisely because a man *must* release, must let go and die to himself, orgasmic ejaculation at the point in the cycle represented by Samhain/Winter Solstice (the sword), is necessary. This is not the release of a man's desire, nor is it the release represented in the cycle by Beltane/Summer Solstice for procreative purposes. Through ejaculation as part of this cycle, the man can release attachment to his linear mode, and give over to the inner, fluid unknown, so the cycle of transformation can go on.

The Cycle of the World Tree. Visualize the circulation of energy with you and your partner as the World Tree. This adds further power to your lovemaking. The tree's roots provide a visual metaphor for union with the source (stone). The roots of the tree are the sexual organs. The trunk of the tree (cauldron) is the trunk of the body. The trunk provides the internal focus necessary for the rising of energy, and the branches and crown (spear) express the abundant outpouring of the in-turned sexuality.

Circulate the energy and pleasure generated at the source through your body, up through the mouth and the crown of the head, and back down outside your body. The parallel is to visualize the energy passing back through the body of your partner. This makes the cycle dynamic and immensely creative. The woman assists the man in getting his linear energies to flow while gaining from the focus that the man brings, and vice versa. When practicing this, with or without coitus, visualize using the (white) power animals mentioned above to direct energy to the head, that is, to the branches and crown of you and your partner as the World Tree. If you are single, then see the World Tree itself, the land, life, and nature as your lover. Visualize nature as a goddess or a god. Enjoy all of their fantastically beautiful manifestations. They will appear dressed in ever new and different forms!

Notes

1. *Diarmuid and Grania*, "The Quarrel," recension based on Cross and Slover (1936), P. W. Joyce (1897), and Lady Gregory (1904).

2. *Longes mac n-Uislenn*, the "Exile of the Sons of Usnach" forms another *remscéla* or prequel to the *Táin Bó Cuailnge*. The recension is based on Thomas Kinsella (1969), Jeffrey Gantz (1981), and A. H. Leahy (1905).

3. *Tochmarc Emer*, the "Courtship of Emer," recension based on Thomas Kinsella (1969) and Lady Gregory (1902).

4. Ashley Montagu, *Touching*; quoted from Margo Anand, *The Art of Sexual Ecstasy*, p. 33.

5. "The soul-substance is the seminal substance; the genius is the genital in the head. We would then all be carrying our seed in our head, like flowers." Norman O. Brown, *Love's Body*, p. 136.

6. The "Battle of the Scythe Chariot," from the *Táin Bó Cuailnge*, recension based on Thomas Kinsella (1969) and Lady Gregory (1902).

7. The *Championship of Ulster* is the sequel to *Bricriu's Feast*; our translation follows Lady Gregory (1902), Jeffrey Gantz (1981), and Cross and Slover (1936).

Chapter 7

HOLDING DRUID CEREMONIES IN YOUR BACK YARD

The ritual Fire of Tiachtga was lit on the eve of Samhain, when the druids of the four provinces of Ireland gathered there to offer sacrifice to all the gods ... It was an obligation, under penalty of fine, to quench the fires of Ireland on that night. The men of Ireland were forbidden to kindle fires except from that fire.[1]

A solid area of evidence about ancient Druidic activities concerns their four festivals, halfway between each equinox and solstice. This chapter offers ritual ideas for each cross-quarter day, based on the Celtic meaning and intent of those occasions.

Druid Cross-Quarter Festivals

From some Graeco-Roman reports, surviving customs, and from myths set in Celtic lands—such as the quote above—we learn details about how the Druids celebrated sacred times. Although it might be hard nowadays to renew the land's fires from one central one, this material is so rich and evocative you can be confident you will be incorporating some authentic, traditional aspects of ritual into your modern creations.

The festival celebrations were the social highpoints of the year. They provided markets for labor, tools, livestock, food, clothes, and, above all, luxury items such as wine, ornaments, and other finery. Music, poetry, storytelling, games, and horseracing provided entertainment, and there was always the chance of meeting a lover or a potential marriage partner. In Ireland, the *feis*, such as the Feis Tara, was a feast attended by representatives from the whole country. The *dal*, or *mor-dal*, "great assembly," met to take care of regional affairs. At these gatherings the Brehon judges and chiefs heard the people on legal matters and took care of political affairs. The festivals were sacred times. No one dared violate the peace. Quarrels or combat were an insult to the founder in whose memory the festival was held, and were even punishable by death.[2]

The four cross-quarter days—midway between the equinoxes and the solstices—were considered the most auspicious time for ceremony and festivities by the Celts. Imbolc is celebrated on or near February 1, Beltane on May Day, Lughnasadh around August 1, and Samhain at Hallowe'en. Two of these festivals revolve around goddesses: the cailleach or hag at Samhain represented by Tlachtga in Ireland and Ceridwen in Wales, and the maiden at Imbolc, represented by Brigit. The other two revolve around gods: Bel or Belenus in the fullness of his masculinity at Beltane, and Lugh the sun god at Lughnasadh. Lugh founded this festival in honor of his foster mother, Tailltiu.

There is little evidence that Celtic Druids celebrated the equinoxes and solstices, although many modern Druids and pagans do. Sun hours are equal to dark hours at the equinoxes. Sun hours are shortest at Winter Solstice and longest at Summer Solstice, and the rising position of the sun on the horizon seems to stand still (the *stasis* in sol*stice*, from the Indo-European root "*sto–*" meaning "to stand") for a few days. In contrast, the cross-quarter days mark pastoral and agricultural turning points. These were the times when herds moved to different pasture land, animals were born or slaughtered, sap started or stopped flowing in plants, and crops were planted or harvested. The Druids determined these times by a combination of natural events, including the sun's journey in the heavens, the moon's phases, animal mating patterns, and deciduous tree cycles.

The Celtic year ended with the final harvest, around the first week of November. That time is Samhain, translated as "summer's end," and starts the void period between the year that is finishing and the new one. Contrary to the current practice of many pagans, the Celts probably did not begin the new year on the day after Samhain. The authors ascribe to the view of the late Ross Nichols, former Chief of the Order of Bards, Ovates and Druids in Britain. He writes that early people "semi-hibernated, taking no account of time, sleeping a great part of the days and eating dried foods until the sun reappeared, say in February."[3] He continues: "The year began in February . . . Imbolc was its first stirring of life . . . probably it had ended much earlier, at Samhuinn in November, the period between the two observances being a no-man's land of darkness and propitiation to the dark gods." Accordingly, we will begin our look at the festival year with Imbolc, the date most identifiable as the New Year of the Celts, in the first week of February.

Imbolc

Imbolc ("around the belly") is also spelled Oimelc or Oimelg. It is known as Candlemas Day in the Christian tradition, St. Brigit's Day in Ireland and Scotland . . . and Groundhog Day in Punxatawny, Pennsylvania! The time is February 1 or 2, which often coincides with the worst winter storms in the Northern Hemisphere. In Celtic lands, though the weather may still have been bitter at the beginning of February, the animals and trees knew that the heavy hand of winter was beginning to loosen its hold. Sap begins to move sluggishly in the trees, and the grip of the year's darkness that began at Samhain now yields to the returning sun.

Ewes give birth at this time and produce milk to feed their lambs. The possibility of fresh milk and cheese brightened the winter of the Celts, urging the celebration of rebirth and renewal of life energy. The myths depict this transition by having the cailleach or hag of Samhain transformed into the spring maiden. Since traveling long distances for great assemblies was difficult in February, the Celts celebrated Imbolc close to home. This explains why no hill or sacred site is traditionally designated as the gathering place of all the Irish tribes at Imbolc.

The connection between Imbolc and Brigit remained in Christian times. St. Brigit's monastery at Kildare in Leinster province was where nuns kept an eternal flame alight from the sixth century C.E. until Henry VIII ordered the dissolution of all monasteries in 1539. This flame was the Christian extension of the pagan fire festival of Imbolc. Later, the Catholic Church began the custom of blessing all candles for home use on this day, again associating Imbolc with fire but replacing Brigit with St. Blaise (a variant of "blaze"?).

Our sources mention Brigit in the same breath as Danu, first Mother of All, and so she takes on the attribute of Mother. This thread linking thousands of years serves to exalt Brigit to the greatest position of any Celtic goddess. So great was her influence and revered status that the Christians could not displace her with Christ or Mary. Consequently, the Irish Catholics again gave her the position of Mother, this time as foster Mother to Jesus and relative-friend to Mary. According to legend, St. Brigit was born of a Druid father in 453 C.E.

For our sample Imbolc ritual, we work with Brigit, the fire festival, and the home. The Celts did not have our penchant for analyzing and dividing things into categories, preferring instead the continuum concept. We see this with Brigit, who is at once the most ancient goddess (and therefore the cailleach), the Mother or giver of milk, and the Maiden or reborn form of the hag. She is at once pre-Celtic, Celtic, and Christian. She is goddess to the Irish, Scottish, British, and the Gallic peoples of continental Europe. We recommend that you study and work with Brigit until her energies and gifts become clear to you.

Perhaps because of the fertility of spring, Imbolc is a women's festival. Until recently, women in the Outer Hebrides Islands would resanctify their houses each February, bringing Brigit into the croft in the form of these items: new fire, Brigit's sun-wheel cross, and her plaited straw belt or *crois*. All the occupants would pull the Brigit belt over their heads and down their bodies, repeating the track of the sun-fire goddess Brigit, stepping through "the zones of heaven and earth."[4]

The Hebridean women acted as midwives to Brigit, the goddess-saint. The house and everyone in it were reborn out of the darkness towards the light. "Her fire was the central feature of every house," writes Michael Dames, "and constituted one end of a flaming axis reaching to the chamber of pure imagination. She put the family in direct touch with ultimate mysteries."[5] The Irish built their homes to duplicate the cosmos. The rooftree of the house represented the world axis. The goddess Brigit was present in the center pole of each house, the *cleithe*, which also means the crown of the head. On a larger scale, she was in the sacred ash of Uisneach at the mystical center of Ireland, and in the sacred oak of Leinster at Cill Dara (Church of the Oak, Kildare). These are the building materials—symbols, locations, customs—to create a magical Imbolc ritual. We encourage you to create your own ritual, using the Druidic and Celtic elements provided here.

Let the ceremony center around your home. To start the New Year, fabricate the maiden Bridhe by wrapping a sheaf of straw inside some article of clothing that a family member uses frequently, especially one in a dangerous occupation (for example, on the west coast of Ireland the muffler of a fisherman would be used). The wrapping represents Bridhe's magical mantle or cloak, the *Brat Bride*. Her mantle/cloak is often mentioned in poems and stories because it covered the entire house and thus protected it.

Place the Bridhe doll outside the back door, the door signifying winter. After the house has been cleaned, a man brings Brigit into the home through the front door, signifying spring and summer, while the women inside call out a welcome to her and to the season. The oldest woman of the house, representing the cailleach, extinguishes the hearth fire, which is only done for the fire festivals. The youngest female, representing the maiden, enters through the front door with a lighted candle, or wearing a crown of lighted candles and a white garment. The hearth is re-lighted from the fire-bearing maiden's candle. The goddess-Brigit doll is placed upon anyone (including animals) who needs healing, as that is one of her powers.

At the core of your ritual, you might work with the hearth fire and the returning sun. You could also work with healing, completing your unfinished business in the dark of the year, with childhood, starting or seeding new projects, or other areas that seem right to you. If you have not had a house blessing or house warming for your abode, this is definitely the time to bring that forth. Hebridean women welcome Brigit with this chant:

> *May Brigit give blessing*
> *To the house that is here . . .*
> *Both stone and beam;*
> *Both summit and foundation;*
> *Both window and timber;*
> *Both foot and head;*
> *Both man and woman;*
> *Both young and old.*[6]

Our Grove's last Imbolc was on a snowy day. Indoors by the fireplace we all worked on a big chart that spelled H-E-A-R-T-H. Under each letter we filled in our personal intentions for spring, the time of the rising sap in ourselves. "H" stood for things like healing (physical and emotional pain), and for home, opening it to those we care about. "E" stood for energy, exercise, and empathy. "A" stood for artistry and actualizing. "R" stood for relationships and rejoicing at our well-earned growth. "T" stood for truthfulness—the core value of Druidry—and for teaching and learning in new ways. "H" stood for happiness after conquering some fear, and for heart.

We wanted this activity to actively manifest in our hearth—our cauldron of life— what was in our hearts. To do this, we used the three attributes of Brigit: healing, craft or livelihood, and inspiration. Each Grove member applied water from a Brigit well in

Ireland to an ailing body part or to the heart for emotional healing. Each put on the central altar something she or he had made, produced, or composed recently and asked for that craft or skill to continue under Brigit's guidance. Finally we each thought of a divination question and asked for an inspired answer from Brigit, muse of creativity, imagination, and spirit.

Not having sheaves of corn, we make a new Bridhe doll each Imbolc in a different way. We start with a sock filled with herbs, then dress it with bits of material and any objects that want to be on it. The first time Maya made a Bridhe doll, these words came: "Blessings we ask from the healing goddess who hangs her cloak on the rays of the sun."

During your ritual, if you call the four directions you might relate them to Brigit's elements. You might say: "Eternal flame of Brigit's forge, come into my work; waters of her sacred springs, heal me; cleansing winds of the air, be my inspiration; Brigit, ground me at the center of the world you protect." If you follow the custom of sharing bread and wine you can bake hot cross buns or soda bread with a crisscross to represent Bridhe's cross. You can drink cider from the last apples of fall or wine from the grapes of the last harvest. End your ritual by caring for your home in a special way: cleaning, rebuilding, decorating, establishing a new altar, preparing for spring.

Beltane

This holiday, also spelled *Bealtaine* ("Bel's fire"), is the word for the month of May in Irish, named for the god Bel. This is a lively, happy, lusty time! It is the second of the spring planting/herding festivals, coming as many days after Spring Equinox as Imbolc came before. Beltane inaugurates the summer season. The Celts only went to war in the six months following this time, until Samhain. Herds were passed between two fires before going to higher pasture, and humans lit their sexual fires and loosed them on each other. Many pagan groups today choose a King and Queen of the May to enact the mythic mating of the goddess of the land to the perfect king. The couple chosen may do this symbolically or actually. They light a "bale" fire on May Eve and jump it naked with friends and partners, proclaiming friendship or relationship with shrieks and laughter. Brehon Druids solemnized the matings made at Beltane with weddings at Lughnasadh. Modern bale fire rituals and the "mating" of King and Queen feel like ancient rites, but there is no way of telling if they are authentically Druidic.

We return now to the tale that begins this chapter. It is from a twelfth-century book of *dindsenchas* or stories of place. In this case the place is the Hill of Uisneach, the sacred center of Ireland. At Beltane, Druids and chieftains from all over Ireland came to Uisneach to light their torches from the royal fire tended by the king's Druid. These lights then went to all the provinces, and from them the people ritually rekindled their domestic fires.

The annual assembly of Druids at Uisneach matches what Julius Caesar wrote about Druids in Gaul. He reported that they gathered on a fixed date each year in a consecrated spot at the center of Gaul (thought to be Chartres in present-day France).[7] According to the medieval writer Geoffrey of Monmouth, Uisneach was the source of the stones which Merlin, the chief Druid of the Arthurian legends, took to Stonehenge. Although geologists and archaeologists have since found that those stones came from mountains in Wales, this story reaffirms the connection of Uisnech with Druids.

Erecting a Maypole is fun, though not a Druidic custom. The pole acts as the phallus, lowered into a deep hole that acts as the vagina. Men can chant and dance with the oiled pole before inserting it into the hole that women have dug and garlanded. The upright Maypole is wound with colored ribbons in gorgeous patterns by having ribbon-holders dance and weave around each other, finally braiding May blossoms into the bottom area.

We recommend erecting a Maypole, because chanting and dancing around it as the ribbons are wound—signifying the feminine embracing the masculine—is great fun even for onlookers. The dance creates an altered and magical state that probably was its long ago purpose. If you direct a Maypole wrapping, give extremely clear and accurate directions to participants or the weaving will become a tangle! Work this out well ahead of time. Music is essential during the winding: to the sound of massed drummers, we sing chants composed by local people or favorites from other sources. The Maypole is the site of crowning a new May Queen and King, selected by the royal couple of the year before.

The Maypole at noon and the bale fire at night comprise the chief rituals at many pagan gatherings for Beltane. We now have the elements of a Beltane ritual: plenty of fires, ushering in summer, gearing up for the year's biggest output (the modern version of cattle to the hills and plants in the ground), goddesses and gods, lustiness, fertility, happiness, play, color, flowers, Druids!

For your ritual, gather a crowd of people. Beltane traditionally was the first major assembly after the grip of winter and more people ensure more merriment. Costumes are in order; go wild with creative ideas. Someone might represent the hobby horse (an old British tradition), or, even more appropriate, the Green Man. This vegetal god was so powerful in pre-Christian Europe that he never really disappeared. A close look at cornices in Gothic cathedrals will reveal him peering from trees and vines, with foliage pouring forth from his mouth. Have someone dress as the Green Man, his face and body covered in foliage. He circulates in the crowd, raising the presence of masculine sexuality and seeking its counterpart among those exuding feminine sexuality.

At dusk on May Eve, light the bale fire! You can design this fire pit and ritual imaginatively. We dig the pit in an oval or yoni shape, deep enough for several logs to be placed below ground level, and lay in a proper fire of tinder, kindling and larger wood. We surround the shape with flowers, firs, candles, ribbons, and other burnable, bright decorations. The sheath of woven ribbons is removed from the Maypole and held by the Queen and King as they lead a spiral dance around the fire pit. When everyone is summoned by the movement and drumming and the first stars appear, the excitement builds to the lighting of the fire.

Last Beltane our Fire Goddess entered the fire-pit circle on a palanquin borne by four men as honor guards. She was seated ornately, sky-clad, surrounded by gauze to mystify the spirits. She lighted a rustic torch, descended from the palanquin as flame-bearer, and applied the torch to the kindling. The effect was striking, moving, even frightening for some who were present because the raw power was so evident. Endless hours of jumping the fire followed, to the accompaniment of energetic drummers. Some people sit by the fire until the last embers die out, giving way to the dawn of summer.

Lughnasadh

The Celts named Lughnasadh ("Lugh's feast") for Lugh, the pan-Celtic solar god. Lugh Lámhfada—literally, "light of the long arm"—was one of the few deities known throughout the many Celtic lands. In modern Irish, *Lúnasa* is the word for August. *Nasadh* is thought to mean games or assembly, and probably comes from Naas, Lugh Lámhfada's wife. She died at the place in southeast Ireland that now bears her name. Naas was the seat of Leinster's kings and a festive gathering place for Celts in that province. The Christian name for the feast day is Lammas or "First Loaf," similar to First Fruits celebrations at the beginning of harvest world-wide. Whatever grain or important crops ripen first are honored by dancing, chanting, and feasting. In New Mexico, the Pueblo Indians celebrate with corn dances in August.

In truth, the largest August gathering for Celts from all over Ireland was not at Naas, but at Tailltin (anglicized as Telltown). The goddess Tailltiu was foster mother to Lugh. She cleared the forest of Bregia near Tara to make fields for planting, and died from the effort. Her foster son Lugh told the people to gather yearly at Tailltin in her honor, and that place became a sacred site. According to Michael Dames, the sun rises over Tailltin on August 1 in a direct line from Ireland's sacred center at Uisneach.

At Lughnasadh, just as the goddess Tailltiu sacrificed herself, we commemorate the event by symbolically sacrificing the first fruits in our gardens, cutting them down with a Druid sickle. We honor Tailltiu as a harvest mother. She knows how to nurture and then cross over to the Otherworlds. She bridges the mundane and the mythic worlds.

Maya personally feels drawn to this goddess and to this feast because of her ancestry. Maya's grandfather was born a few miles from Telltown, which today shows little evidence of its importance apart from some huge earthen mounds. Maya's tribal ancestors were called *Ui-Mic-Uais Breagh*, "descendants of the tribe of the nobles of the Plain of Bregia." The Plain of Bregia is the level swath on Ireland's east coast just north of Dublin, which includes the Boyne Valley and some of the great Neolithic passage mounds such as Knowth and Newgrange. The myths call this topography around Telltown *Mag Mhór* or Great Plain, a euphemism for the Otherworlds, the primary Plane of Existence. The Celtic words for the land around Tailltin therefore show it to be a place between the worlds.

Coming back to Lughnasadh, we can now understand why the sun god Lugh told his people to celebrate this passage from full sun to darkness at a sacred opening between the physical and spirit worlds. The last known Olympic-style games held at the Tailltin feast were on August 1, 1169, under the last High King of Ireland, Ruraidh ó Conchobhar.

A description follows of the ritual that our Grove created for Lughnasadh, the cross-quarter day in August. We gathered on beautiful land in the mountains and set the wards for protection. One member of the Grove, dressed and masked as the Harvest Mother, invoked the goddess Tailltiu and created our space as the sacred plane by calling the welcome *"Fáilte a Tailltin!"* Another member challenged each of us to enter in much the same way as the gatekeeper challenged Lugh concerning his skills before gaining entry to Tara. Our Grove member asked in what name did we come and what skill did we bring to our assembly at Tailltin. Inspired and truthful answers came forth from this rare opportunity to state openly what our talents are and how we would like to use them.

Another member then asked each of us, by Druid name: "Are you present as a Brehon Law judge?" This was because Druids applied the Brehon Laws at Lughnasadh to settle all disputes, and everyone had to assemble in peace. We were asked how we had recently settled an important dispute or conflict. To our surprise, each of us had handled a difficult, emotionally laden, or legal conflict during that exact week! Most of them had resolved in unexpected and positive ways.

Next we learned the magical Heron Pose that Lugh used at the Second Battle of Moy Tura. This battle was instrumental in establishing Order throughout the Cosmos. We stood on one leg with an eye covered by one hand. We drew in Lugh's magic, concentrated on establishing order, focused it as we wished, and then sent it out rapidly into our present-day universe, to create harmony and balance.

Another member of the Grove eloquently envisioned the Wheel of the Year spinning in our presence. We passed the wheel of energy around, then released it upward, turning from full summer to fall harvest. For his poetic visualization, we elected this member to the Bardic Chair for the day. We feasted on Irish soda bread and soy milk, a vegetarian harvest drink. We closed with the appearance of the Green Man. He danced through the forest to earth-mother music, bringing us fruits and vegetables, sprinkling us with fairy dust. He invited us to dance and cavort in and out of sunshine and raindrops until we were replete with the magic and beauty of the ceremony.

As a practical Druid you can ask yourself these questions, arising from the myths of Lugh and Tailltiu (about Lughnasadh): What clearing do I need to do to make way for learning and growth? What am I willing to give up in order to harvest something in myself or my life? How can I bring more peace and order into my life? What recent gathering have I been part of that gave me a sense of belonging to the tribe?

Samhain

Samhain ("summer's end") is the Irish word for November. It is the cross-quarter day between Fall Equinox and Winter Solstice. This is about November 6, when the sun is 15 degrees Scorpio. Like the other cross-quarter days, the date of the festival has shifted and Samhain is now celebrated on Hallowe'en, October 31. The Celtic festival traditionally extended for a week or more over this whole period, so you have some leeway in selecting the exact time to celebrate these days. For example, in 1997 the dark of the moon occurred on October 31, making it the obvious choice.

This end-of-the-year period is the third of the three traditional harvest festivals, following Lughnasadh and Autumn Equinox. Celtic legend says that all crops were to be harvested by this day, since anything left in the fields belonged to the cailleach. She is the hag embodied in the final sheaf of oats that sickle-bearing reapers ritually severed from the earth and preserved inside the cottage until the next planting. In Welsh mythology, the Wild Hunt with the Hounds of Hell occurs at this time. The riders come from Annwn, the Welsh Otherworld, to gather up the souls of those who have died since the previous Samhain, taking them through the gates to the spirit world.

Samhain is the most powerful time of year for Druids, unparalleled for opportunities to enter the spirit world and share profoundly with ancestors, dark goddesses, and gods. This season vibrates with death and renewal, the descent into dark realms, and deep insights. Do your inner work at Samhain. As farmers neither plant nor reap in the winter, as seeds neither germinate nor die, so we take this time in the Wheel of the Year to be still also. At Samhain, we hibernate with the very roots of our life forces, the very depths of our fears, the cavern of our insights, the core of our being. Let this time of encroaching cold and dark call to you! Go within, to levels you would normally have no time for during the heat of the year. Let your focus shift from the physical side of life to the spiritual, when the Goddess lays out her summer lover upon a bier of leaves and the Dark God emerges.

Although all the festivals are border-times, evoking time out of or between normal times, Samhain is the Celtic period of the opening to the Otherworlds that ends the Druid year. You will hear that the "veil which divides the worlds is thinnest" at this time. What do these concepts mean and how can you utilize them in your spiritual practice? At Samhain there is no ordinary time. Released from the bond of the temporal, the gates between the worlds can open, and the dead and the living can mingle. Samhain is the magic death of time. It represents the season of consulting the dead and is among the most primitive ceremonies known. Those who have passed over can return to the material world. When the dead draw near to us, we can ask for guidance and even prophecies. Those in this world can look into the depths of timelessness. As in ancient days, we may choose to wear masks and strange clothes to make the wandering dead believe that we in costume are also spirits! The Great Mystery is revealed to the living: every ending is but a new beginning.

Maya's day of birth is at Samhain and there is no stopping her from plunging into this sacred time for an entire month. Like many Scorpios, she is fascinated with death, darkness, and the occult, and Hallowe'en provides them all. She is likely to be part of half a dozen rituals to start the descent to the Underworld of winter. The following sample ceremony for Samhain comes from our own Druid Grove.

We assembled in costume out of doors, with a large cauldron blazing and candles outlining the circle in the dark of the moon. One member of the grove came around to each of the others with the gift of information about that Druid's chosen tree in its attributes and powers for this time of year. He named the guidance from the tree, almost like an arboreal horoscope. Parts of each member's sacred tree—leaves, needles, berries, bark—were mixed into an incense and we all bathed in the smoke.

For the occasion we built a *sídhe* or Fairy mound next to the circle, and entered through a dolmen. We piled oak leaves inside in the center. We rustled, tossed, and smelled them, then settled into the visions of guided imagery. When the large drum stopped its quiet heartbeat we laid it in the center of the oak leaves. We turned it, turned it as the symbolic Wheel of the Year, calling out prayers and incantations faster and faster, spiraling ourselves kinesthetically down into the waiting chambers of the Dark Goddess and God. We were transported in space-time and for a long time became still.

After this plunge into psychic darkness we emerged from the *sídhe* mound and went to a permanent circle of stones. There we were met and given a lighted taper by the black-robed goddess Tlachtga, Druid daughter of the most magnificent and famous Druid of all—Mog Roith—or Devotee of the Wheel. He carries the solar wheel of the year and his daughter Tlachtga is a giver of fire. Her name means "earth-spear" and may reflect ancient origins as from the cosmos. Indeed, the pillar-stone associated with her might be a meteorite, as is the Kaaba revered by Muslims in Mecca. In Celtic times, the great Druids from the four provinces of Ireland gathered on the eve of Samhain at her Hill of Ward in Co. Meath.

Each of us was beckoned in turn to approach the dark goddess Tlachtga, the wise patroness of Druidic skills. We knew that the moment of the fire tradition was upon us. By ancient law, all fires in Ireland had to be extinguished at Samhain. They could only be relighted by flames from Tlachtga's fire, which chieftains and Druids from all provinces received after travelling to the Hill of Ward. She stood by a fiercesome pillar or touchstone. Those unprepared in Druidic skills would die if they touched it, be blinded if they saw it, and deafened if they heard it.

In our ceremony, a large statue was draped in fiery material and each Grove member approached, extinguishing the lighted candle. Each indicated preparedness by burning some dead plants from the garden in the blazing cauldron, representing the sacrifice Tlachtga made of herself in order to bring forth fire from deadness. Since it was Hallowe'en, it was easy to purchase things that had brilliant light, moaning sounds, or vibrating action. These were activated as each member saw the pillar stone, touched it, heard it and survived! With hand on the "touchstone," each spoke clearly of the wisdom they had received in the *sídhe* mound and promised publicly to carry that wisdom into the world. Tlachtga lit the taper of that person from her magical source. Our Grove closed the ritual and feasted on the autumn harvest.

In other years we have focused on the plant deities. With stalks, vines, and dead vegetables, we made an effigy of the dying Summer God and laid it in a grave, in the body of the earth goddess. We buried symbols or things we needed to part from and covered all with soil and dead leaves. We have looked into a fire in the cauldron to scry in the flames, reading there our personal connection with Samhain in the inner and outer worlds.

Maya has spent several Samhains in a small Mexican village where the native people celebrate *el Día de Los Muertos* on November 2. They sit all night at the tombs of ancestors amidst profuse arrays of flowers, candles, and offerings of "bread for the dead." It is an honor to pray with people partaking in an unbroken spiritual tradition.

Activities

These activities focus on Samhain. Please adapt them for the other cross-quarter festivals.

Earth. Go to a cemetery or select a special rock and decorate it as a tombstone. Put photographs and memorabilia there along with autumn harvest and candles. Then commune with departed family members and friends. Especially mourn those who died during the past year. Listen for any guidance or requests. Allow messages, images, feelings, and thoughts to come. Ask yourself, "What do I want from my dark side? What do I want from my spirit at this time?"

Sky. Visualize yourself approaching the edge of time and space. Bring yourself forward in imagery until you look over into the dead world. Go there if you wish, and take in all you can.

Sea. Go to the edge of the sea, a river, or a body of water. Honor the spirits that reside there. They may receive an offering or anything you would like to release and give away.

Plant. Cut the last growth from your garden or field and make a corn dolly or cailleach sheaf to keep until next year. Create a ceremony to compost the rest of the garden remains, mindful of the power of placing things that give food and life back into the earth that is the source of all.

Animal. Study the migration paths of birds in your area and visit bird sanctuaries. Druids learned much from the pattern of flocks and the behavior of birds. Study the wintering habits of animals in your area. Set aside times to use imagery for connecting with wild animals, looking in on them, checking their well-being, asking for guidance.

Deity. Call on Tlachtga for her Druid wisdom through working with fire. Extinguish all lights. Create ceremony with Tlachtga. Chants and incantations will come to mind. At some point, ask Tlachtga to light her Samhain fire. This is the time to let go of things by burning them in her fire. You might ask for life-preserving warmth, for fiery passion, for transformations, for greater understanding of the fire element. Then rekindle your candles.

Notes

1. Michael Dames, *Mythic Ireland*, p. 224.

2. For more information on Lughnasadh and the Feast of Tailltiu see Lorraine MacDonald, *Dalriada Magazine*, 1992; or http://www.dalriada.co.uk/archives/ lughfair.htm

3. Ross Nichols, *The Book of Druidry*, pp. 94–5 and p. 85.

4. G. Keating, *Foras Feasa Ar Eirinn* ("The History of Ireland"); quoted in M. Dames 1992, p. 254.

5. Michael Dames, *Mythic Ireland*, p. 247.

6. Ibid., p. 253.

7. Berresford Ellis, *The Druids*, p. 73.

Chapter 8

SELF-INITIATING AS A PEREGRINE DRUID

Firstly, I was formed in the shape of a handsome man,
In the hall of Ceridwen in order to be refined.
Although small and modest in my behavior,
I was great in her lofty sanctuary.[1]

Self-initiating is a requisite step to becoming a Druid, whether it happens purposely or spontaneously. This chapter elucidates both methods. Initiation in a larger sense is the same as the hero/ine's journey. The peregrine is our term for a Druid who travels along the inner path, by means of both initiation and the hero/ine's journey. A guide to taking the sometimes perilous route of Separation, Descent, and Return concludes this chapter.

You can hold Taliesin in your mind either as the title of a mythic shaman or the historic bard who lived in Wales during the latter half of the sixth century C.E. In bardic poetry, he describes his training and initiation with the sorcerer Ceridwen. This amazing goddess is a key figure in the training of initiates. She brews the wisdom of all ages in her cauldron of inspiration. Her cauldron brims with rich symbolism, representing a potion for initiates to drink, the womb of the mother in which the infant gestates, the chief stages of spiritual development, and the trials of journeying from ignorance to magical inspiration.

As with all apprentices—be they artists, educators, or shamans—initiates must emerge from the belly of their teachers, coming into this world to do their work. Taliesin knew this:

While I was held prisoner, sweet inspiration educated me
And laws were imparted me in a speech which had no words;
But I had to flee from the angry, terrible hag
Whose outcry was terrifying.[2]

How Orgasm and Initiation Differ

We propose that you must initiate in order to become a Druid. Initiation moves you along in power and experience and keeps you from stagnating in "wanna-be Druid" waters. We are not saying you should "be initiated," which implies that someone else knows something you don't and does something to you: this relationship makes you passive. Rather, we propose that you self-initiate and stay open to the possibility of doing this several times in your life. This may occur according to your own plan, or the Universe may spring a profound experience upon you!

To initiate means not only to begin, but to originate. Initiation often means you do take in certain teachings, but also that you start to bring forth inner wisdom and proceed through a rite. What you learn and what you experience will decisively change your status and spiritual path. Initiation affects us profoundly, unalterably, once we connect with the Universe in this powerful way. Through risk and trial, by ordeal and revelation of self-knowledge, we come through and thus earn the rights and responsibilities of being a Druid. The rite of passage transports us to this new stage.

One thing we know: initiation requires deep personal experience. It gets into our molecules and cells and changes us forever. You cannot "read about" it to achieve it, any more than you can learn to swim by reading. Unlike orgasm, you cannot fake initiation! It is an inner, intensely personal experience. Another person, spirit, or animal might be a guide, teacher, or keeper of the circle, but essentially we take the journey alone.

About the word peregrine: in settling on a unisex term for the heroine and hero on spirit journeys, we chose "peregrine." Not only does the word *peregrina/peregrino* mean "pilgrim" in Spanish, the verb "peregrinate" also means to journey through foreign and alien places, to travel *through* the inner path. The Celts had a heroic society that included both women and men in all roles such as warrior, wise person, and adventurer. In the teachings found in this book, we do not wish to perpetuate the male as hero (One Up) and the female as rescued (One Down). This would not reflect the Celtic view of their world. The Celts probably would have liked the term peregrine and its underlying meaning. We chose the word to refer to both sexes as equals and to connote the alien world through which the initiate must travel many times.

Initiating Oneself

Many Druid organizations exist to guide people through structured steps of training and initiation, while others provide guidance but do not structure that process. For those who prefer to do it themselves, this chapter offers two processes: planned and spontaneous initiation. Maya relates her formal self-initiation as a Druid, the rite of passage to her inner True Self. Nicholas tells of a powerful, unplanned initiation in a forest in Ireland. The rest of this chapter lays out Druidic initiation, following the age-old pattern of the Heroine's or Hero's journey: Separation, Descent, and Return. Since much has been written about the hero's journey, we will concentrate on the heroine as the spirit pilgrim in this book.

If you plan to self-initiate, set yourself on a direct course. Set a date one year and one day in the future for holding your initiation ceremony. Prepare monthly, then weekly, then daily as the date approaches. Admit areas that are weak and practice skills in those areas until you strengthen those spiritual, mental, and ethical muscles. Set yourself a course of study and complete it rigorously, on time. Learn all you can. Simplify and cleanse in all aspects of your life so that you quiet the buzz, the chatter, the frenetic patterns. Substitute patterns of calm, certainty, and direction. Start to announce in gatherings what you are doing and notice the responses: notice who supports your efforts and who pulls away. As your self-study increases and your goals become clear, set out written intentions that you will meet or exceed by the appointed date of initiation. Line up a close group of people who will assist you. Remain open to ideas and guidance that will move through you from subtle sources.

Recording the steps you take to initiate yourself as a Druid is a valuable form of path-working. In Celtic style, you become a bard reporting on your deeds and thoughts, your shapeshiftings and inner travels. After a powerful experience, Maya traced a purification initiation through time, recording each era in which she felt she was present in some form. She asked for inspiration of how things used to be, and the writing came to her during a session with that well-known modern Druidic device, the computer! This is how the account of this experience begins:

> You are inside a large cave, in the womb of the giant Earth Mother. The flickering orange light of the central fire bonds you to the others of your tribe. Drums sound the rhythm of the group's heartbeat. The chanting and drumming echo back from the high stone ceiling and resonate inside your bones.

The skins you wear smell more of your body than of their original fox owner. The heavy musk of your clan joins with the odors of loamy herbs boiling, with burning wood, with lighted oil smoking in bowls outside the circle. The memories are old. You pray together often, when the sun shows her heat or hides it, when the moon shows her light, or hides it—as tonight. It has always been this way.

A Planned Self-Initiation (Maya)

You are welcome to take some of the following elements from Maya's ritual as a guide to your planned self-initiation. Sometimes reading about a successful, completed ceremony with all its flow and elements in sequence, is more helpful than deciphering a list of things needed to prepare for a ritual. Please modify these ideas to suit yourself.

Bumping Up Against It

A decade ago my friend Amy called me a "Druid Princess." The title felt attractive but unearned. The Universe drew me along until I had accumulated enough knowledge to teach a community college course called "Dragons, Druids, and Sacred Stones" and make slide presentations to Celtic organizations. My speed of learning increased. During a visit to Wales, a native-speaking Welsh friend introduced me to the Chief Bard of Wales. He recited his award-winning poetry to the accompaniment of his wife's harp, and then I spoke with the Arch-Druid of that land. I was certain that I had done this before. We know when we are ready for the next step in our spiritual development because, as a Native American man said to me, we "bump up against it." We start asking questions, feeling that something is on the other side of a gateway. When we want to proclaim this personal growth, we are ready to self-initiate. We come to these gateways more than once in life.

Groundwork

I prepared for a year and a day before self-initiating as a newly minted Druid. That is the mythic amount of time it took Ceridwen to boil down her wisdom to its essence in her cauldron. My preparation followed three avenues: study, ritual, and inspiration. During the year of study, I devised a reading list and worked through it, building a base of knowledge. I took each Druidic piece of information and reworked it until it became mine.

Creating and participating in rituals became frequent in my life, and marked the cycle of the seasons. I learned more of the other worlds we enter through altered states in ritual, the importance of inner preparation, setting the intention, protecting the circle, participation by everyone present, and using music and movement. Four months before the big event, I began a pilgrimage to the four directions. In the East I communed with Air by hiking along a 10,000-foot high mountain crest through a gale to a spot where I did ritual with some friends; we got our fill of air! For the South and Fire at Samhain I went to an Indian village in central Mexico. I spent the night with native people on the tombs of their ancestors, in a graveyard lighted by thousands of candles, where I asked permission to do my own Druid ceremony. For the West and Water I bathed in winter in Oak Creek near Sedona, one of the most beautiful water-carved canyons in the West. For the North and Earth, I spent the night in a white alabaster cave with cold wind from the interior keeping vigil with me.

During the year of inviting inspiration, I passed from generic devotion to The Goddess to connection with specific goddesses. At the initiation I invited Ceridwen to make me a vessel of preserving Celtic wisdom. I asked her for the powers she gave to her descendants through Taliesin—memories of Celtic images long gone, inspiration for people of today, and secrets of days to come. Like the elusiveness of fairies, who can be seen only out of the corner of the eye, the cauldron of inspiration opened to me not on demand but by attunement to it.

The Unexpected and the Enigmatic

My search moved deeper and took on a life of its own. An unplanned outcome was being impelled to tell the truth. Instead of the polite neutrality I had learned as a people-pleaser, out of me now came honesty in all forms. I send apologies to the few who did not want this, and welcome the many with whom I have closer connections because of it.

Initiates are always asked questions. I decided to decipher the enigmatic question attributed to the bard Amergin: "Who but I knows the secret of the unhewn dolmen arch?" Dolmen means table-stone in Breton, the Celtic language of Brittany. I had been inside many of these cave-like passages built of megaliths by the Neolithic people, and now worked at getting inside their spiritual structure. They serve as entrances to the Underworld. Initiations took place inside dolmens, and people were reborn spiritually through the birth canal of the stone passage. The dolmen later symbolized the Celtic structure of knowledge, the Ogham alphabet, with data on the outside. What did the space inside the entrance mean? The breath of the deities blows inspiration through us, as air blows into the entrance of the dolmen. The inside represents wisdom, which is more elusive than knowledge. The message of the unhewn dolmen was to open my mind and heart, the inner chambers from which come creativity and finest endeavor.

Ceremonial Transformation

The thirty people at my initiation each took on a part of the ritual, as clans did in days gone by. They helped with face painting, gatekeeping, cauldron tending, dancing, reading, dramatizing, and grounding the energy. Having friends contribute from their strengths and talents enriched the event greatly. As we sat around the circle of stones on that sunny February day, a friend dramatized a poem she had written. It begins: "Maya was born of an egg and a bone, a hollow bone the Druids blew her soul through." I proclaimed the serpent-dragon as my power animal, quoted my life credo and named my path of destiny. I was tested with sacred questions by a friend, a nationally known pagan. I called out the contribution of my lineage. In this way I connected myself with my forebears, the Keeper-People of wisdom and of ancient teachings. I was learning from them the earth-sky-sea science. I could work the alchemy connecting the mundane to the sacred, the ancient to the modern, the intuited to the learned.

Coming Full Circle

For a conclusion to your ritual it is a good idea to let yourself know what you have learned. Others (both with and without bodies) might be listening too! I ended the ceremony with:

> Here ancestors, is my answer! I know the secret of the unhewn dolmen because you have led me there, because I went into the cave, because I dove down in the flames of the cauldron. The secret is this: I am the temple and the inner world is my divine self. The dolmen is all the branches of knowledge from my ancestors. The milky substance of fear and doubt drops away from my eyes like a snake shedding its skin. Because I am Celtic, I do magical workings and hear the music of fairies. Asleep, I travel through the portal of the

dolmen to the Otherworlds. Awake, I have visions that are not in this space and time. You are witnessing my rebirth, my life as a Druid. Blessed be!

An Unplanned Initiation (Nicholas)

In 1985, on a visit to Ireland with a small group of friends, Nicholas had one of the most extraordinary experiences of his life. In a secluded wood near Glendalough, County Wicklow, he met a presence that he could only call the Green Man, Herne, the Lord of the Forest. He also had the experience of being many creatures. Above all, he awoke to himself, his tradition, his ancestors, and his connection with all things. He relates the experience fully in *His Story: Masculinity in the Post-Patriarchal World* (Llewellyn, 1995). He considers this his initiation into himself and his Druidry, and the implications of it continue to have far-reaching effects on his life.

He found that the experience of reconnecting with his ancestral lineage at special and sacred places in his native lands triggers an unfolding of knowledge and imagery from within. He does not find much meaning in initiations that come from outside, and are, for example, rites of induction into a group. Instead, he feels that initiation is a process that connects a person with his or her internal self. It is an inner process of preparation, pilgrimage, and opening to the Self and the spirits of place. After some further experiences in Scotland, Nicholas discovered that his ancestry, previously thought to be English or Anglo-Saxon, all went back to Scotland. His family lineages: Watson, Fleming, Adam, Lockhart, Laurence, Livingston, Read, McClellan, and McCleod, all originate in Scotland. Another family name of Brennand is possibly of Irish origin and Mann, a sept of Clan Gunn, may have come through the Isle of Man.

It is possible that, as time goes by, a Celtic "tribe" could be recreated within which the initiation of young people is performed. At present this social entity does not exist, so it remains up to each one of us to recreate initiations for ourselves—not an easy task. A pilgrimage is ideal, as it removes us from routine habits and opens us up to the special, the synchronous, and the unknown. A retreat also works, especially a time alone in the wilds or with others intent on the same task, but this is not for everyone.

The purpose of an initiation is to reconnect us with the awareness of the eternal Self. It is to provide us with an experience that floods us with the wisdom of our many lives and allows a glimpse of the infinite. When this takes place the challenge is to integrate it into ourselves. The initiation will come like a signpost, which we can either heed or ignore. If we ignore it, the initiation process won't be at all meaningful, and eventually we will forget it happened, like a dream. If we heed initiation and let it guide us, then it will become increasingly meaningful in our lives. It will become larger and more significant the more we understand what took place. The result of an initiation is that it helps you know who you are. After an initiation you become truly comfortable and "at home" within yourself for the first time in your life.

During this experience, Nicholas felt he had come home to his spiritual path. He also understood that along with self-knowledge, initiation carried a certain responsibility: it was now up to him to play his part in keeping the Celtic Druid tradition alive! It was up to him to sustain the practices, mythic images, and symbols of the tradition that inspired him, so that others could come to these things themselves and receive their own initiation. This initiation, among other things, showed him the path of being an author, storyteller, and artist, in the matter of his own tradition. The experience was the guiding signpost of his life and bestowed on him his Druid name.

There are some clues that can let you know an initiation is drawing near. You might hear music that has an incredible effect upon you. Snatches of it might come to your ears from a distance, and sound like the music of your soul—which, in fact, it is. Synchronous events increase and profound meaning is everywhere. Do not fixate on these things or be drawn into the glamour of them, but keep going on your path: events will occur that seem fated, like destiny itself is taking you.

Friends play an important role. You might meet someone you feel you have always known, perhaps you will even feel that you met the person in a past life. Whether this is true or not is unimportant compared to the feeling you are having, triggered by the friend, that you have always known something. It may or may not turn out to be the friend, who is simply the mirror of your Self. The feeling you have is ultimately about knowing your eternal Self.

Each Self has a signature, an essential feature that it carries through time. When your signature is triggered by love, music, nature, poetry, or friendship, remember it is the sound of your own eternal Self and let it come close. In the same way as you might grow tired of a piece of music if you hear it too often, so the Self withdraws when subjected to rational analysis, overexposure, or repetition. Keep on good terms with the inner world, maintain it as a mystery, and this eternal realm will show you everything you need to know.

The Peregrine's Journey

Following the worldwide tradition of the hero/ine's journey, and more specifically the Celtic tradition, we will now explore how to take your own peregrine's journey. The Celtic myths contain initiatory lessons within two great categories of stories: *tochmarcha* or courtships, and *tána* or cattle raids. In the courtship stories, the female often has magical powers and knows the developmental steps to wholeness and the balance between earthiness and airiness, so it is she who guides the male hero (see chapter 6 on sacred sexuality). Both partners must go through trials and perform tasks to deepen their personal development within the relationship as well as with the world outside. In the cattle raids, males and females undergo rigorous training and then, surprisingly, experience opportunities to test their skills and courage in magnanimous adventures.

Prepare yourself for traveling now, on paths where you've not ventured before. Remind yourself that we initiate many times in life, sometimes consciously, sometimes not. Be awake to feelings and sensations, yearnings and fears, callings and hesitations. Surround yourself with Druid tools such as a wand for directing energy, a protective robe, a sickle to cut through emotional chains from the past. We recommend a sword of truth for those times when it is difficult to be honest with yourself. Hone your shapeshifting skills so you can picture yourself as a bird if you are falling, as a fish if you are drowning, as a particle of air if you are burning, and perhaps as a weasel if you are suffocating. Use your Druid methods of divination so you can "see" where you are going. Contact your inner cauldrons of inspiration and regeneration. Be an apprentice at the side of Ceridwen. Ready? Let us depart from the ordinary, from the known . . . .

Separation

Usually a powerful event triggers the Separation, the period of remaking ourselves, somewhat like the experience of leaving home that we had as a young adult. What are some life-changing events that can trigger a life transformation? Negative situations include mental illness, loss of a role, loss of a lover or family member, abuse, and addiction. Other negative situations are isolation, fear and anxiety, midlife crisis and spiritual aridity. Positive situations include finding a soul partner, giving birth, important birthdays, starting or completing school, career successes, creative products. We may not control the trigger, but we do have a choice about how to handle the separation from the known. To give these life events a Druidic turn, think of them as markers or stages on your spiritual path. Then mental illness becomes a visit to altered realities, fear becomes the signal for more warrior training in that area, creativity becomes the outlet for Celtic inspiration.

Life-changing events often occur unexpectedly. We may be unwilling to make changes but feel a compulsion to do so: something pulls us down the initiate's path. Typically, our lives play out a pattern in which there are periods of relative stability interspersed with periods of upheaval, crisis, and turmoil. These crises cause changes in us and, like skilled teachers, put us in touch with important truths.

When we are ready to separate from the known—actually *before* we feel ready—we are led on the journey. The separation can happen suddenly after a traumatic event, gradually during a life transition, or consciously by triggering it ourselves. Nicholas and Maya operate on the basis that the dark god and dark goddess are our guides. Like Gwion, who turns from ordinary uninspired worker to the incredibly creative Taliesin by means of initiation with Ceridwen, we will shed skins until we face our naked truth. In this sense, shapeshiftings are the twists and turns we take to make ourselves into the semblance of what others want, until we graduate to the truth that we are who we are.

Starhawk, one of the leading figures in Wiccan spirituality, says the purpose of ritual is to create situations in which we feel the great tides moving through us. Ritual can *cause* life-changing events but, more commonly, ritual gives us the courage to make changes and gives us a way to focus when we are suffering from confusion, pain, and fear. If you are wrenched away due to a Separation event, getting out of denial as fast as possible and getting into sacred space will help. Ritual provides a way to mark a passage through a crisis, to mark the path of descent to and return from the dark goddess and god. Therefore we recommend that you plan (or at least take note of) each of your initiations and mark the stages ritually. You could have a ceremony of loss for what you are leaving behind. You could set the wards strongly around yourself when you feel vulnerable on a peregrine's journey. Seek your animal guides and protectors, stay close to your trees, ask your ancestors for guidance and wisdom.

There is comfort in knowing about this journey: others have experienced it. The separation and descent are required in order to make the pilgrimage through the spiritual rooms and caves of life. Women report more depression than men, and depression can be a medical term for the separation and descent of initiation. Women often experience depression in their lives, possibly because they experience more loss and separation and are willing to face the dark goddess. Women admit to their inner feelings more readily. Because of their fertility women understand that life is a cycle and there is no renewal without the death of the old.

The peregrine's journey is a direct route to transformation. It allows us to shed exterior pretenses and social roles, revealing the inner Self with whom we can travel for the rest of our lives. Like Gwion and Ceridwen, once we swallow the seed of the dark, we can never go back to the status quo. We give birth to our true Self. The divine presence in us awakes and, by this presence, the trappings of the past can no longer hold us. We may be terrified, but we are released!

Joseph Campbell said we find the goal of the quest to know ourselves at the "burning point" within. The journey into our dark selves takes courage, sending our personal warrior into battle for us. This is the soul in movement, the essence of the mystery of life. The dark journey helps us find the energy at our center. The exact meaning of the Grail image, of the source, of our coming into being, can be apprehended at the cusp of this journey.

A word of encouragement: we come out the other side with fewer bonds. Even though we are afraid, we have left more baggage behind. This makes us feel raw and naked, but it also makes us free. This is the mystery, the eternal truth, that the myths tell us. We have within us the cauldron of rebirth. We can set *ourselves* free! As the Wiccan Charge of the Goddess says: "Know that your seeking and yearning will avail you not, unless you know the Mystery: for if that which you seek, you find not within yourself, you will never find it without."[3]

Descent to the Dark Goddess

The basic source called "goddess" or "god" has at least two aspects: the light and the dark, which correspond to the light and dark times of the year. We will concentrate on the goddess here.

To talk about the dark goddess requires no belief in a separate thing called goddess, nor need it arouse any fear of the dark. People gain access to the dark goddess with no more threat than occurs by going into winter. The dark goddess speaks through the very old, very natural but unanalytical parts of us. She speaks through intuition, gut feelings, shadow, dreams, instinct. She is in the stored information we hold in our bodies and in the lower parts of our brain. Like lunar energy, she illuminates the secret dark of our inner life forces. This goddess knows the power of our anger and aggression, our love and life-giving. Ceridwen is champion of all the forces that refuse to fit comfortably into the social order!

The descent to the dark goddess is a slow, probably painful period of self-discovery. We have to admit what lies beneath the social persona, the ego, the conditioned self. We return to a way of knowing through the body, not through words. Haven't you ever experienced that the body knows and has stored all that has happened in our lives?

The ancient, lowest part of the human brain (called the reptilian brain) is similar to that in all animals with at least the development of reptiles. All it knows is survival, not even whose body it is in. The next layer up, called the mammalian brain, urges us to survive on the tribal level. At this level we are aware of the small group around us, either our family of origin or made family, or an unrelated family of friends and soul-mates. These below-consciousness places in our brain know about the dark. Our feelings, our body, our gut, our physical intelligences know about the dark because they have always lived there. They knew about the dark before there were words on earth, before there were power structures and analytical brains that told us how to behave.

Ceridwen was one of the dark goddesses of the Druids. She is mistress of initiation and descent. Ceridwen and other dark deities send out scouts to round up souls of the dead and bring them to the Otherworlds. They meet all dead souls at the gates and take them to the magical cauldron for renewal. They are dipped into it and are reborn. In today's terms, we can renew ourselves if we are willing to take the journey to the dark world of our unconscious and let go of the dead parts of ourselves. Then we can dip in the cauldron of transformation and renew our lives by what we find there, the missing pieces of ourselves we have neglected, denied, or forgotten. Then we can "re-member" ourselves.

Ceridwen is in charge of the caves of the earth and of our minds, the mines of inspiration and rebirth. The Celts held the mystery of rebirth in wonder. They felt that transformation could only come after shedding the dead aspects of ourselves, just as the earth is renewed only after decay in the dark season of the year. We renew ourselves by sending down to the cauldron those parts of us we want to release, and by bringing to light the rebirthed Self. Ceridwen demands nothing less than death in the dark and then grants renewal in the light.

A kind of Celtic immortality comes to those who see death as an integral part of the cycle of life. We renew ourselves whenever we drink fully and fearlessly from the cauldron—the womb, the Grail, the chalice of life. We *are* the Grail, the cauldron of renewal. By descending to the transforming fires of our dark side, the cauldron renews us.

We are compelled to make the descent, whether by conscious decision or not. We fear what this dark side of ourselves will do to us. We might try to avoid it, but when we need to make the peregrine's journey, often we are drawn down before we realize it. Although it can be an excruciating experience, we become more ourselves than when we began. Myths tell us that going beyond our normal behavior will stretch us and make us reach into the dark to gain the wholeness contained there.

The descent to the dark consists of a test or period of learning in order to come to new knowledge of ourselves. This is a good definition of initiation. As Druids we are free to initiate ourselves, since no one else has more wisdom than we do. The descent takes us back to our roots, to ancient connections through the body, the gut, and the old parts of the brain. Like a pilgrimage, the descent and initiation are *supposed* to be difficult because the giving of ourselves is what causes the transformation and lets us know we are different than before.

Now that you have absorbed the ideas, how do they look in application? How can you navigate the storms of Descent and emerge as a self-initiated Druid? How can you do this over and over in life? Let us start with awareness. You can use your mind, the core organ for students of Druidry, to help you prepare. Tell your mind to be alert to major shifts that presage life changes. Take charge of yourself in ways that keep you prepared: physical well-being, mental clarity, keeping journals and other creative outlets that keep your well of inspiration pumping. Practice flexibility. This can be physical, through yoga and tai chi, mental through poetic expression, and spiritual through prayer and meditation. Make some Druid tools to protect yourself and add to your power during the Descent. Keep your position in family, social groups, and the community-at-large clean and ethical. Give priority to your spiritual needs: listen to your soul. Read works that contribute to putting you in the way of major inner shifts. Take on the difficult. Have a few people around you who, like opera, require a stretch instead of easy listening.

Return and Integration

In the *Mabinogion*, Branwen is the sister of Britain's king; she marries the king of Ireland, where she goes to live. The royal couple's initiation into relationship fails, as communication and vows are broken. Unfortunate consequences send her to live below ground as a scullery maid, beaten by the butcher, abused and scorned by her former subjects. All communications with her homeland and royal brother in Britain are cut off.

If we see this as the peregrine's journey, she had gone to the Otherworlds, faced trials, been stripped of royalty, and lost her former Middle World life. She has descended to meet the dark goddess. What she must do is find her missing self, heal the wounded self, yearn for wholeness, and finally integrate her soul-retrieved parts. For a woman this often requires ceasing to be the all-receiving receptacle—as wife, lover, king's consort. She must fill her womb-cauldron with fire, power, energy, and strength. She must become a warrior, leader, and queen in her own right. This process gives a woman her wholeness. Only then can she be her full True Self, with no need for anyone else to complete her

Branwen, from the depths of her helplessness, befriends a bird and teaches it to speak. The bird flies to Britain and speaks in the ear of her brother, who happens to be a giant as well as a king. He brings all his forces to Ireland—armies, navies, bards, harpists, warriors—and secures his sister's release. Branwen (unlike ourselves, we trust!) remains a tragic figure and commits suicide on her return home to Anglesey. She fails the heroine's final test of integrating the soul-retrieved parts into her essence. She fails to drink fully and fearlessly from the cauldron of life. As with any crisis, one of the realistic outcomes can indeed be misery, regression, and death.

We complete the "Return and Integration" phase of the peregrine's journey on a more positive note, because the other realistic outcomes of spiritual journeying are growth, wisdom, and new ways of being in the world. Among the Celtic myths, hero–gods usually achieve renown after their initiation, whereas heroine–goddesses often meet sad ends such as Branwen or Rhiannon. However, the sun goddess Grania will be an excellent model for us here, since she is a heroine-goddess whose long initiatory journey changed her significantly. See how her story might parallel your own.

Grania was engaged to marry a much older man, Fionn, a rather wild warrior leader. At the wedding feast she locked onto young and innocent Diarmuid with whom women fell in love if they saw his "love spot." She persuaded Diarmuid to break his vow to be faithful to the warrior troop Fianna, to leave without notice and to run off with her although she was promised to his leader, Fionn.

Did you ever do things in your youth of which you were not proud? Have you ever made another person break a promise in order to win favor with you? Have you ever taken someone away from home, family, and friends? Grania did all this, and her actions set her up for a peregrine's journey.

Indeed, Grania and Diarmuid are the quintessential peregrines of Celtic mythology, since they wandered for sixteen years before learning all their lessons. The crux of the tale is that Grania had to learn behaviors other than being selfish, demanding immediate gratification, hurting others, and causing furor; even goddesses have to grow up. Years later, after Fionn had arranged Diarmuid's death, one version of the myth has Grania marrying Fionn and having children with him. She apparently sees the virtues of old age and earthiness; recall that she was a solar deity, flighty and full of the fiery passion of the sun. She achieved her balance by embracing empty parts of herself connected with patience, aging and being down-to-earth.

The authors have made the peregrine's journey more than once. Maya valued her sanity and clear-thinking with pride until undergoing clinical depression; the outcome was an insider's understanding and empathy for those with mental illness. She had a parallel experience with physical health: as the paragon of stress management, nutrition, and exercise, she started a university wellness center, businesses, and publications in those fields. When menopause arrived, all the natural approaches failed and after much distress she accepted hormone replacement as the answer.

Nicholas left the United States after eight years, to live again on his native soil, closer to his family in Britain, among the familiar trees and seasons. That was the Separation phase. He underwent a tumultuous Descent, an unexpected soul crisis on every level. For the Return, he was spat out the other side with a one-way ticket back to the U.S. His new essence, his new way of being, had leapt oceans and continents and would not be sidetracked by old patterning.

We hope that these tales will match some of the learning you yourselves do, and help you to integrate lost or missing parts of yourselves on the way to wholeness. Like Grania, we hope that you have the courage to see your flaws, embrace the learning of new ways, and thrive in a range of life situations.

To apply the Integration experience that ends every peregrine's journey, we suggest that you map out what has happened during your entire journey. In drawings, clay sculptures, drama or writing, lay out the patterns and learning along the way. Notice which parts of yourself you discarded, which parts you manifested for the first time, and how this structure now fits together to represent your Self in this moment. Have a ceremony of "re-membering" or putting together your member parts. You can lay this journey out in real space on the floor, in a forest or magical circle. Walk the pattern, picking up symbols for each treasure guarded by your dragons: each discovery, each wound you healed, each little death, each piece of your soul retrieved, each gift or boon, each contribution to wisdom. Proclaim what every aspect of the journey meant to you, what you lost or let go of, and what you gained. Declare who you are now and what you will do with this Self. Thank yourself for the courage and persistence to be the peregrine, who has traveled through alien lands and arrived home.

Activities

Planning an Initiation Ritual. In chapter 5, you created your Ph.D. study plan for becoming a Practicing Holistic Druid. This is your guide to determine where you are on your learning journey. At significant points during that journey, initiation rituals are in order. Your learning journey is lifelong, and you certainly don't want to wait until the end to proclaim that you are beginning a new phase!

- Reread your Ph.D. study plan now. Determine where you are in each strand of it.

- If the time is right, set up an initiation ceremony alone, or with a trusted group.

- If you prefer, go to a sacred space in nature, put yourself in communion with the spirits there, and wait for a spontaneous initiation.

New Beginnings. Create rituals for all new beginnings, which in their own way are initiations: birthing, naming, house blessing, wedding, passing over. Integrate Druidic principles from your study and reading, along with ritual formats and materials and symbols you have learned. When you feel accomplished at this, you might create an initiation ritual to name yourself a ritualist!

The Hero/ine's Journey. Druids need to learn to drink fully and fearlessly from the cauldron of life. Each of us is somewhere on our Grail Quest. The Grail is the wisdom of our ancestors, our connection to our roots, the renewal we dip into as we travel the spiral of existence. The Quest is our spiritual journey, the search for our fully authentic Self. We make pilgrimage to our inner selves to search for meaning. As with all initiations, there will be fear and danger as we confront the unconfrontable, unmask fears, and free blocked energy for spiritual purposes.

Part of the Quest is to ask "QUESTions." Where are you on your life journey? Ask yourself the Grail questions as you follow these steps:

Separation. Leaving the old behind. Grail Question: Whom does it serve? How can you break away from the known, from your childhood conditioning, from everyday-ness? Go on a Druidic retreat, take a backpack trip, visit a Celtic land, study Celtic myths, learn something completely new. How can you become free of things that no longer serve?

Descent. Death of the Old. Grail Question: What ails thee? When we transmute we face dangers. Seek experiences that will shift your focus from wounds and healing to the life-pulsing question: "Why am I here?" By contacting the Otherworlds represented by death, danger, animals, and the unconscious, we open ourselves to alchemical change from within. All the ancestors, divine beings, and guides provide inspiration and wisdom during this stage.

Rebirth. We return with answers. Grail Question: What is the Grail? We bring back gifts. Bran's cauldron of rebirth is the assurance that we will return from "death." The Dagda's cauldron provides bounteous plenty in which we each find our own most satisfying nourishment. The Grail becomes whatever each of us needs and wants.

Notes

1. From the poem "Song of His Origins," John Matthews, *Taliesin*, p. 281.

2. Ibid.

3. Starhawk, *The Spiral Dance*, p. 91, after Doreen Valiente.

PART II

FROM PAST
TO PRESENT

Part II covers the timeline from ancient Celts and Druids to becoming a Druid today and visiting the Celtic lands that remain. We summarize the history of the Celts, discuss how Druidry developed along with Celtic culture, and explore ways of defining oneself as a Celt.

Chapter 9

What Is a Celt?

It was at Inver Slane in Leinster that the Sons of the Gael made their first attempt to land in Ireland. They were under the leadership of the sons of Miled, with Donn, Eremon, and the poet Amergin among them. It was from the South they came, and their Druids had told them there was nowhere for them to settle until they came to Ireland. "And if you do not get possession of it," they said, "your children will."[1]

We'll set this stage of your journey into Druid magic by bringing to life the society in which the ancient Druids lived, the society of the Celts. The Celts were an enormously diverse people, speaking variants of what is now known as the Celtic family of languages. They occupied central and western Europe in the first millennium B.C.E. Defeated by the Romans, pushed west by later invaders such as the Anglo-Saxons, the Celtic peoples today survive along the northwestern margins of Europe. The Celts shared the traits of pride, fearlessness in battle, and fondness for feasts and ceremony, although they did not share a unified ethnic or political identity. They didn't even call themselves "Celts": this term is derived from Graeco-Roman descriptions of them. Some Irish, Scots, Welsh, Manx, Breton, and Cornish people today accept the Celtic label, but most prefer to call themselves, and their language, after their own names.

A Brief History of the Celts

The Druids were the wise men and women of the Celts. A convincing picture of ancient Europe is emerging from recently unearthed evidence, one that sees the original wise men and women in the role of shamans. Each tribe or subtribal group from Paleolithic times had shamans who did the healing, midwifery, rites of passage, dream interpretation, divination, calendar-keeping, and so on. Anthropologists and historians once dismissed the value of shamanic knowledge and practice, but are now coming to respect its role in tribal society. It is likely that these shamans assisted in the first widespread flowering of native European culture, with the development of megalithic structures, such as Stonehenge, from about 5000 B.C.E. onward. These impressive structures required a large degree of social organization, but we know little about their Neolithic builders, and cannot say how their shamans organized themselves into a supervising group at this time.[2]

From about 1800 B.C.E. on, a new cultural impulse flowed across northern Europe.[3] It descended from Indo-European roots, and brought with it new technologies, especially in metalworking. Its people spoke the family of languages that we now call Celtic. By the first millennium B.C.E. and the Iron Age, this culture dominated central and western Europe. Evidence suggests that this domination did not occur forcibly, but by a process of slow assimilation with the earlier peoples. It is likely that the Native European Tradition in its shamanic form continued in an unbroken line into this, the Celtic period (see more about the Native European Tradition in chapter 10).

A specifically "Celtic" style appeared in central Europe as early as 1200 B.C.E. with the advent of the Hallstatt Culture. This culture declined after 600 B.C.E., but there arose from it a new and vigorous cultural impulse known as La Tène. These peoples, composed of many different tribes, had contacts with the Mediterranean world, and were soon migrating southwards. Celtic Gauls sacked Rome in 390 B.C.E., while other tribes moved eastwards, occupying the Danube area and threatening Greece. The Celtic culture was at its peak in the third century B.C.E. Although still extremely diverse, the many tribes shared the exquisite artistic traditions of La Tène. They possessed a similar social structure, were able to understand each other, and thanks to this enjoyed an immense wealth in the form of ideas, stories, myths, laws, values, wine, weapons, and trade goods.

By the fourth and third centuries B.C.E., urban centers and social stratification increased. Charismatic men, and sometimes women, gained power through control of trade and resources with the support of a warrior elite. Some of these centers verged on statehood, with cities, "national" boundaries and sanctuaries, nobility and kings, and several classes of subjects. The wise men and women comprised one of these classes: they gathered around the halls of the aristocracy to supply their needs. Their functions included entertainment and genealogy—music, songs, and the telling of stories and poems, especially those that praised the exploits of the ruler and his warriors. We surmise that they served the old shamanic functions such as herbalism, healing, divination, soothsaying, and dream-interpretation, but took these abilities in a new direction to serve the needs of the more complex society. These people were the Druids.

But by the end of the first century B.C.E., Celtic society was crumbling before the power of Rome. Resistance in Gaul was at an end, and Julius Caesar had already launched the first invasion of Britain. With the second, the invasion by the Emperor Claudius, the Druids were singled out and massacred on the beach of Anglesey. The Romans deliberately undermined Druid leadership and power among the conquered Celtic peoples. But in the long occupation of Britain that followed, from 43 to 410 C.E., local Celtic practices merged with Roman to produce a synthesis that helped maintain many ancient customs.

Pressure from the east finally ended both the Roman Empire and Celtic society: nomadic tribes from the Caucasian steppes invaded Europe in the fourth century C.E., and lack of space made the Germanic and Scandinavian peoples move west. The Angles, Jutes, and Saxons defeated the Celts of Britain, newly independent from Roman rule, and drove them into Wales, Brittany, and the never-defeated Celtic fastnesses of Ireland, Scotland, and the Isles. It is unlikely that the Druids ever staged a comeback at this time. The triumphant tales of King Arthur and Merlin represent what might have been if the Celts had been successful in defeating the Northmen. Christianity followed hard upon the heels of the Germanic invaders, and challenged the power of any remaining Druids. These forces irrevocably changed the face of Celtic culture forever.

Who Is a Celt Today?

The question "Who is a Celt?" is extremely important for its implications. Leaving aside that the Irish like to call themselves "Irish," and the Welsh, "Welsh," the question goes straight to the issue of cultural rights: does someone from outside the Celtic culture, or any culture, have the right to adopt its ideas, spirituality, styles, artefacts, and behavior?

There are some who argue that a Celt must belong to one of the few surviving ethnic enclaves in Ireland, Scotland, Wales, the Isle of Man, and Brittany, where people speak a Gaelic language and where Celtic culture persists (Cornwall is a Celtic land, but the last native speakers of Cornish died almost a century ago). Actually, there are far more people who can claim a Celtic heritage living outside of these Celtic countries. Over one-fifth of Americans, or more than 50 million people, can claim some Celtic ancestry. The persecuted people who emigrated from Ireland alone landed by the millions on the shores of Canada, the U.S., Australia, and New Zealand, and have produced large families ever since. All the descendants of these people can call themselves Celts by virtue of their bloodlines.

The original Celtic tribes also shifted and moved across Europe, and even into Asia. The story at the beginning of this chapter gives a version of how the Celts came to Ireland from Spain. The many different tribes made no attempt to unite in national groups or impose their shared customs and beliefs upon others, the way the Roman Empire did. Because Celtic culture was liquid and difficult to define, we will examine the concept of culture to see if this further clarifies what it means to be a Celt today.

Is culture defined by such solid facts as geography, language, and race? It would be easy if this were so, but history shows that cultures move and are capable of absorbing different racial strands. American cultural anthropology defines culture as being composed of many distinct elements: linguistic, racial, ethnographic, religious, and material. This mindset tends to give culture an artificial feeling of solidity. While it is practical to describe the people of an area by a name and to describe their culture after them (for example "Wales" and the "Welsh"), people often originate from elsewhere, borrow from their neighbors, invade, are invaded, and intermarry or migrate. They also adopt ideas, strategies, and technologies from elsewhere and integrate them into their culture—usually making them appear homegrown. As a result, we must turn to something more subtle to define what is meant by culture.

People of many different racial origins all become "American" under the aegis of common cultural convictions such as "liberty," "democracy," the "American Dream," or by living within the geographic borders of the United States. The Jews had no land for a long time, spoke many languages, and came from different races, but they possessed a common set of beliefs. To become a Jew, therefore, one had to adopt their belief system. In Northern Ireland today, the line of division between antagonists is defined precisely by belief. One is either "Protestant" or "Catholic" despite all other cultural elements being the same. As you well know, belief is more than simply an idea or a religious system. It is the thing inside that makes you belong with others of the same worldview, and share with them the same outlook and perceptions. Belief, therefore, is a major defining element of cultural distinction.

Given that culture is not solid, that it has always been traded, imitated, and subjected to geographic movement, we submit that those who choose to define themselves as "Celts" . . . are Celts. Those who adopt a Celtic mindset are Celts. Millions of Americans are of Celtic descent and when they return to their roots, or trace genealogy, groove to Celtic music and art, gather at Celtic fairs, or read the myths, then they are Celts.

Because European immigrants to the U.S. had no blood ties with Native Americans, only their own self-definition could make them "Americans" within the last few centuries. If the immigrants did not immerse themselves in the American worldview, did not seek citizenship and learn the language, then they remained by choice whatever they were before they arrived. There may have been a multitude of reasons for this, but it was essentially self-definition that made the cultural transition. Indeed, it may be argued that multiple self-definitions are of more value in the modern world than a single one. Nicholas is a New Mexican, a Briton, a Scot, a Celt, and a European, without any inherent contradiction. Maya is both American and Irish by citizenship, as well as a citizen of the European Union; by red-headed looks she is unmistakably Irish, and by long residency she is New Mexican.

The authors are glad that Celtic culture is spreading around the world. We like to see the plaid worn, hear the pipes, and recognize components of Celtic tradition in American social practice. We recognize there is a pop Celtic culture: books that teach Celtic lore; art that uses knotwork; music with harps, pipes, and pennywhistles. In the Celtic diaspora there is a blended Celtic culture, while in northwest Europe there exists a core, native Celtic culture tied to the land.

In the same way as ancestry and self-definition remain the major standards of inclusion for Celts, so self-definition also applies to Druids. The Celtic societies in which ancient Druidry existed no longer survive; because of that fact, today's Druids must make their self-definition explicit. We cannot be the Druids of the traditional Celtic people, any more than we can claim to be the Flamens and Augurs of the Roman Republic; but we can say what Druidry is today and how we define ourselves as Druids. The next chapter takes up this topic.

Activities

Sit with a friend. Alternately finish these sentences. Repeat about ten times:

- A Celt is . . .
- A Celt is not . . .

Try to avoid reversing what you said one time when you give an answer for the alternative. Instead, originate something new each time and you will go much deeper into your current understanding. Take your time.

Take a swim in the Celtic Renaissance. Explore maps of Celtic homelands. Listen to Celtic music. Get a how-to book and draw some Celtic patterns. Study a Celtic language with the use of cassettes, since the pronunciation differs wildly from the written form. Attend meetings of a local Celtic society. Study your bloodlines, or talk to elders in your family before it is too late and they pass away. Get into the Celtic mindset, and dream.

Notes

1. From *Leabhar Gabála*, the "Book of Invasions," recension based upon Lady Gregory (1904).

2. Ronald Hutton (*The Pagan Religions of the Ancient British Isles*) provides an excellent view of these periods of European history from a critical academic standpoint.

3. The subject of Indo-European migration is open to debate. It is likely that the Indo-European peoples originated in the area north of the Black and Caspian Seas, and began moving outwards from there in the fourth millennium B.C.E. There is a long period of time between then and the first evidence of "Celtic" culture, but this does help explain why Europe became Indo-European-speaking in the interim.

Chapter 10

WHAT IS A DRUID?

I am Tuan.
I am the stag-horned, eagle-feathered one.
I see all things.
I have been since before the world began.

In the likeness of Queens and Princes,
In the likeness of salmon and boar,
In the likeness of heather and gorse,
Of bold oak and maiden birch, I am.

Before the nine trees of wisdom,
Before the filling of the bag of secrets,
Before the telling and weaving of every craft,
Before Manannán's Feast of Age, I am.

With the Raven I have seen the beechmast on the plains of battle.
With the Hound I have read my fate in tall stones.
With a lament beside deep lochs
I have bled out my heart in the agony of the grave.

In the lofty chambers of the winged ones,
In the passing of geese and swans,
In the triumph of the riddling rhyme of words,
I have filled my heart with every rising of the sun.

I am Tuan, the stag-horned one.
I have been since before the world began.

Before the poets on Cader Idris
My song sang of the earth, the sky and sea,
Of the adder's back, the starry web, the dance with eternity.[1]

This chapter defines what Druids were, and what they are today, as well as what they never were! It gives examples from Celtic mythology of Druids as diviners, healers, mediators, and magicians. The chapter lays the foundation for readers to build their own structure of life as a Druid.

The Original Druids

After about 500 B.C.E., in the northern and western part of the patchwork quilt that was Celtic Europe, wise men and women emerged as the Druids. They arose from the old, indigenous, shamanic worldview. They provide us with the first evidence of an established organization within the Celtic branch of the Native European Tradition. By this term we mean the wisdom tradition that arose among the people of Eurasia from the earliest times. This shares much in common with other traditions of Indo-European origin. The Druids organized knowledge, passed it on through oral tradition, and served the political, social, and spiritual needs of the people.[2]

The primary purpose of this emerging class of scholars and bards was to supply an increasingly sophisticated society with words and images about itself. The Druids remembered stories, songs, and myths; they knew ancestries, prophecies, pledges, treaties, alliances, and legal codes. Increasingly they had to organize, to systematize and then pass on this growing body of knowledge. They became arbitrators, lawyers, and judges. They were advisors to the kings, selecting the time and place of war, negotiating peace, making prophecies, receiving honors. They became teachers, and took into their schools children who showed skill in any of the branches of learning. And as poets and bards, they praised and celebrated the achievements of their nobles, their champions, and their tribe.

We believe, from our research, that the organization the Druids brought to the Native European Tradition had a price (see chapter 9). It meant that they no longer participated in the "grassroots" level of society, where traditional shamanism continued to thrive. At this point, there was a distinction, but not a split, between Druidry and shamanism. At best they complemented and recognized the strengths and weaknesses of each other; at worst, they competed. Another distinction was that the

Druids, serving the elite, became increasingly male-dominated, while women continued to serve the needs of the far-greater body of the common population.

As mentioned in the Introduction, the name "Druid" may have applied to any woman or man wise in the native tradition of their ancestors. The herbalist, the midwife, the seer, and the storyteller may all have been called druids, generically meaning "truthful," "firm" (as a tree is firm), or "wise ones." The training of many Druids began at the most basic social level, and many would have remained there, serving the people. Only a few went on into the service of the king or clan chief, and there they established schools and selected the pupils who would be their successors. By the time the Romans conquered Gaul and Britain, it is our opinion that a distinction had arisen between Druids, who advised the nobility, and local practitioners, mostly women, who birthed babies and cast spells. As providers of cradle-to-grave magical care, these people came to be known as witches and sorcerers. The Romans set about systematically exterminating all organized Druidic practice, while it is likely that the "hedgerow" witches with their ancient shamanistic roots survived.

It is interesting to note that early Irish literature uses "witch" and "Druid" in a similar way: both personages can be either men or women, though men appear more often as Druids in the stories, especially in the royal courts. The stories list shape-changing, illusion-making, and weather-craft as the particular skills of witches. Both witches and Druids were oriented to nature and had reverence for the ancestors. This was all part of the flavor of pagan spirituality at the time. The negative connotation of "witch" derives from later Christian transcribers of the early Irish texts and, subsequently, the Inquisition instigated by the Catholic Church.

Throughout the early history of Europe, we can trace an unbroken line of native lore and tradition, the Native European Tradition. Sometimes this became organized—for example, with the megalithic builders and the Druids—but practice usually remained on the grassroots level. This ancient tradition had its origins in shamanism, a practice which depends on the extrasensory and intuitive skills of the individual, as well as on the deliberate transmission of material in oral form. In later times, shamans and witches received some traditional teaching, but mostly they had to rely on their intuitive skills. Repression of the native tradition by "revealed" religion was particularly severe through the medieval period and down to the last century. By the twentieth century in Europe, only the Romany, better known as Gypsies, and "family tradition witches" retained some native practices. Even those who went to the

American colonies to avoid persecution found no more freedom there, and much ancient practice was marginalized to the level of folk tradition.

Some argue that Wicca stands in this unbroken line, despite the repression, loss of knowledge, and difficulties of transmission. But most modern Wicca draws more upon the nonhistorical work of writers (Sir James Frazer and Margaret Murray), and the ceremonial magic of recent eclectic practitioners (Gerald Gardner), than it does upon traditional native European spirituality. Modern Wicca departs frequently from what we do know about the Celtic tradition as organized and practiced by the ancient Druids. Wiccans tend to worship *the* Goddess and God, while Druidry was pantheistic.[3]

In summary, the Druids codified and developed the knowledge of the Celtic branch of the Native European Tradition. They organized traditional knowledge, taught it in schools, and served the needs of a complex, growing society. Druids were exterminated to such a degree that no one can claim to have received anything in a direct line from Celtic times to the present. Although the context in which Druidry operated is now entirely lost, the early literature of Ireland and Wales records their work. On the other hand, some witches and folk tradition survived. Despite persecution they have handed down some of the ancient ways to the present day. Folk tradition, however, was not organized to the philosophical level of Druidry and came to fulfill a different social need.

Druids in Celtic Mythology

Early sources that record Celtic myths and legends are full of things called Druid spears, Druid cloaks, Druid wands, rods, spells, songs, harps, and other instruments that seem to be in the preserve of almost every character: just about anyone could apply "Druid herbs," and some people who are obviously not Druids have access to "Druid wands." At times the sources use "Druid" as a catchall description for anything mysterious, especially if it comes from the Fairy World. In the *Fate of the Children of Lir*, for example, both Aoife and Bodb Dearg of the *Sídhe* use "Druid rods" to effect transformations. In *Diarmuid and Grania*, Aonghus Óg of the *Sídhe* of Brú na Boinne uses a "Druid cloak" to conceal and help Grania fly away from several entrapments. This frequent use of the word "Druid" to describe a magical object probably entered the texts during the Christian era. Apart from this usage, there is another class of Druid descriptions that refer to specific Druids, often named, who feature in the stories. These descriptions are of special interest as they are likely to have originated in the pre-Christian era.

Druids as Teachers and Diviners

In chapter 19 we will see how the Druid Cathbad of Emain Macha, the royal house of Ulster, uses a divination technique to foretell the fate of Deirdre in her mother's womb. Cathbad also foretells the fate of Cuchulainn and gives him his name. We usually find Cathbad employed in the capacity of a diviner, but in the *Boyhood Deeds of Cuchulainn* we have a brief description of him that combines this role with that of a teacher. It is intriguing to ask whether Cathbad was divining from the stars or from other portents.

> *One day, Cathbad the Druid was in his house . . . teaching Druid lore to many studious men, and a pupil asked him what the day would be lucky for.*
>
> *"The man who takes up arms today or mounts his first chariot today will have his name enduring for ever in Ireland with his mighty deeds," Cathbad said. "But his life will be short."*[4]

The role of diviner was a critical one for Druids in Celtic society. The *Courtship of Etain* describes a method of divination using the Ogham figures that we considered in chapter 4; we will visit these again in chapter 17. One episode in the story known as the *Hidden House of Lugh* is particularly interesting for showing that Druids used astrological divination in their role as advisors to the king.

The *Fate of the Sons of Usnach* makes the role of the Druid as teacher especially clear. The female Druid, Levorcham, is not only an herbalist, astronomer and natural scientist, diviner and dream interpreter, but also a poet.

> *Deirdre was raised in a remote place so that none should see her until she was ready to be the wife of the king of Ulster. Only her foster parents were allowed to be with her, and the old woman Levorcham, a satirist, to whom nothing could be refused. Deirdre grew up straight and clean like the rush on the moor, her movements were like the swan on the wave or the deer on the hill. She was the woman of the greatest beauty and the gentlest and kindest nature in all the provinces of Ireland. Levorcham taught her every skill and knowledge that she had herself. There was not an herb on the ground or a star in the heaven or a bird in the wood that Deirdre did not know the name of, and besides these skills Levorcham taught her the Druid crafts of poetry, dreaming and seeing.*[5]

Druids as Healers

There are many references in the texts that describe Druids as herbalists and healers. The following extract is typical. The great epic known as the *Táin Bó Cuailnge*, "The Cattle Raid of Cooley," has as its centerpiece the combat between Cuchulainn and Ferdiad. After a day of fighting the heroes break off for the night:

> *Cuchulainn and Ferdiad threw their spears into the arms of their charioteers, and came up to each other and put their arms around the other and exchanged three kisses. Their horses passed that night in the same enclosure, and the charioteers shared the same fire and they made up beds of rushes for the wounded men. Druids came and put healing herbs in Cuchulainn's wounds, but they could do little but chant spells and lay magic amulets on them to staunch the spurts of blood for the deepness of the wounds.*[6]

The ancient goddess Brigit was so revered in all Celtic regions across Europe that the people in Ireland transformed her into the greatest female Christian holy person, St. Brigit. The historical Brigit, of the fifth century C.E., was born of a Druid father. In both her pagan and Christian forms she was patron of healers and midwives. To this day, women pray for health by bathing in the sacred waters of "Brigit wells" in Scotland and Ireland.[7]

Druids as Counselors

The Druids had immense authority in the great houses, and their word was law. Sencha the Great could "pacify the men of the world with his three fair words." This account of Sencha at work is from *Bricriu's Feast*.

> *Then chairs flew and tables overturned. One side of the hall filled with the fire of clashing swords, while the other side was like a flock of white birds from the glaze flying from the surface of the shields. There was a great alarm and fear for their lives on the people of the gathering. King Conchobor and Fergus were angry to see two men fight together against Cuchulainn. But no one moved or dared to part them, until the Druid Sencha rose.*
>
> *"Part these men," said Sencha.*
>
> *Conchobor and Fergus stepped between the fighting men and made them drop their hands to their sides.*

"Will you do as I advise?" said Sencha.

"We will," said the three men.

"Then divide the Champion's Portion between the whole of the gathering tonight," said Sencha.[8]

Druids also acted on matters less than affairs of state, and advised individuals. In the story of *Diarmuid and Grania*, Princess Grania wishes to know about the handsome men around her father's table, and so she asks a Druid.

"Tell me now," said Grania lightly, "who is that man on the right of Oisin?"

"That is Goll mac Morna, the terrible in battle," said the Druid.

"And who is that on the right of Goll?"

"That is the youthful champion Oscar, son of Oisin."

"And who is that graceful-legged thin man beside Oscar?"

"That is Caoilte mac Ronan, the swiftest man in the world."

"And who is that proud warrior beside Caoilte?"

"That is Lugaid of the Strong Hand, nephew of Fionn mac Cumhail."

"And who is that freckled soft-voiced man," said Grania, "with the raven-black curls and the gentle countenance who sits to the left of Oisin?"

"That is Diarmuid of the lovely face, grandson of Duibhne, the best lover of women in the whole world."[9]

Druids as Power-Brokers

There are several episodes where Druids mediate between opposing forces. Although the Druid fails in this extract from the *Death of Cuchulainn*, it is nonetheless informative for his method.

"Cuchulainn is upon us," said Erc. "Let us form a fence of our shields, and let three pairs of men appear to struggle here and there among us. They must call on Cuchulainn to help them resolve their dispute, and have a Druid beside them to ask him for his spears. We must get his spears, for it is in the prophecy of the daughters of Catalin that a king will be killed by those spears in this battle, and it will be hard for him to refuse the request of a Druid."

. . . Cuchulainn came to one of the pairs of men that were put to quarrel with each other, with a Druid beside them.

"Help us put an end to this quarrel," cried the Druid. "Give me your spear."

"You are not so much in need of it now as I am," said Cuchulainn.

"A bad name upon you if you refuse me," said the Druid.

"I have never had a bad name put on me yet on account of a refusal," said Cuchulainn. He threw the spear, handle foremost, at the Druid and killed him.[10]

Druids as Magicians

In the seventh-century Irish text known by scholars as the *Cauldron of Poesy*, the cauldron stands for oneself, the fire of one's whole being. In her commentary on the text, Erynn Rowan Laurie says:

Traditional Irish poetry is a mix of grammatical rules, metre, voice, and silence, and a certain balance is necessary for the entire composition to hold together in a powerful and pleasing manner. Irish magic was largely a matter of poetry, composed and chanted for particular purposes. The rules of grammar, therefore, might be thought of as the building blocks of magic. The proper creation of poetry, and of magic, is [according to the text] *"the path and function of my cauldron."*[11]

Magic is a common task of the Druids in the myths. It often involved shapeshifting or the creating of illusions. When Cuchulainn becomes distraught on learning that he has killed his son, the Druid Cathbad casts a spell of glamoury upon him that makes it seem an army is coming against him from the waves. Cuchulainn fights against the waves until his fury and hurt are spent. On another occasion the *Táin Bó Cuailnge* describes Cuchulainn as follows:

Then the hero Cuchulainn took his battle-array of contest and strife. On his head he put his crested battle-helmet, from whose recesses his scream echoed so that his enemies thought the fiends of the air called out from it. And about him he cast the cloak of concealment, made of cloth from Tir Tairngire, *the Land of Promise, that was given to him by his foster father, an expert in the magic of Druidry.*[12]

Finally, in the mythic narratives of the *Book of Invasions*, it falls to the magical abilities of Birog of the Mountain to bring Cian to Eithlinn. The result of their union is the pan-Celtic deity, Lugh. Here Birog effects a gender disguise, travels on the wind, and easily puts people to sleep.

Cian went to the woman Druid, Birog of the Mountain for help. Birog gave Cian the appearance of a queen of the Tuatha Dé Danann, dressed him in woman's clothes and took him on the winds to the tower where Eithlinn lived. She called out to the women in the tower and asked them to shelter a high queen from some hardship. Because the women did not like to refuse a woman of the Tuatha Dé Danann they let them in. When they were inside the tower Birog cast a spell on the women to send them to sleep. Cian went to Eithlinn, and the moment she saw him she recognized his face from her dreams and gave him her love.[13]

Druids Today

If you have taken in the history lessons so far, you may be wondering what a Druid is and how on earth anyone can be one today! Let us reiterate that the title refers both to women and to men. Although being a Druid originally meant being of the magical order of the Celts, today it is essentially a matter of self-definition. It may sound like a circuitous definition, but being a Druid means identifying oneself as a Druid (as shown in chapter 9), and choosing to follow the tradition of the Druid path.

You may be thinking, however, that simply declaring oneself a Druid does not a Druid make. There must be something—a belief or training perhaps—that graduates and qualifies the aspirant into the title of Druid. At present, this is difficult to answer, and until an answer appears you can do what we and many of our friends do: consider yourself a "Druid in training."

One of the central meanings of the word Druid throughout this book is "tree wise." What it means to be "tree wise" will become clear as we consider the depth of direct experience in nature that the Druids set for themselves. A friend of ours captured this intensity in the line: "When your forests were cut and burned it was my hurt, burning on my skin."[14] The face of the Green Man with vegetation disgorging through his open mouth is an image from the surviving European folk tradition of Druids uttering "tree wisdom." Incidentally, we do not believe that Druids are limited to knowledge of trees specifically mentioned in the Celtic tradition. The Druids adapted wherever they went, and if they had gone to America or Australia they would have worked with the trees they found there.

To give an idea of what a Druid is today, we suggest you look deeply into what the word means to you. Druids are appearing now in greater numbers than ever and they come in all shapes and sizes, occupations and locations. It is possible to find a huge variety of people from all walks of life who practice Druidry. Indeed there are many differences among those who call themselves Druids as to what they are. Most agree that a Druid is a man or a woman who walks a spiritual path founded upon the Celtic branch of the indigenous European Tradition, but there appear many divergent views of exactly what is "Celtic," "spiritual," "indigenous," or "traditional." This surely, is a healthy situation.

If there is one thing Druids may have in common it is a reverence for life: for nature and the Earth. The degree to which they carry this into their public lives is entirely a matter of choice. So is the manner in which they practice. Some Druids may look more like solitary botanists, while others participate in full regalia celebration of solar festivals at public monuments like Stonehenge.

To help explain these differences it is useful to keep in mind the view taken in this book: Druidry is not a religion, a faith or a belief. Celtic mythology presents no creator, no force outside of the universe that is responsible for it. There is only our experience of the impermanent, ever-changing nature of life. The Druid Tradition helps to locate us in life, in all that we are, surrounded by all that is. It points us to the wholeness—the emptiness and fullness, light and shadow—of our soul and its eternal nature in an infinite universe. Whether this view defines a Druid is impossible to say. There are still many Druids who carry on the patriarchal traditions established by the revivalists of the last few centuries, and, to them, an off-world creator god is very significant. One unifying factor among all contemporary Druids of whatever order or inclination is very likely the wish to give something back to the earth. This is indubitably something the Druids of old did, so here indeed is a common tradition. In the same way as the ancient Druids presided at rituals where offerings were made to the earth—massive deposits of valuable objects in lakes and rivers providing the best examples in Britain and Ireland—so Druids today are rediscovering the results of gifting. Offering things of value to the earth, to the waters or to fire however can easily be misunderstood. The word "sacrifice" for example, evokes unpleasant images in the popular imagination, and it will take time for Druids (or paganism in general) to restore a true understanding of this act.

Let it be said here that offering gifts to the earth does not involve the taking of life for modern Druids. Indeed, the exact opposite! The Druidic practices of generosity, hospitality and beneficence are ultimately acts of great compassion. It is through gifting that service to life begins. It is through gifting that it becomes possible to arrive at a true understanding of our place in all things. We are indebted to life. We are sustained in every moment by water, earth, fire and air. Coming into an understanding of how we can give back to these things allows the possibility of consciously re-entering the sacred web of reciprocal relationships that make up all life.

Druids today comprise a kind of special web around the world, unaligned yet holding to certain values and working towards certain goals. The challenge facing Druids today is to emulate the *Aes Dana*, the Gifted People. At the time of the Celts, the *Aes Dana* were a learned class that included Druids—poets, healers, judges and law keepers—as well as blacksmiths, and other craft-workers. Their gifts and unusual skills were given in the service of Celtic society. Druids who associate themselves with the *Aes Dana* are blessed by Danu, the most ancient Celtic goddess from whom the magical Tuatha Dé Danann descended.[15]

To pursue this connection further, the Gaelic word *dan* means gift, craft, calling, or destiny (recall that *dur* means "to give" in Spanish, as does *donner* in French). Your *dan* might consist of abilities in poetry or music, the arts or sciences, organization, or weaving people together. Druids today, therefore, are charged with examining their calling and gifts, and bringing those forth as part of a long and magical ancestry. It is important to call on your ancestors. Their magic is within you! Where else would it have gone? If you honor your ancestors, their gifts and wisdom will flow through you and the traditions will never die.

Dana also means bold, daring, and confident. If you "follow your bliss" and share with the world your gifts and talents, you will likely be bold and confident in the work you do. The term *Aes Dana* for today's Druids, then, means all of us at our best, producing wondrous things from our talents, and sharing them.

The Gifted People of the Celts could walk between the worlds, help people through conflict, sickness, and death, and communicate lofty or earthy impressions through music and poetry. You, too, can do this, with training. Recall that poets in Celtic society held a revered position and worked closely with the leaders. Today they would be historians, genealogists, writers, teachers, publicists, and high-class performers. The Celtic musicians were charged with regulating society by means of their music. They were highly trained and could make people become joyful and lively, sad and tearful, or relaxed and sleepy. Society was kept in harmony by bards instead of by police. It is gifts such as these that today's Druids can offer in their communities.

What do you have to give to the world? What do you do with your gifts? What wisecrafts do you know? You have this promise from the Tuatha Dé Danann: the source of inspiration is within you. The magic is within you. The gifts are within you. You become one of the Gifted People by using your gifts, talents, crafts, and abilities. You do it by learning more, by training, asking relatives and experts. And significantly, you do it by using Celtic sources of inspiration such as the well and cauldron.

The sacred waters of inspiration are guarded and are only dispensed to the true of heart. When you are true to yourself, the waters of inspiration will always open to you. You have to draw on your True Self, and then put your talents to work in the best fit you can find between your gifts and ways to earn a living. As a Druid today you are challenged to pass on your gifts—not just through your children—but to all who have ears to hear and eyes to see. Your ancestors are waiting!

Activities

Druid Training. Cormac mac Airt was a wise king of the Irish. If he actually lived, it was in the third century C.E., when Celtic kings were required to receive Druidic training. Practice some of what he said he learned as a youth:

- I was a listener in the woods.
- I was a gazer at the stars.
- I was strong towards the powerful.
- I was not arrogant though I was wise.

What Makes You a Druid? Sit with a friend or with a notebook and state all the aspects that make you a Druid. What ceremonies do you carry out? What Druidic knowledge are you pursuing, such as tree wisdom, poetry, or talismans? How do you act from your Druid Self at work?

Giving and Receiving. Find a local sacred space. It may be a tree, grotto, spring, somewhere in your garden or close by. Enter into a relationship with it by leaving a gift on a regular basis. You will have to think carefully about what is appropriate. As time goes by, notice the bonds developing between you and that place. Allow yourself to receive from the place when the time is right.

Ancestral Circle. Lie down and have your ancestors lie in an imaginary circle all around you. From their heads and hearts, allow them to flow into you their wisdom and knowing, their skills and gifts. Receive all this. Sit up and record what came to you.

Personal Myth. Joseph Campbell suggests that we each find the song of life, which tells us how to find our own way. Nobody can give you this personal mythology, but in it, you'll find the key to putting your talents into the world. You'll find guidelines for living the best way you can. You'll find your code of ethics, which all Druids live by. Meditate for a while and then complete these mythic lines:

- I come from a people who …
- My gifts are… and I pass them on by …
- I carry the bloodlines of the *Aes Dana* because …

Notes

1. "Tuan," a poem by Nicholas R. Mann.

2. The Native European Tradition can be divided into many branches: Celtic, Germanic, Norse, Slavic, Finno-Ugric, Greek, Latin, etc.

3. The Wiccan Rede, "Do what thou wilt an it harm none," is oriented to the individual for its ethics. Wicca relates the elements of earth, air, fire, and water to the four directions and describes the Earth and Moon as feminine and the Sun as masculine. Druidry emphasizes community responsibility, civic duty, and restorative justice. Druidry has the Sky, ruled by the Sun (fire); the Sea, ruled by the Moon (water); and the Land, ruled by the Earth. These change gender according to attributes, and the elements are not equivalent to the directions. Wicca is eclectic, while Druidry roots itself in Celtic mythology for its spirituality, magical practice, and teaching.

4. *Boyhood Deeds of Cuchulainn*, recension based on Lady Gregory (1902), Thomas Kinsella (1969), and Cross and Slover (1936).

5. *Longes mac n-Uislenn*, recension based on Thomas Kinsella (1969), Lady Gregory (1904), and A. H. Leahy (1905).

6. *Táin Bó Cuailnge*, recension based on Thomas Kinsella (1969), Lucy Faraday (1904), and Lady Gregory (1902).

7. Miranda Green, *Celtic Goddesses.*

8. *Fledh Bricrenn*, recension of Lady Gregory (1903), and Jeffrey Gantz (1981).

9. *Diarmuid and Grania*, recension of Cross and Slover (1936), P.W. Joyce (1879), and Lady Gregory (1904).

10. See note 7.

11. Erynn Rowan Laurie, *The Cauldron of Poesy.*

12. See note 7.

13. *Leabhar Gabála,* translation from Cross and Slover (1936), R.A. MacAlister (1956), and Lady Gregory (1904).

14. Cam Smith, *Notes from the Mountain.*

15. Peter Berresford Ellis, *Dictionary of Celtic Mythology*, p. 19; Ward Rutherford, *Celtic Mythology*, p. 26.

Chapter 11

WHAT IS DRUIDRY?

I am the wind upon the sea
I am the wave upon the ocean
I am the murmur of the strand
I am a stag of seven points
I am a bull of seven battles
I am a hawk upon the cliff
I am a ray from the sun
I am the fairest of flowers
I am a valiant wild boar
I am a salmon in the pool
I am a lake on the plain
I am the skill of the craftsman
I am the word of knowledge
I am the spoil-seeking spear of battle
I am the god that fashions fire in the head
Who but I spreads light in the assembly upon the mountains?
Who but I can tell the ages of the moon?
Who but I knows where the sun rests?
On whom do the cattle of Tethra smile?
Who but I knows the resolution of battle, the wind upon the sea
And the secrets of the unhewn dolmen arch?[1]

This chapter explores the nature of the existences in which Druids live, move, and practice their arts. It defines the Self and its immortality, the land of paradise, the Fairy World, ancestors, deities, and the living Earth. It gives teachings from the myths to understand the emphasis Druids give to trees and to the World Tree in particular.

Since Druid means "true," "wise," or "firm" in the knowledge of trees, then Druidry is the practice of the wisdom derived from the trees. A Druid aphorism coined by a member of our Grove states: "Knowledge of the trees is knowledge of the Self." To understand Druidry you must understand what Druids mean by the Self, by the trees, and by all the realms of the Celtic worldview. That is the goal of this chapter.

Before we start, let us mention that Druidry is not a neat package. It does not exist as a body of knowledge, as an organization, or as a single entity made up of members today, as does Vedanta or Lions International. Instead each one of us comes to understand Druidry only by making the effort of getting inside the many layers of Celtic cosmology from the past, and by practicing Druidic principles in the present. Because so much of ancient Druidry is unknown, the core of the tradition is like an iceberg where we can only see the tip. We, the authors, are mapping out the whole of the iceberg of Druidry by studying and living on the visible "tip." Much of what we say in this book, therefore, is and can only be our interpretation, but our work is as thorough and well grounded as our study and experiences can make it. We invite you to take the same kind of adventurous journey as ourselves in discovering the new territories of Druidry.

The Eternal Self

The Self is an eternally existent entity that we often call the soul. The early Irish and Welsh sources clearly say that the soul never dies. To be a Druid is to live from this basis. The Otherworlds of Celtic mythology would make no sense unless something continued after physical death. The myths speak of slain warriors dipped in a cauldron of regeneration and restored to physical form. A plate on the exquisite Gundestrup Cauldron depicts this act, which happens not only at bodily death but also when the spirit is reborn though rites of initiation. The poem that opens this chapter tells of many lifetimes in animal forms, and of existence as sheer energy forms: wind, wave, and sunlight.

In this book, Nicholas prefers to call the immortal entity the eternal Self, and Maya prefers the divine or True Self. You may prefer another term such as soul (*anam* in Irish), spirit, or an entirely different word.

Druidic teachings say that the Self is immortal and dwells in a *tuirgin*, or a "circuit of births" or "existences." *Cormac's Glossary*, in a mixture of Celtic and Christian language, describes a *tuirgin* as:

> *. . . the birth that passes from every nature into another . . . a transitory birth which has traversed all nature from Adam and goes through every wonderful time down to the world's doom.*[2]

If we leave out the Christian content, such early sources show that the Celts thought of their lives as the passing of the Self from one existence to another. The Greeks knew this continuous process of rebirth as "metempsychosis"—the transfer of the soul to living form. Christians added the part about creation through an "Adam," and an end in doom. The Self comes into this world through assuming a body, usually human, but it might also be any animate or inanimate form. It may be something that seems fleeting, such as a shout, a wave, or a fleck of light. We now know from quantum physics that these things do make a lasting impression upon the cosmos.

The Celtic bards Tuan, Taliesin, and Amergin go to great lengths to describe the manifestations of their immortal souls in every form of existence. In the *Hostile Confederacy*, Taliesin repeats a common theme:

> *I have been a blue salmon,*
> *I have been a dog, I have been a deer,*
> *I have been a goat on the mountain,*
> *I have been a trunk, I have been a beech,*
> *I have been an axe in the hand.*[3]

Some scholars question the authenticity and age of the work of these poets. Taliesin is thought to have lived in the late sixth century C.E., but many of the poems ascribed to him cannot definitely be linked to his hand. Some scholars doubt whether the reincarnation of the Self expressed in the "I am . . ." or "I have been . . ." form of verse really derives from the age of the Druids; they argue that the idea of the soul dwelling in nonhuman forms was introduced later and is actually Pythagorean in origin. Further, they point out that Graeco-Roman sources describing Druid beliefs mention only transmigration, that is, the passing of the immortal soul into physical, human form.

Early Celtic sources describe reincarnation in every physical form, especially in the realm of animals. These references are too numerous and too consistent to dismiss so easily. If it was not part of Druid lore at the time of the Classical Greek and Roman writers, it was certainly fundamental to the Celtic tradition by the time scribes began recording Irish and Welsh myth and poetry, sometime in the seventh century C.E. Other writers, such as John Matthews, argue that many of the poems ascribed to Taliesin are far older than the sixth century, and therefore provide us with an excellent window into the Celtic worldview. As this book proceeds, we will describe many examples of existence in forms other than human. Please make up your own mind on the issue!

The Land of the Living

When the body dies, the Self returns to a paradise realm that has many names. *Tír na n'Óg*—the Land of Youth, is the name often found in the myths. It is also called *Tír na mBan*—the Land of Women, *Tír Tairngire*—the Land of Promise, *Emhain*—the Isle of Avalon, *Tír na mBeo*—the Land of the Living, and the Blessed Land. For convenience, in this book we shall call the paradise realm the Land of the Living or occasionally *Tír na n'Óg*.

The Land of the Living lies upon a mythic island in the western sea. It is reached by crossing the ocean—*Magh Rein*, the Plain of the Sea, or by crossing a plain—*Magh Mell*, the Plain of Honey, or *Magh Mhór*, the Great Plain. Up to recent times in Ireland, departing souls were often equipped with a stout pair of boots to last them on their walk across *Magh Mhór*, while in earlier instances the shoes were symbolic, perhaps made of one piece of metal. It was the custom of pre-Christian Celts to provide souls with food and drink for their journey, and nobles were often buried with a chariot and horses to take them on their way across the worlds.

Can you picture the Land of the Living? Visualize having none of the limitations of the body. Imagine a place where there is no sickness, no suffering, and no death. There are only delights, sports, feasting, music, and every kind of wonderful and beautiful experience. Here, the Self is fully aware of its eternal and majestic being.

A woman bearing a silver branch appears to a mythic chieftain called Bran, and tells him of "the fairest land in all the worlds."

> *There is no use for keening;*
> *There is nothing harsh or rough;*
> *Only sweet music on the ear,*
> *In this familiar well-tilled land.*

Without grief, without sorrow,
Without death, without sickness,
These are the signs of Emhain.
Behold! It is no common wonder.[4]

The Celts sometimes greeted a birth with mourning, because it meant an end to existence in that beautiful realm, and they saw death as an occasion for joy, because it meant a return to *Tír na n'Óg*. When the Self wishes to leave *Tír na n'Óg*, it is reborn into this world, usually with complete forgetfulness, although it is possible to remember something of one's previous state. Bran is an unusual example because he is able to return to our world and tell the experience of his voyage to the Land of Women. When he returns to Ireland after about a year, Bran tells people his name and they respond: "We know of no such man; but the *Voyage of Bran* is in our ancient stories." Thus, time is counted very differently in the Land of the Living than in this world.

Have you thought that reincarnation might occur out of sequence with the linear time of this world? There is nothing in Celtic cosmology that would prevent the Self from returning to a body prior in time to its previous incarnation. There is no Celtic law of karma determining what the form of incarnation will be. Neither good nor bad deeds determine the status of life in a body: the purpose of incarnation is rather to extend the Self's experience of being into all the many different forms of existence. These existences are not constructed in a hierarchy, nor is it better or worse to incarnate in forms other than human. When the Self knows what it is like to be an animal, a tree, an elemental form, then it becomes wise in the craft of Druidry.

The myths indicate that the Law of Returns operates in every realm: what you give out will ultimately come back to you. In the *Fate of the Children of Lir*, the stepmother Aoife is ordered to dwell in the wind until "the end of life and time" for changing her sister's children into swans. The application of the Law of Returns here appears to suggest a hierarchy of being, but it is not that. The children are not swans for anything they have done, nor, as swans, is there any loss of sentience. Being a spirit of the wind is not punishment for Aoife: the punishment is that she can never change into another form again.

The Land of the *Sidhe*

There is a realm that stands apart from the Land of the Living, called the Fairy Realm or, sometimes, the Otherworld. It lies closer to this world than the Land of the Living. It is just beyond the apparent surface of this world, and is inhabited by the fairy folk. It is the Land of the *Sidhe*, the Ever-Living Ones. We will introduce this topic now, and will return to it throughout the book; you will find its full flowering in chapter 20.

The fairy folk were once the *Tuatha Dé Danann*, the "tribe of the goddess Danu," who were among the original inhabitants of Ireland. Their name *Aes Dana*, "people of skill," or *Aes Sidhe*, "people of peace," is sometimes also given to the Druids. When the Celtic Gaels came to Ireland, the *Sidhe* went to live in the earth itself, and gave their names to many of the hills and mounds. The *Sidhe* are the source of much that is beautiful, especially in art and music; but the beauty of the Fairy Realm can be dangerously seductive. The Realm of the *Sidhe* is the view of the eternal realm that is available through the physical senses. It is not the Land of the Living, nor is it this world: it is a never-never realm somewhere in the middle. The Fairy Realm is also the realm of the ancestral spirits, the animal powers, spirits of place, and the gods and goddesses.

The world of the *Sidhe* is essentially a timeless realm. A visitor can return immediately from there but feel as if it was a visit of many years; or, after what seems like a brief visit, return to find that many years have passed in this world. In the *Adventures of Nera* for example, Nera enters the Fairy Realm through the Cave of the Cats near Cruachan, settles down, marries a fairy woman, conceives a child, and returns to Cruachan at the moment he departed. This may seem an advantage, but one of the perils of the Fairy Realm for humans is precisely that nothing ever changes.

Ancestral Spirits and Deities

The relationship of the Self to the spirits of the ancestors and to gods and goddesses is subtle. The deities possess autonomous existence in the Fairy Realm but depend upon human consciousness to engage with them and bring them into manifestation in this world. Deities become greater the more people think of them or otherwise engage with them over time. This is especially true of the ancestral or tribal deities. In Gaul, the main deity of the tribe was known as Teutates, which derives directly from Celtic words for "tribe," *touta* and *tuath*. Thus, when a Celt swears or makes an oath, what translators usually render as "by the gods," is better translated as "by the spirit of my tribe." This is often given in a compromise form: "I swear by the gods my people swear by." But in most cases the original text makes no direct reference to deity at all.

When we remain close to the Celtic sources, we find that our notion of gods and goddesses barely exists in the ancient traditions. They are not powers greater than, separate from, or outside of the world, as we often conceive them. Celts loved ambiguity, the shading between dimensions, the possibility of the infinite in anything. About all we can say is this: Celts were normal, adventurous humans who loved their heroes and heroines. They mythologized and elevated heroic characters and ancestors to superhuman status with magical abilities and incredible strengths. After a long passage of time, these might become what we call deities, but the Celts rarely used this conception. Only the outside observers of the Celtic world, the Romans and the Greeks, identified the divine figures of the Celts with their own ideas of gods and goddesses.

There is no Celtic creation myth, nor is there a creator god. There is no mediating divine savior. The word for god, *dé* in Irish, is added almost as an afterthought to mythical beings, if used at all. *Dé* also means "breath," just as *spiritus* means "breath of a god" in Latin. *Dé* distinguished sky beings from earth and sea beings, the *andée*. Apart from supernatural forces such as Danu, described as the "Mother of the Gods" and never heard of again, the "gods" are ancestral deities or spirits inhabiting a specific place. Of the 400 or so Celtic deities mentioned by classical writers or named on inscriptions, well over 300 are mentioned only once; the remainder just four or five times. They were specific to a place, such as a spring, a pool, or a river, and it is in such locales that people honored them with votive offerings and rituals.

If you were a Celt, you would pray to your mythic ancestors whose spirits dwell within the universe. You would know they live in the earth, the waters, and the sky, where their presence makes those places sacred. They are intensely powerful in certain places, in groves and especially in the hills of the *Sídhe*. These include the megalithic mounds dotting the European landscape, places that were already ancient at the time of the Celts.

When we visited Scotland in search of the ancient homelands of our clans, we were puzzled by the number of clan places, battle cries, and mottoes that translated simply as the name of a particular hill. On the Isle of Skye we sought the ancestral home of Clan Nicholson—the name of one of Maya's great-grandmothers. The clan motto is *Scorr a Bhreac*, which we translated as "the grey, speckled, or variegated ridge." We had no idea what this meant, and it seemed rather dull for a battle cry. Then we arrived at the ruins of the ancestral crofts; above our heads stood a beautiful, long, grey ridge. This feature provided the motto and war cry of Clan Nicholson because it represented the dwelling place of the clan spirits and ancestors.

If you are familiar with Jungian thinking, the concept of archetypes provides another way of understanding the Celtic notion of the deities. They constellate aspects of human experience and consciousness. The Dagda is the good father, Danu the good mother, The Morrígan is the crone and battle goddess, Math the god of wisdom, Arianrhod the virgin queen, Lugh and Grania are male and female manifestations of the youthful solar spirit, Mabon is the divine child, and so on. Each deity assumes attributes that enable members of successive generations to recognize a similar form, although these archetypal qualities may manifest differently for each individual.

The Living Earth

In the Druids' cosmos, everything is alive. The ancient Celts knew that trees, rocks, and springs possessed an inner presence. Every place had its story to explain how it got its name, how it was formed, and what dwelt there. Modern folk tradition often remembers this special quality of place as a kind of fairy or supernatural being, as an auspicious or inauspicious power, or as buried treasure. In this way of thinking, the numinous is accessible, and can be called on at any time for inspiration and energy. As a Druid, imagine yourself as a moonrise, "white softness growing tall from the juice of the earth."[5]

If we take the teaching of reincarnating into every form of existence to its logical conclusion, the whole world brims with the passage of incarnating souls or aspects of the Self. The *Sídhe* or Fairy Folk, the ancestors, the tribe, the animal powers, the spirits of place, and the Goddesses of the Land also infuse the living earth. These spirits inhabit specific places such as hills, springs, and sacred groves, and awareness of their immanent or indwelling presence is easiest in those locations: this is pantheism.

The following extract from the *Fate of the Children of Lir*, adapted rather than translated from the Irish by Ella Young, beautifully illustrates these themes. The Children of Lir, in the form of swans, have returned home to find everyone they knew gone, and their father's house in ruins.

> "*The mountains are dead,*" said Conn, son of Lir.
> "*The mountains are not dead,*" said Aibric. "*They are dark and silent, but*

they are not dead. I know. I have cried to them in the night and laid my forehead against theirs and felt the beating of their mighty hearts. They are wiser than the wisest druid, more tender than the tenderest mother. It is they who keep the world alive."

(The Children of Lir then tell their tale to Nephin, a mountain in the West of Ireland.)

It looked dark and sombre against the fading sky, and the sight of it, discrowned and silent, struck chill to the hearts of the wild swans: They turned away their heads to hide the tears in their eyes.

But Aibric stretched out his hands to the mountain and cried out: "O beautiful glorious Comrade, pity us! [Tír na n'Óg] is no more, and Moy-Mell is lost forever! Welcome the Children of Lir, for they have nothing left but you and the earth of Ireland!"

Then a wonder happened.

The star-heart of Nephin shone out - magnificent - tremulous - coloured like a pale amethyst. The swans cried out to each other: "The mountain is alive! Beauty has come again to the earth! Aibric, you have given us back the Land of Youth!"

A delicate faery music trembled and died away and was born again in the still evening air, and more and more the radiance deepened in the heart of Nephin. The swans began to sing most sweetly and joyously, and at the sound of that singing the star-heart showed in mountain after mountain till every mountain in Ireland pulsed and shone.

"Crown yourselves, mountains!" said Aodh, "that we may know the Sídhe are still alive and Lir's house is built now where old age cannot wither it!"[6]

The World Tree

Trees played an important role in this divine and magical world of the Celts. In the Irish story the *Sickness of Cuchulainn or The Only Jealousy of Emer*, Cuchulainn's charioteer Laeg visits the land of the *Sídhe*. This is one of the best descriptions we have of the Fairy Realm, and it is noteworthy for the prominent place given to trees, especially the singing silver tree.

They passed over the Plain of Speech and by the Tree of Victory. They crossed the Racing Plain and came to the Gathering-Place of the Woods. They went to the Isle of Labra and passed over the lake before it in a little ship of bronze. On the island they came to a mound and upon it a great house. Laeg thought he had seen it before, but it was all strange and wonderful to him. By the western gate were two herds of horses, one grey, the other chestnut. The trees by the eastern gate were purple and crimson with flowers that lasted all the year round, and in them birds sang sweetly and long.

The tree in the forecourt was of silver, and when the sun shone it glittered and was as brilliant as gold. From its leaves came the constant sound of sweet, soft, and low harmonies. There were three times twenty trees there whose tops touched and then did not touch. Three hundred people could be fed from the fruit of the trees, and the fruits were all different and always ripe. There was a vat of mead in the court, and although the custom was to continuously distribute it the household, it was always full.[7]

The trees in Druidic consciousness are symbols of multiple aspects of creation. Think of the correspondence like this: to chemists, the Periodic Table of the Elements represents all the solid, liquid, and gaseous forms of existence; to astrologers, the sun, moon, planets, and their movements through the zodiac represent layers upon layers of meaning and explanations of existence; to philosophers, matter, being, and essence are the stuff of existence. To Druids, then, the many trees represent everything in existence: each tree has attributes that correspond to related human, nature-based, and spirit essences. The symbology provided by the entire assembly of the trees puts order into all the realms in the universe.

It seems right that the Druids represented and ordered existence by means of the trees that so dominated the European continent following the last Ice Age. The oak tree, for example, represents a climax in ecological succession: it hosted and helped hundreds of dependent plants, insects, and animals to evolve, while also providing nourishment, fuel, and enduring shelter for humans. So it is appropriate that the oak tree was the essential emblem of the Druids.

Each tree has qualities that associate it with other things: minerals, plants, herbs, animals, birds, ancestors, spirits, seasons, and every other category you can think of. For example, the ash is associated with air, the south, noon, midsummer, quartz crystal, the eagle, the feathered serpent, the burning spear, and the god Lugh. It derives these associations mostly from the quality and uses of its wood. The ash provides long, flexible, and strong shafts of wood ideal for handles of tools and weapons. As the haft of a spear, the ash represents the zenith of masculine power, identifying it with the sun at noon and midsummer. Another tree, the elder, is associated with earth, the moonstone, magic, the raven, the Fairy Folk, and their world; the Celts prohibited the cutting or destruction of the tree. Such associations may arise from the ability of elders to grow miraculously from cuttings thrust into the earth, the uselessness of its wood for any practical purpose, and its abundant flowers and berries.

Trees provide the symbols with which to order the world, and because the spoken word creates order through naming and stories, each tree is a phoneme in the composition of speech, and a letter in the alphabet of language. We shall examine these points in finer detail in future chapters.

Collectively in the Celtic tradition, the trees form the World Tree. If we imagine all the species of trees and the aspects of existence they represent arranged in a circle, then at the center where all their qualities converge is the World Tree. This is the *axis mundi*, the axis that runs through the center of the Upper, Middle, and Lower Worlds, or, in the Celtic cosmology, sky, earth, and sea. As the World Tree is composed of all the trees in existence, it is therefore the source of all knowledge, harmonizing and braiding together the many letters of the individual trees. Access to the realms of Otherworlds is through the roots and branches of the World Tree.

An unverified Druid tradition is that whoever wishes to learn "tree wisdom" must remain upon a tree representing the World Tree for three days and nights. This corresponds to a Norse tradition where Odin hung upon the World Tree, *Yggdrasil*, to gain the runes—the letters of wisdom—equivalent to the Celtic Ogham. These stories are shining signals from our past, depicting Nature as the source of wisdom and trees as central to Nature. The stories are symbolic ways of saying that knowledge is gained not from *studying* trees as scientists do, but by dancing with and *being* like trees—staying still, waiting, listening, changing, living in harmony with the greater cycles of life.

Celtic mythology is rich with magical trees that broaden our understanding of the World Tree within the Druid mindset. In the story quoted above, the singing silver tree is in the Fairy Realm. Fand appears as a Fairy Queen who tests men and initiates them into their power. It is noteworthy that there is a continuously full "vat of mead" in her house. This can be none other than the Celtic Cauldron of Plenty, the equivalent of the Well of Knowledge and Inspiration that appears at the foot of the World Tree in other European mythologies.

In the *Voyage of Bran*, the woman bearing the silver branch from the "apple tree of Emhain" describes a marvelous tree:

There is an ancient tree in bloom
Full of birds calling in song,
Every hour they call in harmony,
On the broad silver plain to the south.

This suggests that the apple tree of Emhain (i.e., Avalon) not only nourishes the otherworldy inhabitants, but that time itself is ordered around it. The Irish story of Diarmuid and Grania provides a pivotal scene where they slay a giant and take refuge in a magical quicken or rowan tree. Their pursuer, Fionn mac Cumhail, finally catches up with them there. He remains on the ground while Diarmuid and Grania make their escape by flying through the air into the tree branches. It is likely that Diarmuid and Fionn are Lords of Summer and Winter, respectively, both competing for the hand of Grania, the Solar Goddess, around the cycle of the year. Their confrontation is therefore appropriately played out on the axis of the World Tree.

All these Celtic stories of trees lead directly to the concept of a World Tree, the *crann beatha* in Irish, also known as the Tree of Life. The Celts in Ireland possessed several sacred or World Trees: the ash tree that stood on the Hill of Uisneach was especially significant, for the Irish perceived it as standing in the center of Ireland.

Awareness of the eternal Self is at the core of many spiritual traditions, including Druidry. Because the Self has existed in all times and realms, it learns a timeless and dimensionless awareness. To understand the saying "Knowledge of the trees is knowledge of the self," we must understand how the trees reflect every possible aspect of existence. Once a person understands the forms of existence through many experiences of reincarnation, then she or he arrives at awareness of the whole and is a Druid. The symbol of the whole is the World Tree.

Strabo records that, when Alexander the Great asked the Celts what they feared most, they replied: "That the sky will fall on our heads," meaning they feared nothing. When the time came to die, to go beyond this world and the interpenetrating—and sometimes dangerous—realm of the Fairies, and make the journey to the Land of the Living, the Celts had no fear. The journey meant joyous reunion with all that was magical and eternal. It meant awareness of all lives a being had ever lived. It was a celebration among all that was sacred, in the land of the eternal Self, upon the Tree of Life.

The Celtic Cosmos

The Land of the Living. The Land of Youth, Women, the Blessed Ones. The dwelling place of the eternal Self when it is not with a body. This realm infuses, surrounds, and contains the World of the *Sídhe* and the Human World. It is infinite, knowing no corporal, spatial, or temporal limit.

The Fairy Realm. The World of the *Sídhe*, Gods, Goddesses, and Ancestors. The Otherworld of the Fairies infuses the Human World at all times with its power and numinosity. It can be seductive and dangerous. It is the view of the Land of the Living provided by the physical senses.

The Human World. The world of Humans, Nature, Life. The Self is accompanied by a body in this world, and its perceptions are determined by the natural senses. Druids can learn awareness of the eternal Self while incarnate and thereby gain some understanding of the interpenetrating World of the *Sídhe* and of immortal existence in the Land of the Living.

Four Pillars of Druidry

This section summarizes the principal ideas of Druidry described above. We do not present these "Four Pillars of Druidry" as articles of Druid dogma or belief, but as four tenets that are demonstrated in reliable Celtic sources. As we said at the beginning of the chapter, because so much of Druidry is unknown, these tenets represent the tip of an iceberg. The bulk of knowledge is lost to view, but we can surmise it is there from what is visible on the surface. However, we might be surmising incorrectly. Think about these four tenets: multiple lifetimes, spirit in all things, reverence for ancestors, and multiple worlds. Feel how these elements fit together to produce a coherent worldview. What is missing? The Goddess of Sovereignty? The World Tree? Pursuit of Truth? Maybe there are other pillars that you can add to the list.

Multiple lifetimes. The Self or soul (*anam*) comes and goes in an eternal cycle of lives. Between lives in this world, the Self dwells in the Land of the Living. The Self may incarnate in any form, animate or inanimate. The Self loses memory of the details of each individual life but carries the result of the experience across the worlds in the form of wisdom. This may manifest as inspiration (*awen*—Welsh, *imbas*—Irish), music or poetry, as the Truth of Sovereignty (see chapter 15), or in other ways. There is no evidence to suggest that the experience of the Self as it journeys between the worlds and between lifetimes is sequential. The experience is better understood as being contracted or expanded, shallower or deeper, inner and outer. The beauty of death is that it erases memories of the life, while leaving the soul with the wisdom that the lessons of the life have imparted.

Spirit in all things. The whole universe is alive with immanent presence. Water, rocks, fires, hills, and rivers, even thoughts, shouts, waves, and the wind, are all alive. The spirits of place, and especially the Goddesses of Sovereignty, represent this power in the land. The Druids revered the landscape, worshipped within it, and let nature be their guide and teacher. Druids taught that humans belong to the community of all life.

Reverence for ancestors. The awareness or wisdom that each soul brings into existence is both individual and collective. The lineage and tradition into which the soul incarnates shapes the consciousness of the individual Self. The Druids honored the ancestors and tradition, usually expressed as honor for the clan or tribe, as it makes each person what they are now. The community of the tribe is made up of the dead as well as the living. The community is invariably associated with a particular place: a rath, *dún*, mound, hill, or ridge in which the spirit of the tribe dwells. Within each lineage dwell particularly significant ancestral beings, whose mythology has exalted them to the stature of the divine. Being specific to tribes and places at the time, these divine beings rarely achieved a pan-Celtic status of god or goddess. Only a handful, such as Brigit, Lugh, and the battle goddesses, resonated in the mythic imagination to the degree that they were honored all across Europe. Every ritual or spiritual act presided over by a Druid began with an acknowledgement of the ancestors.

Multiple worlds. In addition to this world, there are two others: the Land of the Living and the Realm of the *Sídhe*. These worlds coexist and interpenetrate each other. It is possible to journey between the worlds, but to do this in human form is dangerous. Time in the Otherworlds is nonlinear, and glamour and the subjective limitations of the physical senses may seriously affect the traveler's experience. These many worlds can be imagined as a wheel: we live on the rim of the wheel and experience time on the journey around its perimeter. The spokes of the wheel are the many other worlds (Irish myth mentions thirty-three!), and the Self passes through these to get to the hub. The hub is the Land of the Living, where the experience of the Self is not constrained by birth, death, or time. The Celts were part of a vibrant, dynamic cosmos that was lush with possibilities.

Activities

The Self. Relax comfortably in some quiet place. Watch the rhythm of your breathing rise and fall of its own volition. Notice how the body functions on its own. Try not to control these things, just observe them happening. Now notice how thoughts come into the mind, or feelings into the body. Again, do not accept or reject these thoughts and feelings, just let them arise and then fall away.

Now reflect on what is perceiving these thoughts, feelings, and physical events. Notice how there is always this perceiver but it is never possible to perceive the perceiver because it is also always the observer. Remain in that place of pure perception for a while.

Next, dwell on the pureness of the perceiver: it is the Self. Recall how it can perceive in dreams. Recall how it can remain unharmed outside of the body at times of stress or danger. Your genetic inheritance cannot touch it. It has a body now and this is its experience, but there will be other times perhaps without a body, or in a different one. Notice how the Self is aware of its bodily experience and gets information from sensory organs, but is always outside the experience. Try to imagine exactly what of this experience is carried through death. What will the Self perceive beyond the body?

The Power of Place. Go to a quiet place in nature. Feel yourself to be a tree. It may be one you have identified with, are already working with, or any one that suits the moment. Feel your roots, your trunk, your branches. Feel the experience of being a tree.

Now transport yourself to another land. It may be a place you hold sacred. It may be in the Celtic homelands. It may be now, it may be long ago. You may be in a grove, you may stand alone. Put your roots down into the soil of this place. Extend your branches into the air of this place. Feel the power of your trunk, and the elements of the place playing on your body. Now feel the spirits of place enter the scene. Allow whatever is there to emerge and manifest around you. Feel the energy of the place enter your being. Then lift up your roots and return to your quiet place.

A Tree in all Worlds. Relax in some quiet place. Visualize in your mind's eye a broad, green, gentle plain, covered by a vast expanse of blue sky. Now see a tree upon the plain: imagine any tree you like. Clearly visualize its properties. When you have a clear image of that tree, imagine another. Slowly visualize as many trees in as much detail as you are comfortable with, making sure that they form a circle around you, with you at the center.

When you have created a good number of trees, and sensed their particular qualities, begin to dissolve those qualities into something more abstract. Sense the quality that makes a tree what it is, the quality that makes it appear again and again in the same form throughout the world. What is the essence of each variety of tree? Does it appear as a form? A color? A sound? Let the quality of each tree dissolve so it is free to blend with the qualities of other trees. Put yourself at the center and feel these qualities join and mesh with you. Be the essence of "treeness." Reverse the flow. Make the quality of one tree's essence stronger than the others, then bring up another tree's essence. You are at the center, orchestrating the world that the trees create. You are the World Tree.

Feel what it is like to be a tree in all worlds. Feel your branches, and your roots. There may be an opening in your trunk through which it is possible to go and visit one place in the creation. There may be a message you wish to take some-where, or a place you want to visit in order to ask a question. The World Tree is infinite and reaches into the past and the future.

Now dissolve the World Tree, allowing each tree to go back to its place upon the broad green plain. Give thanks to each tree for the quality it provides. Release the image you have created of the circle of trees. Come back to yourself.

Notes

1. From the *Leabhar Gabála*, the "Book of Invasions." This recension based upon the translations of Robert Graves (1952), R.A. MacAlester (1956), and Cross & Slover (1936).

2. *Cormac's Glossary*, Whitley Stokes (1868), also Caitlín Matthews (1994).

3. Translation by D. W. Nash, *Taliesin, or the Bards and Druids of Britain* (1858), given in John Matthews, *Taliesin*.

4. From *Imram Brain maic Febail* (translated literally into English, the "Rowing-About of Bran son of Febal" or the "Voyage of Bran"). The version given here relies upon the translations of Kuno Meyer (1895) and Lady Gregory (1904).

5. Cam Smith, *Notes from the Mountain*.

6. From Ella Young, *Celtic Wonder Tales* (1910).

7. This story is preserved in the eleventh-century *Leabhar ne h-Uidhri*. Recension based on Lady Gregory (1902), A. H. Leahy (1905), and Cross and Slover (1936).

Chapter 12

WHY BECOME A DRUID?

Among all the tribes, generally speaking, there are three classes of men held in special honor: the Bards, the Vates [seers], and the Druids.[1]

This chapter looks at reasons for becoming a Druid and describes what it is like to come home to your tradition. At the end, we ask you to bring your personal reasons to the surface.

Were you ever so drawn to something that you could not resist it? That happened to Maya on the first day she drove through New Mexico: "I wanted to stay, and I did. I couldn't explain it totally, but it felt like a hand in the middle of my back had guided me to this place." You may feel a hand in the middle of your back guiding you now. Because you are attracted to Druidry is an excellent reason to become a Druid. ". . . Druidism," writes Edred Thorsson, "can be for anyone who feels drawn to the Celtic way of life. For if the attraction is there for you, it is as sure a sign as any that the Celtic Way is a meaningful path for you to follow."[2]

Here we will explore reasons why people are becoming Druids: bloodlines, the feeling of returning to their native tradition, mystery, intellectual emphasis, and spirituality without religion. We hope you will add others to the list.

The Druid in Your Mirror

The Irish, Scots and Welsh, the Manx, Breton, and Cornish people retain traditions and linguistic proof of their over 2,000-year-old Celtic ancestry. That ancestry also runs in their blood. If your people are from those areas, Celtic blood runs in you. In the miracle of life, DNA passes live from parent to child, parent to child, over thousands of years. Therefore particles and living traces of the actual bodies and minds of your ancestors are within you now.

Many of us Westerners left the formal religion of our upbringing and searched in other places for religious teachings. The intense study of Eastern philosophies spurred by the hippies and gurus of the 1970s led many to embrace Asian spiritual traditions. You must know people—perhaps yourself—who turned to Taoism, Zen Buddhism, Vedanta for spiritual inspiration. These same people may have followed those paths for two, ten, or twenty years, only to return to the cycle of searching. Maya was one of these perennial seekers:

> *While I was teaching a university course in Women's Rituals as the 90s began, a guest speaker came to the class to present a ritual invoking Lilith. The speaker was a radical feminist rabbi who had refused to leave her native Judaism though her political views made her many enemies. The rabbi gave this advice: Go to your roots. Those four words catapulted me to immerse, to bathe, to inhale the Celtic culture of my forebears, in place of the plain vanilla "American" culture I grew up in.*

If you look at the inner side of your forearm through the thin skin, you will see the veins that carry the blood of your ancestors. If you imagine looking inside every cell, you will see the chromosomes that came from your parents. If you look at the DNA inside the chromosomes you will see the living genetic messages, half from your mother and half from your father, that make you who you are. If you look in the mirror you will see the presence of your ancestors.

Was some of your genetic material present when the Romans destroyed the Druids on the Isle of Anglesey? Was some of that living material present when the boy Taliesin stepped forth on the shore, dazzling the king's men with his poetry? Could be, if you are of Welsh descent. You needn't hold to the idea of reincarnation at all. You needn't have been there on the shore; instead, some of your DNA might have witnessed the scene and carried that memory into you.

Was some of your DNA present when Maeve disregarded her Druid who said "I see crimson, I see red," and threw the forces of Connaught against Cuchulainn and the troops of Ulster? Was some of your DNA listening when the Druid Cathbad foretold that the beautiful child Deirdre would be fair and comely, yet her beauty would bring banishment and death on sons of kings? Could be, if you are of Irish descent.

Was part of you present when storytellers first enchanted their listeners with tales of the Grail and the Druid Merlin? Could be, if you are of Breton descent. Did part of you try to make the shamanic leap across the perilous bridge to reach the otherworldly Isle of Skye where the female warrior Scáthach lived? Could be, if you are of Scots descent.

The bloodlines we carry are the keepers of more than hemoglobin. They store genetic survival tales, cellular memories of times past, desires to accomplish what our ancestors did, talents in music and poetry and art. Legends of the people in our past stir our blood. When we wonder about the ancient Druids, our bloodlines already carry the information that we need to know.

We urge everyone who reads this book to go to the homelands of your ancestors (see chapter 14). There is no substitute for this experience: by seeing people who look like you, hearing the speech your distant ancestors spoke, standing by the hills and lakes they saw, you will start to have their dreams and visions. If you want to know why the Druids used nature as their teacher, go to the patches of nature where they lived. You can no longer see the great groves in which the Druids performed ceremonies, but you can still sense sacred places and create your own among the same mists and earth.

Coming Home

For many of us in the Anglo-Celtic-European world there is a sense of displacement, of being uprooted and disconnected from the native tradition of our origins. It is hard for many of us in the U.S.A., Australia, or anywhere around the world, to find our present identity. Some people seek out the traditions of the countries they are naturalized into. The nature-based spirituality of the Native Americans or the Aborigines of Australia is enormously attractive. Native traditions have maintained a connection with the earth, with life and with nature, which the transcendent and revealed religions have not. Today there is much interest in the ways of native and tribal peoples. The trouble is that many native peoples do not want newcomers adopting their spiritual traditions, and it is doubtful that the outsiders can really grasp them without becoming fully native themselves (if that is even possible).

As you have probably guessed by now, our answer to this sense of loss and displacement is that we already have our own native tradition! A feeling often expressed among those who have turned to the Druid Path is that of coming home. Becoming a Druid feels like returning to oneself, and to the ancient tradition of one's ancestors. Even if there is no known lineage that connects a person to the Celtic tradition, this feeling often exists, and may be expressed as a connection through other life times. Native

Americans and other indigenous people would be happier if we sat around the fire with them, listening to their stories, and telling the myths and legends of our own native tradition, rather than if we tried to copy theirs.

On the path of Druidry you can feel knowledge and energy welling up from within. It may even be an advantage that there is no direct continuation of the Druid tradition across the centuries! There is no institution, no Order with a Book of Teachings, no dogma and instructions on how to do things. The evidence from the past shows that the Druids had no books or creeds, and possibly no ordination into their Orders. Each Druid learned all the particular skills of the practice mostly through an oral transmission or handing down of knowledge. This may have taken a long time —the Graeco-Roman sources mention twenty years—until they themselves could demonstrate their abilities to others in a way that was incontrovertible.

This sense of knowledge and energy welling up from within is very important on the Druid Path. Druidry can easily become intellectual, scholarly, or abstract because it is a path that emphasizes the spoken word rather than the body. Practitioners must constantly ground themselves both in the experience of the Self and in the experience of nature.

Druids today are synthesizing the historical rift of dualism which dominates the Western worldview. Druids have no rift between spirit and matter, intelligence and creation, the divine and nature. The Druids of old taught the indigenous European Celtic spiritual tradition before it was subsumed by patterns of dualistic thinking. They held a very different worldview. Spirit, the sacred, intelligence, the life force, were everywhere and in all things. Druids revered nature and the body as divine. The true Self or soul was sacred and immortal because it is a part of nature, not because it is separate from the natural world. Creatures and plants were not lower on the scale than humans. Though there was a social hierarchy, and Druids were at the top of it, they earned it through study and not through heredity. Kings and chieftains were elected by the people, and could be as freely deposed. Power did not come from above but from within. Only through manifesting their innate divine power could human beings demonstrate the virtues the Celts held in most esteem: truth, honor, generosity, hospitality, strength, courage, and justice. It often comes as a relief to discover that we can come home to ourselves. We do not have to be anything other than what we are.

As we explore these core thoughts of Druidry, let us remember not to take anything on trust. There is nothing to believe here. If we cannot feel inside ourselves that something is true, then it is not true. We know that truth is central to Druidic thinking, and it is truth that makes and shapes ourselves and the world.

Mystery

People love mystery! If something comes from a time and place long ago and far away, it carries an aura of mystery even if the people living at that time and place thought it was commonplace. So might it be with Druidry. People 2,000 years ago probably thought it was a prosaic part of their lives. As one moves away from the center of a field of knowledge, uncertainty builds up, followed by confusion and, finally, mystery. That has happened with Druidry and brings us to the present time.

Mystery arouses and tantalizes us because it is unexplained, perhaps inexplicable. Since we were children many of us loved uncovering secrets. Something puzzling or unknown brings up our curiosity. Druidry sounds esoteric, understandable only to those with special knowledge, to those admitted to secret rites. Indeed, secret rite is exactly what "mystery" means in Greek, from their word meaning "to initiate, to close the eyes or mouth," and therefore to keep secret.

It is fascinating that most of the world's religions have a branch for mystics, to which ordinary practitioners do not belong. Mysticism is a spiritual discipline where the divine is directly accessible by intuition, usually through meditation and trance-like contemplation. Whereas a religion's priests or ministers fulfill public roles, a religion's monks typically are the mystics, be they Essenes, Trappists, Qabalists, or Lamas. If you are drawn to the mystery of Druidry, you may resonate with the rituals, the contemplation, and the study of unusual powers.

For you, does the mystery of Druidry lie in the unknowns? In the power of those Celts trained to be spiritual leaders? In the broken strands of teachings, or the hatred and persecution against them? Are you attracted because you want to delve into the shadow side, the occult? Do you want to be part of the practice of magic? For some people, the mystery lies in the effect on their friends and acquaintances when they say they are a Druid!

For those who want mystery, Druidry is ideal because much of it must remain an enigma. We have scant information from the time when Celtic Druids lived—from Classical Greek and Roman writers inimical to them, from myths recorded centuries later, and archaeological evidence being revealed now. We must use intelligent guesswork to fill in the gaps. Those who want mystery can create or invent Druidry in the present time, guided by their intuition and wisdom.

Another aspect of mystery that requires a little more caution is glamour. Are you attracted to Druidry because it comes close to your fantasies of attracting the perfect lover, or of becoming a magician, or of losing yourself in the dreams of the Fairy World? Make no mistake, Druidry is about self-knowledge and becoming whole. It is about working hard to understand the core themes of existence. It requires that we resolve struggles we all get involved in for power, status, security, and love. The Celtic world recognized the Fairy Realm as a place of glamour. It offers power, authority, knowledge, feasting, love, sex, and wealth. A visit to the Fairy Realm may be intensely enjoyable. You may even win "spoils" that can be brought back to this world. Often this is at enormous cost, and usually the gifts of the *Sídhe* dissolve in the reality of this world.

Intellectual Emphasis

Compared with New Age "feelie" religions, or the requirement to accept dogma on faith in the revealed desert religions (i.e., Christianity, Judaism, and Islam), Druidry comes from the head. It does not uphold any belief. It upholds the pursuit of truth as the supreme virtue. This appeals to people who value reason, logic, and left-brain thinking. Educators call these the "critical thinking skills." People who bring forth their inner realm into words instead of pictures tend to like the cerebral emphasis of Druidry. Celtic Druids were intellectuals with highly trained memories. They were learned carriers of cultural, magical, and spiritual traditions. Druids today are carriers of these traditions through the study of philosophy, law, politics, history, healing, music, science, and other fields.

The Celts revered the head in ways we find unusual today. A distinctly Celtic necklace, the torc, may have served to highlight the powers of the wearer's mind. A torc was a thick metal circle worn around the neck, with an opening or fastening in the front. We surmise that it marked the territory of the warrior's or chieftain's mind and perhaps the soul. Some torcs were of gold and wrought in exquisite patterns of twisted and curved golden wires. The precision, beauty, and quantity of torcs which have been found reveal their importance, even if their exact significance is lost. In addition, Celtic warriors thickened their hair with wet lime so that it bristled out fiercely from their head. Skulls of warriors were embedded into walls as badges of honor and prestige. Enemies' heads were severed and tied to Celtic chariots, both to display the warriors' ferocity and to gain access to the spirit of the dead.

In a shamanic display that guaranteed victory, the hero Cuchulainn went into a "warp-frenzy" that sounds like a Celtic description of crown-chakra fireworks!

> *Terrible was his transformation when sorely oppressed by his enemies. At such times among the aerial clouds over his head were visible the virulent pouring showers and sparks of ruddy fire which the seething of his savage wrath caused to mount up above him. His hair became tangled about his head, as* [if] *it had been branches of a red thorn-bush stuffed into a strongly-fenced gap . . . Taller, thicker, more rigid, longer than* [the] *mast of a great ship was the perpendicular jet of dusky blood which out of his scalp's very central point shot upwards and then was scattered to the four cardinal points.*[3]

With this emphasis on the head, it is only one step more to understand that it was the spoken word which the Celts revered—that which issued from the head through the mouth. Celtic honor was a matter of life and death. Giving one's word was a promise kept even beyond death, when a person's family was obliged to carry out the matter of honor. Celtic excellence at storytelling is renowned. You might be lucky enough on a visit to Ireland to encounter *seanachies* in pubs, keeping audiences rapt with tales told many times before.

Celtic reverence for poetry is legendary. To this day, bards in Wales hold Eisteddfod poetry contests. Maya met the chief bard of Wales, an old Druid, several years ago. He had won so many bardic "chairs," (awards given to the winner of each Eisteddfod), that he no longer competed so that younger bards would have a chance. Though Maya does not speak or understand Welsh, something about the way he recited his poetry for her leapt the language barrier, reached inside her head, and made her one with it. The cadence, alliteration, his wife's accompaniment on the harp, all called up cellular memories. At the end Maya asked if he had been speaking of ancestors and forefathers on the land and indeed, that was the topic of his bardic poem!

The Celtic reverence for nature appears in poems that extol birds, flowers, sea spray, wind, and streams. The Druid ability to castigate by word appears in reports that satirists could raise welts on the skin of the one being denigrated (see chapter 1 on *mallachtí*). The ability to charm and entice with words is evident in this mythic invitation to join the fairy army on the Plain of Honey:

They are beautiful in battle.
A host with high looks, rushing, avenging.
It is no wonder they have such strength;
Every one of them is the son of a king and a queen;
Manes of hair they have of the colour of gold.
Their bodies smooth and comely;
Their eyes blue and far-seeing; their teeth bright like crystal …
White shields they have in their hands, with patterns … of white silver;
Blue shining swords, red horns set with gold.
They are good at killing men in battle;
Good at song-making, good at chess-playing.[4]

The emphasis upon the head and the spoken word means more than simply being intellectual. Your thoughts are indicators of the quality of your life. They indicate the consciousness of your whole being. Thoughts and words steer our lives in the direction we wish to go. Becoming a Druid is not so much about the powers we may have, or what we may do, or how much we can learn or remember: it is about the wisdom of the lessons we have learned in our whole existence, manifesting in the consciousness of the present moment and directing the way we live now.

Spirituality without Religion

Imagine practicing your spirituality freely, without guilt, without wondering whether you are doing it "right". That can only happen when there is no one but you to say what is "right." Only you can be in charge of your own spiritual development. This is the case with Druidry. While there are many Druidic organizations, there is no church. There is no single administration that says what is inside and what is outside the fold. Indeed, Druidry is nothing like a religion in that sense.

Make no mistake—the Celts and Druids of 2,000 years ago were patriarchal, hierarchical, war-dominating people. Some of the Druid groups today continue this hierarchy, while others are more politically correct and sensitive to modern achievements in equality, peace, and ecology. Some groups today have strict rules and lock-step procedures for entry and initiation to different levels. A single leader may have created this atmosphere. Others forego such control; they offer material for self-study and encourage self-determination of one's progress. It is this noninstitutional basis that attracts some to Druidry. Without starting from scratch, the free thinker can found her or his own "religion" by practicing present-day Druidry.

Druidry offers no set of beliefs or dogmas. Despite the writings of eighteenth- and nineteenth-century Druids, it has no theology or creation mythology. It has no God or supreme power, at least in the way we understand this today. It has no book of scriptures, nor a clergy to interpret them. Druidry relies upon the experience of the senses, the experience of the body in nature, the experience of the soul, and the pursuit of truth.

Druidry does offer a coherent system of ethics and values. These became enshrined in the Brehon Laws of Ireland that sought justice by having the offender directly compensate the victim for the offense. Justice was therefore based upon restoration rather than on punishment. This Druid system of ethics may be enormously attractive to some people in our time. Much of modern-day paganism or alternative spirituality has an anarchic, individualistic, freewheeling style. This quality may be valuable to some, but many of us require a coherent approach to the complex ethical issues that confront us in our everyday lives. Druidry offers such an approach as it is based upon honor for the self, for the earth, for tradition, and for the community.

Practitioners of Druidry might differ in what brought them to this study—bloodlines, their native tradition, mystery, emphasis on the word, freedom from institutional constraints. Most have felt an inner pull toward it, like planets toward the sun. So we return to this core reason that people become Druids: because they feel drawn to set their foot upon this path. For many of us, the fact that Celtic DNA runs in our bodies compellingly ends the search for other paths and brings us to Druidry. Quite possibly, when it is right for us, we do not *choose* a path; it chooses us. When our spirit follows its bliss, we call that a spiritual path. In the end, it is *our* tradition in language, in thought, in perceptions, in our racial memory and biological code, that will allow us to sit down around the fire of the council of all beings and add our note to the collective harmony of all traditions. This is why it is good for those who feel it to be their path to become a Druid.

Activities

Why do you want to be a Druid? Slowly ponder the reasons in this chapter as well as the following additional reasons, then compile your own personalized picture of what brought you to this point.

- Truth
- Ancient connection
- Earth-honoring tradition
- Immanence or power-from-within
- Magic
- Prophecy
- Celtic arts
- Natural sciences
- Ethics

Druidry in your life. Ask yourself the following question numerous times and record your answers. After the first five or ten times, you will notice a shift to deeper, more creative levels. This is typical in brainstorming.

What Druidry brings to my life is . . .

Your own path. If Druidry had never existed and you had to found your own religion or spiritual path, what would it consist of?

Notes

1. Strabo, *Geography* IV.4.4.

2. In Tadhg MacCrossan, *The Sacred Cauldron*, p. xiv.

3. Standish Hayes O'Grady, *Silva Gadelica*.

4. Lady Augusta Gregory, *Gods and Fighting Men*, p. 122.

Chapter 13

How Do You Form a Druid Grove?

At a fixed time of the year [the Druids] *meet in assembly in a holy place in the land of the Carnutes, which is regarded as the center of the whole of Gaul.*[1]

This chapter explains the process of joining an existing grove or a virtual grove, as well as forming a new one in your area. It describes Internet and print resources for contact and study purposes.

Locating Existing Groves

Your path of study and practice in Druidry can be enhanced and steadied by joining with others of like mind and intention. You may find it easiest to join an existing group of Druids because a group offers direction and energy due to the sheer number of involved participants. Druid groups are called Groves, in honor of the trees that formed and still form the preferred meeting place.

You might locate a Grove near where you live. There is likely a pagan community already in existence close to you, and you can contact pagan groups through local bookstores and other sources. The chances are, however, that they will be Wiccan in orientation rather than Druidic. At present, Druids form a very small percentage in the world of pagans. You will find drumming circles, shamanic groups, goddess circles, ceremonial magicians, Wiccans—even Celtic Wiccans—but Druids, rarely.

Networking with Druids Worldwide

If a group of Druids is not nearby, you could communicate for a while with an electronic grove, via e-mail. This is an excellent way to get started on the Druid path, since anyone with a computer can contact a Druid organization. We can guess that the Druids of 2,000 years ago would have found the electronic magic of computers a superb addition to their abilities! Nearly all the following groups and more can be found on the Internet by entering the keywords "Druid" or "Celtic" on your search engine. If you write to them, send a large, self-addressed envelope with plenty of stamps or international postage: that way they can most conveniently send you their materials.

The Order of Bards, Ovates and Druids, P.O. Box 1333, Lewes, East Sussex, BN7 3ZG, Britain. This organization has thousands of members worldwide and offers a correspondence course and mentor program. We recommend it highly; it will help start you on the Druid path, although the already motivated and scholarly student might wish for more content in the courses. Their current Chief is Philip Carr-Gomm. Contact **OBOD** electronically at http://www.druidry.org and explore their pages of links. Their monthly newsletter is *Touchstone*; subscription details available from the above address.

The British Druid Order, P.O. Box 29, St. Leonards-on-Sea, East Sussex, TN37 7YP, Britain. This is an excellent Druid organization if you have shamanic leanings. They also produce *A Druid Directory* and a magazine *The Druid's Voice*. Write for details, enclosing a stamped self-addressed envelope or international post coupon. Philip Shallcrass is the founder and joint Chief of the **BDO**.

The College of Druidism, 4A Minto Street, Edinburgh, EH7 4AN, Scotland. The College offers a correspondence course and some very interesting publications. Kaledon Naddair, the founder, is at once stimulating and exasperating, gifted and bombastic and, as a result, the College is highly influenced by his personality. The same may be said for **GOD**, the **Glastonbury Order of Druids**, Dove House, Barton St. David, Somerset, TA11 6DF, Britain. Its founding members do have a sense of humor. GOD has also been persistent in claiming the right to celebrate at Stonehenge on the Summer Solstice and for this they are to be commended. They produce an annual magazine, *Druidlore*, the "official magazine of The Council of British Druid Orders."

A'r nDrai'ocht Fe'in (ADF), P.O. Box 9420, Newark DE 19714-9420, U.S.A. This is the Druid organization in North America most likely to have a Grove near to you. They offer teaching materials and publications. Contact them electronically at http://www.adf.org.

Henge of Keltria, P.O. Box 33284, Minneapolis, Minnesota 55433, U.S.A. This organization offers a correspondence course, journals, and other publications on matters Celtic and Druidic. Contact them electronically at http://www.keltria.org.

Reformed Druids of North America (RDNA), c/o Michael Scharding, Carleton College, 300 North College Street, Northfield, Minnesota 55057, U.S.A. Many Druid groups in North America can trace themselves back to the **RDNA**.

Druid Clan of Dana, Clonegal Castle, Enniscorthy, Eire (Ireland). Founded in 1992, the Clan is based on the work of the Fellowship of Isis.

Imbas, P.O. Box 1215, Montague NJ 07827-0215, U.S.A. One of the aims of Imbas is to reconstruct Iron Age Celtic religion based upon home, family, and tribe. To join their organization or Internet discussion group, write them or explore their website at http://morrigan.alabanza.com.

Finally, there are pagan magazines that often run articles of Druid interest. These include *Green Egg* and the *Hallowquest Newsletter*, the latter edited by John and Caitlín Matthews: BCM Hallowquest, London WC1N 3XX, Britain (U.S. $20 subscription).

Usenet newsgroups allow discussion on a whole variety of topics. Get on the Internet and search alt.mythology, alt.religion.druid, or soc.culture.celtic, which may produce some interesting tidbits. Very interesting Celtic material can be found at http://www.clannada.org, http://www.summerlands.org, or at http://celtic.stanford.edu/clipart.html.

You may prefer to join a privately maintained e-mail group. *Nemeton*, for example, holds "Celtic reconstructionist Pagan and Druid discussions" which are well worth attending. Details are available through the Nemeton Webring Homepage: http://www.nucleus.com/~valhalla/nemeton/index.html. OBOD also has Internet forums; find details at http://www.druidry.org.

Starting a New Grove

Forming a Grove can be quite easy and informal. It only requires a few members at the beginning: more will come later. At first it helps if there are at least four committed members. Our experience in other groups has shown that having over twelve to fifteen members becomes difficult in terms of space and coordination. If this became the case, a Grove could divide in two. We will share our experience in forming a new grove as a practical example of how it might work for you.

We were members of an electronic virtual grove, communicating via the Internet with Druids in Britain. Two people in Albuquerque asked to study Druidry with us, and this created enough of an impetus to form a face-to-face Grove. At the time, we had no way of knowing how much interest in forming a Grove existed in our area. New Mexico is sparsely populated and as large as Spain. Although some avid Druids exist in other towns, only five of us lived close enough to form the core of the Grove.

We needed a diverse pattern of participation in the Grove. One level is for those who keep in touch by e-mail and mail; another is for those who live at a distance and can only attend a few meetings a year. Still one more level of participation is for those beginning on the Druid path who attend the open study meetings that take place eight times a year, in the months without a cross-quarter day. Newcomers attend a year of these study meetings before joining the Grove. Only full Grove members may attend the four main rituals we have each year at the cross-quarter days.

Early on we wrote the following declaration, which was extremely useful for providing us with a definition and direction. This declaration is not copyrighted and may be used by other Druids to help form their own statements of intent.

Declaration of the Sandia Mountain Grove of Druids

The Sandia Mountain Grove of Druids is committed to the wisdom teachings of the Celts—a Native European Tradition. It strives to uphold the knowledge of the Celtic peoples wherever they are in the world. The Grove recognizes the quest for self knowledge in the Celtic tradition and honors the keepers of their lore and wisdom, the Druids.

The Sandia Mt. Grove recognizes the central role of the trees in the teachings of the Druids. All nature is divine. The Druidic Grove is the Temple of the Divine. Each tree holds a station in the Temple of the Grove and embodies a particular aspect of nature. All who enter the Grove hold the trees in honor, and, through the structure and inspiration the trees provide, so they honor all of creation. The Sandia Mt. Grove expects those who initiate into the Druidic Native European Tradition under its auspices to hold a station of a tree and bring its qualities and powers to the Grove for at least one year and a day.

The Sandia Mt. Grove is committed to continuing Druid wisdom through teaching, ritual and other practical and spiritual work. It holds learning circles, makes information accessible, develops reading lists, treatises and other publications and conducts ceremonies. The Grove celebrates four festivals with formal rituals around the wheel of the year, namely: Imbolc, Beltane, Lughnasadh, and Samhain, with the equinoxes and solstices being celebrated however Grove members desire.

The Sandia Mt. Grove recognizes and respects the many Orders of Druids and other groups teaching the Native European Traditions around the world but is not affiliated with any of them.

The Sandia Mt. Grove is autonomous and sovereign unto itself and draws its power from the wellspring of earthly wisdom as it is revealed through the trees and their representatives, the Druids. There is absolute equality in the Grove. Like the trees, the members of the Grove are who they are through their inner nature, and none is greater or lesser for it. Each Druid stands equally in the Grove, manifesting power from within, contributing to the power of the whole.

The Sandia Mt. Grove of Druids upholds the pursuit of truth, the sanctity of the self, natural virtue, self-responsibility and earth veneration. It supports civic duty, social diversity and feminine-masculine balance. It respects the right of all peoples everywhere to their own spiritual paths.

The Sandia Mt. Grove studies traditions of the Celtic and pagan past while being aware of the romance attached to them. It understands that much of what is known as "Druidry" is an invention of recent centuries. The Grove aims to remain true to the existing Celtic source material and to promote critical research of it, but is not confined by it. The Grove remembers the past and draws inspiration from it while incorporating the advantages of the present to create a new synthesis of Druidic practice.

> *We seek the wisdom of our ancestors*
> *Not so we may walk where they walked,*
> *But so we may travel further.*[2]

A quarterly publication known as the *Live Oak Oracle* was founded at the same time as the Grove, and all members, indeed all Druids, are welcome to contribute to it. Rather than being a newsletter, the publication is a means of clarifying and recording ideas and rituals. It provides a way of reaching out to a greater number of people interested in Druidry, including those who live at a distance. It also allows the local pagan community and general public to receive well-researched material about Druid lore and Celtic myths. We are not suggesting that every Druid or budding Grove create a publication or a website, but some means of recording the spoken word is essential, given the nature of Druidry.

An excellent way of forming a Grove is to begin with a course of study. The Order of Bards, Ovates and Druids offers a correspondence course, and they connect each student with others in the locality. Alternatively, a group might begin by studying a text such as Philip Carr-Gomm's *Elements of the Druid Tradition* or this book. As the members get to know each other and common commitments emerge, the basis for a Grove will be formed. We highly recommend this approach. Studying a chapter or two of a book once a month, or more frequently, provides a common objective, educates, sets clear parameters, allows individuals to participate at the depth they choose, and commits no one to anything they do not want or are not ready for.

After a core group of people emerges that is committed to a common Druid path, the next step is to decide where, when, and how you would like to meet for activities other than study. Our Grove meets for rituals to celebrate the four main festivals of the Celtic year. We plan this in advance, and if the weather permits meet outdoors. We are lucky to live in the beautiful desert of the southwestern United States, and members of our Grove own land in the mountains where we can conduct ceremony in virgin forests. At other times we select a special place beside a river, in a canyon, or in the mountains. We are planting a grove of sacred trees on one of our home properties, and this will create a dedicated outdoor setting when the opportunity does not exist to go to the forest. Otherwise, we meet indoors in a ritual space.

Our rituals are the centerpiece of a day out on the land together; eventually we will have longer retreats. For the cross-quarter day rituals, we select a time closest to the actual date, adjusting this for dark or full times of the moon. The cross-quarter day itself sets the theme for the ritual. Each member of the Grove prepares something separately, and then when we gather we share our parts. We find that a wonderful synthesis always takes place, and we prefer this to having one or two people prescript the ritual. This is an entirely appropriate process, as so little authentic Druid material remains. We find it better to follow our talents, inspiration and intuition rather than our minds in this matter. One person may bring a cauldron visualization, another a poem or drama, another a tree observance, another a historical re-creation. These always merge in a seamless fashion and create a beginning, middle, and ending for the ritual. A description of some of our ceremonies is given in chapter 7.

This should give you some ideas about forming your own local Grove, which may be easier than finding one already in existence. The Druid renaissance is a relatively recent phenomenon and now is a good time to ride the crest of the emerging wave.

Reading the Sources

We recommend that every serious student of Druidry read the Celtic myths in the original Irish and Welsh, or else in several translations (in order to derive a fuller understanding of how the original texts can be read). We give a list of source texts in the Bibliography. There is *no* other source material (apart from history and archaeology, which have limited use). Only then will it be possible for you to read the many modern books on the Celtic and Druid tradition and know what the authors are talking about, or what they are inventing!

Works in Translation

T. P. Cross and C. H. Slover
Jeffrey Gantz
Elizabeth A. Gray
Lady Augusta Gregory
Thomas Kinsella
Proinsias MacCana
Cecille O'Rahilly
Whitley Stokes
Others whose work is available from the catalogs given below.

Original Books

Philip Carr-Gomm
Peter Berresford Ellis
Miranda J. Green
Ronald Hutton
Simon James
Katherine Kurtz
Erynn Rowan Laurie
Morgan Llywelyn
Jean Markale
Caitlín and John Matthews
Alwyn and Brinley Rees
Anne Ross
Philip Shallcrass
Evangeline Walton

With these recommendations, we will also include here a list of books on Druidry we urge you to avoid, at least until you are quite familiar with the mythic source material. These include works by Lewis Spence, Robert Graves, James Bonwick, Murry Hope, Stuart Piggot, and Iolo Morganwg (aka Edward Williams, whose work pops up in many guises). One should run a critical eye over many popular books with claims to Celtic wisdom. Caitlín Matthews and Michael Dames, for example, are highly recommended, but they are intuitive writers who do not always clarify their sources.

Write for a catalog of translations of Irish texts to . . .

The Irish Texts Society, c/o The Royal Bank of Scotland, Drummonds Branch, 49 Charing Cross, Admiralty Arch, London SW1A 2DX, Britain.

The Dublin Institute for Advanced Studies, 10 Burlington Road, Dublin 4, Ireland.

One mail-order bookshop for Celtic books is Three Geese in Flight, P.O. Box 454, Bearsville NY 12409, U.S.A.

Activities

Becoming a Druid Researcher. The Druids were wisdom-keepers and so must we be. Take steps towards finding more information. The library, bookstore, and the Internet are helpful. Some suggestions:

- Search the Internet using keywords such as "Druid" or "Celtic." Try websites such as: http://www.summerlands.com or http://www.uoguelph.ca/~bmyers/druid.html.

- Subscribe to an e-mail list concerned with Druidry. Read the threads that existing subscribers discuss, then contribute when you are ready. This could constitute an electronic Grove for you.

- Put the word out to your friends and to pagan groups, so people know you are searching. Someone will have a connection. Did you know that if you tell a desire or wish of yours to twenty or twenty-five people, one of them will have the next connection you need?

- Join an existing Druid grove, or reach out and make at least two contacts with other Druids, either by e-mail, letter, or in person. Utilize the resources given above.

Declaration of Druidry. This declaration is waiting to be written—by you! It will clarify your purposes and your thinking. You may want to borrow ideas from the Declaration of the Sandia Mountain Grove of Druids given in this chapter.

Druid Renaissance. The movement to live authentic Druidry needs your voice. Write an article for publication or join an Internet list and speak up. Draw, dramatize, or put to music your Druid intentions and practices. Be here!

Notes

1. Caesar, *Bellum Gallicum* VI.13.

2. *Live Oak Oracle* 1, Winter 1996.

Chapter 14

So You Want to Visit the Celtic Homelands?

O, the life of the Druid is the life of the land.[1]

For Druids, and for others wanting to connect with their Celtic ancestry and inheritance, visiting the lands of origin is immensely exciting and rewarding. This chapter describes places of Celtic antiquity in Ireland, Britain, Wales, Scotland, and Brittany.

Mapping Your Ancestry

In chapter 5 you laid the groundwork for researching your family genealogy. We urge you to do all possible research at home, because Europe is no place to begin ancestral searches: it is the ending place, the triumphant conclusion to your search! While you are still at home, locate ancestral haunts on large-scale maps. In Britain, Ordnance Survey 1:50,000 maps show excellent detail. Order them through the type of store or catalog that sells surveying materials, Geological Survey, and foreign maps. Also, obtain a motoring atlas for each country, with three or four miles to one inch so you can wander on the plentiful back roads without making a wrong turn. You might want to pinpoint your route so that it covers all known locales of your ancestors, including ports of emigration, as well as informative tourist centers. In this chapter we highlight special sites that we have visited and can recommend. After your first trip, you will be in a position to select your next itinerary based on the inside knowledge you've gleaned from your experience.

Planning the Sacred Journey

Your trip to Celtic homelands will probably be made up of a combination of reverence, research, and fun! As Druids, standing where others before us conducted ritual has a profound effect. The journey will be sacred because you are going to lands that have been inspirited for countless thousands of years. You are going to places where every spring, rock, and mountain was named and revered. Your genealogical research might be spurred by seeing where your ancestors were born and raised. Traveling the roads they must have walked and the hills they must have climbed is a momentous experience. Planning will pay off for any length of trip at any time of year, because you will accomplish more of what you want and encounter fewer frustrations and disappointments. Of course, we hope you leave room for spontaneity and for the amazing and frequent moments of magic that occur in Celtic lands. Take plenty of photographs when in magical, sacred, or unusual places, because what is sensed but not seen often turns up on film.

We travel annually to our Celtic homelands. Nicholas was born in Britain and lived there until 1988. Maya is an Irish citizen. Each year we like to have a theme or purpose. Our most rewarding theme is to follow the routes of the Celtic myths as they appear in place names and in the landscape. Please consider doing this yourself. After you learn some of the myths thoroughly, map them and then walk, bicycle, or drive the routes. The Celtic era will leap into your consciousness and reveal treasures unobtainable to the ordinary visitor.

Our usual pattern is to fly to London and rent a car at the airport for the duration of our stay. Ferries can take you and your vehicle to Ireland, the Western Isles of Scotland, and to France, or you can take the Channel Tunnel across to the continent. Rental car and ferry reservations can be made in the United States. Having a car door-to-door is expensive, and when we stay for longer periods we use public transport. This option limits the places that can be reached, but you can meet more people that way. At times we like to bury ourselves somewhere without transport and simply be on the land for a while. Public transport is very good in Britain and Scotland, and works quite well in Ireland—but this method will not get you to remote sites. Try to avoid the peak season in late July and all of August, when all continental and insular Europeans go on vacation at once! In August you might not even get a seat on a train or be able to drive without bumper-to-bumper traffic.

Ireland

When we first visited the Republic of Ireland in the 80s, the exhibits of the National Museum in Dublin were extremely disappointing. A few gold and bronze objects, exhibited dustily, were but a fragment of the hoards of Celtic artefacts that have been found in Ireland. Celtic culture of immense wealth and sophistication had existed there long before the coming of Christianity, but seemed of little interest to the exhibits' curators. When we visited in 1996 and 1997, however, the National Museum had created a Bronze Age exhibition called "*Ór*, Ireland's Gold." It was a breathtaking experience to see such a celebration. Beautiful objects of gold displayed the power and inspiration of the Celtic world, and brought to life the social, daily, and heroic life in the past.

While the museum's objects themselves spoke powerfully to us, the conditioned thinking of recent centuries could also be heard. The audio-visual display allotted the incredible achievements of the megalith builders only a few pictures, and the Celts a sentence or two. Then it sonorously proclaimed that "Irish history begins with St. Patrick." Officials in the Republic of Ireland do not yet seem ready to take on their magnificent pre-Catholic history.

Do not fear, though, for the landscape itself in the Irish Republic upholds the past. And the Irish character is full of the blarney and imagination that is so recognizably Celtic in origin. The "word artists" of modern Ireland such as Yeats, Beckett, and Heaney continue the bardic tradition, as do her storytellers and musicians. Irish writers are the midwives to rebirthing the Celtic sacredness of words based on myth not logic, imagery not history.[2] So visit the National Museum in Dublin, pay your respects to the splendid statue of Cuchulainn in the post office in O'Connell Street, down a pint of Guinness while listening to stories in a pub, and then go to Tara.

Ireland's ancient sites go almost unmarked along the roads. There are no huge signs or parking areas, sparing visitors any theme park atmosphere. The ride along narrow lanes to Tara, the ancient ceremonial site of Ireland's High Kings, preserves a natural aura best experienced early or late in the day. This also helps avoid other visitors to the site, many of whom—missing the theme park feeling—can be heard to mutter, "There's nothing here." There is indeed nothing at Tara but a few sod-covered banks and ditches, a Neolithic mound, a stone, and a church converted into a visitor center. What is there depends upon the mythic imagination of the visitor, and the more you know of the legends of Tara the richer will be your experience. When the staff there found that we were well versed in Tara's meaning, they spent all their time making our visit more wonderful; we hope that happens for you. They let us see the Mound of the Hostages with its carved megaliths—the earliest structure to crown the hill. They discussed whether the phallic stone standing high at the center of Ráth na Ríg is the original *Lia Fáil*.

There is, of course, a political aspect to the life of modern Ireland. As of the time of writing, travel to Northern Ireland is safe. The "Agreement" signed by most of the concerned parties points the way ahead toward peace.

One site should not be missed in Northern Ireland. As you know, each Celtic province used to have a ceremonial center. In Ulster, the king presided over ceremonies at Emain Macha, now Navan Fort in Co. Armagh. In the days of the epic hero Cuchulainn, the Druid Cathbad was advisor to King Conchobor at Emain Macha and maintained a school for Druidic lore near there. Today you can see the remains of a great circular structure, almost half a football field in diameter, that was used for rituals in about 100 B.C.E. and then, a decade later, ritually set afire. The outer enclosure of this ceremonial area ranges for acres and verges on a lake where four exquisite trumpets with La Tène designs were found. The prehistoric and Celtic eras are flawlessly presented in the interpretive visitors' center, housed in a conical building of Celtic design.

Up north, in Co. Donegal near Derry, there stands the reconstructed stone fort Grianán Aileach, once the province of the Northern Uí Néill, the O'Neill dynasty that ruled Ireland. The Grianán was probably built in the second century C.E. The outside diameter of this circular fort is more than seventy-five feet, with walls fourteen feet thick at the base and sixteen feet high. Interior walls are terraced with steps. Whether it was a royal seat or a tribal center, the structure is a fine early example of architectural art.

The ceremonial center for the province of Connaught is astonishing in its four square miles of mounds, raths, and linear earthworks. Its name is "Cruachan of the Enchantments," found on maps as Rathcroghan near Tulsk in Co. Roscommon. Recent soil-resistivity surveys add more amazing information about this "royal house" of the legendary Queen Maeve. The greatest mound (eight yards high, ninety-six yards in diameter) was surrounded by a perimeter fence with a diameter of almost half a mile, twice the size of the enclosures at Tara or Emain Macha. It was the site of an annual fair and very large-scale pagan rituals.[3]

Cruachan also claims one of the mythic entrances to the Underworld. After much poking about and intuitive searching, we located the opening to the "Cave of The

Cats." Its entrance stone is barely visible beneath a hawthorn tree. The narrow, muddy opening reveals a classic slab-lined *souterrain* or *fogou*, and then goes into a rapidly descending natural cave. The place is not to be visited out of idle curiosity: it has many guardians, masquerading as cattle linebackers, disappearing farmers, and dogs, birds, and feints of the landscape leading one astray. When Nicholas took a picture of a nearby ground fissure, not only did a crow beat the air within inches of his head, but the photo shows steamy emanations pouring out from the earth. Within the cave itself the sense of Underworld power is even greater. He wasn't able to take pictures or go any distance into the depths that first time, though on a second visit one of his two cameras worked and he managed to reach the bottom of the cave. Legend says that "fearsome beasts issue from it to ravage the countryside."[4] We believe it!

While in Queen Maeve's territory, we recommend that you drive and hike to the top of Carrowkeel in Co. Sligo. On the summit there are over a dozen mounds containing stone-lined chambers built over 5,000 years ago. Of course, the mounds were constructed before the Celtic period, but sitting inside them will work some memory-magic on you. We also recommend visiting the mountain because of the view. From there you can see the huge stone-covered mound known as Maeve's Grave on Knocknarea (which you can also climb) to the northwest. You can see exquisite loughs and the plain of Moy Tura (*Magh Tuireadh*), scene of two mythic battles where the divine Tuatha Dé Danann defeated the indigenous Fir Bolg and the Fomorians with the magical help of The Morrigán. The dead Fomorians were more numerous than "the snowflakes of winter or the waves of the tempest," and the standing stones of the plain are said to mark their graves.

Not far away, treat yourself to visiting two large, rounded stones intricately carved with La Tène designs. We prefer this outstanding type of Celtic design to the later Christian-era knotwork made famous by the Book of Kells and modern graphic artists. The Turoe Stone is gorgeous in shape and design; it can be found by inquiring around Loughrea in Co. Galway. The Castlestrange Stone in Co. Roscommon, like the Turoe Stone, was carved in the last few centuries before Christ. Both have a circular iron grille around the base that we deduced was not a reconstruction of something Celtic but merely a sheep guard! Both stones have been moved to their present positions but must have quite a history. We like knowing that Celtic hands and minds made these superb, magnificent patterns over 2,000 years ago.

Deep in the *Gaeltacht*, the Irish-speaking region, off the west coast of Co. Clare lie the Aran Islands. There on Inishmore ("large island") was built one of Europe's most spectacular Iron Age forts, Dún Aenghus. Its semicircular design sits on the cliff edge, needing only landward defense which it had in abundance. The fort is surrounded by multiple walls and a very deep and dense *chevaux-de-frise* or forest of jumbled rocks; this prevents approach by cavalry and defies approach on foot without broken bones! Recent interpretation holds that Dún Aenghus was not only a fort but also a ceremonial site, perhaps for royal inaugurations and offerings to the sea. A quick toss off the enormous cliff could have dispatched ritual victims and enemies alike!

The Burren, in Co. Clare bordering Galway Bay, is a treasure chest for travelers. Limestone crevasses streak like gray tweed across the bare hills, hiding one of Europe's most unusual and varied collections of flora. Also hidden are holy wells, Celtic raths, and the ruins of a Brehon school of law at Cahermacnaughten. Tourists can enjoy Aillwee Cave and the striking Poulnabrone dolmen. The coastal town of Ballyvaughan boasts a tea shop where you can purchase an all-important map of the Burren while savoring the not-to-be-missed desserts—if you need such justification!

Just southwest of the Burren are the spectacular Cliffs of Moher, awash with crashing waves and the strains of Celtic music from vendors. A Brigit well nearby can replenish your supply of ritual water. As you continue south along the coast, you enter fairy territory: Co. Clare has retained palpable strands of Fairy Faith, mounds, lore, and superstitions. Of the 40,000 raths once making up Ireland's landscape, quite a few remain untilled and unoccupied because they are thought to be inhabited by fairies. On the road out of Lehinch, three raths lie in a row and are particularly appealing. One has a pilgrim's path wrapping around it, and under a wind-blown hawthorn we have found altar offerings of shells, feathers, and ribbons. Most residents will claim ignorance, but many of them stay on the safe side when it comes to the fairies.

Near Shannon Airport and Limerick in the southern part of Co. Clare are restored castles, post-Celtic but still interesting. Bunratty is a Disneyland type of place, to be avoided, but Knappogue Castle near Quin is more peaceful and captivating, complete with popular musical dinners with a medieval theme. Just miles away at Craggaunowen you will find a reconstructed *crannog*, a Bronze-Age lake dwelling complete with furniture and tools, as well as a ring fort with a *souterrain*. The museum houses a leather boat of the type that may have been used in the sixth century to sail to America.

Our final suggestion for understanding Ireland is to view the seasonal celebrations from the hills where the Celts gathered for the cross-quarter days and other purposes. Michael Dames, in his book *Mythic Ireland*, orients readers from the ancient center of Ireland, the Hill of Uisneach. *Uisce* means "water" in Irish and is the source of the

English word "whiskey," the water of life. Dames writes in an intuitive way that will serve you excellently when traveling the mythic routes, though his facts can't always be verified. Uisneach in Co. Westmeath was also called the Hill of Mide, the legendary fifth province of Ireland belonging to no king. It is on a rise which is not remarkable to look at except to sense it as the hub of a wheel on which the entire mystical island of Éire turned. On a sunny day we trooped across fields to get there and found a small crowd awaiting a BBC film crew. The Irish were rolling around on the hill with laughter as their cattle misled the English technicians, laden with equipment, on a circuitous route destined never to reach the hilltop. A different kind of cattle raid, indeed!

Bear in mind that very little if anything built by Celts remains on these hills, but some majestic trees are there, and the view is the same as our Celtic forebears saw. From Uisneach the hills and landmarks in many counties can been seen—the living goddess Ériu stretching across the land that is named for her. Myth tells us that the first Druidic fires were lit there, on Beltane. Michael Dames points out that if only two concentric rings of bonfires surrounded Uisneach, each fire in line of sight of the next from hilltop to hilltop, simultaneous fires on sacred occasions could have been lit all across Ireland, right to the seacoasts! Imagine what a fabulous web might have connected all the Celtic tribes to mark the turning of the seasons, and imagine yourself as one of the Druids in charge of lighting the fires.

One of the hills probably used for fire signals is Dún Aillinne in Co. Kildare. According to myths, this was the home of the great leader Fionn mac Cumhail of the Fianna and, according to history, it was the ritual center of Leinster kings. Today it is a vast circular enclosure, hinting at long use, possibly as the site of an annual fair for large tribal gatherings.

The royal centers in all four provinces no doubt held seasonal ceremonies for the cross-quarter days. In addition, it seems that occasional gatherings of people from all over Ireland took place in a few central locations of what is now Co. Meath. Two that are known are Telltown (*Tailltin*) and the Hill of Ward (see the rituals in chapter 7). Telltown was the site of a great August feast of Lughnasadh to start the harvest. Olympic-style games and marriages completed the festival. It is near Kells and very close to other major places of interest in Co. Meath, so go stand there and see what comes up for you. You will see the Telltown earthworks centered on Rath Dubh, "Black Fort." The Hill of Ward, near Athboy, was the burial place of the goddess Tlachtga and thus the scene of Samhain gatherings to welcome spirits and enter the darkest time of year. Tlachtga was the patron of Druids and the keeper of Life and

Death. Druids gathered on that hill at Samhain, extinguished every fire, and sent out brands from the rekindled fire to all parts of Ireland. Stand there, at Samhain if you can, and visualize the scene when most of the Druids of Éire worked magic in consort to bring back the light.

Celtic Britain

Strictly speaking, this heading should include Wales and the Welsh, who were the original Britons; but we shall look at Wales separately, and call what is now England after its Celtic name, Britain. It is likely that this name derives from one of the largest of Celtic tribes, the Brigantes: their goddess of the land is related to the pan-Celtic goddess Brigit. Later Anglo-Saxon occupiers of the land took up that name for the nation's current goddess of sovereignty, Britannia.

Although the country of England is outwardly Anglo-Saxon, the pattern laid down on the land by the Celts runs deep. The memory of symbols and images like Britannia in the national consciousness tend to push the British people toward their Celtic neighbors rather than toward the continent. This identification has become fraught with tremendous grievances, due to prejudicial English and London-centered attitudes that have dominated and cruelly exploited the Irish, Welsh, and Scots over the course of history. Many Britons lean to their Gaelic roots which, if not existing by blood, exist in romance, or simply by virtue of dwelling on the insular shores. So let us look at Britain, not from the perspective of London, but from its land and coastal fringes where the Celtic spirit still dwells.

The hillforts represent one of the most remarkable legacies of the Celts on the British landscape. As you travel you will see many a hilltop sculpted by banks and ditches into a mighty and memorable form. In his book, *Hillforts of the Iron Age in England and Wales*, J. Forde-Johnston gives an account of British hillforts that becomes tedious simply from the sheer volume of evidence. The figures are astonishing: a regional survey shows distribution of hillforts increasing in number toward the southwest of Britain and Wales: Cornwall 184, Devon 101, west Wales 145, Somerset 63, Wiltshire 49. The total number of hillforts for all counties is set at over 1,600. Those in the west tend to be small, with the larger ones bunched in Wessex and the Welsh border region. Most hillforts are single enclosures: about 300 are irregular in shape and enclose 5–30 acres, while about another 500 are round and tend to be less than 5 acres in size. About 40 are up to 50 acres, and these are multivallate (having many banks and ditches) with elaborate entrances, such as the ones at Maiden Castle (45 acres), Hambledon Hill, and Oldbury (50 acres).

The really big hillforts, over 50 acres in size, combine univallate and multivallate defenses and perhaps had a specialized function, e.g. Hamdon Hill (210 acres), Bindon (with an outer enclosure of 260 acres), and Hengistbury Head (200 acres). Most of the Celtic hillforts date back into the early Iron Age, circa 800 B.C.E., for the beginning of construction, but some earlier ones were begun in the years after 1200 B.C.E. on Neolithic foundations. The end of all construction and occupation is marked by the Roman invasion of Britain in 43 C.E. Defense was certainly a function of these hillforts, as well as quartering and protecting livestock from raiders—most forts are located close to upland pasture. Yet Maiden Castle, with its access to the coasts and control of trade routes, clearly served a different purpose than the numerous one-acre ring forts in west Wales. Therefore, hillfort functions and types form only a part of a complex pattern of needs and environmental concerns developing over many centuries.

The power of these hillforts becomes clear from a visit. With circular huts rising on a crested interior above a series of massive earthworks and surmounted by their revetments, the hillfort must have looked extremely impressive in the Iron Age landscape. They are statements of identity, power, wealth, and culture. If they were used for cattle, the mud at the entrances must have been awful; most likely they were the visible symbols of the power of the tribe. They must have had ritual, festive, and assembly functions over which the Druids presided, and only in the last resort did they become fortresses against an enemy.

We recommend visits to Maiden Castle near Dorchester, Old Sarum near Salisbury, Danebury near Andover, Cadbury Castle near Yeovil (the best claimaint for the title of legendary Camelot), Yarnbury Castle near Stonehenge, Uffington Castle near Wantage because it lies above the White Horse, Barbury Castle near Swindon, and Herefordshire Beacon near Great Malvern.

There is increasing evidence that the huge figures carved into the hillsides of Britain originated in the Celtic era. Three are worth visiting: the White Horse at Uffington, the Long Man of Wilmington near Lewes in West Sussex (mentioned in chapter 3), and the Cerne Abbas Giant north of Dorchester. The first has an aura of Celtic sanctity, and is connected with an early Celtic date—around 1000 B.C.E. The second, perhaps because of recutting, has lost some of its original quality, but still feels pre-Christian. The third is decidedly pagan, with its enormous phallus; but is more likely to have been carved by Roman soldiers stationed nearby than by the Celts.

For present-day Druids, sites close to nature have an especially compelling power. Nowhere is this more true than in Devon and Cornwall. You can enjoy spectacular coastlines, including the notable headland of Tintagel and nearby Rocky Valley. The moors of Exmoor, Dartmoor, and Bodmin possess streams, pools, rivers, woods, and rock formations where the spirit of the ancestors clearly dwells. A stop at Merrivale and Vixen Tor on West Dartmoor, for example, will take you past ancient stones from the late Neolithic and early Bronze Age eras. Go on down into the nearby valley of the River Walkham and experience the many ancient elemental presences awaiting you there.

In Cornwall, veneration for sacred springs is still in evidence, and it is worth tracking down some holy wells in the region to obtain a flavor of this. Take an offering of flowers or perhaps a prayer tie that will eventually disintegrate. Visit some very pleasantly located Iron Age settlements such as Carn Euny and Chysauster, complete with their underground passages or *souterrains*: that will give you a taste of Celtic stonework. Recent years have seen the revival of Celtic traditions in Cornwall. The language, once dead, is again being taught (if not yet commonly spoken), and folk customs are jealously preserved. It may even be possible for you to attend a Cornish Gorsedd (assembly), the first revival of which was held in the beautiful setting of the stone circle Boscawen-Un.

From the Middle Stone Age through the Celtic period and Arthurian era, peoples migrated and traded frequently between western Britain, the Isle of Man in the Irish Sea, and Ireland. The Irish god Manannán and the Welsh Manawydan seem to derive from the same ancient source, and may have given the Isle of Man its name. There is even tenuous legendary evidence of a Druid school on the island.

Other exhibitions of the Celtic tradition in Britain are worth seeking out. Butser Ancient Farm in Hampshire, for example, provides a longstanding recreation of the Celtic way of life, complete with roundhouse and agricultural projects. There is another reconstruction of a Celtic roundhouse near Meare outside Glastonbury in Somerset. The Iron Age lake villages there have provided some of the best artefacts of the Celtic era in Britain. Glastonbury too is certainly worth a look, though little evidence from the Celtic era has been found there on the ancient Isle of Avalon. It is likely that the island itself, with its unusual woods, hills, and springs, was a sanctuary and may even have been a Druid center.

Somerset and Wiltshire provide a good starting point for investigating megalithic sacred sites. These have nothing to do with the Druids, but Stonehenge has of course figured greatly in the history of the Druid revival. Nearby is Stanton Drew—"stones of the Druids"—named by antiquarians because of its fancied association with Druidry. Recent soil-resistivity surveys there have found concentric rings of free-standing oak columns within the main circle. Such timber monuments predate the Druids by two or even three thousand years, but there is evidence that the Druids also constructed circles of timber posts. The whims of the antiquarians are therefore fulfilled, but not in the way that they thought!

As far as museums go, the British Museum in London holds the best treasures. Unfortunately, Celtic history is given a low priority and far more space is devoted to foreign culture than to the native European one. However, it's worth going to the "BM" to view the massive gold torcs, the Battersea Shield, the Waterloo Helmet, La Tène mirrors, weapons, and other priceless objects that represent a fraction of what is in the vaults.

Wales

Wales is a treasury of Celtic material. Many places in the landscape evoke this past. Breiddin Hillfort in Powys is well worth a visit, as is Dinas Emrys, Gwynedd, with its interesting Arthurian/Merlin associations. A reconstructed Iron Age village stands at the Museum of Welsh Life at St. Fagans just outside Cardiff. In west Wales, Castell Henllys offers a more extensive reconstruction of Iron Age life, and Celtica at Machynlleth offers an excellent audio-visual exhibition.

You should investigate the Isle of Anglesey off the northwest coast of Wales and one of the major ports for Irish ferries, even if Anglesey only yields its secrets after some diligent seeking. The Roman army destroyed all the Druids of this island, and it is the burial site of the legendary Queen Branwen. We think we have discovered the place near Holyhead where the spinning castle of the icy Queen Arianrhod was sucked into a whirlpool in the Irish Sea.

In fact, many of the best artefacts of the Celtic era have been found in water. As the boundary between the worlds, water took on symbolic meaning in Celtic ritual. As a result, many lakes, pools, and rivers were the scene of ritual deposits: for example, at Llyn Cerrig Bach in Anglesey hundreds of metal objects were thrown into the waters of the lake between about 200 B.C.E. and 50 C.E. This makes the lake one of the most important sacred sites thus far found in Britain. These finds lend support to the claim made by the Romans that Anglesey was an important Druidic center. Most of the objects are on display at the National Museum of Wales in Cardiff.

The Welsh, perhaps moreso than any other Celtic nation, have proudly maintained their traditions. They speak the Brythonic branch of the Celtic language (as distinct from the Gaelic branch), and Welsh children are now bilingual. The Eisteddfod—a festive celebration of music and poetry—has been presided over by Druids for hundreds of years. The Eisteddfod encourages Welsh language, Welsh identity and nationalism, and maintains the standards of Welsh literature. The present form of the Eisteddfod can be traced back to 1176 C.E., and some say even as far as the sixth century. The celebration was founded to distinguish between the many itinerant poets of Wales, to license some and censure others. In this way, bardic standards could be maintained, and poets could receive a proper fee from their noble patrons. Subsequent Eisteddfodau were events under the patronage of the rich who welcomed associations with the past as a means of elevating their prestige and status.

The poets of the Middle Ages were very aware of their Druidic predecessors, and it was customary to attribute poems to early bards such as Taliesin. This custom continued into recent centuries, culminating with Iolo Morganwg (1747-1824) who claimed Druidic teachings were never lost in Wales. Iolo's work now seems far more patriarchal and Christian than it does Druidic. Many people were taken in by Iolo Morganwg, and his forgeries and claims are still repeated to this day. The Eisteddfod, known as the Welsh Gorsedd of the Bards, is a hugely enjoyable event and a visit is recommended. Unfortunately, its anachronistic pretensions—the archaic but muddled symbols, the stone circles, the long flowing costumes—have made it an easy target of criticism. The result is that the Welsh whose interest is in poetry and music try to distance themselves from the ritual aspects of the Eisteddfodau. Those who seek the spiritual dimension would have been better served if Iolo had not tried to pass off his work as ancient and authentic Druidry.[5]

Nevertheless, the more secular festivals such as the annual National Eisteddfod provide a tremendous focus for Welsh culture. There is minimal Druid content, but as an outdoor event emphasizing the spoken and sung word, the Druid connection is evident. An International Eisteddfod is held annually at Llangollen.

Related native culture can be found on the nearby Isle of Man. Similar to the Welsh events, annual festivals of music, song, and poetry called *Yn Chruinnaght* can be found on the island. The motorcycle road race that popularized the Isle of Man must be looked upon by Celtic spirit-charioteers with great favor!

Scotland

In the section on Wales above, we wrote of the deliberate and self-conscious preservation of Celtic culture perhaps being greater there than in any other Celtic nation. This would seem odd when in Scotland one can hear the pipes, see the dress, and meet the fiercely independent spirit that exemplifies the Celts as a people. Indeed, at this time, Scotland is aiming toward self-government and more sovereignty. It must be pointed out, however regrettably, that much of what is now Scottish culture arose out of military history under the English heel during the past few centuries. Wales focuses on bardic traditions for its Celtic identity, and on a spiritual tradition based upon Druidry, however remote it may be. In contrast, much of modern Scottish identity is founded on a history of militarism, first as enemies of the British and then as the soldiers of its empire. Most of the tartans, dress, and tunes of the pipebands, for example, arose out of regimental tradition and not from the Gaelic past.

The plaid with its distinctive tartans was indeed the dress of the ancient Highland clans. That said, they would probably not recognize most of today's tartans, which originate after 1746—the date of the battle of Culloden when the Scots were finally defeated by the English. It was at this time that regimental tartans were created. The kilt itself is a comparatively recent invention. The original plaid was a long piece of rough crofter's tweed that could be worn in a variety of ways. Under this wrapped woolen cloak, Scots usually wore trews—an ancient and peculiarly distinctive Celtic style of trousers. The original pipe music was known as *pibroch*, and was a lilting, timeless style of playing, passed from teacher to pupil. *Pibroch* is a far cry from the marches that predominate today. Finally, whereas in Wales and Ireland, the Celtic language is either flourishing or beginning to return, the Gaelic of Scotland is still on the decline and is likely to be heard only fleetingly in the Western Isles.

Despite all that, it is still possible for you to go to Scotland and experience much that is of interest to students of the Celts and Druidry. The whole history of the Pictish kingdom is fascinating. It is well worth tracking down the extraordinary Pictish Symbol Stones (many of which are now in museums) and royal seats of the kings on the east coast. But it is on the west coast, the Highlands and the islands that the most intriguing Celtic sites remain. Most of these are hugely complemented by the striking beauty of their settings. If you are interested in tracking the mythic past, then Scáthach's Castle on the Sleat peninsula of the Isle of Skye will prove a fascinating visit. Although the ruins of this small castle are medieval, the sea-girt location with the dramatic Cuillin Hills across the water make it easy to imagine the Celtic heroes arriving here from Ireland to receive their warrior training.

Less mythic but equally stimulating to the imagination are the many *brochs* scattered throughout western Scotland. Brochs are Iron Age Celtic structures, some of which remained in use into the first few centuries C.E. You can visit the Broch of Mousa in Shetland, or the more accessible brochs of Gleann Beag near Skye, and Dun Carloway on the Isle of Lewis. Brochs are tall, circular, double-walled stone structures that allowed cattle to enter below and people to live above. A central fire caused warm air to rise and heat the double walls, which also allowed moisture to evaporate. The brochs were effective, defensive drying kilns that allowed comfortable habitation in a wet climate. We may imagine the first "Lords of the Isles" gathering in the brochs and being entertained by their boat-carried bards and Druids.

The National Museum of Antiquities of Scotland in Edinburgh is well worth a visit, especially if you are interested in the Picts. If you have Scottish ancestry, a visit to the clan center after which your family is named or associated is always rewarding. Some centers have genealogical resources and we have found the staff at each center to be invariably helpful. If there is no clan center, make inquiries until you turn up a friendly person who can direct you to the pre-Culloden places of clan-significance. There are also genealogical centers in Edinburgh where research can be done, but go prepared: if you don't know what you are looking for, or do not have much information about your ancestors, the results are likely to be disappointing.

Brittany

If you have megalithomania, Brittany has tall monoliths, dolmens, and forests of standing stones around Carnac. If you are looking for remnants of Celtic civilization, however, Brittany doesn't offer much that is visible. La Roche-aux-Fées, "Rock of the Fairies," is a Stone Age structure with a Celtic name. You might come across *ceilidhs* (dancing evenings) called *Fest-Noz* or "evening entertainment." Until recently, the horned god and the cult of cattle were traditionally fêted on September 13 in Carnac under the protection of St. Cornely, the patron saint of domestic horned animals. Maya was there on that date a few years ago, only to find no celebration, no parade of cows to the church, and no one who would even admit knowledge of what she was talking about!

Still, we recommend visiting this peninsula located on the very northwest tip of the European continent. Since ancient times it has been called Armorica, "the land facing the sea" or the "armor" against the Atlantic Ocean. Armorica is the finale of the huge Eurasian land mass that stretches from the Pacific Ocean, the area that spawned the Indo-European ancestors of the Celts. Separated geographically, Brittany only became part of France politically in 1532, and remains separate from France in the minds of many inhabitants. The native language of western Brittany is Breton, one of the remaining Celtic languages. Today, a million or so people speak Breton, or at least are conversant in the tongue. They are descendants of the native people of Britain. Forced by invading Germanic tribes to move, by 400 C.E. many Britons had crossed the Channel to northwest France. There the Celtic-Gallo-Roman population fought and mixed with the newcomers, who eventually gained control. Within two hundred years, the Britons became the Bretons, Armorica became Petite Bretagne or "Little Britain," many of the customs and social structures changed, and the language became the Brythonic of the Cornish and Welsh.

For thousands of years a mutual love has existed between the people of Brittany and the land, sea, and sky of this region—mystical affinities which seem decidedly Druidic. In 1910 a French professor at the University of Rennes collected Breton death-myths about fairies which remind us of the Tuatha Dé Danann.

> *In truth, in the Breton mind, the dead are not dead; they live a mysterious life on the edge of real life . . . and as soon as night falls [and] the living . . . give themselves up to the temporary sleep of death, the so-called dead again become the inhabitants of their earth which they have never left. They resume their place at their former hearth, devote themselves to their old work, take an interest in the home, the fields, the boat; they behave, in a word, like the race of male and female fairies which once formed a more refined and delicate species of humanity in the midst of ordinary humanity.*[6]

Findings from the Iron Age can be seen in the Musée de Bretagne in Rennes. The museum in Nantes has material from a rich, late La Tène tomb. Outside of Brittany, the famous Druid-composed Coligny Calendar is kept in the Musée de la Civilisation Gallo-Romaine at Lyon. The town of Chartres may have been the site of a Druid college a thousand years before the mysterious and alchemy-inspired Gothic cathedral was built there: please go and see what you think, now that you know more about the history of the site. A full-size Romano-Celtic temple has been reconstructed at the site of an excavated shrine at Oisseau-le-Petit near Poitiers. In Maya's opinion, the finest French museum for all the ancient eras is the Musée des Antiquités Nationales in Saint

Germain-en-Laye, a short train ride from Paris. You will find everything from the best-loved Paleolithic figurines to key finds from Celtic graves and camps there.

Activities

Travel! Call your *taistil* (travel agency), peruse the flight schedules and your maps, pack what you need, and take off for the Celtic homelands!

Notes

1. Philip Shallcrass, "The Druid and the Land," poem, 1994.

2. Michael Dames, *Mythic Ireland*, pp. 16–17.

3. "The Balance of Power in Ancient Ireland," *Science*, vol. 278, 17 October 1997, p. 386.

4. Proinsias MacCana, *Celtic Mythology*, p. 126.

5. Dillwyn Miles, *The Secret of the Bards of the Isle of Britain*. This book rather tediously traces the history of the Eisteddfod in Wales, and reveals none of the secrets of the title.

6. W. Y. Evans-Wentz, *The Fairy-Faith in Celtic Countries*, p. 194.

PART III

ADVANCED TRAINING

Part III journeys deeper into Druid teachings. It opens the doorway to the creation of sacred space, the wisdom of the tree alphabet, the bardic schools, the cauldron of inspiration, and the Otherworlds.

Chapter 15

Upholding the Truth of Sovereignty

An Fhírinne in aghaidh an tSaoil!
The Truth facing the World!

This chapter examines the crucial Druid concepts of Truth and Sovereignty, their expression through poetry and the spoken word, and the relationship between the Self and the Goddess of the Land.

Druids uphold Truth as the supreme virtue. In the old Irish stories, telling an untruth made blemishes appear on perpetrators' skin and the building collapse where they stood. An untruth could remove them from their post, make their cause fail, and even lead to their death. Only speaking *fír flathemon*, which means the "Truth of Sovereignty," could rectify these things. When King Lugaid in the story below gives a false judgement, the courthouse begins to fall. When Cormac Mac Airt gives the right judgement the people cry out: "This is the Truth!" The truth magically restores the courthouse, and Cormac becomes sovereign. Note that the appearance of a king or queen in Celtic myth symbolizes our divine Self, our true and sovereign Self. This is important because acting from inner truth has magical power. In the story, Cormac became king not as a reward for virtue—as in honest George Washington becoming president—but as a magical transfer of power to a right and just source.

> *When the young Cormac was in fosterage at Tara the king, Lugaid Mac Con, gave judgement against a man whose sheep had grazed the woad in the garden of the queen. His judgement was that the sheep should be forfeit for theirtrespass. As he spoke the courthouse began to fall down the slope of the rath. "It is not so," said Cormac. "The wool from the sheep is enough*

205

*in compensation for the woad, for both will grow again." "This is the Truth!"
the people cried, "and the man who has given it is the son of a true king." At
once the courthouse ceased in its fall. For the year afterwards that Lugaid
remained king at Tara no grass came out of the ground, no leaves grew on the
trees, nor grain on the corn. The people of Ériu expelled Lugaid from the kingship and elected Cormac Mac Airt as king.*[1]

If you are searching for a guideline for living that is irrefutably Druidic, you have
found it here: *fír flathemon* is the most solid rule of conduct we have. Druids in particular and Celts in general consulted the truth of their eternal and sovereign Self in
order to conduct their lives in the way a wise and just king would rule the kingdom.

Previously we examined the Druid teaching on the immortality of the soul. We saw
how the eternal Self travels between this world and the Land of the Living in a circuit
of births transcending linear time. On this journey, the incarnate Self has free will,
responsibility for its actions, and wisdom accumulated from experience in every form
of existence. The wisdom learned from these experiences over many lifetimes determines destiny. The Self in its central position within the individual expresses this wisdom as the Truth of Sovereignty.

What does the Truth of Sovereignty mean, especially when truth is such a subjective
concept? To be sovereign means to be self-governing, independent, exercising personal
power from the overarching viewpoint of wisdom. What does this mean when it is
applied to truth? What does it mean for a Druid to say that Truth reigns supreme?

The injunction to maintain truth as sovereign is subtle. It does not supply a direct
moral code, like the Ten Commandments, or the Buddhist Eight Noble Truths. It is
ethical rather than moral—based on self-responsibility rather than authority. It is
open-ended like the Golden Rule ("Do unto others as you would have them do unto
you") or the Wiccan Rede ("Do what ye wilt an ye harm none"). Each of us must take
responsibility for acting in the best manner we can in every situation. There is no outside force imposing rules on us; no one else can tell you what your truth is, but you
know it just the same. You know when you act from the inner place where your divine
Self reigns. And you know when you go against it: in those cases, you feel your ethics
being trammeled, your conscience becoming numb, or the flow of your life being
pushed out of its channel.

The Truth of Sovereignty puts enormous responsibility on each of us. There is no
external God watching us. There is no church ordering our behavior. There is, however, the Goddess of the Land.

Lessons from Queen Maeve

When Queen Maeve of Connacht initiates war against Ulster in the *Táin Bó Cuailnge* (the Cattle Raid of Cooley), it is neither right nor wrong. It will harm many people, yet it is her truth to fight in order to obtain the bull she wants. It is in her nature and she is queen. It is also in the truth of Cuchulainn's nature to defend Ulster against Maeve and her forces. This conflict of interests is what makes a good epic. The bards sing the praises of both sides. When Maeve imposes her will over a Goddess of the Land, however, failure follows.

Prior to marching her army to Ulster, Maeve sought out a Druid for a prophecy regarding the outcome. She was unsatisfied with his reply, and on the return to camp she met a young woman:

> *. . . in her hand lay a shuttle of white bronze, and she wove something in the shape of a web with it.*
>
> *"What is your name, woman?" said Maeve.*
>
> *"I am Fedelm of the Sídhe of Connacht," she said.*
>
> *"Have you the power of seeing?"* (imbas forosna)
>
> *"I have that power," she said; "and, as you are Connacht's queen, it is yours to ask."*
>
> *"Then Fedelm the Prophetess," said Maeve, "tell me how it will be with our hosts."*
>
> *"I see crimson on them. I see red," said Fedelm.*
>
> *"That is not true," said Maeve; "for Conchobor and the men of Ulster are lying in the weakness brought upon them by the curse of Macha. Look again and tell me what you see."*
>
> *"I see crimson. I see red."*
>
> *"That is not true," said Maeve; "for we need not be afraid of anyone in Ulster when Cormac and Fergus are with us in their exile. Look again and tell me truly what you see."*[2]

Twice more, Maeve is unsuccessful in ordering Fedelm to change her prophecy of defeat and death. By denying the truth spoken by Fedelm, Maeve sets up the failure of her cattle raid. As a member of the *Sídhe* of Connacht, Fedelm represents the sovereignty of the land—she is of those who dwell within the earth. Maeve as Queen of Connacht pits herself against the source of her own sovereignty. On a more human level, Maeve puts her desires ahead of the truth. Her refusal to see that truth predetermines the outcome of the *Táin*. She loses her own Self-sovereignty and ignores the sovereignty of the land.

Maeve repeats this mistake when she insists that the Connacht champion Ferdiad fight against Cuchulainn, his friend, foster brother, and possible lover. She offers Ferdiad gifts, including marriage to her daughter Finnabair, as well as the "friendship of her thighs." Ferdiad refuses to fight Cuchulainn for these things, so Maeve tries to undermine his loyalty to Cuchulainn, violating the hero's Self-sovereignty. The king of Ulster, Conchobor, duplicates this violation on the other side. By placing his will over the truth, Conchobor drove the Ulster champion Fergus into exile, establishing a major cause of the *Táin*. In the end, Fergus vindicates himself against Conchobor, and Cuchulainn defeats Maeve.

The *Táin Bó Cuailnge* describes the ability and inability of the figures in this great Celtic epic to pursue their inner truth of sovereignty. We may not know in the vast scheme of the Universe whether an action is ultimately good or bad, but it is the goal of the Druid to know if it came from a place of truth.

For us today, the lessons contained here include recognizing the inner source of our sovereignty, being true to it, and not violating it in others. Think about the source of your being. Reflect on where you have come from: the life-stream, the planet, your family and ancestors—your origins, connections, and rootedness. Now think about this in others. Make sure your actions do not come between them and their source.

The *Eric*, the *Geis*, and the Law

In Celtic times, each person had an *eric* upon them. The *eric* was an honor-price, a value established by Brehon Law and a measure of self-honor. If an offense was made to a person's honor or a physical injury done to them, the *eric* set the compensation to be paid. Although the honor-price was a material assessment of worth and displayed the social hierarchy, it is possible that it also served to reinforce the sense of the eternal Self. The Roman geographer Pomponius Mela reported that the Celts did not view death as the end of life and even promised to repay debts in a future world.[3] Perhaps the Celts were confident that their *eric* was carried across lifetimes and would stand them in good stead when they returned.

A *geis* (plural *gessa*) was quite different from an *eric*, but it served a similar purpose. It was an obligation placed upon a person, often at birth, by a Druid. It could either prohibit something or magically determine the destiny of the soul. Cuchulainn's *gessa* forbade him to eat dog flesh or to refuse food offered at the roadside. His destiny was to be one of Ireland's greatest heroes. When he accepts dog meat on the road to a battle he meets his death. Breaking a *geis* could deeply harm an individual, as it symbolically broke one's honor. In our discussion here, it would violate one's sovereignty and truth, a fate worse than death. While apparently harmful, the *geis* in fact marked out a person as truly individual. It instructed Celts about individual uniqueness, putting them on notice to guard their honor and their eternal Self over the length of their lifetime.

These subtle inner ideas of truth and sovereignty were complemented by the necessary moral and ethical outward forms of Brehon Law. Druids established many schools where they taught the legal tradition. Some Irish Bardic Schools, complete with Druidic roots, survived until the sixteenth and possibly even the seventeenth century. The Irish Brehon Law, part of the largest body of early European literary material outside of Greek and Latin, taught a strict code of moral behavior and gave precise penalties against any wrongdoing. The Brehon Laws respected the rights of all, including women. The concept of primogeniture—the right of the eldest son to inherit the entire estate—that is central to patriarchal power was alien to Celtic thought. Brehon Laws recognized impulsive acts of love and accounted for their consequences. They required that the position of every official, including the king, be based on merit and election only.

Yes, the Celts had honor-prices and obligations, as well as the books of Brehon Law with their endless lists of compensations for this injury or that wrongdoing. Still, it was not the letter of the law that they applauded: it was *fír flathemon*, the Truth of Sovereignty.

The Sovereignty of the Self

The Celts loved material success and splendor, but they revered the powers of the eternal Self more. These powers can be visible in human actions, but are most pronounced in words emanating from the head: in fine speech, in the giving of law and justice, in poetry, song, and storytelling. For this reason the Celts revered the head; as we have already seen, the quintessential piece of Celtic jewelry, the torc, was worn around the neck to signify one's ability to draw upon the power of the Self and manifest it in this world by means of the head's power.

The Druids revered truth above all else. This was more than the worldly truth of law and morality: it was *an Fhírinne in aghaidh an tSaoil*, the "Truth Facing the World."[4] This Druid saying, usually translated as the "Truth against the world," does not mean there is a transcendent truth opposed to worldly truth. The truth and sovereignty of the eternal Self is not something over and above the world: it is something present in the world, meeting reality in a direct "I-Thou" relationship.

This immanent truth springs from the wisdom of the eternal Self. The ancient *Testament of Morann* quoted below is the source of the pivotal concept of *fír flathemon*. *The Dictionary of the Irish Language* translates this as "truth, or justice, of the ruler." *Fír* can mean either "true" or "just," or "truth, right, or justice," depending on sentence structure and usage. *Flathemon* is the genitive singular, "of the ruler." It derives from *flaitheas*, "sovereignty," which in old Irish is *flaithemnas*. We therefore find the full meaning of *fír flathemon* is best expressed when translated as the "Truth of Sovereignty."[5]

Praise and honor went to those who spoke the Truth of Sovereignty. They possessed self-knowledge. Their words sprang from the wisdom of many lifetimes lived in every human, animate, and inanimate form. As we shall see in the next section, *fír flathemon* also emanates from the lineage of ancestral and tribal spirits, as well as from the gods and goddesses of the land—especially the Goddess of Sovereignty. Early Celts who accessed these powers were respected lawgivers, bards, poets, and diviners on the path of Druidry. Such a person was called a *file* in Ireland, a Vate in Gaul, and an Ovate in Britain. The rightful sovereign or ruler was one who joined with the Goddess of the Land.

The Greek Pythagorean teachings "Know thyself" and "To thine own self be true" are in the direct tradition of Druid philosophy; some even allege that the sixth century B.C.E. Pythagoras learned his philosophy from visits he made to the Druids! The world-center lay beneath the feet of every Celt, just as the Druids appear to have placed the Self at the center of the world in their cosmology. The greatest honor came from pursuing self-knowledge and remaining true to the sovereignty of the eternal Self. Through knowing ourselves, without setting ourselves over or under others, without self-pride or self-condemnation, we come to know the truth of the sovereignty of Self.

To the Romans, the Self-sovereignty of the Celts came across as what appeared to be a touchy sense of honor. In today's terms this might range from machismo to what is called self-valuing and affirmation. Some of that might be desirable and some not. The question is, how can we best apply Self-sovereignty today? One answer is to acknowledge our personal strength, wisdom, and power flowing from within. By the time you are this far along in the path of Druidry you have probably spent years or decades developing your true Self. Think about the things you will stand up for, fight for, and even die for. What issues are you willing to speak out for in public? What cause do you support with your heart and head, and not just with your monetary donations? Acknowledge those things, act on them, and let them empower you.

The Goddess of the Land

In the Celtic worldview the eternal Self as the true sovereign of the human being finds its counterpart in the ruler as the true sovereign of the land. When the Self is the center within each individual, there is health and harmony within the body; when the rightful ruler is upon the royal seat in the cosmological center, then order and abundance prevail throughout the land. The Celtic tradition represents the sovereignty of the land as a female figure, a goddess, whom the ruler must marry so that order and abundance will prevail in the land. This goddess has several distinguishing features: she personifies beauty, and she gives her name to a cosmological center—usually a hill or mound. She bears a cauldron or chalice which is a neverending source of abundance and inspiration.

In the story known as the *Hidden House of Lugh*, the King, Conn of a Hundred Battles, touches a stone upon the Hill of Tara that cries out. Conn asks his Druids what this means and they tell him: "The name of the stone is the *Lia Fáil*, the Stone of Destiny. It was brought here by the Tuatha Dé Danann. It was placed here and it is here in Tara that it will stay forever. Whenever there is a gathering at Tara the stone will cry out when touched by the rightful king, and when there is no king for the stone to exult in there will be hardness upon the land." Here the earth itself recognizes and responds to the presence of the true ruler.

The remainder of the story expands on this theme. Lugh himself introduces sovereignty to Conn in the form of the Goddess of the Land. Conn comes to a finely built house near Tara that he has never seen before. The text continues:

> *In the house was a young woman. She had such fine looks and so steady and graceful a bearing he thought she must be a queen. She had on a green cloak that waved around her as she walked. It was fringed with silver and pinned by a marvelously wrought clasp of gold that reached across her breasts from shoulder to shoulder. Her brow was smooth and high, her eyes wide and bright, her cheeks flushed and playful, and her lips were as full and as red as the berries of the rowan tree. She had a band of gold on her head to stop her*

shining long hair from falling loose. From out of the sleeve-holes of her dress her long straight arms, white and as soft as the foam of a wave, held a silver vessel with rings of gold about it. It was full of fine red ale. She had a gold ladle and a gold cup to serve with. She said to the man on the seat of the host of the house: "Who am I to serve?"

"Serve Conn of the Hundred Battles," the man said, "for he will gain a hundred battles before he dies." And that is how Conn got his name and knew his destiny.

"This woman," the man of the house said, "is the Sovereignty of Ireland. She will be in this place forever. As for myself, I am Lugh of the Long Hand, son of Eithlinn."[6]

This woman is the embodiment of the land itself. It is she who appears in later Grail mythology bearing a cup from which she serves the company. We know from the Celtic myths that the king had to marry the Goddess of the Land, the embodiment of Sovereignty. In *Tochmarc Etáine*, for example, the people tell the new king Eochaid: "There can be no king in Ireland without a queen." Etain's identity as queen of sovereignty is clear because she is found beside a Fairy mound, has a cauldron beside her, and subsequently serves from a cup in a distinctive way. The mythic imagery is congruent: when the Self is sovereign within the body, when the king is wed to the ancestral spirit of the land, not only is all well within the individual, but all is well throughout the land.

You should be able to see the pattern now: the *internal* sovereignty of the Self is connected with the Goddess of the Land, the *external* spirit of sovereignty, through the tribe and the ancestors. The ancestors form part of the *tuath* or tribe. Their presence dwells within the land itself.

We note that this power of the ancestors finds its earliest expression in Europe in cave art, and subsequently in the megalithic structures of the late Neolithic age. These chambered mounds, dolmens, and portal tombs were ancient when the Celts arrived. How resourceful for the Celts to make the stone-age structures into abodes for their divine ancestors, the *Sídhe*! They were dwelling places of the "Mother of the Gods," the sovereign spirit of the ancestors made mythic in the form of the divine feminine. This Goddess of Sovereignty is the embodiment of the "other" in the I-Thou relationship between the Self and the community of tribe, ancestors, and the earth. The mounds may well have held that meaning and purpose for their original builders, who were as distant in time from the Celts as the Celts are from us.

What we can be sure of is that, for us today, the Goddess of the Land represents the principle of care for the Earth and all who live upon her. When we marry ourselves to her and treat her as a living, breathing being, then harmony prevails; we are all one body on one living earth. In the Druid vision of the land as an all-inclusive goddess, we find the right relationship between our eternal Self and all others.

Develop your own image of the Goddess of the Land. When the image comes clear you may want to draw or sculpt it, make a mask of the Goddess, or compose a song in her honor. Personify the landscape and your immediate surroundings in a manner that allows a direct, intimate, and personal relationship with her. Further ideas on how to do this are given as an Activity below.

The Truth of Sovereignty

The Book of Leinster records that the sixth or seventh century C.E. Brehon Druid, Morann mac Moín, wrote these instructions for a Pictish king:

> *It is through the truth of the ruler* (fír flathemon) *that plagues* [and] *great lightnings are kept from the people.*
>
> *It is through the truth of the ruler that he judges great tribes* [and] *great riches.*
>
> *It is through the truth of the ruler that he secures peace, tranquillity, joy, ease,* [and] *comfort.*
>
> *It is through the truth of the ruler that he dispatches battalions to the borders of hostile neighbors.*
>
> *It is through the truth of the ruler that every heir plants his house-post in his fair inheritance.*
>
> *It is through the truth of the ruler that abundances of great tree-fruit of the great wood are tasted.*
>
> *It is through the truth of the ruler that milk-yields of great cattle are maintained.*
>
> *It is through the truth of the ruler that there is abundance of every high, tall corn.*
>
> *It is through the truth of the ruler that abundances of fish swim in streams.*
>
> *It is through the truth of the ruler that fair children are well begotten.*[7]

If you hold to the truth of the eternal Self, you will speak the Truth of Sovereignty. If you discriminate between the subtleties of unique situations, use right judgement, and care for the well-being of all life, you will speak the Truth of Sovereignty. Not only will you thrive, but the promise is that your community will thrive, the fields will increase in abundance, the rivers, lakes, and oceans will become more productive, the harvests will never fail, and the wild and domesticated animals will always flourish.

The Celts recognized speakers of sovereign Truth through the inspired words that flowed from their lips. Poetry, above all other forms of creative expression, was the proof of their abilities. It was the magical power that brought all into unity. At some point in the seventh century C.E., an Irish *filí* or poet composed a poem on the source of wisdom and poetry. The text, preserved in a sixteenth-century manuscript and attributed to Amergin, was named the *Cauldron of Poesy* by modern scholars. An important extract runs as follows:

> *Where is the source of poetry in a person; in the body or in the soul?*
> *Some say it is in the soul, for the body is one with the soul.*
> *Others say it is in the body where the poetic arts are learned, passed through*
> *the bodies of our ancestors . . .*[8]

This text clearly states that the ability to speak from self-knowledge and sovereignty derives both from the Self or soul, and from the body through the lineage of the ancestors. It is time to tie these complementary sources together, through the images and symbols described in the previous chapters.

In chapter 11 we spoke of the World Tree harmonizing or being the sum of the qualities of the many kinds of trees. Every variety of tree sounds a particular note, captures a particular radiance, constellates an aspect of existence, and forms a letter in the Celtic alphabet. In total, these form the World Tree, the symbol of the whole of creation. It stands at the center of the world, and forms the world axis. Its roots lie in the sea or the lower realm, its trunk rises on the earth or middle realm, and its branches reach into the sky or heavenly realm. Trees grow upon, nurture, increase, express, and provide the land with form and spirit; they compose the symphony of all aspects of creation.

Now let us add the Goddess of the Land to this imagery, and the journey of the Self through the many worlds. The Self incarnates in one form and so comes to know that aspect of the whole. Over many lifetimes, in many different forms, the Self becomes wise in all the aspects of knowledge that are constellated by the trees. The wisdom of the eternal Self, awake in this world, allows the individual to speak from the source of sovereignty. The Self becomes the World Tree, capable of travelling freely between the many realms. It is the sovereign at the heart of creation, who knows and composes the poetic symphony of the trees.

In Welsh, the word for wood, *gwydd*, and the word for wisdom, *gwyddon*, are similar. Indo-European philosophers call wise utterance the Divine Word, the *logos* of creation. The Word is the creative power of the Universe. Through naming and language the Universe comes into being, and everything finds its place within it. When we speak from our place of sovereignty, our words are then truth. When we align the truth of our sovereign Self with that of the Goddess of the Land, then our words are one with the earth, the tribe, the divine powers, and ancestors.

> Walk with me in the world of appearances,
> Mossy velvet green covers the forest floor of memory
> But I know where wisdom waits.
> Ragged juts of truth like paths of limestone
> Make solid steps between the worlds.
> What lifts my foot up from the crevasse
> But the salmon of wisdom leaping from that world to this?
> I am bird, I drink the air.
> I am fish, I eat the sea.
> I am wisdom.[9]

When we accomplish the marriage between our eternal Self and the Goddess of the Land, then we speak the Truth of Sovereignty and the Universe thrives. This is the magical goal of Druidry.

Activities

Truth in Action. Begin to think of a vow you could make to yourself about pursuing, upholding, or speaking the truth. Think in terms of truth not only being spoken but being acted. Is there any place in your life where truth needs greater application?

Truth for Change. What act of truth could you undertake that would change something around you?

Truth with Magic. If you are a scientist you are probably already familiar with the pursuit of one kind of truth, but the Druidic Truth of Sovereignty suggests a magical principle. What could you do to bring more magic into your pursuit of truth?

Your *Geis*. We no longer have Druids to set a *geis* upon us at birth, and maybe that's just as well: we can do it for ourselves. You know yourself well enough to glimpse the destiny of your soul. In the spirit of the Bardic Tradition, write a poem that expresses your obligation to your Truth, to your eternal Self.

Self-sovereignty. If you spoke from the sovereignty of your eternal Self, what is the first thing you would say or do that might benefit others?

The Goddess of the Land. Picture the land where you live and envision it as a Goddess. If you don't want to do this where you live, go to a special place. Meet her in the trees, the creatures, the rivers, rocks and hills of the land. Communicate with her. Invest her with sovereign powers. Create a ceremony in which you ally yourself with her. Dance to her and write poems and songs about her. Extend the Goddess to include the community in which you live. What can you do for your community that expresses her? What does she wish to do for the community? Imagine her touch guiding the actions of the leaders of your community, your people, your land.

The Truth of Sovereignty. Write a short piece that explains the chain of causality between the Self, poetry, the Truth of Sovereignty, the Goddess of Sovereignty, and the increase of health and peace in the land. Let us know what you come up with!

Notes

1. Standish Hayes O'Grady, 1892, p.96f.

2. *Táin Bó Cuailnge*, based on the recension of Thomas Kinsella (1969), Lucy Faraday (1904), and Lady Gregory (1902). For *imbas forosna*, see chapter 19.

3. *De Situ Orbis* III, written in the mid-first century C.E.

4. Thought to appear for the first time in a ninth-century Irish gloss on a geographical tract by Diciul (eighth century). *Aghaidh*, usually translated as "against," also means "face" as in the original meaning of "confront," i.e., face-to-face. The motto in Welsh of the Gorsedd of Bards of the Isle of Britain: *Y Gwir yn erbyn y byd*, usually translated as "Truth against the world," is also ambiguous. *Yn erbyn* "against" or "by" (the latter in the sense of "by noon"), contains the verb *erbyn* meaning "meet" or "receive." This yields: "Truth meeting the world." (Thanks to Meredith Robbins for help in the translation from the Welsh.)

5. We thank Searles O'Dubhain, e-mail correspondence 11/23/97, for his help in the translation.

6. From *Baile in Scail*, the "Prophecy of the Shadow," otherwise known as "The Hidden House of Lugh," recension based on Lady Gregory (1904).

7. *Audacht Morainn*, the "Testament of Morann," translation by Fergus Kelly, p. 7.

8. Recension from Erynn Darkstar, *The Cauldron of Poesy*; P. L. Henry, "The Cauldron of Poesy," *Studia Celtica* 14/15, pp. 114–128; Liam Breatnach, "The Cauldron of Poesy," *Ériu* 32, pp. 45–93.

9. From "I Know Where Wisdom Waits," a poem by Maya Magee Sutton.

Chapter 16

LEARNING THE DRUID PATH FROM NATURE

They came upon an ancient and sacred grove, never violated during long ages. Its interlacing branches enclosed a cool central space into which the sun never shone, but where an abundance of water spouted from dark springs.[1]

This chapter explores the relationship between Druidry and nature. The parameters for creating sacred space are given. Methods by which Druids learn from trees and animals are revealed. Finally, the chapter offers a view of feminine and masculine energies around the cycle of the year.

Sacred Space: The Druid *Nemeton*

Observers from the Roman Empire wrote that Druids sought remote areas of the forest for their ceremonies. This is true, but it could give us a false picture; the fact is that Druids also owed their chieftain or king some service. For this, the Druids presided over public ceremonies and official religious duties at sanctuaries built to hold large assemblies. The Celtic ritual sites provide us with a common pattern that we can use to create sacred space today. In Ireland the major examples are the raths of Tara, Emain Macha, Rath Cruachan, and Dún Ailinne; in Gallic France, the shrines of Roquepertuse, Entremont, and Gournay.

These ritual spaces consist of an approach, a single gateway through an outer boundary, and a central altar, shrine, or ritual platform. The boundary is usually a fosse—a ditch and bank—either circular or square, often surmounted by a palisade. If there was more than one temple at a site, the outer boundary enclosed a vast area, such as we find at Tara. Scholars once thought that the Irish raths or ring-mounds all featured a covered space in the center. That was because postholes were found upon them, usually arranged in a circle or concentric circles. It is now thought that most of the temples were open to the sky, and the postholes supported free-standing wooden columns. Emain Macha, the "royal seat" of Ulster, offers the single possible exception to this pattern: an enormous circular roofed structure apparently dominated the summit of the hill for a brief period of time.

Is it possible that the Druids also used the megalithic sacred sites, already thousands of years old when the Celts arrived? Many Neolithic sites such as Stonehenge and Stanton Drew featured concentric rings of freestanding wooden columns in addition to their stone circles. The similarity between these and the concentric rings of postholes found at Celtic sites is very great and suggests a continuity of ancient practice, notwithstanding almost 3,000 years separating the columned sites of the Neolithic and the Celtic periods. The intervening years, however, were more than enough time for the wooden posts to completely disintegrate, leaving only the stones. In addition to this, archaeological excavation has never found convincing evidence of ritual use of megalithic sites in the Celtic era. There is therefore no proof that the Druids imitated or used the Stone Age sites. Indeed, Irish legends say that the stone circles, passage mounds, and dolmens were avoided as being the abode of Fairy Folk—the *Sídhe*.

The spiritual was integrated into the daily life of the Celts. The most common setting for spiritual practice by ordinary people was the home and its surroundings, while the Druids most commonly frequented areas around trees and water. Druids may have presided at the great raths and shrines, performing rituals for their chiefs and kings, but their inclination was toward nature. They worshipped in woods and caves, among rock formations, beside rivers, lakes, and springs. These were places where spirits moved or were felt to dwell. The central shrine on the hill top of Emain Macha, mentioned above, has revealed only one short, intense period of ritual use, compared to evidence of huge and continuous votive activity at the pools and lakes in the surrounding valleys.

Classical writers such as Lucan (quoted at the opening of this chapter) noted that a clearing in the forest or a prominent tree or group of trees was the Druid temple of choice. The Irish name for such a holy place is *nemed*, but it is the Gallic name, *nemeton*, that is used most frequently by authors and Druids. The term usually refers to a sacred grove, and there are even instances of a deity named *Nemetona*, who was, therefore, a goddess of the grove. What do we know about the approach, boundary, and center of the *nemeton*, and how can one be created?

The Approach

The nemeton requires an approach that creates a conscious awareness in you, befitting the sacred purpose. For Druids, an excellent approach is through a variety of natural settings. As the approach leads to and focuses upon the center, so the time spent upon the approach allows your mind to focus upon its destination. An approach over a broad and open plain creates a very different state of mind to one along a narrow path through an enclosing forest. Think about your intention for visiting the nemeton and on this basis decide which approach is most appropriate.

The approach is very important and should never be neglected. Please do not be tempted to drive as close as you can get to a sacred site. Always include the preparation time that a walk provides. The element of mystery is essential, and it helps if the sanctuary reveals itself slowly or is invisible until the last moment. The hilltop raths of Ireland concealed activity on the center platform as much as their dramatic setting revealed their location. The bottoms of the ditches remain invisible until the visitor is upon them, and the elevation plus any palisades or wooden posts would have veiled the summit of the central mound. If you are thinking of creating a *nemeton*, perhaps by planting a grove, then make an approach that only allows glimpses of the center.

The Outer Gate and Boundary

The Greek word for the boundary of a sacred place, *temenos*, is related to the word nemeton. It contains the dual meaning of "temple" and of "time." The *temenos* defines a distinct dimension in time and sacred space, quite separate from the world about it. It is the "template" for the dimension of the sacred.

An ideal boundary for the Druid *nemeton* is a circle of trees, shrubs, and other plants. There is evidence that some of the original Druid groves were enhanced by additional planting. If you do this, the position and kinds of trees are obviously very important. If you are interested in a more formal boundary, then you could create a fosse, with the bank on the outside. Or you might create a ring of tall, straight posts, knowing that this was not only a Celtic practice but one that reaches back 6,000 years into the Neolithic period.

Many references can be found in history and legend to the *temenos* and how it was defined. The Romans demarcated an enclosure for a new city with a furrow, the *sulcus primigenius*, ploughed by a team of oxen. The god Terminus then dwelt in the stones set up to mark the boundary and cursed any who violated it. The prime ceremonial center of ancient Ulster was the hill of Emain Macha. Legend says that its massive ditch and bank boundary was modeled on the brooch from the cloak of the goddess of war and of the horse, Macha. The New Jerusalem of St. John has a geometrically precise *temenos*, as does Plato's ideal city of Magnesia, capital of Atlantis. These transcendent cities are intended to be the perfect terrestrial expression of the divine heavenly order. In all these traditions, the boundary is sacred: it must not be violated and should be reinforced annually by ceremonies such as a perambulation or a "beating of the bounds."

Unless you are attracted to the more formal displays of public ritual, we recommend that the Druid *temenos* or boundary of the grove be naturally formed. Do not create an ideal, mental, geometric, or abstract expression of the divine order in your mind and then impose it on the earth. The Druid *temenos* represents an order that is intrinsic to the earth. It may possess a geometry, but this emerges from out of the geometry of the natural world. The *temenos*, and thus the *nemeton*, is protected and maintained by the residing *genius loci*, the spirit of place. It is not necessary for Druids to cast a circle or resanctify the temple each time they wish to use the *nemeton*. The sacred power is always present and emerges from within the natural world.

The gateway into the *nemeton* should be well defined: it is here that the ordinary outside world is left behind. An experience of compression and then expansion into the inner space supports and enhances the feeling of transition between the worlds. Create an entrance in the shape of an archway of branches or a rough-hewn timber portal, or perhaps two simple wooden columns let into the earth.

The Inner Gate and Center

Within the *temenos* there is a central area. Within the central area there may be an altar, shrines, or other features. There may be an inner gateway that defines transition to the center and these special features. The inner gateway may consist of a simple façade decorated with objects that define its sanctity and purpose. It may consist of steps to a platform or a covered area. The stone façades of the Gallic shrines at Roquepertuse and Entremont include sculptures of animals and niches for human skulls. You need not go this far in creating your façade! You may want to set an emblem on your inner gate that is symbolic of the earth, sky, and sea triad, or the three drops of inspiration, or another symbol of your Druidic practice.

The center itself may contain any number of things: it may be entirely empty, or have an altar, a fire pit, a stone, a tree, or whatever is particular to the place. There may be further internal entrances and altars.

Many places sacred to the ancient Druids were beside springs, pools, or rivers. The point of transition to the center was clearly made by the water's edge. In these cases, it is doubtful that people entered the water, but they certainly deposited votive offerings in it. The water beside many *nemeton*s has revealed prodigious amounts of expensive and finely wrought objects ranging from weapons, trumpets, and chariot mountings to jewelry. For example, at Llyn Cerrig Bach, a small lake on the Isle of Anglesey, hundreds of valuable metal objects were cast into the water between the second century B.C.E. and the first century C.E. The objects included swords, shields, cauldrons, chains, and chariot mountings, and were ritually broken or bent before being offered to the waters. There are a few well-known examples of humans beings who were ritually drowned in bogs, perhaps as superlative offerings!

If an obvious natural feature such as a spring, an earth fissure, or a cleft in a tree is lacking for your *nemeton*, you can create a central focus. The center is the place of access to and from the inner worlds. You can represent this with an appropriate artificial opening: a cup, a cauldron, a drum, a holed stone, a candle, or any temporary feature. As the center is the place of the World Tree, you may like a gnomon, a single majestic tree, or some other more permanent symbol of the *axis mundi* to stand there. Ancient *nemeton*s reveal that either oak, ash, or yew were trees of choice, and the properties of these trees show that the spirit of each grove was very distinct.

This opening in the center of the grove, or the axis of the World Tree, is the route for you to connect to sun, moon, stars, the Fairy Realm, the spirits of place, the Land of the Living, and the eternal Self in its dance with the infinite. You might bring symbols of these powers and realms to the grove, according to your ritual intention. Remember that Druids do not confuse the symbol with the thing itself, and portents from the natural world are always preferred. The Druids went "back to nature." They rejected the elaborate geometrical and astronomical complexity of the megalithic sites, and allowed their groves to be filled with the powers of the natural world.

Learning from the Trees

We will make only some general remarks about learning from the trees here, because chapter 17 and the section entitled "The World Tree" in chapter 11 cover this topic in more depth. For Druids, trees constellate the world order. They are symbols that represent the many aspects of existence. The Ash, for example, harmonizes with the Summer Solstice, noon, the south, the Spear of Victory, the Burning Spear, the god Lugh, and the eagle. It is useful to imagine the trees arranged around a circle or in a mandala, whose many stations and divisions represent the aspects of life. While this provides a means of conceiving and ordering the world, it is important not to see this as a fixed and rigid system. It is more of a poetic than a utilitarian device.

The Druids worked with the trees they found in their locality. The significance of the trees would have varied greatly according to other plants, latitude, altitude, climate, soil, and drainage. It is likely that there never was a "tree system" as outlined in the following chapter. The significance of the trees varied too much from location to location for such neat and universal distinctions to be made. There were as many different meanings associated with a particular kind of tree as there were local spirits of place. Travelling Druids were attuned to the power of place, and trees are enormously influential in effecting this "tuning in." Druids arriving at a new location could sense the configuration of natural and spiritual energies by reading the pattern of the trees!

Trees were revered by the Celts: some were forbidden to be touched, others were put to practical use. The properties of each variety of tree were well known and understood by all. Life and livelihood depended upon the trees. Shelter, food, hedging, defenses, utensils, furniture, shields, handles, boats, bridges, doors, wheels, chariots; fires for light, warmth, cooking, and smelting; dyes, tanning, medicine, and glue: all were derived from trees. Every Celt knew which wood burned long, hot, quick, or slow; which rotted and which resisted water; the time when trees blossomed, leafed, and fruited. Indeed, these events determined the cycle of the year and the activities of the people. The trees described the calendar, defined time, and contributed to the spirit of each place. If a locality and its people were thriving, Druids could expect to read this from the pattern of the trees.

Nicholas had a vivid dream a short time ago in which he was flying over Ireland. The thing he remembers most from the dream was the pattern of the trees. The feeling was of Ireland a long time ago, and the trees dominated the landscape. Hilltops, rivers, and open fields appeared through a dense green mantle of foliage. The trees themselves swirled across the landscape in curvilinear forms. When he drew in for a closer look, the patterns made by the trees were like the designs on the carved stones or metalwork of the La Tène era. He finally arrived over the Hill of Uisneach, considered the geomantic center of Ireland. On the summit of the hill, a great ash tree formed a node around which all the curving patterns revolved and from which they originated. Nicholas awoke with the thought that if the brooch of the goddess Macha was the pattern for the sacred center of Emain Macha, then the trees of Ireland formed the pattern on her robe in its entirety.

The index of the health of the land, and thus of its inhabitants, can be measured by the health of the trees. Trees create the context in which all living systems thrive and increase; the modern concepts of woodland gardening and permaculture support this. Permaculture demonstrates that more food can be grown in an area rich with trees. Reforestation and tree planting of our rural and urban environment is possibly the only model for a sustainable future for humans on the planet, given our current rate of growth. In his book, *How to Make a Forest Garden*, Patrick Whitefield writes:

> *Growing new trees is one way to take carbon dioxide out of the atmosphere . . . They also enable the soil to store more water and release it more slowly, preventing both flood and drought. They protect soil from wind and water erosion. They give shelter from wind and sun . . . and help to moderate excessive heat and cold. They form part of the habitat of wild plants and animals. In their falling leaves they recycle soil nutrients and provide organic soil matter. They prevent excessive buildup of salts in the topsoil of irrigated land . . . . If we have a choice between feeding ourselves by growing trees or by another means, it is likely we will do more good to the Earth by choosing trees.[2]*

Modern Druids would do well to learn from the trees. These wonderful life forms provide us with symbolic, magical, poetic, aesthetic, and spiritual resources. They also bestow down-to-earth, practical benefits upon all life. The British-based Order of Bards, Ovates and Druids has a tree planting program, and all Druid groups worthy of the name promote ecological awareness.

Learning from the Animals

Through contact with animals, humans find the ability to be in the present moment. In the world of animals, we feel who we are. Animals are at one with the needs and the drives of their bodies. When an animal is tired, it sleeps; when it is hungry, it eats. Going after what it needs, an animal is what it feels—unlike humans, whose feelings are often controlled by conditioning. Animals also teach us how to use our inherent power to transform our situation. An animal can move in its entirety from one state of being to another. From this we learn to let go and move away from outmoded mental states and beliefs.

Because they are at one with their life force, animals provide humans with reality. Their way of being is made up of actual, tangible things and somatic experiences. Animals provide us with a means of knowing that certain experiences really do exist and are not merely ideas. There is no separation between the animal and the world, just as there is, in fact, no separation between us and the world. Only the development of abstract and written vocabularies in which things appear to have an independent existence makes it seem that we are separate from the world. In many cosmologies, "God" created the world, therefore establishing the divine as separate from the world. Animal language, in contrast, is of the body-mind, with all its subtle nuances of perception.

Druids, with access to the Otherworldly powers of animal forms, were the representatives of a particular animal and claimed it as their totem. A totem is the divine and perfect form of an animal's or a plant's manifestation of universal energy. Over time, this manifestation is joined by collective human projection. Totem powers exist in the nonlinear time of the Fairy Realm, and are always accessible; they can take over and produce Otherworldly visions and even physical markings (*stromata*) for those willing to dive into their nature. Such shamanic phenomena depend upon lively discourse with the Otherworlds. This was one of the original tasks of the Druids, who kept alive the vision and knowledge of a magical realm, one interpenetrating and transforming the human one.

When a power animal is evoked by a Druid, there is no separation between the human, the animal, the divine, the spiritual, and the experiential worlds. Druids fly and see with the vision of a bird; they walk with the grace, caution, and agility of the deer; they move with the strength of the bear; they swim with the fluidity of the fish; they hear with the sensibility of the otter. They work with the tenacity of the insect. From these acute and direct perceptual experiences, Druids learn how to be and how to behave in a world where there is no division between spirit and matter. Druids walk in the community of all life. As animals possess sensibilities that far exceed those of humans, the animal powers become the supreme mediators of transformation—and the facilitators of journeying between the worlds. They, and their totem, can be used to facilitate rites of passage—transitions from one stage of life to the next. This is a far cry from the usual position ascribed to animals in Western society that sees them as being somewhere lower down an evolutionary scale, without feeling, and thus deserving of domination and exploitation.

Druids see animals as powers that introduce transformational qualities. The power of the boar can be summoned when seeking the strength to move through a long process. The quality of the eagle can help us see the way to an outcome and achieve it swiftly. The rabbit can get through low undergrowth, a fawn can remain still and concealed, a butterfly can go from one life stage to another. This transformational ability works within our psyches directly. The eagle does not symbolize farsightedness: rather, it is farsightedness that is present in our experience of the eagle.

The language of our perceptions already divorces us from direct meaning, so we must be careful not to lose the direct experience provided by animals. Fortunately, they are always with us. Simply exposing ourselves to them restores meaning within our minds. Animals live in the universal realm of all being and, despite our depredations, they will never give up their independence and sovereignty. Not only do they speak to us with their real presence, but they can speak to us in dreams, in inner journeys, and in encounters with the archetypal realm: so, for example, the archetypal power that is "fox" will unfold its message within us as we choose to journey toward it. Like Manannán—the messenger between the worlds—the trickster fox will turn things around in our minds and then dart away like quicksilver whenever we get too close. If we are fortunate enough to become fox, to move totally within its energy, then we will know a cunning, humorous transformational power is working within our lives. If we can dream of the fox, the horse, the boar, or the deer, then no barrier exists between the human and the animal, its dream presence and real presence.

Imagine that we appear in the dreams of animals! This would make the cycle of reciprocation complete, allowing everything to be in its place. Animal dreams probably involve a reality as tangible as their lives. It is likely that the world was shaped and created by animal ancestors just as it was by human ones. Thus we share with the animals the origin of life. Indeed, paleontology reveals that they far precede us as the source of life on earth. And so, in the deepest recesses of our biological arising, animal dreamings shape our cognitive and limbic modes. Their archetypal powers structure the collective unconscious of our lives.

Just because we may attribute such processes to the "instinctive" part of the brain does not mean animals are in any way inferior or lacking in intelligence. Indeed, the instinctual modes of animals generate sublime experiences which give immediacy and power to human forms of expression. The dance of birds (the beating of their wings), the coordination of horses (the rhythm of their gait), the articulation of reptiles (the symmetry of their motion), the sinuousness of water creatures (their undulating pace): all these translate into the highest forms of art.

Think of it: in all the Arts we draw upon the powers of animals. The brilliant colors of painting, the swirls and meanders in decoration, the fluid patterns in dance, and the changing rhythms of music draw upon the powers that we share with the animals. Letters themselves are said to be derived from the observation of a flock of cranes "which make letters as they fly."[2] The contribution that animals make to the wealth of our inner lives is immeasurable. And, as the outer and the inner reflect each other, so it is that in the legends of all people it is the animals who first existed and gave shape to the world.[3]

The Wheel of the Year

The spiritual traditions of the world are rich in examples of ritual cycles that correspond with the seasons of the year. Some of these follow the advent and demise of particular deities. Dying and rising gods are especially frequent, while the goddess appears to pass without dying from one form to another between the seasons. Persephone, for example, dwells in this world in the summer months and in the lower world in winter. A God of the Waning Year or "Holly King" presides over the winter; he then dies or gives way to a God of the Waxing Year or "Oak King," who presides over the summer. You may find much of value in connecting with these archetypal images as they turn around the yearly cycle. They give meaning to the calendar because they help us accept the inevitability of change, especially the cycle of birth, youth, maturity, old age, and death.

The changing goddess and the dying-rising god represent a ritual cycle of the year rooted in nature and in the Celtic worldview, but there is no evidence that it is particularly Druidic. We use this cyclical pattern in our Druid ceremonies and find that it becomes more relevant and appropriate as time goes by. We hope it is useful to you as well. Feel free to adapt it to suit your locality, climate, and needs. For convenience we will describe the annual movements by separating the cycle of the goddess or the feminine from that of the god or the masculine—but bear in mind that these attributes together turn this wheel of the year.

The goddess in this wheel does not die and resurrect herself: rather, she is continually transforming. Like women in procreation, she is always giving birth to new forms of herself. She has many aspects. In midwinter she is deep, dark, down among the roots of the trees, preparing within her womb the conception of the year to come. At Imbolc, in early spring, she is the maiden, celebrating the return of the light. At Beltane, in early summer, she is the lusty young woman. In summer she is the rich, mature mother, giving birth to the fruits of the year, at the same time as she conceives within her womb the dark season of the year to come. At Lughnasadh, in the fall, she is the harvest mother, spreading out her cornucopia of abundance while advising us to lay in stores for the winter. At Samhain, in early winter, she is the crone, laying out the ghost of the year past, preparing to go deep within for wisdom.

Meanwhile, the god in this wheel has two aspects, dark and light, one giving way to the other. Like men in the act of procreation, the god is always rising and falling. Rather than giving birth to new forms of himself, he must die to be reborn. In mid-winter, the Dark God is at his greatest power. He is the god of fertility for the seeds of the earth. He meets with the goddess in her winter aspects and together they conceive the tiny spark that will become the Light God. At Imbolc, the Dark God rules but is waning; the Light God is growing and the festival is one of quickening, of helping his child spirit along. At Beltane the Light God flourishes, and we hear no more of the Dark God. The Light God increases in strength and energy up to the Summer Solstice. There at the peak, the god and goddess of summer conceive the season of the year to come, harvest and the darkness of winter. At Lughnasadh, the Light God celebrates his harvest festival as the Dark God begins to grow. At Samhain, the Light God dies, and the Dark God comes into his own. He continues to grow up to midwinter, putting deep roots down into the earth, using frost and wind to break things down for the year to come.[4]

Activities

Your Own *Nemeton*. Design and create your own *nemeton* or Druid Grove. As far as possible, do not work this out ahead of time in your mind, but allow the spirit of the place to emerge and tell you how to do it. The approach and *temenos* need careful preparation. How can you make these? Do you want the boundary to be solid, formal, informal, permeable, seasonal, flexible? Will it be a circle or a square? What kind of entranceway do you want? What will be in the center?

Tree Planting. Think carefully about the role of trees in your nemeton, and in your garden as a whole. Read a book that explains permaculture and woodland/forest gardening and see if your garden would benefit from some tree-planting. Is planting a grove of every different kind of tree with Druidic associations really such a good idea? Tune into your locality and let it tell you what kinds of trees are most beneficial. Get involved with a neighborhood tree planting project if it exists. If it does not, find out what it would take to create one.

Knowledge of Place. Druids had an intense connection with the earth, trees, and animals found in the exact place where they lived and taught. Obtain books on geomancy (Nicholas has written *The Isle of Avalon*, Llewellyn, 1996, and *Sedona, Sacred Earth*, Brotherhood of Life, 1989, both based on this art/science). Study your neighborhood and geographic area for clues from the earth as to power spots, geopathic areas, and areas conducive to good living. Every place from small to large has its own teaching to offer.

Herbal Lore. Grow flowers. Seek them out in the wild. Learn enough about herbs to start a small herb garden. Grow some medicinal and some culinary herbs and learn to use them well! We recommend *A Druid's Herbal* by Ellen Evert Hopman.

Nature. Find a special spot in nature near where you live—a place in the woods, by water, near boulders, in the mountains, on the beach, in a meadow. Go there at least once a week. Take no pen or paper. Have no agenda. Sit, lie, dream, sleep, walk, and listen to the messages from nature. Watch the animals. Enter their world. Read *Talking With Nature* by Michael Roads to learn how to hear direct speaking from nature. Learn how to be told by your favorite animals what is happening to them or what ails them.

A Power Animal. Perform any activity you now perform from the place of an animal. Walk as a deer would walk in the forest. Run as a horse would run. See through the eyes of a fish, a bird. Ask an animal to be your totem for a year or so, and work with its innate abilities and powers. What role did certain animals have for your ancestors, and can you feel this coming through you today?

The Wheel of the Year. Draw up your own Wheel of the Year. Base it upon your observation of nature where you live, and place upon it those things that you would like to celebrate. Invite any archetypal images such as gods, goddesses, animals, or symbols that will help you do this.

Notes

1. Lucan, *Pharsalia* III.400–404.

2. Robert Graves (1952), p. 459.

3. Patrick Whitefield, *How to Make a Forest Garden*, Permanent Publications, 1988, p. 2.

4. These ideas are developed by Nicholas in chapter 6 of *His Story*.

5. These themes, especially that of the dark half of the year, are thoroughly explored in *The Dark God*, Nicholas R. Mann.

Chapter 17

USING THE CELTIC TREE ALPHABET

Bran told the people the story of his journey to the Land of Women. He told them to inscribe it on yew in sixty quatrains of Ogham. Then he bade them farewell, and his wanderings from that time on are unknown.[1]

This chapter describes the Celtic Tree Alphabet and the difficulties surrounding its modern interpretation. The valuable idea of gaining wisdom from the trees is discussed, and the chapter concludes with a description of the letters and qualities associated with each tree.

Early Irish texts record several alphabets, over which there is considerable and heated controversy. Issues include the age and authenticity of the alphabets, whether they are Druidic, and how the trees that name each letter correlate to the calendar of the year. The quotation above, for example, might not be reporting a typical edict given by a Celtic chief. It might be what later transcribers of the story of Bran thought was an appropriate instruction for him to give. A total of sixty, four-line verses in Ogham would be painstaking, hard to organize, and would use up a lot of yew! The concept of the Celtic tree alphabet itself is more important than any controversy. The symbolic wealth of the system should become obvious to readers, who can then make up their own minds about the issues.

Before we begin, allow us to make two observations. First, the letters of our modern alphabet have little meaning in themselves, whereas each letter of the Celtic tree alphabet hosts a constellation of meanings that, when added to each other, articulate a complete cosmology. Second, the ancient Celtic calendar did not divide time into linear uniform units, such as seconds, minutes, and hours measured by clocks. It was based upon direct observation of the natural cycles of the day, the season, the sun, the stars, and the moon. For the Celts, time was not a constant. It had a cyclical, relative, and emergent periodicity, which might fluctuate for different individuals.

The Wisdom of the Trees

One day inside Nicholas' favorite wood on Dartmoor in southwestern Britain, he fell into a conversation with a spirit he calls Awen. The record of this conversation, as he remembers it, will serve as an introduction to the trees.

"The first systematic attempt to work out the stations of the trees around the calendar was made by Robert Graves in *The White Goddess*," I began. "But while being very thought-provoking, Graves did some injustice to the Celtic tree alphabet by rearranging the form in which it is handed down. He created an order that was based more upon his classical scholarship than upon Celtic research."

"Well, that is an interesting theory," said Awen, settling herself upon a log. "Tell me more about it."

"I'm not going to say there is a right and a wrong form of the tree alphabet. In this situation we are walking in the forest of our deep memories and in the multidimensional realm of symbols. Our unconsciousness may arrange the symbols in quite different ways for each individual, and each way is valid. So I'm not going to contradict anyone here."

"Good," said Awen.

"In *The White Goddess*, Graves ordered the trees around a thirteen-station lunar calendar. He made the data fit his theory by using only thirteen instead of twenty trees. As the name of his book implies, he was pursuing the goddess at the time, and this is how she appeared to him. It's a legitimate interpretation, but uniquely his own. He didn't know about the Celtic Sun Goddesses which might have changed his whole system, and he ignored the Green Man. The problem is that almost everyone has unquestioningly followed his interpretation ever since."

"There must be some original sources for the tree alphabet from which Graves got his evidence," said Awen. "What do they say?"

"One of the sources is the seventeenth-century Irish writer Roderick O'Flaherty," I replied. "He said his work *Ogygia* was in the 'true bardic tradition,' but he never substantiated his claim."

"Well, where did O'Flaherty get it from?"

"The first authentic Celtic alphabet that we know of is called Ogham, which means 'language.' It is said to be named after its creator, the god Ogma Sun Face. Ogham is a basic signaling system that uses the fingers rather than a true alphabet. It was used for secret conversations between those who possessed the cipher. Although it is nice to imagine it being used in this way by Druids, we have no evidence of this. What we do have shows Ogham being used for inscriptions of a more prosaic nature: territory markers, cenotaphs, and so on. This sort of inscription was carved on stone from the fourth and fifth century onwards, when Druidry was in decline, and ceased to be used by the ninth century at the latest.

"However, the early Irish myths often say that when heroes and heroines die, an inscription of their name is carved on a stone in Ogham and set up over their mound or grave. When Fionn mac Cumhail buries the three Sea Champions, for example, he orders their names to be written on stones 'in branching Ogham.' The trouble is that we have no inscriptions that can be dated to the time when the Fenian Cycle is thought to have developed—the last few centuries B.C.E. to the first few centuries C.E. But it is exactly the kind of action that the tenth- to fourteenth-century Christian scribes would have ascribed to Fionn because it gave the right archaic touch.

"The most invaluable main sources on Ogham are the *Book of Leinster* and the *Book of Ballymote*. The first was compiled in the twelfth century C.E. and the second in the fourteenth from earlier sources. They refer to many Ogham systems. Although apparently a writing system employing notches on a stick or stone, it can also use the fingers of the hand. Ogham is made up of four sets of five signs. Each begins with a single 'finger,' then two, and so on up to five, including the thumb. Here, I'll draw it out." I found some paper and a pencil and drew out the sequence. As I drew I commented that the inscribers used an edge of the stone as the vertical dividing line, with notches made to both sides of it. Awen made up some Ogham signs of her own with twigs.

"Returning to O'Flaherty," I said, "he gives two forms of a 'tree alphabet' that correspond very closely to the Ogham system. They are made up of four sets of five letters. Each one of the twenty letters represents a tree, and that is the essence we're looking for. Now, whether these alphabets arose out of an original Ogham script used by the Celts we just don't know. O'Flaherty could have made it up. The first alphabet is called the *Boibel-Loth*. It goes like this." I drew out the following:

B L F N S H D T Cc(Q) M G Ng Y R A O U E I

"Fascinating," said Awen, her forehead furrowed in concentration as she wove together a garland of ivy. "What's the second alphabet?"

"The second form O'Flaherty gives—and no one really knows which is older—is more well known. Its opening sequence is BLN, and it is called the *Beth-Luis-Nion* alphabet after the birch, the rowan, and the ash. O'Flaherty shows it having thirteen consonants. This is the form Graves developed to get his lunar tree calendar of thirteen months. He shoves the vowels to one side, which is very odd. It goes like this."

B L N F S H D T C M G P R

"The P here is the equivalent of Ng, *ngetal*, or the reed. However, the *Book of Ballymote* gives the alphabet its full twenty letters including vowels, and this is the form most commonly followed." I drew it, with Awen following me closely.

B L N F S H D T C Q M G Ng Z R A O U E I

"The opening sequence is also given as BLFNS, as in the *Boibel-Loth*. But this doesn't make sense when Irish tradition has always called this alphabet the *Beth-Luis-Nion*. It's hard to get at it from other sources as they have been muddled by later transcribers."[1]

"Is there any other early source which is unaltered and could decide the matter?" Awen was now chewing on a piece of birch.

"What might clinch the original form is an inscription on stone from Callen in County Clare," I replied. "It's thought to date to as early as 300 C.E. and goes like this."

B L N T S B D T C Q M G Ng Z R

"If we replace the recurring consonants T and B by F and H, then this would seem to substantiate the BLN form."

"All right," said Awen, adjusting herself to examine the substantiated fifteen-consonant, five-vowel form, "show me how they correspond to the Ogham script."

Between them they drew out the following sequence, and added the names of the trees for good measure.

B	Beth	Birch	⊢
L	Luis	Rowan	⊨
N	Nion	Ash	⊨
F	Fearn	Alder	⊨
S	Saille	Willow	⊨
H	Huath	Hawthorn	⊣
D	Duir	Oak	⊣
T	Tinne	Holly	⊣
C	Coll	Hazel	⊣
Q	Quert	Apple	⊣
M	Muin	Bramble	⅄
G	Gort	Ivy	⅄
Ng	Ngetal	Reed	⅄
Z	Straiph	Blackthorn	⅄
R	Ruis	Elder	⅄
A	Ailm	Scots Pine	+
O	Ohn	Gorse	‡
U	Ura	Heather	‡
E	Eado	Poplar	‡
I	Idho	Yew	‡

"The central line or stave of Ogham is the dividing line," I explained. "So a piece of script might look like this."

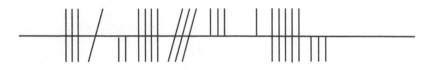

"You can see how it had its limitations. Originally it was probably like a sign language for silent communication. The *Book of Ballymote* mentions using the nose or a shin for the baseline, but just about anything could have been used. Robert Graves suggests that the letters are located on the digits and tips of the fingers and the thumb. To send a message, all you have to do is point to those places using the finger of the other hand. This would be effective, but very laborious, and there is no ancient evidence for it."

"Gosh, there is a lot of speculation, isn't there?" said Awen. She picked up a drawing I had made that correlated the calendar with the tree alphabet. "How on earth did you arrive at this?"

"I was afraid you would ask me that," I said. "It's a question that vexes all Celtic researchers. I think it's up to each person to place the stations of the trees around the calendar. Some may prefer Graves' thirteen stations, but I like the twenty, as it feels like a complete sequence. The ash tree at Summer Solstice, the hawthorn in May, the ivy and reed at Winter Solstice, the apple at Imbolc, all feel right to me. Some trees may appear at several points in the cycle. The oak for example, may reappear briefly at Summer Solstice and the yew at Winter Solstice. It would be a mistake to force an exact fit. And besides, what about climatic differences? The Druids of Gaul probably had a very different set of meanings associated with each tree than did the Druids of Scotland."

"Yes," said Awen, "Druidry works with the natural world around it. The tree alphabet is more of a model for understanding the interconnectedness of all things rather than a mental system to be imposed upon nature. In each place things are different."

"Well," I said, a little defensively, "you can see how neatly this system divides the year into four parts by having five letters lie between each cross-quarter day."

They drew out a large circle, marked in the calendar, and began placing trees, the Ogham, and the *Beth-Luis-Nion* alphabet around it. Awen wondered if the gods, goddesses, and the animals could also be placed in their appropriate stations, and soon the whole circle came alive. Awen put Brigit and her animals at Imbolc, and the solar and horse goddesses at Summer Solstice. Nicholas placed Bel and his animals at Beltane, and Cernunnos and his creatures at Winter Solstice (see illustration of calendar on page 241).

"Look!" said Awen, scratching some leaf debris out of her long shining hair. "The calendar goes one way around the circle and the tree alphabet goes the other. How do you explain that?"

"I don't know," I said. "There is absolutely no evidence that the Celts ever represented it like this. We're just making this up. But there isn't any rule that says script has to run in one direction either. Ogham script is read upward on a stone."

"Has anyone fully worked out this form?" asked Awen, as she firmly placed bees as the animal associated with Ura, heather, at the Autumn Equinox.

"In their publication *Inner Keltia*, edited by Kaledon Naddair, a group in Scotland has developed this particular form," I said. "But I still think all those interested should work out their own form, using the trees of their geographic location, before loading their minds with Naddair's, Graves', or anyone else's information."

"Are you saying this is no use to anyone but ourselves?" said Awen rather testily.

"Well, the order of the trees and their Oghams is good," I said. "But the rest is just a heuristic device."

"I see," mused Awen. "It's just too rigid a model. We need something more four-dimensional. After all, these are symbols and powers that emerge from the deepest level of the natural world. Letters arranged in a two-dimensional model are mere reflections of the living world. No wonder the Druids avoided writing!" Awen studied the drawing for a few more minutes, endeavoring to place the sprigs of wisdom in a pattern that approximated the order of her inner world.

"For me," I said, "what makes it alive is the cycle of the year. When I keep in mind how everything is changing, that the natural world is going through its cycles, and how central the trees are to all that, then I don't lose sight of the dynamic of the tree alphabet."

Awen stretched. "You scholars are all the same. You try and explain everything. 'Heuristic' indeed . . . just live it! Dance to it! Words are only alive when they come streaming out from the heart, the center of life."

The Celtic Tree Alphabet and Calendar

The chart on page 241 shows the 20-letter *Beth-Luis-Nion* Alphabet, associated trees and Ogham, and the stations of some gods, goddesses, and power animals around the cycle of the Celtic cross-quarter day festivals. This calendar is subjective and intended as a model for local redevelopment and interpretation. For cross-references to other systems of Ogham, see notes.[3]

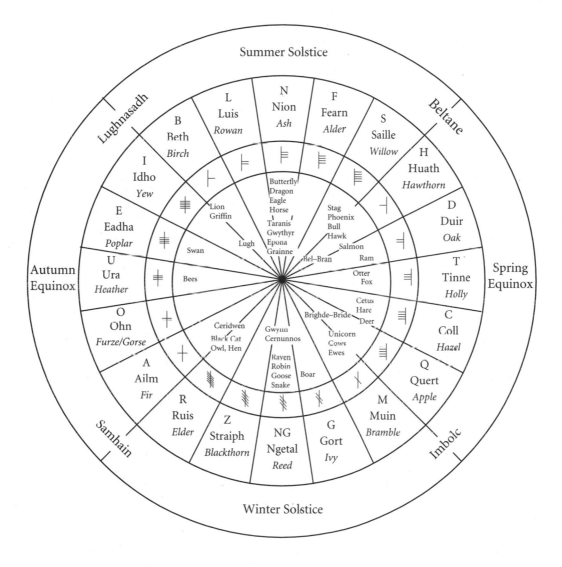

The Celtic Trees

B   **Beth**   **BIRCH**   **Air**

The birch is the first tree to quickly cover new ground, especially in light sandy soils on exposed uplands. It is associated with new beginnings. It has white silvery bark and casts little shade. It does not root deeply and is easily blown down. The wood decays quickly and burns fast and hot. Use birch twigs for cleansing sacred space, and the wood for making protective charms.

L   **Luis**   **ROWAN**   **Air**

The rowan, quickbeam, or mountain ash is a graceful tree that grows fast, but not tall, on high ground. It has clusters of white blossoms in spring that bear red berries in autumn. It is one of the three "witch trees," and has divinatory and protective properties. It burns long and hot, and fires of rowan were used for summoning the spirits of the dead.

N   **Nion**   **ASH**   **Air**

Sister to the rowan, the ash is a tall and slender tree that presides over the Summer Solstice. The last tree to leaf in spring, it is among the first to shed its leaves and winged seeds in autumn. It has the best wood for burning, and for making the handles of axes and the shafts for spears. The Nordic World Tree, Yggdrasil, is an ash. Three of the five sacred trees of Ireland, at Tortu, Dathi, and Uisneach, were ash. It is also associated with Lugh, the sky god, who in Welsh myth rests in its branches in the form of an eagle.

F   **Fearn**   **ALDER**   **Water**

The alder loves to grow with its roots in water. It prefers to cluster in groups of small trees. In winter it adds a red hue to the riverside scene. Red dye can be extracted from its bark. The wood burns poorly and decays fast when dry, but resists rot as long as it remains wet. It is the tree of Bran the Blessed, who at one point wades across a sea, lies down across a river, and has hurdles laid upon him to form a bridge with his body.

S   **Saille**   **WILLOW**   **Water**

The willow grows beside water, often reaching large and beautiful dimensions, especially in its "weeping" form. It is associated with the moon and witches. The words "willow," "wicker," "wicket," "witch," and "wicked" all derive from a common origin. It is a preferred wood for divination and developing psychic powers. Use its osiers for basketry and for the binding of broomsticks.

H   **Huath**   **HAWTHORN**   **Fire**

Hawthorn graces the landscape in spring with its dense blossom in shades from white to deep pink. The blossoms crown the May Queen, but marriages are put off till June because Beltane energy is not lasting. Its blossoms and aphrodisiac effect contrast with its long thorns. The tree does not grow tall, but can become old, and is covered in autumn with rich red berries that birds love. A hawthorn beside a spring is auspicious, and a desirable place for prayer ties or other messages.

D   **Duir**   **OAK**   **Fire**

The Celtic name of the oak, *duir*, is connected with Druidry and with an opening or door. It is a tree of enormous strength; you cannot drive a nail into it once its heartwood is aged. Oak forest was the climax of ecological succession in Europe after the Ice Age, giving rise to a host of dependent plant and animal species. The Latin name for the acorn is *glans*, and the tree's masculine beauty is often noted. The wood burns long and was preferred for ritual fires at Summer Solstice. Oaks grow very old, with roots as great as the branches. The Dagda's oak club of myth could create at one end and destroy at the other.

T   **Tinne**   **HOLLY**   **Fire**

The holly, with its evergreen leaves and fiery red berries, gladdens hearts in the late winter months. The traditional holly club or axe tests strength and courage. The holly makes excellent charcoal, and its Celtic name, *tinne*, is the origin of our word for tinder. It is associated with Cu Roi mac Daire and the Green Knight.

C   **Coll**   **HAZEL**   **Fire**

The hazel grows abundantly in the woods of Europe, especially in conjunction with oak. It was regularly coppiced to provide timber of useful sizes for building, fences, and temporary structures. It is one of the preferred woods for divination. It is very easy to carve Ogham upon it. In Irish myth, the coll (cob) nuts of the nine hazels of poetry and inspiration feed the five salmon of wisdom. It is associated with the heron.

Q   **Quert**   **APPLE**   **Air**

The apple tree's sweet blossoms and fruit provide the food for the dwellers in the Otherworlds. It is the tree of paradise, of superhuman nourishment, and its orchards often mark the entrances to the Otherworlds, as found in the orchards of the Isle of Avalon.

M   **Muin**   **BRAMBLE**   **Earth**

One of several non-trees in the tree alphabet, the bramble or "vine" of fruitfulness can intoxicate. Its thorns impede progress and its briars entangle the seeker. Bramble surrounds the place where lost parts of the soul sleep and the soul must emerge through its thorny passageways. At Imbolc it promises wholeness in the coming year.

G   **Gort**   **IVY**   **Earth**

Ivy thrives in winter by clinging to its dormant hosts, the trees. It does not destroy its host unless the tree is old and dying. The ivy nourishes deer through bleak times, and its berries feed hungry birds. Ivy thrives in shadows and facilitates transformation. It is willing to go into dark places and bring down the old to ensure rebirth. Associated with Hern or Cernunnos.

Ng   **Ngetal**   **REED**   **Water**

Though not a tree, the reed is assured of its place in the alphabet because it once covered vast areas of marshy land in Europe. It still provides material for floors and roofs, as well as a rich habitat for wildlife. The reed has the power to draw deep from its roots in cold waters and a dormant landscape. It can flex and bend. A broken reed is the symbol of all that is untrustworthy, for it shows something that is rigid and inflexible. Reed is associated with the salmon of wisdom and most waterfowl.

Z	Straiph	BLACKTHORN	Earth

At first sight the blackthorn appears to have adverse qualities. It forms dark, spreading, impenetrable thickets protected by stiff thorns. But it also provides ample shelter and food for wildlife, and its early blossoms are sweet and a pleasure to behold. When befriended and trained, it makes the best of all hedgerows.

R	Ruis	ELDER	Earth

The elder is a sacred tree. The Celts so strongly forbade anyone from cutting it that violation may have meant execution. It is the prime Fairy Tree and should never be disturbed. The elder does not reach much stature with its pithy and flimsy wood but it has the power to regenerate perpetually. A cutting that is thrust into the ground will quickly grow. The pungent clusters of flowers and dark purple berries make rich food for animals and excellent wine for humans.

A	Ailm	SCOTCHPINE	Air

The Scotch pine or fir presides over the dark half of the year and marks the entranceway to dark places within. It is the favored tree to bring indoors and decorate at Winter Solstice. It burns with a quick, bright flame. You can often find it in high and auspicious places.

O	Ohn	GORSE	Fire

The gorse, the furze, and the broom thrive in poor soil, and all have yellow blossoms. At times their blooms are so bright they appear to set hillsides aflame. But the fiery, spiny nature of the gorse is difficult and unhelpful. When trained, however, the gorse makes a strong ally.

U	Ura	HEATHER	Earth

Like the gorse, the heather shrub covers poor, high ground, and when in bloom the plant transforms hillsides into purple carpets. Unlike gorse, its nature is soft and yielding. Its sweet-smelling flowers are longlasting and have many varieties of color. Heather is lucky, especially in matters of love.

| E | Eado | POPLAR | Water |

The poplar or aspen is the trembling tree, the whispering tree, "the tree that talks." It is a keeper of language, a magical tree, but it can keep no secrets. It is kin to grain in that it grows quickly, can be cut down and will grow back, making it a tree representative of death and rebirth.

| I | Idho | YEW | Water |

The yew is the tree of death and transformation. The wood is used for making coffins, weapons such as longbows and dagger handles, and for carving inscriptions. When wounded, the tree continuously bleeds red sap. Its leaf-needles and red berries are toxic to humans. Nothing can grow in its dense shade. The yew attains great age, huge girth, and is capable of eternal renewal, as shoots grow out from its hollow core or from the ground about.

Activities

Your Sacred Tree. Study about sacred trees, then select one as your teacher for a year. Learn about its medicinal properties, uses, and symbolism. Visit a tree of that species frequently, sitting beneath it, sleeping by it, climbing it, smelling it, listening to it, talking to it, singing to it, studying it during all four seasons. Ask to be its friend. Ask to get in touch with its spirit and learn from it.

The Celtic Tree Calendar. Draw out a Celtic Tree Calendar on a large piece of paper. Mark in the seasons and the major festivals. Mark in the *Beth-Luis-Nion* alphabet and the corresponding Ogham script. Place this on a convenient wall and mark, in the appropriate place, any animals, trees, plants, or deities that come to you over the cycle of the year. Rather than copy anything from the Tree Calendar in this book, make sure everything on your calendar is placed meaningfully for you.

What you are creating with this exercise is your own set of correspondences. This will be for your own magical use. The trees of your own locality are likely to be more appropriate for you to work with than ones from northern Europe: remember that the symbols and meanings that have collected around some European tree may collect around a different tree in your locality. In New Mexico it is fascinating to work out the correspondences of the trees, which are mainly cottonwood, willow, juniper, piñon, ponderosa pine, cedar, sycamore, aspen, and several varieties of oak.

Oghams. Make a set of Oghams by carving them on the wood of the trees to which the letters correspond, or on local wood. We recommend sticks about the size of a finger, on which you can engrave or burn the Oghams. These are known as *Coelbren(i)* or "omen sticks" (if this technique is beyond you, try drawing the Oghams on tongue depressors or craft sticks). Make a ritual of thanks and dedication beside any tree when you obtain wood from it. Someday you can undertake a pilgrimage to Celtic lands to find wood from the trees the Celts themselves used. What a challenge to inscribe Ogham on a reed! Keep your set protected in a bag and use them for divination, as described in chapter 4.

Notes

1. From the *Voyage of Bran*.

2. Steve Blamires, *Celtic Tree Mysteries*, gives an excellent discussion of these issues (and opts for the BLF form).

3. Further reading: (1) Kaledon Naddair, "Some Secrets from the Shamanistic Calendar." (2) Edred Thorsson, *The Book of Ogham: The Celtic Tree Oracle*. (3) For references to other Ogham systems see: "The Ogham Tract," *Auraicept na nÉces,* George Calder (1917), quoted in Caitlín and John Matthews' *Encyclopaedia*.

Chapter 18

Training the Druid Mind

I have been a drop in a shower,
A sword in a hand,
A shield in battle,
A string in a harp.
Nine years in enchantment,
In water, in foam,
I have absorbed fire,
I have been a tree in a covert,
There is nothing of which I have not been a part.[1]

This chapter examines the training of Druids, and gives poems and other original source materials that provide a view into the Druid mind. It also describes surviving bardic traditions and shows readers how to cultivate these skills in themselves.

The Bardic Schools

From what historical sources tell us of the Druids, great emphasis was placed upon training the mind. Apart from techniques of inspiration, which we shall examine in the next chapter, Druids underwent many years of mental development. This emphasized memorizing the vast body of oral tradition and learning to compose many highly complicated poetic measures, structures, and canons. We may imagine Druids at an early age beginning to learn a huge number of poems. Taliesin mentions that 300 poems was a minimum, and says he knew 900 more. To this was added stories, history, genealogies, and laws. At the royal courts, Druids were expected to repeat from memory huge amounts of information. They were the walking libraries of the Celts!

Eloquence in reciting from memory was highly praised. Druids not only had to provide information, but deliver it in authoritative, well-turned lines, often to the accompaniment of music. A great deal of this was effected with the help of formulae and by repeating familiar tales. When it came to poetry, however, Druids could praise, critique, satirize, elevate, and surprise listeners with extemporaneous compositions, provided they followed a recognized poetic form.

The Celts revered the head, and it is likely this reverence originated in the power they attributed to the spoken word. The words of a Druid, it is said, could stop battles, separate warriors, lift spirits, bring laughter, and, conversely, bring sorrow, tears, scorn, curses, or sleep upon the assembly. This power of the word lay in the head. Here was the window to the wisdom of the soul. Druid training focused on developing verbal skills and abilities that expressed the soul.

The Bardic Schools of Ireland, Scotland, and Wales maintained this tradition. Daniel Corkery, in his book *The Hidden Ireland*, writes: "In common with almost every other institution of the Gael, the Bardic School as a factor in the life of the nation, has not been so much misunderstood or underestimated as entirely omitted by those [Englishmen] who . . . write Irish history."[2] The literary tradition in Ireland was central to Irish intellectual and spiritual life, and this tradition had its origins in the Druidic practices throughout Celtic civilization.

The Bardic Schools functioned as lay universities alongside the monastic institutions. They were free of the confines of the Church, and thus differed markedly from the institutions of learning throughout the rest of Europe. Notice the reason for this: the Bardic Schools maintained a lively and fertile exchange with the people by studying—not the history, laws, and literature of Greece and Rome—but the history, laws, and literature of Ireland in the Irish language. Can you feel yourself in training to be a poet, through the following remarkable description of an Irish Bardic School? It is from the *Memoirs of the Marquis of Clanricarde*, published in 1722.

> *The poetical Seminary or School . . . was open only to such as were descended of Poets and reputed within their Tribes . . . The Qualifications first requir'd were reading well, writing the Mother-tongue, and a strong Memory. It was . . . necessary that the place should be in the solitary Recess of a Garden . . . far out of the reach of any Noise . . . The Structure was a snug, low Hut, and beds . . . each within a small Apartment without much Furniture of any kind . . . No windows to let in the Day . . . The Students upon thorough Examination*

being first divided into Classes . . . The Professors . . . gave a Subject suitable to the Capacity of each class, determining the number of Rhimes, and clearing what was to be chiefly observed therein as to Syllables, Quatrains, Concord, Correspondence, Termination and Union, each of which were restrain'd by peculiar Rules. The said Subject . . . having been given over Night, they work'd it apart . . . the whole next day in the Dark, till at a certain Hour in the Night . . . they committed it to writing . . . afterwards . . . in a large Room, where the Masters waited, each Scholar gave in his Performance. Every Saturday and on the Eves of Festival Days they broke up and dispers'd themselves among the Gentlemen and rich Farmers of the Country, by whom they were very well entertain'd and much made of . . . The People . . . sent in by turns every Week . . . all manner of Provision towards the Subsistence of the Academy, so that the chief Poet . . . got very well by it. It was six or seven Years before a Mastery or the last Degree was conferred . . . .

As every Professor, or chief Poet, depended upon some Prince or great Lord, that had endowed his Tribe, he was under strict ties to him and his Family, as to record in good Metre his Marriages, Births, Deaths, Acquisitions made in war and Peace, Exploits, and other remarkable things . . . He was likewise bound to offer an Elegy on the Decease of the said Lord, his consort, or any of their children, and a Marriage Song when there should be an Occasion. But as to any Epick or Heroick Verse to be made for any other Lord or Stranger, it was requir'd that at least a Paroemion or Metre therein, should be upon the Patron . . . The last Part . . . was perform'd with a great deal of Ceremony in a Consort of Vocal and Instrumental Musick. The poet himself said nothing, but directed and took care that everybody else did his Part right. The Bards having first had the Composition from him, got it well by heart, and now pronounc'd it orderly, keeping even pace with the Harp . . .[3]

When the English descended on Ireland again in the seventeenth century, they enacted cruel and oppressive laws not just to subjugate the people but to break them and their culture forever. This is the modern beginning of "The Troubles." In their own country, the Irish were forbidden to vote, own the land of their ancestors, start businesses, practice Catholicism, be represented by lawyers in court, or speak their native language! The Bardic Schools rapidly declined, and with them died the teaching and formal practice of the Brehon Laws.

Also forbidden was the unparalleled literary tradition that the Irish had maintained through the Dark Ages. The English attempted to stifle the native brilliance of the past. They attempted to destroy the only European literary bridge back to the oral excellence of the Celts. They attempted to impose their law and letters on people who had an older, different, and sophisticated tradition. They systematically punished the native Irish intellectual, spiritual, and cultural pride and identity. Most Europeans and North Americans today are never taught this enlightened mythology, literature, poetry, and music, and indeed they are led to believe it never existed. We call this a crime against humanity.

As we shall see, however, excellence with the written and spoken word survived in other forms. The Irish maintained some of their rich cultural tradition despite persecution. Maya's grandfather was born in Co. Meath in 1867 and came to the U.S. about ten years later. In his first decade in Ireland, with only two years of schooling but much exposure to the oral tradition around the hearth, he had memorized countless poems and stories. Till he died in his 90s, he could recite rhymes and legends pertinent to any occasion. The knowledge in his bardic mind filled many reels of tape during recording sessions. Think of what people must have learned over a whole lifetime, if a farm child could take in so much! The beloved Robert Burns of Scotland as well as Yeats and Joyce of Ireland and dozens more male and female poets and writers, have enriched our literature with the bardic gifts of the Celts. The Welsh have maintained a connection with the mental training of Druidry through the Eisteddfod, described in chapter 14; to this day, the rules of their poetry competition recognize twenty-four distinct poetic forms.[4]

Your advanced Druid training requires a commitment to developing the power of the spoken and written word. The revival of the Bardic Schools begins in your living room! Nothing less is required than for you to start a Bardic School yourself! Gather with a few other dedicated and motivated Celts, once a month without fail. Have everyone bring five unusual and stimulating topics written on separate pieces of paper. Place them in a bowl and have one of you select a topic. Each participant writes poetry for ten or fifteen minutes on that topic: this is called timed writing. The only rule is that you may not stop writing, even if your pen says, "This topic is boring and I feel like snoring." Read your poems aloud without comments from anyone. The next person picks a topic from the bowl and everyone write on a new subject. And so it goes for two hours. You are there to compose and stretch your bardic mind, not to criticize.

If you reread the description above of the old poetic seminary, you will get more ideas of how to practice. Memorize ferociously. Memorize every poem you have ever wanted to know. Memorize those that rhyme and those that use freeform. Study the few books that describe the embedded meters and the complicated layers of form that the Celts loved. Read aloud poems written in Welsh, Irish, and Scots Gaelic. It matters not that you cannot pronounce the languages; you will feel the rhythms and stressed syllables, along with the repetitions they use for emphasis. You may be able to obtain tapes of native speakers reciting this poetry.

Make cassettes of your own poetry, and give them to family and friends. Have evenings when you read your own or others' compositions aloud. Offer to perform at people's homes during a literary or Celtic cultural evening. Give the gift of your poetry for every occasion—marriage, birth, death, graduation, and birthday. Include at least a few lyrical and original lines with a card. Offer to say toasts and eulogies and make satires on political events. Sing at weddings if you have the talent. Recite to harp music. If you play an instrument, carry it with you and be ready to give of your talent.

Essential to becoming a bard is to take part in Burns Night! Robert Burns lived 200 years ago in Scotland. He had the Celtic way with words, composing "Auld Lang Syne" and hundreds of favorites, including bawdy toasts and droll rhymes. Every January 25th, to celebrate his birthday, people of Scots descent around the globe gather for dinner, toasts, and poetry. Bagpipers herald the entry of the traditional haggis dish of mutton, oatmeal, and herbs. You will hear poetic flourishes that people have been perfecting since the year before. A Burns Night will connect you with bardic history in a flash. Attend one, or create your own!

Read and read and read poetry that you love, then emulate it. After reading a tremendous favorite of yours, lie down, do some relaxation exercises, and then compose the next two verses after the poem ends. You may not believe you can do this: after you've done it, you may not believe how easy it was. Any time the urge comes, lie down, cover your face, and compose while listening to music. Train yourself not to write down your poems until the next day. In the dark, before sleep, pose a theme to your bardic mind and drift off, knowing that the words will come from the muse of your dreams. Your eternal Self has been waiting a long time to speak.

The War of Words

When he arrived at Emain Macha, Bricriu invited Conchobor and the whole company to his feast.

"I am willing to go," said Conchobor, "if the men of Ulster are willing."

"We will not go," said Fergus and the others. "For if we do, the dead will number more than the living, as it is likely Bricriu intends to set us quarreling with each other."

"Well, if you refuse to go," said Bricriu, "I will stir up anger between kings and chiefs, champions and warriors."

"We will not go to avoid that," said Conchobor.

"I will set father against son," said Bricriu.

"We will not go to avoid that," said Conchobor.

"I will set mother against daughter," said Bricriu, "and the breast of woman beating against the breast of woman."

"Then it would be better for us to go!" said Fergus; "but first let us consult together."

So they gathered together, and Sencha the Druid advised them what they should do. "Put eight swordsmen around Bricriu," he said, "who will make him leave the house the moment he has laid out his feast."[5]

So begins *Bricriu's Feast or The War of Words of the Women of Ulster*, in which Sencha repeatedly displays the thinking and powers of a Druid. Later in the story he, as the resident Druid, orders three fighting champions to be parted—Cuchulainn, Conall, and Laegaire. Instantly King Conchobor and his champion Fergus leap up and part the men. Later still, when the wives of the three champions resume the struggle, Sencha says: "It is not a war of arms that will be waged here tonight, it will be a war of words."

In this manner, Sencha skillfully diverts a potentially deadly situation into one that is resolved through the eloquence of speech. The Celts were notoriously quick to take offense, and to settle such matters by the force of arms. But if there was one thing they admired above battle it was the well-turned word, the music of the bards, and the poetry that came from the depth of the Druid mind. It is fascinating to note that it is three women, not men, who compete in the "war of words." Celtic society respected women as speakers and poets. Here is a sample of the speech by Emer, wife of Cuchulainn:

There is no woman who comes near to me in the beauty of my appearance and my form. None have my wisdom, my brightness of eye, my kindness and my bearing. None have the joy or the strength of loving that I have. All Ulster desires me. I am the nut of the heart. If I were a loose woman there would not be a husband among you tonight who would still be with his wife on the morrow!

The power that you have as a speaker begins with a statement of self-definition. Your eloquence comes from the confidence that springs from the heart of the eternal Self. Build this confidence by writing a poem using the "I am . . ." form, and read it at a gathering. This is not a time to be humble or shy, rather you should let your words speak in place of your ego. Set yourself a theme and write ten statements about yourself that pertain to that theme. An example might be "My cauldron is burning with . . ." Pick the most significant answer and weave it into a conversation tomorrow. With the skill of a Druid diplomat, stop a fight or settle a conflict or mediate a deadlock. Keep yourself honed to step forward as a skilled word warrior.

The Fire in the Head

In what may be the oldest poem ever recorded on the insular Celtic shores, the *Song of Amergin*, the poet declaims:

I am the god that fashions fire in the head.
Who but I spreads light in the assembly upon the mountains?

Think about the meaning of the line above, "fire in the head." Could the fire in the head be the illumination in the minds of those gathered for the hilltop assembly? Do you think it is the spoken word that resonates with truth, beauty, and power? Do you think the "god" was a Druid who had cultivated great eloquence? We know that the life purpose of Druids was to contribute the Truth of Sovereignty to every situation (see chapter 15). This came from knowledge memorized in their long training, and from the wisdom obtained through the experience of many lifetimes. Above all, their training concentrated upon developing their verbal, poetic, and bardic skills.

Among the verbal skills available to Druids was satire. It is certain that Druids used their skills not only for peace but for war. In chapter 1 we learned how the poets of the Tuatha Dé Danann used satire against the Fomorians in the Second Battle of Moy

Tura. The great epic *Táin Bó Cuailnge* has more to say about this when Queen Maeve attempts to persuade Ferdiad to fight Cuchulainn.

> *Maeve sent messengers to bring Ferdiad to her, but he would not come as he knew what she intended. So Maeve sent Druids and satirists to make the three hurtful satires on him of mockery, insult and ridicule, but still he would not come. So Maeve told the Druids to make the three hilltop satires on him that would raise the blisters on his cheek of shame, blemish, and reproach. Ferdiad then came to Maeve's tent for he thought it better to fall by spears than by satires.*[6]

For people whose existence depended upon their honor and the reputation of their name, the spread of one satire was sufficient to cause their complete downfall, even death. A common satire was one that criticized a king or chieftain for lack of generosity. In what is said to be the first satire ever composed in Ireland, the poet Cairbre brought downfall upon the king, Bres, by giving back to him in words his lack of hospitality. The satire is essentially a reversal of the royal blessing.

> *Without food ready on the dish,*
> *Without cow's milk for the calf to grow on,*
> *Without shelter in the darkness of the night,*
> *Without payment for storytellers,*
> *May that be the condition of Bres.*[7]

Another verbal skill of Druids was praise. Taliesin has much to say in his works about the "shallow" and "foolish" poets who fawned upon the rich and powerful. He himself does this by praising the kings of his time, and heaping compliments upon his benefactor, Elphin. Yet when we examine the works of Taliesin, the main theme is praise for the soul that retains self-knowledge in lifetime after lifetime. When we read the "I am" or "I have been" forms that Taliesin excels in, we have to ask ourselves, who is the "I" that is speaking? What is the nature of the "I" that makes the following claim?

> *I was instructor*
> *To the whole universe.*
> *I shall be until the last days*
> *Upon the face of the earth.*[8]

The extraordinary poetry of Taliesin perhaps grants the best glimpse into the Druid mind that we have. The poetry is later than the Druidic era, but it resounds with images of those ancient times. Celtic myth and legend were kept alive in Wales in the sixth to the tenth centuries C.E. The pattern of itinerant bards speaking in the halls of the powerful must have been the same in Taliesin's time as it was 1,000 years before. Contact with Irish counterparts was frequent. Although Taliesin alludes to Christian influence, the pagan Druid content of the Celtic age shines through in every verse.

Develop your skills as an orator. Pay attention to words and their meaning. If something as light as "Darn!" originated as a curse, think about how you use it. If satire can destroy so completely, think about the way you employ it. The Celts would not agree that "Sticks and stones may break my bones but names will never hurt me." Is teasing really as beneficial and funny as you intend it to be? What is the opposite of satire? Say what you like and admire in others, and learn to praise sincerely. Regarding the fire in the head, when have you spoken passionately and eloquently? What sparked that fire? Can you do it again? The next time you need to discipline your child or communicate with your partner about something important, or make a presentation at work, do it with fire in the head. Let the cauldron of inspiration bear your message. Speak from the center of yourself and the world will listen.

The Spiral Castle

In the next verse of the poem quoted above, "Primary Chief Bard," Taliesin says:

> *I have sat in the perilous seat*
> *Above Caer Sidi.*
> *I shall continue to revolve*
> *Between the three elements.*

This terse, enigmatic verse contains so many allusions to the mysteries central to the Druid mind that it repays serious study. The perilous seat or chair is the place from which the poet speaks knowledge. The chair of the bard is the pinnacle or the center of all human experience. It is hard to gain it, but the word spoken from there has the power to change the world. Even today in Wales, the winner of bardic contests is awarded a miniature chair. There is a dramatic Welsh mountain known as Cader Idris. Legend says that those who spend a night on a natural rock chair on its summit will either die, become insane, or become a poet. This is in direct reference to "the perilous seat above Caer Sidi," but here we must plunge deeper into the Druid mind.

Some say that Caer Sidi is the revolving, shining castle of Arianrhod. Caer Sidi in Welsh means spiral or "revolving castle," while in Irish it can mean a place of the *Sídhe*. Arianrhod is the sister of the great magician Gwydion ap Don. She dwells in a castle off the coast of Anglesey, from where she controls the tides. Her name means "silver wheel" and she seems to be a lunar goddess. Arianrhod's name also refers to the Corona Borealis, and possibly to the Pole Star as well. Her castle is likened to the *axis mundi*, which does not itself turn but around which the world turns. Robert Graves translated the above verse to bring out the meaning of stillness in the center more clearly. He renders the last lines as: ". . . the whirling round without motion of the three elements."[9]

Under Arianrhod's castle is a bottomless well. A great treasure lies there, but it is also the most perilous one to seek out. Legend says that in a misguided attempt to gain it, Arianrhod opened an entrance to the forbidden depths and the sea overwhelmed her and Caer Sidi. Arianrhod and Gwydion were probably involved in incestuous sex magic. While insisting upon her virginity, Arianrhod is mother to the god Lleu Llaw Gyffes. After she abandons him, he visits her three times. Taliesin says, "Three times I lay in the prison of Arianrhod"; this may refer to the three visits of Lleu to Caer Sidi. The first visit was to gain a name, the second to be armed, the third to gain a wife.

If Caer Sidi also refers to the mounds of the *Sídhe* then we must assume that a Druid's training included vigils at such places. Irish myth makes several references to the *Sídhe* having the power to revolve. The rath of Curoi mac Daire of the Munster *Sídhe*, for example, was impossible to enter after sunset because it spun so rapidly. Visits to the places of the *Sídhe* were certainly perilous, and could bring death, insanity, or inspiration to the intruder.

It is not made clear what the "three elements" are in Taliesin's poem, but they are probably earth, sky, and sea. They might equally refer to the three drops from the Cauldron of Wisdom, to one of the many Druidic triads, and to the three branches of knowledge held by bards, *filidh*, and Druids.

The seat of the bards around which the universe turns is itself still. That seems to equate to the Self around which revolves the Truth of Sovereignty and all our actions in a lifetime. Take this time to practice some spiritual stress management. Calm yourself at the center. Let events whirl around you but not catch you up in frenzy. Hold fast to the certainty that your spiral castle is solidly emanating from your soul. Trust it. Speak from your center.

If you are debating about a life change or a big project, ask yourself, as a Druid: "Is this the perilous seat above Caer Sidi? Do I feel trepidation and excitement both? Is this for my highest good? What is my wisdom saying about this decision?" Perhaps a vigil would clarify your choice. Set up a place to stay connected all night with the Celtic deities and muses. Describe any dilemma in writing or in pictures. State your intention. Use all your Druid powers, your tools, and your magic to conduct this vigil rigorously and profoundly. You will produce the answer you need, though it may not be the one you want.

From this place of exploring the Druid mind, we go directly to bringing forth our creative power of inspiration in the next chapter.

Activities

The Poems of Taliesin. Read the poems of Taliesin. We provide sources in the notes of this chapter and in the Bibliography at the end of this book. Read the poems aloud. Go beyond where they are formulaic and discover where they shift to another level. Study the "I am" and "I have been" form, and repeat these lines to yourself. Stay with whatever they bring up, and add whatever lines come to you.

The Vigil. Druids sought inspiration in nature and had a Celtic version of the Native American vision quest. Taliesin obtained poetic wisdom from a vigil. He was suspended on a fishing weir, in darkness, rising and falling with the tide. In the account of the Bardic Schools the pupils mused on the "said Subject . . . having been given it over Night, they work'd it apart . . . the whole next day in the Dark." The Scottish version of the *Tarbhfeis* tells us that Druids lay overnight beside a waterfall or sea loch for divination and inspiration. Spend the night on the equivalent of the stone seat on the summit of Cader Idris. You will be dead, mad, or a poet by morning!

We recommend that Druids today take some time alone in nature: a visit won't do. You must really be there throughout the whole cycle of a day and a night, or more, enough time to leave the concerns of everyday life behind. We also recommend that this be done comfortably, so that you meet your physical needs while allowing the mind to dwell on deeper things. The Self has a pattern of creating that is very much in tune with nature, and it takes a while just to relax enough to attune to this inner rhythm. When in your secret place, recite the poems of others and those you have composed yourself, until the spontaneous music and poetry of your Self pours through.

The Chair of the Bard. In your group rituals, elect whoever has been most eloquent to the "Chair of the Bard." Have a seat prepared, if you like. Let the person take his or her place on it and feel what it is like to be in the Druid mindset. Invite the Bard-for-a-Day to extemporize.

Storytelling. Commit to memory stories, songs, or poems that contain Druidic teachings. Sketch out the essential theme of the story and fill in around it. It is not necessary to remember the details, as these will fall into place. When you tell the story, be flexible. Cater to your audience. Some parts will be far more captivating to some audiences than others. If you belong to a local pagan community, learn these poems and stories for your Bardic Circles.

The Bardic Circle. If you do not have Bardic Circles in your community, create this wonderful custom. Invite friends over for an evening of recital from memory. Or add a Bardic Circle to already existing festivals or events. The format is very simple: gather around a fire and pass a talking stick or some other object around the circle. When the stick comes to you, it is your turn to recite, sing, or play music. You may pass if you like. Keep the stick moving around the circle until you are certain everyone who wants to present has done so. Do not let one person dominate! You can set a time limit, or say that people will have another turn after everyone who wishes has had a first turn. We hold a Bardic Circle while camping out the evening before Beltane, and also during Burns Night.

Notes

1. Attributed to Taliesin, from *Cad Goddeu*, "The Battle of the Trees," translated by John Matthews, *Taliesin*.

2. Daniel Corkery, *The Hidden Ireland*, p. 69.

3. Ibid., pp. 73–5.

4. Dillwyn Miles, *The Secret of the Bards of the Isle of Britain*.

5. From *Bricriu's Feast*, recension of Lady Gregory (1903), Jeffrey Gantz (1981), and Proinsias MacCana (1991).

6. From "The Combat at the Ford," *Táin Bó Cuailnge*, based upon the recension of Thomas Kinsella (1963), Lucy Faraday (1904), and Lady Gregory (1902).

7. *Leabhar Gabála Érenn*, recension based on Lady Augusta Gregory (1904) and Cross and Slover (1936).

8. From the poem "Primary Chief Bard," found in the *Book of Taliesin*, a fourteenth-century text; translation based on W. F. Skene, *The Four Ancient Books of Wales*.

9. Robert Graves, *The White Goddess*, p. 91.

Chapter 19

LYING IN THE STREAMBED OF INSPIRATION

I know the land by being the land.
By feeling the river run over my face.[1]

This chapter explores traditional practices for achieving Druidic inspiration. It describes the use of symbols, visions, poetry, and the spoken word to effect magic.

The Power of Poetry

From his storm-driven ship off the coast of Ireland, the poet Amergin made the following invocation:

> *They that are tossed in the great fertile sea*
> *May now reach the land of Ireland.*
> *They may now find a place upon its broad plains,*
> *Its rich mountains and green valleys.*
> *They may now find a place in its fruit-filled forests,*
> *On its rivers and deep-pooled waters.*
> *They may now have their assemblies on this land*
> *And their king at Tara, the Hill of the Tribes.*
> *May the Sons of Miled be seen on this land*
> *And their ships find a place there.*
> *It is for this land now under darkness*
> *That I make this keen invocation.*

Let our Druids and our chief poets, let their learned wives,
Ask that we come to the land I now name,
The land of the noble woman, Ériu.[2]

Amergin accomplishes several things in this absolutely wonderful poem. He and his companions, the Sons of Miled who come from Gaelic Spain, have accepted a challenge from the Tuatha Dé Danann to withdraw beyond the ninth wave. If they can find a way back to shore they can assume the sovereignty of Ireland. Raising a tremendous storm, the Tuatha Dé Danann thrust back and almost destroy the ships of the Gaels. Amergin seizes the moment. Drawing upon the depths of inspiration, he hurls his poem into the face of the storm. The storm instantly quiets and the ships draw in to shore.

In this story, Amergin wins Ireland by the power of his poetic incantation. His words calm the elements. Even more amazing, the Goddess of the Land herself accepts the newcomers. From this act, the sovereignty of Ireland belongs to the Gaels forever. Amergin accomplishes through the spoken word what would otherwise have taken many bloody battles, if it could be accomplished at all.

This is the magic that is available to Druids through inspiration. In many ways, the subject at the heart of this book is the power of the word. What can we do with the example set by Amergin? His name means "born of song," and this provides a clue. We need to "rebirth" ourselves as poets. To do this, think of what it means to hold the position of Celtic poet. Our words must befit a person who speaks for the sovereign. Each of us as a Druid is a poet laureate, speaking our own Truth of Sovereignty. Our judgements must contain the wisdom of the ages and merit the attention of our community. We seek only poetic justice. We must hurl truth in the face of injustice. We need to believe in the power of our intention. As Druids, we have the responsibility to think clearly, know our minds and express our considered thoughts in powerful ways. "Poet" literally means creator; to be a Druid poet is to be responsible for creating well-being in our entire sphere of life.

Imbas, and a Confession

When we decided to undertake the writing of this book, it was a question of trusting our imbas, our inspiration. We agreed that direct knowledge of the Druids was next to impossible to obtain, that the historical sources had been hashed over again and again, and that all the data are available through the writings of such scholars as

Miranda Green and Peter Berresford Ellis. We agreed that archaeological artefacts are valuable but cannot speak the stories of their owners. We also agreed that the early Irish, Scottish, and Welsh texts, though imperfect, are the only sources that allow us inside the ideas and practices of the Druids. These Celtic myths and legends provide the most meaningful context in which to interpret the discoveries of archaeology. Everything Celtic or Druidic must arise from these once oral and now written sources. The only other source of material is ourselves, bringing forth inspired work.

Much has been written about the Druids in the last few hundred years, and some of it is inspired. Unfortunately, most of it is pure invention, despite the claims of its authors about being authentic. These writings have indiscriminately entered the corpus of "Druidic" knowledge. More often than not, they tell us more about the mind of the eighteenth- or nineteenth-century gentlemen who wrote such works than they do about the Druids.

Isaac Bonewits has cleverly divided the material on Druidry into three categories. The first, "paleopagan" Druidry, belongs to what we can verify as originating in the Celtic age of the Druids. The second, "mesopagan" Druidry, originated in the minds of (mostly) male antiquarians from the late seventeenth up to the mid-twentieth century; this was an attempt to revive or continue what they thought was paleopagan. The third, "neopagan" Druidry, is derived from the critical scholarship, archaeology, and radically alternative spiritual framework of the latter half of the twentieth century. Neopaganism, according to Bonewits, is "consciously striving to eliminate as much as possible of the traditional Western monotheism and dualism" from its ideas and practices.[3]

We do not wish to dismiss out of hand the work of the "mesopagan" Druids. They include such luminaries as John Toland, Iolo Morganwg, and William Blake. The ideas generated by them, however, have created a mishmash of material. There are now glosses on glosses, speculations upon speculations, and concepts that plainly belong to Christianity in this category of Druidism. We ask that each author who makes a contribution to Druidry state the sources of his or her information. A problem arises if an author claims authentic Druidic origins for something that all the world's scholarship has never before turned up! In contrast, it is refreshing and in keeping with Celtic abilities to write inspired poems and make intuitive contributions, as long as the authors acknowledge them as such.

So we, Nicholas and Maya, stripped the existing body of knowledge about Druidry to the bare bones. For years we have studied what there is to study. Now we are ready to publish our contribution towards fleshing out neopagan Druidry. We keep inviting it to come from our inspiration. Yes, we grant ourselves the authority to create the best book on Druid magic we can! Apart from the early Irish, Scottish, and Welsh sources, no other source of Druidry is more authentic than the *imbas* that streams from those who place themselves in the lineage of the tradition. We designed the activities in this book to help you discover Druidry for yourself. We hope the chapters and the activities inspire your own creativity as Druids. Finally, we are asking you to do no more nor less than we have done ourselves.

Often when our Grove meets we don't know exactly what we are going to say or do. We gather, announce that the Grove is present, and stand there representing our trees. We feel what it means to be Druids after so many centuries of dormancy. We are in no hurry to use a format or ritual that probably originated in the patriarchal religions we grew up with! We actively seek inspiration. We seek the new, by lying in the oldest streamed we know of, derived from our own Native European Tradition. Let us look through the sources of inspiration described in the early mythic literature, and see which ones attract us the most.

The Streambed of Inspiration

Water is central to the imagery used by the Celts to represent inspiration. The salmon of wisdom dwell in a pool, and other watery sources frequently inspire mythic characters. Irish poets of the eighteenth century spoke of "Bathing in the Well of the Muses," no doubt an allusion to such sources of inspiration in their time. In her book *The Elements of the Celtic Tradition*, Caitlín Matthews adapts this theme. She writes, "poetry is like a steady stream running underground," and talks of the "poet's bed." From this Maya created the image of "lying in the streambed of inspiration." This image invites us to enter the brilliant creative continuity that flows throughout the ages of the Celtic tradition. The flow is always there in ourselves, if we align with it.

This book is essentially an invitation to you to lie in the streambed of Druidry and discover for yourself the creative power of inspiration. For the Celtic Druids this usually manifested as poetry, but it might emerge in a different way for you. The common factor here is that we choose to identify with the ancient stream of wisdom called Druidry.

There is a great deal to the idea of genetic or cellular memory. We all can access the tradition of our ancestors through our internal somatic processes. Our bodies are extraordinarily intelligent, performing actions that we are incapable of doing consciously. Indeed, we have to get out of the way of our somatic intelligence for our body to operate. What if we got out of the way of our genetic and cellular intelligence enough to allow wisdom to emerge that provides us with the fundamentals of Druidry? To do this we must put aside many of our old beliefs, some of our thoughts, and even the language in which we think. Language predisposes us to structure our world according to currently held views. Make sure you stay within the tenets of the Celtic worldview.

Connecting with inspiration is one of the most Druidic practices you can learn. We hope you will indulge in the streambed activity at the end of this chapter many times!

The Salmon of Wisdom and the Well of the Moon

The following text contains exceptional information about sources of inspiration and describes three divination techniques that require poetry.

> *Fionn went to learn poetry from Finegas who dwelt on the banks of the Boyne. The poet agreed to teach him, and Fionn told him his name was Demna. For seven years Finegas had sought Fintan, the Salmon of Knowledge, that dwelt in the river. He thought it would come to him, as it was in a prophecy that the salmon would be found by one named Fionn, and from then on he would have all knowledge. Not long after Fionn went into the service of Finegas, the salmon was found. Finegas ordered Fionn to cook it, but on no account must he touch any of it.*
>
> *Fionn began to cook the fish, and seeing a blister rising on its skin, pressed it down with his thumb. He received a burn, and to cool it, brought his thumb up to his lips. Instantly he found himself aware of what was passing in the courts of Tara, Naas, and Emain Macha. He could hear everything, and no secret could be kept from him. Fionn ran to tell Finegas what was happening.*
>
> *"Did you eat of the salmon, my boy?" said Finegas.*
>
> *"No," Fionn replied, "but I burned my thumb when I pressed down a blister that rose on the salmon's back, and to ease the pain, I put my thumb in my mouth."*
>
> *"You told me your name was Demna," said Finegas, "but have you any other name?"*

"I am also called Fionn," he said.

"Then fate is against me," said Finegas, "and it must be to you that the salmon is to be given."

Finegas gave Fionn the whole of the salmon, and it is this which gave all knowledge to him. Whenever Fionn put his thumb in his mouth and touched the tooth of knowledge, then everything was revealed to him. With this knowledge, there also came the wisdom of foretelling and of poetry; although some say this came another way.

There was a well of the moon, guarded by the three women, the daughters of Beag of the Tuatha Dé Danann. They would not let anyone drink from the well. One day Fionn pursued a deer into the rushes beside the well, and the three women rushed out to prevent him from finding it. One of the women had a vessel of well water in her hand. She threw it at Fionn to stop him, and some of the water went in his mouth. From then on Fionn had all the knowledge of poetry that the well of the moon could give. He knew the three ways of poetry: the teinim laida, *the* imbas forosna, *and the* dichetul dichennaib.[4]

Imbas Forosna. "Inspiration of Tradition" is a divination technique of uncertain meaning. The prophetess Fedelm used it to tell Maeve the outcome of the *Táin*. Our guess is that it simply means what it says. Fedelm placed herself in the power of her ancestral tradition and spoke with the foresight of that perspective. This would be similar to Second Sight. To practice this, lie in the streambed of ancestral inspiration as described in this chapter and work on developing Second Sight, as discussed in chapter 4.

One source connects *imbas forosna* with animal practices, and most Celtic scholars follow this source. In the ninth or tenth century a monk wrote *Cormac's Glossary*, explaining *imbas forosna* as chewing on the flesh of an animal sacrificed for divination. Since several myths describe chewing animal flesh, most scholars assume the myths are describing the enigmatic *forosna* technique. Druids did this to have something revealed to them. We recommend using an animal token such as a feather, tooth, or bone instead of raw flesh. Druids made invocations, songs, or prayers over the token, then placed it on the threshold of the dwelling. They then laid down in darkness, covered their faces, and perhaps fell asleep. They arose and immediately recited or recorded the poem they received that could foretell the future or answer the dilemma.[5] *Imbas* forosna delivers the answer in poetic form in the manner of an oracle. At the *Tarbhfeis*, the "Bull Feast," Druids ate the flesh of a bull, then slept, and whomever they dreamed of would become the High King.

Druids also wrapped themselves in mantles imbued with the magical power of animals. We know that the Druid of the *Tarbhfeis* not only ate the flesh of a bull but lay wrapped in its hide to sleep. The bull is an animal of enormous power—probably the most powerful creature the Celts ever met—and so was the harbinger of the next king. Another myth tells of a cloak and headdress made of feathers. There are also numerous accounts of shapeshifting into animal forms and the wearing of the skins of wild creatures. These stories lead to the conclusion that putting on a mantle was a direct means of accessing poetic and oracular inspiration. We discuss this in the section on the Druid Robe in chapter 3.

Teinim Laida. "Breaking Open by Poetry" is a divination technique that uses a poem or song to arrive at an answer to a question or problem. You the Druid sing or recite in a loose and extemporaneous fashion until achieving a trance-like state. The text *Senchus Mór* says the poet composes "without thinking."[6] Like a shaman shaking a rattle over a sick person to discover the ailing part, you shake your voice over the question to find the answer. Some shamans describe aloud in singsong fashion what they can see during their journeys. Commune with the subject until the words of inspiration reveal the answer. You can accompany yourself on an instrument, especially a harp or a drum, or play meditative music. This technique is excellent for solving a mystery.

Dichetul Dichennaib. "Recital through Finger-ends" is similar to *teinim laida* but adds touch to the technique. Druids touched the subject with their fingers and through divination were able to obtain what they sought by spontaneously composing a verse. Since Ogham letters and many corresponding meanings were assigned to each joint, the fingers contained a condensed or telegraphic version of knowledge. Try associating crucial areas of your life with your different fingers and joints. If the situation is about a person who is not present, then touch the finger you have associated with the person, and begin reciting or singing about that situation. Listen to the thread of what comes and your answer will be there. The *Exile of the Sons of Usnach* describes an example of this technique when the subject is present.

> *Cathbad the Druid, King Conchobor and all the men of the Red Branch of Ulster were drinking in the house of Fedlimid one day. Fedlimid's wife was*

great with child. As she crossed the floor to go to her couch, the child in her womb cried out. The cry was so loud that the men made for their weapons. Fedlimid asked her what the sound was. She replied that she did not know: "For no woman knows what she bears within her womb."

Then Cathbad rose, and placing his hand upon her belly, he said:

> *A woman with braided golden tresses,*
> *Green eyes, red lips like coral,*
> *Cheeks purple-pink like the foxglove,*
> *Skin like newly fallen snow.*
>
> *Heroes will battle for her,*
> *Kings will call upon her,*
> *Great Queens will ache with envy*
> *At her pure, faultless, lovely form.*
>
> *Let Deirdre be her name.*
> *It is she who cries in the womb.*
> *For you Ulster will lie in torment,*
> *And jealousy dog you like a flame.*[7]

The Cauldron of Ceridwen

The Celtic tradition has many cauldrons. The Dagda's Cauldron of Plenty was one of the four original talismans brought to Ireland by the Tuatha Dé Danann, from which "no company ever went away unsatisfied." The Cauldron of Bran had the power to restore life to warriors slain in battle, but they lacked speech. The Cauldron of Annwn would not serve food to a coward or an oath-breaker. These cauldrons are powerful, but none possesses the same attributes as the Cauldron of Ceridwen (described in chapter 5).

Ceridwen is the great Welsh goddess who is mother and wise crone, the one who holds our genetic memories, the records of our people. She is a sorcerer, brewing a potion of the wisdom of all ages. She is a prophet, knowing her son Taliesin will be the greatest bard of his people. She is a shaman, shapechanging into animal forms. She is the source of knowledge, the mother of inspiration. How is this goddess alive today? Who is she in your life?

Recall in the myth that Ceridwen wanted to make the gift of wisdom for her ugly child, Afagddu, so he would be looked upon favorably. She gathered certain magical herbs at specific times, and brewed them in a cauldron for a year and a day, waiting until they distilled into three drops of inspiration. A village boy named Gwion Bach fed the fire during that time. On the last day, as you might guess, three drops spurted out of the cauldron and landed on Gwion's thumb. To stop the pain he put the thumb in his mouth. The drops instantly transferred the wisdom of all time into the boy and he knew all there was to know. He "saw" that Ceridwen would kill him for imbibing the potion intended for her son, so he fled.

> She pursued Gwion. He became aware of her and changed into a hare. She became a black greyhound. He ran to a river and changed into a fish. She became an otter. He changed into a bird and fled through the air. She became a hawk. Then he saw a threshing floor, and changing himself into a grain, hid among the countless other grains. Ceridwen became a black, red-crested hen. She picked him out and swallowed him. The grain went into her womb, and she bore Gwion there for nine months. When he was born he was so beautiful that she could not bear to kill him. So she placed him in a leather bag and set him adrift on the sea.
>
> At that time there lived a lord named Gwyddno Garanhir who had a weir on the mouth of the river Conwy. He was accustomed to take salmon from it every May Eve. Gwyddno had a son named Elphin, who up to that time had nothing but bad luck. Gwyddno sent Elphin to the weir and told him all he could find there was his. Elphin began to lament when he found nothing but a small leather bag hanging from a pole of the weir. He opened the bag and inside he saw a bright forehead, and cried out: "Behold, tal iesin!" [radiant brow]. The child within said, "Taliesin it is!"
>
> Elphin carried the child home, and Taliesin composed for him on the way. From that day forth Elphin's fortune changed, and he grew prosperous in the company of his wondrous bard.[8]

Taliesin passes through the cauldron three times. Once he is born as Gwion of a human mother, unaware of his eternal Self. The second time he is born of the goddess of wisdom. The final time he is born of the universal mother, represented by the sea. The symbols of womb, cauldron, and ocean are congruent in the mythic imagination as sources of inspiration. The name of Ceridwen's ugly son means "utter darkness," while her reborn son carries the name of radiance. We see here the sign that training ourselves in the Druid path brings radiant wisdom that is better than light because it never ceases. The wealth from the goddess of wisdom can never be exhausted. Her treasure comes from initiation, from instruction in the old ways.

We learn from this magical story that wisdom takes time to accumulate. Ceridwen hones her existence until it consists only of gathering and brewing mystical knowledge with care and patience. Her cauldron represents our existence, simmering until we awaken ourselves to the wisdom and poetry of our eternal Self. When will you give yourself permission to be wise? What lesson have you learned over and over that you have finally distilled into wisdom? This may come, for example, from parenting, teaching, or practicing a craft. What have you been preparing that is ready to taste? Give yourself extended and intense time to study the mysteries of Ceridwen's cauldron and she will repay you with the great gift of inspiration.

We take from this myth the understanding that Taliesin underwent Druidic initiation via earth, sea, and sky. He spent nine months or years of intense training in Ceridwen's "womb" on land. Then he was set adrift in a skin-boat to prove his seafaring knowledge and his mastery of the celestial spheres of astronomy and astrology. Celtic initiates actually were bound into coracles and set adrift in places where the waters returned boats to shore, after a frightening and enlightening experience! Taliesin and other initiates learned directly from nature and from teachers who passed on a living tradition. If Ceridwen came to you today and you could receive anything she knew, what would that be?

The cauldron has more meanings than there are drops of water in the sea. Cauldrons are filled with liquid, filled with the emotions that pour through us in waves. Our grief and tears make it brim. This is a good time to ask: what inside of you needs crying? What flood of emotions would pour out if you broke open your cauldron? Cauldrons are heated by the fire of transformation. As Caitlín Matthews put it, how could the cauldron help you to transform raw emotion into fodder for inspiration? Could you write of a wrenching experience? Could you dramatize it, put it to music, paint it, or sculpt it? You are the fire, the cauldron, and the contents. The truth is within.

The cauldron represents the fire in the head spouting forth wisdom. Think of it! The Celts venerated the head because they were honoring the oral transmission of wisdom for uncounted millennia. The bards were walking records of the tribes. Their memories and recitations were the mobile libraries of the Celts. The sacred and magical aspect is this: the bards and Druids learned from the oral lessons of their teachers, and they told the next generation, who told the next. Exactly the way DNA is passed alive from parent to child, the Druids passed the sacred and magical traditions of the Celts for centuries: these are within us.

Think of the cauldron as the cup of life and rebirth, into which we can keep dipping as we travel the spiral of existence. The Celts believed that life feeds on death. The more we allow outdated ideas to fall away, the more we pare dead wood from our way of living, then the more alive we become as Druids! The more we give birth to our creativity, the more our cup will brim to refill our imagination. Magical cauldrons are a central image of Celtic tradition, the abiding symbol of travel to the Otherworlds. How can you bring these multilayered meanings into your life today?

Throughout this book we have established that the inspiration revered by the Celts can be found *within* us. By magical and commonsense practices we can align with this power flowing through us. The cauldron is within us, revealed in the awesome power and array of the eternal Self. We journey within as we become our own shaman. We fire up the Celtic cauldron as we become our own oracle. We bring forth our wisdom as we become Druids and bards, inspired to transmit our awakened powers.

The cauldron is from prehistory, predating the Celts by tens of thousands of years. When we think of cauldrons we must recall how ancient, universal, and fundamental to human life they are. A cauldron is essentially a container that transforms its contents into another, more useful form. For thousands of years the cauldron was the dominant object at the center of every house. Many cauldrons dating back to the Bronze Age (1800–800 B.C.E.) demonstrate heavy use and considerable amounts of repair. Boiling everything together in a cauldron suspended over a fire, with some things wrapped in bags and others added directly to the broth, was the standard procedure in the farmhouses of Britain and Ireland. From time to time the broth would be drained, eaten, and a whole new batch begun. Sometimes more water would be added to the cauldron, but it was not changed for weeks. Prolonged boiling and distillation of herbs and other ingredients certainly produced a potion of considerable power.

Imagine the women tending the hearth with its cooking spits and cauldrons. The abundance provided by the cauldron found a parallel in the wombs of the women; the bounty of each was a measure of the wealth of the household. We may also imagine the older women keeping warm around the fire. The knowledge they shared with the mothers and younger women must have seemed occult and mystical to the boys and the men.

From this viewpoint, we can understand how the idea of a cauldron of wisdom took root in people's imagination. The life-giving hearth at the center of the home, tended by women, provides the exemplary image for the source of all nourishment. As the source, the cauldron is the symbol for the inspiration that comes welling up from the place of the eternal Self. It is in the keeping of Ceridwen, at once the mother and the crone, abundance and wisdom combined.

The most remarkable real cauldron from Celtic times was found in a bog at Gundestrup, Denmark. This silver-plated cauldron was probably made in Thrace in the first few centuries B.C.E. It depicts scenes from a Celtic mythic narrative. In one depiction on the interior, a huge goddess-like figure is plunging a man into a cauldron. Warriors line up to have their turn while some horsemen ride away, and three men play massive animal-headed trumpets. The warriors carry a tree on the tips of their spears, while a dog paws the base of the tree. The men and dog may be sacrificial victims, followed by the tree. Such an interpretation comes from actual finds where the Celts dug deep ritual pits and deposited a whole tree on top of animal and human victims. The Gundestrup cauldron, however, shows a cauldron and not a pit. It may be that the warriors lining up were slain in battle, deposited in the cauldron, and then reborn as the men riding away on horses. The tree dividing the two groups would then be a symbol of the Celtic Tree of Life, rather than an offering for the cauldron.

Although the Cauldron of Ceridwen is apparently concerned with poetry and inspiration, her mythic narrative turns on the birthing of her children and then the rebirth of Gwion as Taliesin. It is possible they are all one and the same being. The image on the Gundestrup cauldron is that of a goddess of death and rebirth. The story of Ceridwen and Taliesin makes the connection between poetry and rebirth, so the cauldron as the source of the poetic wisdom of the eternal Self finds congruency at every turn.

The *Aisling* and the Divine Other

As described in the previous chapter, the English made it impossible for the Bardic Schools to continue in Ireland after the mid-seventeenth century. The Schools were replaced by the "Courts of Poetry" but the English gave no patronage to the *cúirt* system and did not preserve Gaelic learning. Soon the poets became poorer, with nowhere to meet except in the taverns. According to Daniel Corkery, however, this produced one remarkable result: the *Aisling* or "vision poem."

The poets were driven by necessity into the field, often working against rack-rents that threatened them with eviction and poverty. They turned to nature for inspiration, and to the age-old vision of the land as a goddess. Corkery says the *Aisling* poems were written in stressed meters, and always had as their content the spirit of Ireland rising as a "majestic and radiant maiden." In many ways *Aislings* are Jacobite poems against the rule of England. They appeal to the native spirit of the land to arise, unite with the king in exile (Bonnie Prince Charlie for the Scots), and so restore sovereignty to the Gaelic nations. The great poet Aodhagán ó Rathaille (Egan O'Rahilly), circa 1670–1726, wrote this *Aisling*:

> *The Brightest of the Bright met me on my path so lonely;*
> *The Crystal of all Crystals was her flashing dark-blue eye;*
> *Melodious more than music was her spoken language only;*
> *And glorious were her cheeks of a brilliant crimson dye.*

> *Oh, my misery, my woe, my sorrow and my anguish,*
> *My bitter source of dolor is evermore that she,*
> *The Loveliest of the Lovely, should thus be left to languish*
> *Amid a ruffian horde till the Heroes cross the sea.*[9]

At the heart of the *Aisling* is the vision of a transfigured land rising to restore the traditional and sacred way of life. It is a singularly Celtic image. This vision is sustained throughout the Druidic tradition, where the land itself is the Goddess of Sovereignty who must wed the monarch or leader in order for abundance and prosperity to prevail. Echoes of this theme are heard even in Britain, where kings are unconsciously perceived as deriving their sovereignty from the queen.

On the spiritual level, the *Aisling* is an expression of the intimate I-Thou relationship between the Self and the World. When we finally come home to the truth of our eternal Self, the Self is confronted by the presence of what we may call the "Other." This, be it a plant, a tree, an animal, a landscape, a person, or many people, is the embodiment of all that is not of the Self. The Other is all that is not "I." The human challenge lies in resolving this relationship, and it is usually done by identifying the Other with an anthropomorphic image of the sacred. Such personifications of the divine involve certain risks. A creator or savior deity is too remote to ever be fully present in the world, nor can it really be intimate with the Self. An unutterable great mystery is too impersonal. An image of a merciful saint or a flawless goddess may mean we do not see the world for what it really is. The Celts chose to relate to the Other in terms of a goddess, but she is often described in the myths as a hag, like Ceridwen.

Once the Self comes into a true relationship with the Other, with Nature personified as a goddess, it understands that she appears in every form. Once we, as Druids, understand the everchanging cycle of life, death, and rebirth and are willing to embrace all this, even in its most hideous forms, then our relationship with the world is one of great wisdom, intimacy, and beauty.

The *Aisling* is an appropriate poetic theme and source of inspiration for Druids today. It arises directly out of recorded Irish tradition, and has its roots in the ancient Celtic world. It focuses upon the source of sovereignty, the Goddess of the Land, and the union between her and the Self that is necessary for increase and harmony to prevail. It is ultimately the same theme that runs throughout the poems of Amergin and Taliesin, who celebrate the sacred alliance between themselves, the people, and the land.

Activities

The Streambed of Inspiration. Create a setting in which you can completely relax and let go of all concerns. Have a pen and paper nearby. Ideally the setting should be one of sensory deprivation: dark, silent, still, at ambient temperature. Lie down with a woven fabric over your face. It may be your tartan, something you wove, or a cloak from a Celtic land. Place your Druid's Egg or another favorite stone on your belly. You need to be aware of your body and not be so comfortable that you will fall asleep. The streambed of inspiration awaits you.

You are going to seek the wisdom of your body, which may come to you in several ways. It may come in images, colors, sounds, feelings, scents, or sensations. At first, simply allow thoughts and words to come, but do not hold onto them. Let them drift away. The goal is to lie in the awareness of the language of your body.

Trust your body. It has walked, run, jumped, seen, heard, held, thrown, stroked, rolled, and done countless other things for you throughout your whole life. It has incredible wisdom and abilities. Listen to your body. Feel your body. Your body has messages for you from the collection of sophisticated cells that make up your being. Take note of these messages.

Now feel that you have not simply popped out of nowhere, but have arisen out of a very long genetic continuity. The intelligence of your body has evolved not just in your lifetime, but over eons. You are lying in the streambed of your lineage. You feel the presence of processes that began millions of years ago flowing through your being. You are one with an eternal stream of life. Feel what it is like to know this. Allow the memory of cellular intelligence to flow through your body.

Does any of this flow come to you in ways that feel Druidic? Be aware of yourself as a Druid in this great stream of life, and see what comes to you.

Finally, bring all that you have experienced to the part of you that thinks in words. Allow the images and sensations to create a poem. Allow the experience to emerge creatively. Take all the time you need to do this.

Now take your pen and paper and write down the poem or tape record it. Don't be critical of what you are writing. If you write it down, pay no attention to spelling or structure. Allow the words to spill onto the page or onto the tape. Later you can return to the poem. You might be surprised how the essence of the experience came out whole, exactly the way you first wrote the poem.

Imbas. Practice the *imbas forosna*, the *teinim laida*, and the *dichetul dichennaib* as described in this chapter.

The Salmon of Wisdom. Obtain a real salmon in a meaningful way, and prepare it for a feast with friends. Bring it to the table declaring its significance. Tell the story of Fionn if you choose. Ask your companions to compose spontaneously after touching or eating the salmon.

The Well of the Moon. Make a pilgrimage to a sacred well or spring at a time when the moon is full. Honor the spirit of the place, and be prepared for divination or composing poetry and song.

The Cauldron of Ceridwen. Find a suitable vessel that will represent the Cauldron of Ceridwen. Keep it in a safe and sacred place where you will see it daily. Light candles or incense around it, put things into it and perhaps take things out of it. Over the course of a year and a day (ideally beginning at Samhain), build up a collection of images, thoughts, symbols, and meanings around the cauldron. Let it be charged by this significance, and let the cauldron hold and alchemically blend these things together. If, at the end of this time, you feel the cauldron has done its work, prepare a ritual in which you will give away or receive the contents. Let the contents be represented by three drops of magical liquid.

The *Aisling*. See the land, a tree, or the spirit of nature about you in the form of a goddess or a great queen. See her rise from the land and come to dance with you. What is she saying? Is she celebrating or grieving? Is there abundance or loss? What does it mean to embrace her? Express all this in a poem or a song.

Notes

1. Cam Smith, *Notes from the Mountain*.

2. From the *Leabhar Gabála*, the "Book of Invasions." The poem draws on Lady Augusta Gregory (1904), and R. A. S. MacAlister (1938–1956) for the translation.

3. Isaac Bonewits, "The Druid Revival in Modern America," in *The Druid Renaissance*, ed., Philip Carr-Gomm, p. 74.

4. From the *Boyhood Deeds of Fionn*, recension based on the translations by Cross and Slover (1936) and Lady Gregory (1904).

5. See *Cormac's Glossary*, edited by Whitley Stokes.

6. *Senchus Mór: The Ancient Laws of Ireland*, edited by W. N. Hancock.

7. From *Longes mac n-Uislenn*, "The Exile of the Sons of Usnach," recension based upon the translations of Thomas Kinsella (1969), Lady Gregory (1904), and A. H. Leahy (1905).

8. From the *Hanes Taliesin*, translation found in P. K. Ford, editor, *The Mabinogion and Other Medieval Welsh Tales*, and in John Matthews, *Taliesin*. Note: this includes the only known reference to the "Books of the Fferyllt" in the Celtic sources and probably refers to the Roman author Virgil.

9. Quoted by Daniel Corkery, from *The Poems of Egan O'Rahilly*, edited by Patrick S. Dinneen and Tadhg O'Donoghue, Irish Texts Society.

Chapter 20

Journeying to the Otherworlds

A host comes across the sea,
Rowing swiftly to the shining stone;
From out of the stone pours forth
The swelling of sweet music a hundred-fold.

Through the length of every age
It sings a song which is never sad;
It is increased by the choirs of hundreds
Who never know the ebbing tide.

Let Bran listen to the wonders
Of the music I am singing;
Let Emhain beside the clear sea
Draw you to its many-colored plains.

Set out upon your voyage!
Go to the pure land over the sea;
And may you, with joy everlasting,
Come to the Land of Women.[1]

This chapter explores the nature of this world and the Druid doctrine of the eternal Self. It investigates the Fairy World, death, reincarnation, and the nature of our existence in the next world.

The Experience of This World

We finally come to the place in this book where we, as Druids, must consider the inevitable end of life in this body. As described throughout this book, the eternal Self or the soul is central to the tenets of Druidry. The Self makes a *tuirgin*, a "circuit of existences," around the many worlds that make up the Celtic cosmos. The primary dwelling place is without a body, in the Land of the Living. There the Self exists in its full and eternal nature. Periodically the Self assumes a body or some other earthly form, dwells within it for the span of its lifetime, and returns to the Land of the Living. The Self may also dwell for a time in the Land of the *Sídhe*, the Fairy Realm. Finally, we learned that time in those other worlds is not linear or sequential. What does this process mean, and how can we apply it to our present existence?

For all of us, the physical body determines our current experience. This life is our priority here, and it colors our point of view. In the Celtic cosmology, the soul totally embraces the body, and the body becomes the soul's experience. The bodily senses provide our life with experience, and it is nearly impossible to see life outside of these senses. Much great Celtic literature celebrates the physical powers of its characters. The *Táin* celebrates feasting, fighting, and lovemaking, and it praises those who develop their physical skills to the utmost.

We must acknowledge that there are boundaries to the physical senses that make it very difficult to perceive beyond them. This is at once a great blessing and a great limitation for humans. The blessing of the body is that it provides the Self with a wonderful vehicle of experience! The body as a vehicle for the Self is an amazingly refined organism that has evolved over eons and is perfectly suited to the nature of this world. Science shows us that the cells forming the body are part of an enormous experiment in cooperation that continuously creates wondrous life forms for the refinement of existence upon the planet Earth. As the great Irish stories point out, incarnation in the human body is a wonderful gift for us to enjoy!

The limitation of the body is that it does not generally perceive and have experiences beyond the physical senses. To be sure, there are dreams, visions, and subtle sensibilities; but we are not as certain of those things as we are about bodily experiences. Communicating between this dimension and others is not as sure as using the telephone. We can have faith about life hereafter, but not certainty, because our life at the moment is contained in the body. It is very difficult to see or obtain affirmation of life beyond death. Nature brings all her organisms to death in the end. Indeed, death is a necessary contributor to the process of the evolving community of life on earth, and without it life would remain static.

To apply these ways of experiencing this world, go to a beautiful place in nature and simply observe it. If you are beside water, directly observe the water, not your concept of water. If you are among trees, pay attention to them until you can really "see" them. The goal here is to allow yourself to be in this world, without a subconscious directive running your life. Allow yourself to be a body in this world; appreciate what a wonderful thing that is.

After a while of observing the special place and allowing your body to be totally present there, call upon the presence of your eternal Self. Invite your Self, your soul, to experience through the senses of the body. Let yourself dance with life, with nature as your lover. What does the soul see in nature? What does the Self share in common with nature? As a Druid in nature, what song, what poem, what words can you create that capture these feelings?

Visions of the Next World

Our sources clearly show that the existence of the eternal soul in dimensions without a body was not based on faith or belief. The reality of dwelling forever in many worlds permeates Celtic literature. Where did the Celts get their certainty, since the body does not have the perceptual ability to experience eternal life? Sometimes we long for a glimpse of the eternal Self and feel empty. In fact, the very emptiness that meets our inner gaze is the guarantee of the ongoing life of the Self. The emptiness we see with our physical, mental, or inner eye when attuned to the eternal establishes that death is doing its job properly, and that the eternal Self is absolutely and entirely free of the limitations of this life.

Sometimes, perhaps only once in our lives, we receive a glimpse of the true nature of the eternal Self; circumstances conspire to provide us with a view of the Land of the Living. It may be an out-of-body or near-death experience, a love affair, a condition induced by fasting, stress, drugs, or a moment of complete ecstasy. We carry these experiences close to our hearts and long to find the key that can explain them or, better still, repeat them.

That we are not meant to repeat these experiences in life is suggested by their rarity. They are difficult to achieve in a positive way. They exact great cost to the quality of life if one endlessly strives to repeat them in sex, food, drugs, ascetic exercises, or other obsessive behavior. Visions of the Otherworlds come just a few times, as signposts to the eternal. They come to remind us of the existence of the Self, not as something to be achieved and lived in this world. The visions are not the Land of the Living itself. They do not fulfill the longing of our hearts. They are only reminders of the eternal perceived through the physical senses. If we cling to the visions as the goal, as the way itself, they dissolve into delusion.

It is likely that Celtic Druids understood psychotropic substances, since they were herbalists. Hallucinogenic mushrooms grow in the meadows of Europe in autumn in great quantities.[2] The use of these mushrooms may have provided the Druids with visions of the Otherworlds, but this was within a sacred and guided context which enabled the experience to be mastered. Few mentions of this context have survived in Celtic sources, except in the teaching stories of the otherworldly journeys. There, the dangers of the realm of the *Sídhe* are emphasized.

It is probable that the Celtic Fairy World is equivalent to the realm entered by shamans when seeking knowledge, often in trance. The many shamanic traditions know this realm by various names, and shamans often access it under the influence of hallucinogens. Remnants of shamanic training can be picked out from Celtic sources. At some point Druidry probably left the shamanic path, which continued to be practiced by those who became known as witches.[3] Until a safe training and code of practice for Druidic shamanism are reestablished, the risks involved are too many for it to be safely attempted.

Preiddeu Annwn, the "Spoils of Annwn," is attributed to the sixth-century bard Taliesin. The following extract describes a journey to the Otherworlds made by Arthur and his companions, and the terrible perils encountered there.

> *Complete is the prison of Gwair in Caer Sidi . . .*
> *A heavy blue chain firmly holds the youth,*
> *And for the spoils of Annwn bitterly he sings,*
> *And until the last days shall he continue his lay.*
> *Thrice the fullness of Prydwen we went into it;*
> *Except seven, none returned from Caer Sidi.*
>
> *In Caer Pedryvan forever revolving,*
> *The first word from the cauldron, when was it spoken?*
> *By the breath of nine maidens gently it is heated;*
> *Is it not the cauldron of the Lord of Annwn in its fashion,*

With a ridge around its rim of pearls?
It will not boil the food of a coward or of one forsworn . . .
And before the portals of the cold place the horns of light shall be burning.
And we went with Arthur in his splendid labors,
Except seven, none returned from Caer Vediwed.

Three times twenty hundred men stood on the wall of Caer Wydr.
It was difficult to converse with their sentinel.
Three times the fullness of Prydwen, we went with Arthur,
Except seven, none returned from Caer Colur.[4]

Caer Sidi is the Fairy castle of Arianrhod described in chapter 18. Gwair is an archetypal youthful prisoner in the castle. Druids and bards such as the Welsh magician Gwydion sought this kind of confinement and initiation in order to become magicians and master poets. The "heavy blue chain" is likely to be water and Prydwen is the ship of King Arthur. Caer Pedryvan ("four-cornered"), Caer Vediwed ("dizziness"), Caer Colur, and Caer Wydr ("glass") are all synonyms for Caer Sidi, the spiral castle of Arianrhod. The poem describes an expedition undertaken to gain the treasures of the Self, like a grail quest. They are seeking the gift of poetic speech, prophecy, wisdom, bounty, and the promise of life after death. The "spoils" or treasure they seek are contained in the magical cauldron of poetry, inspiration, and wisdom. As this is a Welsh verse, it is probably speaking of Ceridwen's cauldron. The destination is envisioned as a huge, ethereal, slowly revolving, shining castle of glass or crystal located at the center of earth, sea, and sky. Of three shiploads who went on the quest only seven men returned, possibly because they were not prepared for this initiation. As suggested in chapter 19, get a good understanding of Ceridwen before you journey to Caer Sidi!

To summarize our discussion up to this point: the evidence for the passage of the Self from one body to another, the passage into other animate and inanimate forms, and finally the passage to the Land of the Living, derives from Celtic sources and contains the essence of Druidic teachings. We interpret this teaching, on the basis of our own experience, to mean that the Self is already complete and whole, but subject to physical sensibilities that condition its state of perception. Without a body, the soul in the Land of the Living experiences pure perception, without any conditioning by physical sensibilities. We conjecture that the Self carries no particular memory of lives over into that state, only the wisdom that is gained from them. The purpose of the "circuit of births" is to extend the experience of the Self into all realms. The multi-lived Self is thus wise because of the compassion that springs from its awareness of unity with all existences.

The Experience of the Realm of Fairy

When the Self assumes a body it undergoes the experience of perceiving through the physical senses. The experience can be confusing especially if the physical-social experience is unduly dysfunctional, painful, and full of suffering. In these circumstances the Self, understandably, is not enamored of the body, and longs for something else. When a spiritual tradition teaches the knowledge of the eternal Self and the passage from one body to another, this longing may be satisfied. Where no tradition exists, or worse, the tradition teaches a distorted cosmology, the longing may lead the individual to obsessions, to vision-seeking, hallucinogens, or any number of extreme spiritual practices. These practices may produce a visionary experience of the Land of the Living, but what we often don't remember is that we perceive this through the subjective sensibilities of the body.

In our considered opinion, the Druids taught that these conditioned experiences are of the Fairy Realm. This lies neither in this world nor in the Land of the Living; it is a realm that produces the sweetest music, the best art, crafts and food, the most tantalizing visions, the most superlative lovers—but it is tremendously deceptive. The Fairy Realm also produces the most intense suffering, bewilderment, illusion, soul-loss, and wandering akin to the description of lost souls in the Graeco-Roman and Christian purgatorial traditions.

We the authors differ on the dangers of the Fairy World. Perhaps because Nicholas was born and raised in England and Maya was raised by Irish-born relatives, our cultural conditioning and even our genetic backgrounds hold the Fairy Realm differently. Nicholas was trained to value the rational while Maya's schooling included superstition and folklore. Besides, Maya was born at Samhain when the ancestors and spirits freely visit us. We encourage you to work through your knowledge and beliefs carefully, so that you are guided in the best way before exposing yourself to potential hazards.

Perhaps because of fear of death, through desire or confused teaching, the Self might pursue happiness in the "never-never world." What delusions can occur! Instead of the ever-existing treasure of the eternal Self, one can end up seeking elusive treasures. You know them well: love, wealth, power, status, beauty, fame. You also know that people seek shamanistic and psychic powers, parlor tricks, even righteousness and grace. These are the glamourous temptations proffered from the Realm of the *Sídhe*. For this reason the Celts feared the Fairy Realm. They took many measures to ensure that newborn children were protected from it.

You, however, are learning clear Druidic teachings. You have an eternal soul that views the ordinary world as a hugely enjoyable passage through physical form. You can access ancestral wisdom through inspired poetry and deep understanding of the myths. There is little reason to seek the glamour and illusion of the Fairy Realms, although you might visit there for teachings from time to time.

In the story of the *Sickness of Cuchulainn or The Only Jealousy of Emer*, Cuchulainn falls in love with a woman from the realm of the *Sídhe*. Her name is Fand, wife of Manannán. Her name means "pearl" or "tear of the fire of the eye." The text says that it was "on account of the pure brilliance of her beauty that Fand was given her name, for there is nothing but a tear in this world or in the world of fairy to which her beauty could be compared."

Cuchulainn is completely besotted with Fand, and his wife, Emer, becomes jealous; we can gather from the story's subtitle that she is not normally jealous. This point is made repeatedly as Cuchulainn passes through his many love affairs without any objection from Emer. This time Emer is jealous because Fand will take Cuchulainn to another world. Not only is Cuchulainn completely beguiled by Fand's glamour, but she demands him all to herself and will do anything to get him. She has already beaten him senseless and let him lie sick for a year. The kind of love she offers is very tempting for its fierce, seductive, possessive, and obsessive qualities. Compared to the love Emer has for Cuchulainn, however, it is the difference between being in love and loving. This story offers a classic example of the dangers of wandering into the Fairy Realm. It is interesting to read what finally cures Cuchulainn of his sickness.

Emer went to Emain Macha and told Conchobor the condition that Cuchulainn was in. Conchobor sent the Druids of Ulster to capture him. Cuchulainn tried to kill the People of Skill, but they chanted magic songs that bound him. After a while some of his wits returned to him and he begged for a drink from their hands. The Druids gave him the drink of forgetfulness, so that he would forget Fand. Then they gave the drink of forgetfulness to Emer, for the state she was in was no better than that of Cuchulainn. Finally, Manannán shook his cloak between Cuchulainn and Fand, so that they should never meet each other again throughout all eternity.[5]

When we are in a body, the physical senses condition our view of the Land of the Living, and what we actually see is the land of Fairy. It is a subjective and less-than-perfect vision of the realm of the infinite and eternal Self. Shamans may be the only people who make it their business to go there; but this requires long training, and it is nearly always deleterious to their health. The purpose of the shaman's journey to the Otherworlds is to contact ancestral spirits, animal powers, the many spirits of place, gods, and goddesses, in order to obtain their guidance for healing, hunting, interpreting omens and dreams, and resolving issues.

Celtic myths with identifiable shamanic content often hint at madness. In the Welsh tradition of Merlin, for example, he goes insane for a while and lives like an animal in the woods. And in the Irish *Frenzy of Suibne*, Suibne exhibits many shamanic characteristics such as flight, transformation into a bird and talking with trees—but he is entirely mad. Keeping these extreme examples in mind, the safest way to bring through the beauty and knowledge of the Fairy Realm is through practicing the Druidic arts, especially the verbal bardic arts of poetry, music, and storytelling.

The Druid path is therefore not particularly shamanistic, although some Druids were shamans. The Druid path is about living in this world and being ready for death and the Land of the Living. Druids concentrate on bringing into this world the beauty, wisdom, and power of the eternal mostly through the expression of the word. The Druids avidly learned to be poets, bards, musicians, storytellers, wisdom-keepers, and speakers of the truth. Inspiration came from the depths, the source within. Although the Fairy World presented a type of easy access to this, it was never really the business of humans to go there. The end will come soon enough: instead of seeing the realm of the ever-living ones through the physical senses, death will ensure that we see it clearly when the time comes.

The Mirror of the *Sidhe*

Let us practice an exercise called the Mirror of the *Sidhe*. The Fairy Realm is reflexive, which means that sooner or later we will perceive in our surroundings whatever we are predisposed to see. The infinite universe, through the fantastic permutations of the Fairy Realm, will shape itself into the ideas, theories, cosmologies, and dreams that we hold about it. Here is the important point: the Fairy Realm of the *Sidhe* is a mirror of ourselves. It shows us the places where we are being run by desires, beliefs, conditioning, and unconscious patterns. If, like Cuchulainn, we are seduced by fantasies of the perfect lover, then the Fairy Realm mirrors this image back to us. If we are on an ingrained path of a religious doctrine, then the Fairy Realm mirrors images of our faith that we have accepted without questioning, such as the images of heaven, paradise, purgatory, and hell.

Journeys into the Fairy Realm are thus enormously revealing. They tell us about ourselves; but we must be careful not to identify with what we meet there. Don't perform the following practice if you are feeling off-center, because you would more likely identify with what you encounter than simply allowing it to pass through the window of your imagination.

Visualize a stone. This is at the center of your being. It is your core, the place you can return to. From this center of stone, imagine yourself to be in the Land of the Sídhe. There is a shining black mirror before you, and you look into it. Allow whatever images there are in the Fairy Realm to come to you. You are solid and strong at your core of stone and cannot be harmed.

Allow your fantasies to emerge and play upon the face of the mirror. Allow your dream lover to emerge and play on the face of the mirror. Allow a perfect and beautiful image of yourself to play upon the mirror.

Do not react to any of these things. Simply allow them to appear and dissolve away. Do not respond to any invitation, or try to speak to any being you may meet. Just watch them emerge and go away again. Do not censor anything; neither react nor respond to it.

Allow whatever god or goddess you choose to appear
on the face of the mirror.
Allow whatever you desire and long for to appear
on the face of the mirror.
Allow whatever you fear to appear
on the face of the mirror.
Allow your imagination to play in whatever forms
the Sídhe come to you.

There is music here, costume and art. There are incredible colors, shapes, and surreal landscapes. Allow whatever it is the Sídhe want to show you. When you are ready to return to your stone, wipe the mirror clean. Say something like: "I am whole." "I am my eternal Self."

Take note of any particular images that strike you. Think about them. Are they running your life, or are you running them? Is there an image of a lover from the Fairy Realm that is preventing you from really being present with your lover in this world? Are you afraid of any of them? If necessary, tell them they are only fantasies, conceptualizations, beliefs. Realize there is nothing to fear: there is only fear itself to confront and accept.

If there is one particular image you would like to work with more deeply, return to the mirror of the Land of the Sídhe, and allow its image to emerge.

If you want this image to become clearer and stronger, be very cautious. This is the magic of glamoury, and what you create here is likely to run your life. It can, however, provide you with information about yourself and others. Women, in particular, may be interested in the magic of glamour. Provided this is used with self-knowledge and restraint it may be an exciting power.

If you want the image to go away, then first you must be certain that you have examined every aspect of it, have really allowed it to pass before you so that you understand it. Very often an image will disperse only when it has become fully conscious. It had power when unconscious, but it cannot stand the clarity of consciousness, and will dissolve away as the fantasy it always was.

Transition to the Next World

After an initial period of absolute wonder, bodily life may appear very limited to the incarnate Self. This may produce a sense of longing in the Self for what feels missing or lost. We like to reassure ourselves with belief that there is a "beyond," but the physical senses cannot perceive it. Nature might seem to be experimenting, and as easily can discard us as it did the dinosaurs. The reassurance that there is a "beyond" actually lies in something that we are all familiar with, and that is death. As Druids operating with immortal souls we must examine death very closely.

Death actually means death. Death means precisely what it means: an end, a cessation, an expiration, a dissolution of the existence of the body. Death assures us that there is an end to the experience of the body. Death assures us that there is an end to the experiences of suffering, shame, guilt, hopelessness, rejection, sorrow, hatred, revenge. Death equally assures us that there is an end to the experiences of love, ecstasy, happiness, and hope—an end to every facet of life. Only with complete cessation can there be complete renewal. As stated earlier, death ensures that things evolve. If even one thing were to carry over from the experience of life in a body, then we would be doomed to live forever in the absence of complete transformation and renewal. Death promises an end to everything that we identify with, cling to, and which ultimately confines us. This conclusion is completely natural: scientists theorize that our cells contain material that is timed to bring about death. The Celts had no fear of death, and, as remarked upon by the Romans, happily met their end in battle or elsewhere, assured of an afterlife.

The *immrama* or "wonder-voyages" of Celtic mythic heroes such as Bran, Arthur, and Maeldun take them to many islands. These islands appear as distractions from the main goal of their journey, which is to reach the Land of the Living and obtain the "treasures" that lie there.

A psychopomp or conductor of souls aids each traveler on the journey. In the *Voyage of Bran*, the psychopomp is Manannán, the sea god of the Tuatha Dé Danann. He appears in his chariot upon the waves and points the way to the Land of the Living, here called the Island of Women. His presence suggests that the way to this land is not easy and requires some guidance. It may be that the way to this land is through the realm of the *Sídhe* which presents some danger to the voyager.

The first island that Bran comes to, the Island of Joy, is in another world. It is not the ultimate destination of the soul. The man who lands there gapes in wonder and laughter, but has no other experience. Bran is now warned, and is extremely careful when he finally arrives at the Island of Women.

In the *Voyage of Maeldun*, the travelers visit a total of thirty-three islands. Each one has a quality similar to the Island of Joy. They exist in another realm and present some fair, foul, or ambiguous archetypal quality that never changes. The danger of the Fairy World is that nothing ever changes. The Self has to remain focused on its ultimate goal of transformation to reach the Land of the Living. This can be likened to the journey through the Bardos to the pure land of the Buddha in the Tibetan Buddhist tradition.

John O'Donohue in his work on Celtic-Christian spirituality, *Anam Cara*, speaks of the "soul-friend," a literal translation of the title from the Irish. The duty of the soul-friend is to hold the bigger picture of another person's soul. The soul-friend supports a soul on its path, especially on its circuit of existences and the journey after death. Although this is now a task almost exclusively reserved for clerics, it was a custom of

Celtic Christians, especially the women. Peter Berresford Ellis writes that the soul-friend "was a concept used in pre-Christian Celtic society, and the role was usually filled by a druid." If each one of us was the *anam ċara* for another person, it would revive a Druidic duty and be of great benefit to us all.[6]

The Practice of Transition

We base the following practice of transitioning from human form to the eternal Self on our analysis of Celtic myths, and on our work with those who are dying. It draws upon our ritual experiences within a death and dying group, and detailed group study of *The Tibetan Book of Living and Dying* by Sogyal Rinpoche. We highly recommend this book. We do not claim that the following procedure is authentically Druidic, although glimpsing multiple worlds is common to both the Celtic and Tibetan cultures. Please use what you are comfortable with and create your own way of helping others to cross over.

This practice is intended to assist a person who is in the process of dying or has recently passed over. The best preparation for this practice is to put yourself in a state of love and compassion for the dying or dead person, as well as for friends and relatives. Sincerity is the true measure of this practice, and its words are most meaningful when springing directly from the heart.

If you feel that this ceremony will be of comfort to friends and relatives of the dying or dead person, invite them to participate. You will then need to respect and accommodate the beliefs of those who attend. Those participating should also be able to contribute support to the passage of the dying or dead person and not be immersed in their own issues of grief. You can do the practice alone, or silently, or at a distance from the deceased.

We write the following practice as if a woman has recently died. If you are helping a dead man or someone still in the dying process, you can adjust the words accordingly.

Prepare the space, either around the body, or elsewhere. Ensure that all is quiet and you will not be disturbed.

Say a prayer to invite the inspiration and guidance that will help you and the deceased.

Invite the others present to bring in their own guidance, which may be divine powers and other beneficent spirits.

Ask all these powers for help in the transition of the deceased from this world to the next world. If you like, you may name the next world, for example: the Land of the Living, the Land of Youth, the Isle of the Blessed, or other terms.

Quietly explain to the deceased what is happening. Explain the situation clearly and frankly. Let her know that existence in her physical body is over, and that any pain and suffering are likewise over.

Explain that she is an immortal soul. Her eternal Self has completed this cycle of birth, life, and death, and is returning to the place from which it came.

Tell her that there is nothing to fear. In fact, this is an opportunity of enormous release.

Say that she need have no regrets, remorse, guilt, or shame about anything she has done or failed to do in this life. She can, without fear or anxiety, let go of any attachments she may have to loved ones, and freely depart from this existence.

Let her know that all present are ready to support her in her transition to the next world. Those present can now say aloud that they have forgiven her, loved her, and let her go.

Remind her again that she is an immortal soul who is passing from this world and returning to the state of her eternal Self. Tell her that she has had many births, lives, and deaths. This is one death in the cycle of her existences. Now she is awakening into the experience of her eternal Self.

If you sense that that there is considerable fear of physical death, or grieving, regret, confusion, or some other suffering present around the soul of the deceased, pay particular attention to this. Soothe the atmosphere. Remind the soul of its true nature, and that release of the body is an occasion for freedom, joy, opportunity, and transformation.

When you feel that the soul and those present are ready, say something along the lines of the following:

Eternal Self, Soul of (name deceased here),
You have dwelt in this body for the span of its life,
Say farewell now to that which has nourished and supported you.
Say farewell to the body that has been such a constant companion and
provider of your life experience!
Look lovingly upon this empty body, thank it for all it has given you,
and now release it.

Eternal Self,
You are not a body.
You are an immortal soul.
Your dwelling is in . . . (the Land of the Living, the Summerland, etc.)
You are ready to continue your cycle of existences.
You are ready to go to the place of your full and divine nature.

Now invite the others to visualize the soul of the deceased above the body. Take time to allow the full sense of the soul to gather in a splendid way.

Say something like: "This is the soul of . . . It is ready to go to the home of its eternal Self."

Now visualize a radiant presence in front of the soul. Invite those present to picture this divine presence in any way they choose. Take some time to allow this wonderful presence to fill the room. Invite the soul itself to picture the divine as a pure, soothing, and inviting presence.

Say something like the following:

Eternal Self, (name deceased here),
This radiant presence is the brilliance of the Divine
It is the mirror of the divine radiance of your being.
It is the true nature of your being.
It comes from where you came, and to where you will return.

Now invite all present to visualize the soul moving from above the dead body into the presence of the divine. See it move toward and into the radiant divine. Reassure the soul silently or aloud that this is the journey it must make. Speak words of encouragement.

When the soul has completely merged with the divine, see the combined presence dissolve and pass away. If you like, you may see the presence move outward from the room on a bridge of light, or as a flash of light moving into space.

If everyone present is familiar and comfortable with the Druid tradition, then it is appropriate at this point to call on a psychopomp, a guide to escort the soul to the Land of the Living. The following example calls on Manannán. After this, make sure that everyone present is firmly awake, and ground the practice by sharing food or beverages.

> *Manannán of the surging sea,*
> *Manannán of the crested waves,*
> *Manannán of the bright seahorses,*
> *Come in your chariot across the beautiful sea.,*
> *And take this soul to its eternal home.*
>
> *Manannán, of the land of the Tree of Life,*
> *Of the land of poetry, truth, and love,*
> *Of the land of feasts and many-colored hospitality,*
> *Carry this soul safely by your side,*
> *To its eternal home.*

The Experience of the Next World

Death finally provides the opportunity for us to enter the next world. As with the entry to this world, the exit from it is an occasion to celebrate. Death takes us to the other shore, and our perceptions no longer come from the physical senses of the body. Lest this appear to be disapproving, the departing Self thanks the body and nature for their provision of the experience of life. Whatever we may be suffering in our bodies, death is the opportunity to release this and be grateful to the body. Although it is extremely sad for us to lose people we are close to, we must make the effort to be a soul-friend to them and celebrate their journey onwards. Perhaps you will hold an event in the tradition of the Irish wake.

Death provides the opportunity to live eternally. We become who we are in the infinite, beyond the sensibilities provided by nature. Nothing can be carried over: no belief, no faith, creed, love, regret, possessions—nothing. Yet the Self is unconcerned.

It is absorbed with experiencing the Land of the Living. In the same way as life in a body provides the way for the self to dance with nature, with the goddess of the land or of sovereignty, so death provides the opportunity for the eternal Self to dance with the infinite.

You can hear this in the tale of the Irish monk entranced by the beauty of a bird singing in an orchard. He hears the bird singing, sees the trees flooded with color and light, and is enraptured by the whole experience. When the moment ends he goes back into the monastery, but the monks do not know him. They consult their records and find that his self-description and the names of his fellows match those who dwelt in the monastery 200 years before. During those 200 years the monk in the orchard was not concerned with thoughts, loved ones, regrets, or memories of this world. He was concerned with exploring the infinite nature of the moment.[7]

Another window into the experience of the Land of the Living is the universal story of the Good Steward who keeps the estate of a great lord in good order. When the Lord returns, the place of honor is given to the steward. The lord is the eternal Self, and the steward is its experience while having a body. The steward cares for self in the community of earthly life. The Lord returns at the time of death, when the full nature of the eternal Self is restored. Celtic kings were stewards of the land. In the *Book of Invasions*, the king of Ireland is Nuada. He is struggling against the Fomor who represent chaos and destruction. Nuada steps down from the throne when Lugh arrives. The immortal Lugh brings sovereignty, leadership, and skill to the land of Ireland, just as we experience the powers of our true Self when we joyously return to the Land of the Living.

> *When Nuada of the Silver Arm saw all these things that Lugh could do, he thought that Lugh would free the country from the tyranny of the Fomor. So Nuada welcomed Lugh, and he came down from his throne and put Lugh on it so that all might listen to him.*[8]

Activities

The Stone of the Self. In the story of the coming of the Tuatha Dé Danann to Ireland, they bring with them the Stone of Destiny. This cries out when touched by the true sovereign. Imagine traversing the inner landscape of your being and coming to a stone that marks the place of your self-sovereignty. What does it look like? Reach out to the stone. Enter into it. What sound does it make?

At the beginning of this chapter the quotation from the *Voyage of Bran* describes a singing stone. Take a moment to reread the poem. This is an image of the eternal Self. What would it feel like to be such a stone?

Select a stone—ideally the Druid's Egg of chapter 3—and use it to focus your attention. At the point of stillness, of center, allow yourself to feel the eternal nature of your Self. Use this stone whenever you go to this place. Charge it with the power of your experiences there. If possible, make arrangements to have this stone accompany you to the grave.

Connecting with Your Ancestors. Go to a place in the landscape where you can feel a connection to your ancestors. Invite your Self to be present, and ask what it shares with those who have gone ahead into old age and death. If you have children, this might be a very important question and answer to share with them. We owe it to those who come after us to leave signposts of the way. What signposts have your ancestors left you, and what will you leave for your children?

Your Own Crossing Over. How would you like to go out from this world? Are your affairs in order? If you wish, think about a script for your wake. Let others know your wishes.

Notes

1. From the *Imram Brain maic Febail*. The version given here is based upon the translations of Kuno Meyer (1895) and Lady Gregory (1904).

2. Psilocybin or "liberty caps."

3. A coherent attempt at recreating Druidic shamanism is being made by Caitlín and John Matthews, for example in John Matthews' *The Celtic Shaman*.

4. *Preiddeu Annwn*, from *The Book of Taliesen*. Recension based upon Robert Graves (1952), and John Matthews (1991), see also *The Celtic Shaman*, pp. 251–2. This poem is more likely to have been composed in Wales in the thirteenth century than the sixth, and its meaning is obscure.

5. From the eleventh century *Leabhar ne h-Uidhri*, transcribed from the earlier and now lost *Yellow Book of Slane*, translation based on Lady Gregory (1903), A. H. Leahy (1905), and Cross and Slover (1936).

6. John O'Donohue, *Anam Cara*, 1997, Caitlín Matthews, 1994, p. 305, and Peter Berresford Ellis, 1995, p. 18.

7. Ibid.

8. *Leabhar Gabála*, based on the translation of Lady Gregory (1904).

Guide to Celtic Deities, People, and Places

A Note on Pronunciation: The accent is always on the first syllable in Irish words. All words are from Irish unless given as (W) = Welsh. In Irish, an "h" means the letter before it is silent, although "ch" is pronounced as in the Scottish loch. An "m" is pronounced either as "v" or "w." Differences in spelling and pronouncing Irish occur due to old and new variations, dialects, traditions, Anglicization, and linguistic concern for showing the root origin of a word. During the time we spent at Emain Macha, for example, we listened to many pronunciations of the name and rarely heard the same one repeated from locals and scholars alike.

A

Ailill—(al-il): King of Connacht and husband of Maeve.

Ailinne, Dún—(doon aw-lin): The huge circular ring-fort on the Hill of Allen in Leinster was established by Nuada, a Chief Druid. He named it after his wife Almu. Fionn mac Cumhail later made it his home. Sometimes spelled "Aillinne."

Amergin—(av-ir-in): "born of song": Amergin White-Knee, poet of the Gaels, enables them to ally themselves with the sovereign goddesses of Ireland. His poetic incantation to Ériu instantly quiets the storm wrought by the Tuatha Dé Danann, and allows the ships of the Gael to land on Ireland's shore.

Anam: The soul. The *anam ċara* or "soul-friend" has the responsibility to guide the soul through the passage of birth, life, and death.

Aneirin—(W) (anayrin): See Amergin.

Aonghus Óg—(ahng-is ohg): The son of the Dagda and Boann, whose home is Brú na Boinne (Newgrange). Angus is the youthful Irish god of love and beauty, foster father to Dairmuid O'Duibne. His name is also spelled "Angus."

Annwn—(W) (anoo-in): The Land of the *Sídhe*, literally the "not-world." Sometimes referred to as Annwfn.

Aobh—(aev): Mother of the Children of Lir.

Aoife—(ee-fe): (1) Warrior princess defeated by Cuchulainn;

(2) the stepmother/aunt of the Children of Lir; and

(3) the lover of Ilbrec, son of Manannán, who was changed into a crane. Her skin was used to make the original Crane Bag.

Arianrhod—(W) (ah-ri-ahn-hrod): "Silver Wheel." Daughter of Don, sister of Gwydion, mother of Lleu Llaw Gyffes. She is the "virgin queen" who dwells in a spiral castle and controls the tides.

Awen—(W) (a-oo-en): Inspiration.

B

Badb—(bav): "Fury." A battle goddess who appears to be an aspect of the Morrigán, along with Nemain and Macha.

Banba—(bawn-va): The "sow" of the Plough is one of the three tutelary and sovereign goddesses of the land of Ireland.

Balor of the Evil Eye: King of the Fomorians. Balor attempts to ignore the fundamental rule of sovereignty by diminishing the power of the women about him. He imprisons his daughter in a tower hoping to prevent the natural law of succession. He ignores the warnings of his wife Ceithlenn. His power turns bad within him and manifests as his "evil eye." Lugh slays him at the Second Battle of Moy Tura.

Beltane—(beal-tinah): The festival at the beginning of May to mark the putting out of cattle and the planting season. Also spelled Bealtaine.

Beth-Luis-Nion: The Irish alphabet named after the trees and originating in Ogham. The letters' names are:

> Beth, Luis, Nion, Fearn, Saille, Huath, Duir, Tinne, Coll, Quert, Muin, Gort, Ngetal, Straiph, Ruis, Ailm, Ohn, Ura, Eado, Idho.

Boann—(bo-un): "White cow," the goddess of the River Boyne and mate of the Dagda.

Bodb—(bohv): Bodb Dearg, the "Red Crow," son of the Dagda and father of Sadb. His *sídhe* (fairy hill) lies in Co. Galway.

Bran—(brahn): (1) Son of Febal who voyaged to the Land of Women;

(2) (W) King of Britain. Bran, "raven," is keeper of a cauldron of regeneration. The raven is the messenger between the worlds.

Bricriu—(brik-ru): The pleasure of Bricriu of the Bitter or Poisoned Tongue is always to create conflict and trouble. Some say this resulted from an old wound.

Brigit—(bri-hed): "High one." Originally a goddess of the land of Leinster and daughter of the Dagda, Brigit became popular throughout the western Celtic world and successfully made the transformation to a Christian saint.

Brú na Boinne—(bru na boyn): "[gods'] house of the Boyne" in Co. Meath, the greatest concentration of Neolithic ceremonial sites in Ireland. In Celtic myth Brú na Boinne refers to the mound now known as Newgrange, the home of Aonghus Óg. It is said that Angus loved Diarmuid, and after his death tried to restore him through enchantment. This proved impossible, but nonetheless Diarmuid would appear briefly to Angus in spirit or light form on one day of the year. Newgrange was built so that at dawn on the Winter Solstice the sun penetrates the long passageway and illuminates the carved chamber within the mound for a brief period of time. Is it possible that here, embedded in Celtic myth, is an account of this extraordinary astronomical event?

C

Cathbad—(kah-ha): The Druid of Emain Macha and King Conchobor Mac Nessa of Ulster.

Celts—(kelts): The name given to the European tribes north of the Mediterranean by the Greeks and Romans. This covered an extremely diverse group of peoples. More precisely, the term "Celtic" refers to the family of languages, of Indo-European origin, spoken across a broad area of Europe and introduced there from as early as 2000 B.C.E. More precisely still, Celtic is the name given by historians to describe the cultural impulse that began in central Europe (Hallstat) before 1000 B.C.E., but which achieved its full flowering with the La Tène era sometime after 500 B.C.E. This culture (with its virtue of combining all definitions) developed urban, centralized, hierarchical, and socially stratified features including nobles, priests, warriors, craftsmen, and farmers, characteristic of its Indo-European origins. Growth depended upon trade with the Mediterranean world, and for many centuries the Graeco-Roman world mirrored the Celtic and vice versa. The Druid class grew in response to these social developments and, like the priests of Etruria and Rome, served the warrior class and nobles. Following the conquest by Rome, Celtic or Gaelic-speaking culture has survived only on the northern and western fringes of Europe. Nevertheless, it has had an enormous effect on the Western world, especially in North America.

Ceridwen—(W) (kerid-wen): The origin and meaning of Ceridwen's name is obscure, but she appears as a Goddess of Inspiration (*awen*,) a sorceress, a Fairy woman, shapeshifter, and crone.

Cernunnos—(ker-noo-nos): See Herne.

Champion's Portion: The portion given by the king to his champion. The allocation of the portions at the royal feast define an order in which every person has a place. In this manner the order of the community becomes visible. Ritually sharing in the body of a creature makes a statement that at once mirrors the divisions of the social order and binds it together. The ritual partaking of a body in a feast in the Dionysian, Orphic, Osirisian, and Christian traditions involves the body of the god and establishes order on a cosmic scale.

Conchobor—(kun-hur or con-or): Conchobor Mac Nessa was King of Ulster after Fergus Mac Roth.

Cruachan—(cru-a-ghin): Rath Cruachan is the ceremonial center of Connacht, traditionally the home and royal house of Queen Maeve. There is a cave there, known as the "Cave of the Cats," that is an entrance to the Fairy Realm. See Maeve.

Cuailgne—(cooli): A province in Ulster where dwelt the Brown Bull which Maeve coveted.

Cuchulainn—(cu-chullin): The Ulster champion, the Hound of Culann. His father is Lugh, his mother Dechtire, daughter of the Druid Cathbad. His most famous exploit was to stand alone against the combined armies of Ireland led by Maeve while the men of Ulster lay under the curse of Macha.

Curoi mac Daire or **Cui Roi**—(koo-ri): Associated in part with the Fairy realm, this powerful deity claimed his earthly home in Munster. He challenges the heroes of Ulster to a beheading game.

D

Dagda—(dag-da): "Good Father." A deity of the Tuatha Dé Danann, the father of Brigit and other tutelary goddesses of Ireland. He has a "cauldron of plenty," and a club which destroys with one end and heals with the other. He is likely to have originated as a fertility god.

Dana or **Danu:** "Mother of the Gods." Danu is mentioned briefly in Celtic myth, then forgotten, unless she is also Anu or Aine, the solar goddess who is honored at many sites, especially the megalithic temples. She may also be the personification of the eternal spirit of the *tuath* or tribe.

Diarmuid O'Duibhne—(dermuit o'duv-ne): Grandson of the love-god Angus Óg, Diarmuid has a "love spot" which no woman can resist. Considered the best champion of the Fianna after Fionn and Oisin, Diarmuid is persuaded by Princess Grania to elope with her. Aided by Angus, they avoid their pursuers for sixteen years. Then Fionn offers peace and the couple settle down. Fionn fails to prevent

Diarmuid from dying from a magical boar's goring. Angus takes the soul of Diarmuid to Brú na Boinne, but can only communicate with it once a year.

Deirdre—(d'er-druh): (1) When the Druid Cathbad foretells that Deirdre would become the most beautiful woman in Ireland, King Conchobor keeps her as his own. She falls in love with Noisiu and they flee to Alba (Scotland) with his two brothers. Conchobor kills Noisiu's brothers, thus betraying the honor of Fergus Mac Roth who has them under his protection. Eventually, Deirdre kills herself.

(2) Deirdre of the Black Mountain, the messenger of Fionn mac Cumhail. The myths imply she was so swift that she could fly. It is possible she was a Druid.

Don—(W) (dawn): Goddess of the Fairy Realm or World of the *Sídhe*. See Danu.

Druid—(current definition): A keeper of the wisdom, laws, history, stories, and values of the Celtic branch of the Native European spiritual path. A practitioner of the Celtic cultural, spiritual, and magical tradition, who honors the land and all things in the animal, plant, and mineral worlds and the earth, sea, and sky.

—(ancient definition): The class of people who presided at divinations and sacrifices of the Celts. They were natural philosophers, scholars, magicians, bards, judges, and political advisors to Celtic chieftains and nobles.

E

Emain Macha—(evin or owin maha): Emain Macha, the royal seat of Ulster, now known as Navan Fort, lies two miles west of the town of Armagh. Emain Macha was the place of sovereignty, the cosmological and ceremonial center and the seat of power of the Ulaid of Ulster. It was laid out according to the brooch from the cloak of the goddess Macha. Emain Macha is dominated by a hill ringed by a huge earthen bank and ditch and topped by a great mound. Around 100 B.C.E. a massive circular timber structure about 130 feet in diameter was built upon the hill and then deliberately destroyed, perhaps after a decade, as part of the rites for the construction of the mound.

Emain Macha was Ulster's equivalent of the royal seat of Tara in Meath or of Cruachan in Connacht. For a long time it was assumed that these places were habitation sites and must have had thrones, banqueting halls, and houses. We now know that the main purpose of the great mounds and circular enclosures was ceremonial. The banks of the enclosures are outside the ditches, not inside as would be needed to defend a habitation site. Few structures were ever built on or beside the central mounds, and reconstruction shows that they were suited for ritual.

The social structure of Emain Macha is indicated by the raths or ring-forts on hills nearby. It is probable that the king lived in a ring-fort on one hill, the warriors of the Red Branch on another, while people such as craftsmen conducted their livelihood in the vicinity. We find mentions of Druids in the texts of Emain Macha. One text describes the foundation of a hospital attended by Druid physicians in 300 B.C.E., the first record of such an institution in Europe. The *Táin Bó Cuailnge* says the custom of Emain Macha was that none could speak before the king and he could not speak before his Druids.

Emer—(eve-er or ay-ver): Wife of Cuchulainn. There is no mention of their having children.

Eochaid—(yoch-i): A name common among the Irish kings. The most well-known was Eochaid Airemh, "of the plough," lover of Etain.

Ériu—(ayr-u): Ériu, of the Sun, one of the three tutelary and sovereign goddesses of the land of Ireland.

Etain—(etoin): The most famous Etain was loved by Midir of the *Sídhe* and the High King Eochaid. Her story contains this classic description of a sovereign Goddess of the Land:

> *The king was going over the green of Bri Leith and he saw at the side of the spring there a woman. She had a comb of gold and silver, and she was washing in a silver basin with four golden birds chased upon it and small bright purple carbuncles set around the rim. A beautiful purple cloak she had beside her, with silver fringes to it and a golden brooch. She had on a dress of green silk embroidered in red gold with marvelously wrought clasps of gold and silver on her breasts and shoulders. The sunlight was falling upon her so that the gold and the green silk shone out. Two tresses of hair she had, four locks in each tress and a gold bead at the point of every lock. Her hair was the color of the yellow flag iris in summer, or the colour of red gold after it is polished.*

She was letting her hair down to wash it, and her arms were out through the sleeve-holes of her dress. Her arms and wrists were long and straight, and as white as the snow of a single night. Her cheeks were as red as the foxgloves of the moor. Her fingers were long and of great whiteness, and her nails beautiful and pink. Her eyebrows were as blue-black as a beetles wing; her eyes were as blue as the hyacinth; her even teeth were like a shower of pearls in her head, and her lips were as red as the berries of the rowan tree. Her shoulders were high, smooth and white, and her long slender yielding side was as soft and as white as the foam of a wave. Her thighs were firm, warm and sleek; her were knees round and small; her shins were white and straight. The bright light of the moon shone in her face; the highness of pride was in her smooth brows, and the light of love was in both her eyes. The dimple of sport was in her cheeks, and in them there came and went flushes as purple and as red as the blood of any calf, and others with the brilliance of snow. A gentle, strong dignity was in her voice; and when she walked her step was as steady and as stately as that of a queen. She was the most perfect of the women of the world that the eyes of men had ever seen. They who saw her thought she must be one of the race of the fairies. [From *Tochmarc Etáine,* the "Courtship of Etain," recension based on the translations of Lady Augusta Gregory (1904), A. H. Leahy (1905), and Jeffrey Gantz (1981).]

Ethlinn—(elin): Daughter of the Fomorian leader Balor of the Evil Eye. Forewarned that he would be slain by his grandson, Balor imprisoned Ethlinn in a tower and forebade her sight of any man. Cian of the Tuatha Dé Danann is disguised as a woman by the Druid, Birog of the Mountains. Cian finds Ethlinn and their union produces Lugh.

F

Fand—(fon or fahn): Fand the "Tear of the Fire of the Eye" is Manannán's wife. She seduces Cuchulainn into the fairy world. Fand also represents the goddess in whose possession are keys to the eternal realm of the soul. It is in her domain that the orchard of sustaining fruits lies. The orchard is full of singing birds—symbols of the higher Self. She herself first appears as a beautiful bird—probably a swan—diving into the waters that represent the subconsciousness. In her court is the continuously full cauldron of plenty. At its door stands the Tree of Life, brilliant as gold, from which issues forth sweet and soft harmonies. Her island realm is reached by crossing the waters where dwell the "masters of music." This realm is a glamourous illusion and more. It finds its equivalent in all the world mythologies. What it means is different for each person, but the imagery nourishes the deepest part of our soul—the longing for union with another, with the divine source, for the experience of the eternal Self.

Fedlimid—(fay-lim-i): Harpist and father of Deirdre. The name of his wife is not given.

Ferdiad—(fer-di-uh): The friend and foster-brother of Cuchulainn who is finally persuaded by Maeve into fighting him in the greatest single combat of the *Táin*.

Fergus Mac Roth: King of Ulster, he is tricked out of the kingship by Conchobor. He becomes Conchobor's champion but the relationship is fragile. When betrayed by Conchobor over the Sons of Uisliu, Fergus goes to Connacht to serve Queen Maeve. His cause, often overlooked by those who see Maeve to blame for the *Táin Bó Cuailnge*, almost wins the day against Ulster.

Fidchell—(fad-hel): A Celtic game equivalent to chess. It involves preventing the king of your opponent from reaching the center of the board. This would seem to confirm that the struggle in the great *fidchell* games of Celtic mythology is one of sovereignty.

Fionn Mac Cumhail—(f'un mac cool): The most famous leader of the warrior band called the Fianna. Collectively, the stories of Fionn and his son Oisin form the Fenian Cycle of early Irish literature. These stories tend to be more magical than The Ulster Cycle, which focuses on the *Táin*, and were perhaps composed at an earlier date. Fionn is also known by the Anglicized spelling "Finn Mac Cool."

Fionnabair—(f'un-a-vir): Daughter of Maeve and Aillill. The second most famous cattle raid of Ireland, the *Táin Bó Fraoch*, is undertaken on her behalf. The Welsh equivalent is Gwenhwyvar, known in English as Guinevere.

Fir Bolg: The "Men of the Bag." The Fir Bolg are among the first inhabitants of Ireland. They are chthonic, and use primitive flint tools although they are on good terms with agriculture.

Fir flathemon—(feer flah-mun): The word, justice, or truth of the ruler: "The Truth of Sovereignty."

Fodhla—(fo-lah): "of the Hazel." One of the three tutelary and sovereign goddesses of the land of Ireland.

G

Geis—(geys), plural **gessa**: There seem to be at least two kinds of *geis*. The first usually takes the form of a prohibition that is laid upon a person early on in life. The *geis* on Cuchulainn is that he never eat the flesh of a dog, his namesake. If he did, he would surely die. The *geis* on Fergus is that he never refuse a feast. It was a *geis* on everyone not to turn the left-hand side of their chariot to Emain Macha. The literature makes it clear that a *geis* has a magical quality about it. More than a prohibition, it is an charge set by a poet or a Druid, that determines the destiny of the soul. The second kind of *geis* was more like a promise, a bond, or an oath of loyalty. Breaking bonds did not necessarily lead to death, but it would reflect upon a person's honor, and honor was held to be worth more than life.

Grania or **Gráinne**: Daughter of the High King, Cormac Mac Airt. She elopes with Diarmuid after being promised to Fionn Mac Cumhail. Fionn pursues the couple for many years, and, as a result, many of the dolmens in Ireland are known as "beds of Diarmuid and Grania." After Diarmuid's death, Grania returns to Fionn. Her name relates her to Grian, the sun.

Gundestrup Cauldron: This exquisite silver-plated cauldron, found in a bog in Denmark, is of Thracian manufacture, and probably belongs to the third century B.C.E. Celtic tribes were settling throughout the Balkans at this time, and the cauldron was likely to have been a gift of allegiance and hospitality for a chief.

Gwydion —(W) (gwu-dion): Son of Don, he was a magician and the father of Lleu Llaw Gyffes through incest with his sister Arianrhod.

Gwynn ap Nydd—(W) (gowin ap nithe): A psychopomp and leader of the Wild Hunt. His appearances are usually mercurial and more threatening than those of Manannán. He often wears horns, rides a great horse, and is accompanied by the white-furred, red-eyed Hounds of the Fairy Realm, the Cwm Annwn. Unlike Manannán, who escorts them over the sea, the Wild Hunt takes travellers and the deceased into the Otherworlds through an opening on land. The Isle of Avalon, for example, is first reached by boat, then the traveller is guided by Gwynn into an opening in the seven-tiered mount, Glastonbury Tor. See Herne.

H

Herne: A horned god of fertility and the hunt. While Herne the Hunter is specific to Windsor Great Park in Britain, the name is known from Roman inscriptions in Gaul as Cernunnos. This name in Gaelic becomes Herne, because the 'c' becomes "ch," pronounced "h," and the Latin suffix -*unnos* is deleted. Probably orginating extremely early in the Native European Tradition as a man dressed in skins and horns to aid in the hunt, his image remained popular into the Celtic era. It is likely Herne who is depicted sitting cross-legged holding a ram-headed snake on the Gundestrup Cauldron.

Hero-Light: The hero-light, the hero-halo, the warrior's-moon, the horns, the "sparks and mists of the Badb," are descriptions of auric emanations from the body that become visible around great warriors such as Cuchulainn. It is customary to provide deities with such auras and halos in the world religious traditions, but they usually accompany states of sublime ecstasy rather than anger and battle madness. The wrathful deities of the Buddhist tradition, and the terrible forms of Hindu deities such as Shiva, Lord of Destruction, also possess such auric manifestations, perhaps providing a better parallel.

I

Imbas—(im-as): Inspiration or intuition; this is the Irish equivalent of the Welsh word *awen*.

Imbolc—(immolc): The festival at the beginning of February which celebrates the returning light, the first lambs, and the flow of ewe's milk.

L

La Tène: The name given to the art style of the Celts that developed in central Europe from the mid fifth century B.C.E. Its abstract, often asymmetrical, curvilinear art of spirals, tendrils, and scrolls took Celtic craftsmanship to a new peak. Irish La Tène decorative work on high-status objects of metal is particularly noteworthy.

Laeg—(loy-gh): Charioteer of Cuchulainn.

Laeghaire—(leer-ry): A champion of the Red Branch of Ulster.

Lleu Llaw Gyffes—(W) (hlu-hlow-gufess): The Welsh equivalent of Lugh, with less than divine powers.

Lugaid—(lew-ih): There are many Lugaids in Irish myth. Lugaid, the son of Curoi Mac Daire, kills Cuchulainn's charioteer Laeg, which leads to the death of Cuchulainn.

Lugh—(loo): Son of Cian of the Tuatha De Danann and Ethlinn of the Fomor. Lugh is fostered by a queen of the Fir Bolg, thereby blending all the races of Ireland. Lugh means "shining" or "bright one." *Lugh Lámhfada* (loo-law-fada) is "Lugh of the Long Arm," a solar deity and the master of all crafts, or *samildanach*. He is the father of Cuchulainn and foster-son of Manannán.

Lughnasadh—(loo-na-sa): The festival of Lugh at the beginning of August that celebrated first harvest, and at which goods were traded, contracts were ratified, judgements given, and games held.

M

Macha—(mah-ha): An aspect of the Battle Goddess, The Morrigán. She is credited for building Emain Macha, and for uttering the curse that lays the men of Ulster low in the *Táin Bó Cuailnge*:

> *From this time forth until the ninth generation,*
> *When Ulster is in need of its greatest strength,*
> *When your enemies are upon you and danger is at every hand,*
> *Then the pangs of a woman in childbirth will fall upon the men of Ulster,*
> *And your pain and your weakness will last the length of five days and*
> *four nights.*

Macha is like Epona of Gaul and Rhiannon of Wales. She is a goddess of horses and a foundation deity, the sovereign and chthonic goddess of place. Macha means a plain. She also appears in the stories of the Tuatha Dé Danann as a crow-goddess feeding on the heads of fallen men. To go against the power of the feminine as it manifests in horses, land, and battle is to invite a curse that will make you weakest in the time of your greatest need.

Manannán Mac Lir—(mahn-uh-nawn moc leer): Sea god of the Tuatha Dé Danann. In the *Voyage of Bran*, he appears in his chariot upon the waves and points the way to the Land of Women. This suggests he is a psychopomp, a guide to the Otherworlds, and a helper of humankind. In the Land of the *Sídhe* he presides over the "Feast of Age." He also has a sense of humor.

Maeve or Medb—(me'v): "intoxicating." Queen of Connacht. In the *Táin Bó Cuailnge* the character of Maeve is established immediately: she is the equal of all, though in her own mind she is better than anyone. She has more wealth, better judgement, is more open-handed, and can beat anyone in a fight. She rules in her own right; she sleeps with whomever she pleases—and her husband had better not be jealous!

Maeve's court is Cruachan of the Enchantments on the Plain of Ai. It was as important a center in Celtic Ireland as Emain Macha or Tara. Today the remains of Cruachan, or Rath Croaghan, cover an extensive area. Ring forts, mounds, and linear earthworks (ceremonial chariot ways?) extend for four square miles near Tulsk in Co. Roscommon. The greatest mound measures eight yards high, ninety-six yards in diameter, and was surrounded by a perimeter fence with a diameter of almost 800 yards, twice the size of Tara or Emain Macha! It was clearly for ceremonial purposes. Cruachan belongs to the great age of the Irish Celts, 600 B.C.E. to 400 C.E., and was the seat of the sovereignty of the province of Connacht. Maeve herself is said to be buried on the dramatic hill of Knocknarea, just west of the city of Sligo. On the summit of the hill is a colossal mound that bears her name, Queen Maeve's Grave. Her spirit does seem to dwell around the place even though the mound of stones belongs to the Neolithic age of passage-mound building, the fourth millennium B.C.E.

Clues like this tell us that Maeve is older than when the action of the *Táin* traditionally takes place. There are in fact, several Maeves. We have a "Good Queen Meb" or "Mab" of Irish and British folklore, a somewhat ludicrous figure for children's bedtime stories or for bawdy tavern jokes. We have a Maeve of the Christian transcribers: shrewish, possessive, envious, vain, shameless, lascivious, immoral, arrogant, bribing her followers, using her daughter, taken over by the weaknesses of women. We have a Maeve of the Celts: a great queen, generous, open-handed, giver of feasts, giver of good-judgements, beautiful, sexy, a warrior, noble, proud, fierce and a great leader. And we have a Maeve who was a figure of myth even to the Celts: a tutelary goddess of the land, a goddess of sovereignty, an ancestral deity, a chthonic figure of fertility, of plenty in the herds, the soil and the wombs of women, the spirit of the tribal mother, the larger-than-life embodiment of the divine feminine.

Midhir—(mee-hir): Son of the Dagda, Midhir the Proud dwells in the *sídhe* of Bri Lieth, Slieve Callory, Co. Longford.

Morrígán—(mor ri-gawn): "phantom queen." A goddess with many names: Macha, Nemain, Dea, and the Badb; and many aspects: battle, victory, sexuality, fertility, sovereignty, and destruction. Lover of the early kings, she helps the Tuatha Dé Danann win the battles at Moy Tura. Later she brings misery to both sides in the *Táin Bó Cuailnge*, especially after Cuchulainn scorns her love. She finally secures his death and settles on him in her form of the raven. She is a shapeshifter and appears as a young and beautiful woman, as a hag, as a raven or a creature of any kind. She appears beside a stream washing the shroud of those who are about to die. The Morrigán is the manifestation of the extremes of sexual desire and viciousness. She epitomizes the lust that verges on the wish to kill, and she delights in mayhem, panic, terror, and overwhelming fear. It may be that the only reason why she originally helps and offers her love to Cuchulainn is because he is the ultimate bringer of carnage in war; in that sense they are a match for each other.

Moy Tura or **Magh Tuireadh**—(moy turra): The "Plain of Towers," site of battles between the Tuatha Dé Danann and the Fir Bolg, and later against the Fomorians. It lies in central southern Co. Sligo.

Muirthemne—(mur-tev-nuh): The Plain of Muirthemne is the home of Cuchulainn. His fortress, Dun Dealgan, is said to be outside Dundalk.

Murna of the White or Fair Neck: A descendent of Nuada and Ethlinn, and mother of Fionn Mac Cumhail.

N

Nemain—(nev-in): A battle goddess who may be one of the three aspects of The Morrigán. Her name means "venomous," and she is described as running and shrieking from spear tip to spear tip in battle.

Nemeton: *Nemed* in Irish. A sacred place. From the Indo-European root word, *nem*, "to lay out." Most continental *nemetons* were square or rectangular, while the insular *nemetons* were circular. A sacred spring or grove.

Nera: One of the few humans to travel safely between this world and the Fairy Realm. He has a son with a woman in the World of the *Sídhe*.

Niamh—(n'iav): "radiance." One Niamh is a daughter of Manannán who dwells with Oisin in the Land of Promise. Another Niamh is the wife of the Ulster champion Conall Cernach who becomes the lover of Cuchulainn just before he dies.

Noisiu—(noy-shu): A Red Branch warrior famous for his singing voice. Deirdre loved him.

Nuada—(nu-ah) or **Nuada Argetlamh**, (ar-ged-lor): Nuada of the Silver Hand, is king of the Tuatha Dé Danann when they arrive in Ireland. When he lost his hand at the first battle of Moy Tura, the great healer Diancecht made him a silver hand. Still he lost the throne, for no man could rule who had a blemish. He eventually was completely healed and regained the throne. The Sword of Truth is in Nuada's possession.

O

Ogham—(ow-am): Ogham is said to be the earliest form of writing in Ireland, and was the gift of Ogma Grian-aineach, "Sunny Face." Ogham is a method of writing letters on wood or stone that originated in a signaling or mnemonic system using the hands and fingers. The inscriptions that survive today from the Celtic era are all on stone. They are read from the ground up and use the edge of the stone as their dividing line. The surviving Ogham stones contain simple statements: a name, the name of the person who caused the stone to be put up, or the name of the person commemorated by the stone, but some could be read as markers that define territory, access, and warnings.

Oisin—(oshen): "little fawn." Son of Fionn Mac Cumhail and Sadb. A great warrior of the Fianna whose adventures included dwelling with Niamh in the Fairy Realm for three weeks. When he returned to this world, 300 years had gone by.

S

Sadb—(sive): "sweet." A daughter of the Tuatha Dé Danann king Bodb Dearg. She is changed into a fawn by a "Dark Druid," and is found by Fionn Mac Cumhail. She resumes her human form and becomes Fionn's first and perhaps only true love. Taken by the Dark Druid, Sadb again becomes a fawn and gives birth to Oisin.

Samhain—(saw-in): The cross-quarter festival between Autumn Equinox and Winter Solstice, celebrated by the Celts for a week or more, but now held on October 31. The time when the doorways to the Otherworlds stand open and the powers of the Fairy Realm run riot through this world.

Scáthach—(skaw-ha): "shadow." The greatest woman warrior in the Celtic tradition, who trained the heroes of Ireland in the martial arts on the Isle of Skye. Scáthach was also a poet and a seer.

Sídhe—(shee): The people of the *Sídhe* were the Tuatha Dé Danann who took the earth, the hills, and ancient mounds to dwell in after their defeat by the invading Gaels. Thus the *Sídhe* means both the people, the fairies, and their dwelling places, the hills (known as *sídhes* or *sídhe* hills). Sometimes legendary figures are described as denizens of such a place: so Midhir, for example, is of the *sídhe* of Bri Leith; Aonghus Óg of the *sídhe* of Brú na Boinne. Interestingly, *sídhe* means "peace" in Old Irish, so the Tuatha Dé Danann were also known as *Aes Sídhe*, the "people of peace."

Suibhne—(siv-ney): A late Celtic king cursed by St. Ronan. He becomes mad, but many of his actions, such as flight, are characteristic of shamans.

T

Tailtiu—(tal-t'c): Daughter of the king of the Fir Bolg, Tailtiu is the foster mother of Lugh. Lugh made Lughnasadh a feast in her honor and this was celebrated at what is now Telltown.

Táin—(toyn): A cattle raid, such as the one described in the *Táin Bó Cuailnge* (toyn bo cooli).

Tara: The seat of the High Kings of Ireland. *Temair* or *Teamhair* in Old Irish, the wall of Tea. Located in Co. Meath, "middle," it lies at the center of the four ancient provinces of Ireland: Munster, Leinster, Connacht, and Ulster. Said to be named after Tea, wife of the first King of the Gaels, Eremon. The hill top shows use as a ceremonial site from before 3000 B.C.E. Ráth na Ríg, the "Royal Rath," belongs to the Iron Age, and although construction of further raths eased off after the coming of Christianity, Tara was still thriving up until the Viking invasions of the late eighth century C.E. See Cruachan and Emain Macha.

Tír na mBan—(tir-nah-mahn): "The Land of Women," one of many names for the Land of the Living.

Tír na n'Óg—(tir nah-nohg): "The Land of Youth," another name for the place souls go after death. Like *Tir na mBeo*, the Land of the Living, the inhabitants always remain young and partake in the "Feast of Age." They drink and eat of the food of immortality, described as boar, mead, and apples.

Tuatha Dé Danann—(too-ha-day-dah-nan): The tribe of the goddess Dana. One of several early groups to inhabit Ireland, they were famous for their magical powers. The Celts from Spain—the Gaels or Milesians—defeated them, and they went to live in the ground below the hills.

u

Uisneach—(oos-n'ech): The hill near the center of Ireland where the precursors to the Gaels, the Nemedians, lit a fire to announce their arrival in the land. The cross-quarter festival of Beltane was celebrated there. Also spelled "Usnech" or "Usnach."

Uisliu—(oos-leh): He had three sons who went into exile for the sake of Deirdre.

BIBLIOGRAPHY

Reprinted works are noted where appropriate.

Translations

Calder, G. *Auraicept na nÉces* (Ogham text). Long, 1917.

Carmichael, Alexander. *Carmina Gadelica*. 1900; reprint, Floris Books, 1992.

Cross, Tom Peete, and Clark Harris Slover. *Ancient Irish Tales*. 1936; reprint, Barnes & Noble, 1996.

Faraday, L. Winifred. *The Cattle Raid of Cualnge*. David Nutt, 1904.

Ford, P. K., ed. *The Mabinogion and Other Medieval Welsh Tales*. UC Press, 1977.

Gantz, Jeffrey. *The Mabinogion*. Penguin, 1976.

———. *Early Irish Myths and Sagas*. Penguin, 1981.

Geoffrey of Monmouth. *Vita Merlini*. Trans. J. J. Parry. University of Illinois Press, 1925.

Gray, Elizabeth A. *Cath Maige Tuired* ("The Second Battle of Mag Tuired"). Irish Texts Society, 1983.

Gregory, Lady Augusta. *Cuchulain of Muirthemne*. 1902; reprint, Colin Smythe, 1970.

———. *Gods and Fighting Men*. 1904; reprint, Colin Smythe, 1970.

Hancock, W. N., ed. *Senchus Mór: The Ancient Laws of Ireland*. 1865; reprint, William S. Hein, 1983.

Hull, Eleanor. *The Cuchullin Saga in Irish Literature*. 1898; reprint, AMS Press, 1972.

———. *Pagan Ireland*. Dublin, 1904.

————. *The Cuchulainn Saga*. George G. Harrap & Co, 1911.

Joyce, P. W. *Old Celtic Romances: Tales from Irish Mythology*. 1879; reprint, Devin-Adair, 1962.

Kelly, Fergus. *Audacht Morainn ("The Testament of Morann")*. Dublin Institute for Advanced Studies, 1976.

Kinsella, Thomas. *The Táin*. Dolmen Press, 1969.

Leahy, Arthur H. *Heroic Romances of Ireland*. 1905; reprint, Lemma, 1974.

MacAlister, R. A. Stewart. *Lebor Gabála Érenn, The Book of the Taking of Ireland*, 5 Vols. Irish Texts Society 1939–56.

Matthews, Caitlín & John: see General Reading list.

Meyer, Kuno. *The Voyage of Bran, Son of Febal*. D. Nutt, 1985; reprint, Llanerch 1994.

O'Grady, Standish Hayes. *Silva Gadelica: A Collection of Tales in Irish with Extracts Illustrating Persons and Places*. Williams and Norgate, 1892. Two volumes: Irish text and English translation.

O'Rahilly, Cecile. "*Táin Bó Cualnge*," from the *Book of Leinster Táin*. Dublin Institute for Advanced Studies, 1967.

————. *Táin Bó Cúailnge*, Recension I. Dublin Institute for Advanced Studies, 1976.

Stokes, Whitley. *Cormac's Glossary*. Irish Archaeological and Celtic Society, 1868.

Greek and Roman Sources

Caesar. *Bellum Gallicum*.

Dio Cassius. *Roman History*.

Lucan. *Pharsalia*.

Pliny the Elder. *Naturalis Historia*.

Tacitus. *Annales; Historiae; Agricola*.

The authors Timaeus, Timagenes, Polyhistor, Polybius, Livy, Athenaeus, Diodorus Siculus, and Strabo mention the Celts, but none presents a firsthand account, tending instead to exaggerate the sophistication of the "Noble Savages" they are writing about.

General Reading

Amber K. *True Magick: A Beginner's Guide*. Llewellyn, 1991.

Anand, Margo. *The Art of Sexual Ecstasy*. Putnam, 1989.

Anderson, William. *Green Man*. Thames & Hudson, 1990.

Ashe, Geoffrey. *Dawn Behind the Dawn*. Holt, 1993.

Bahn, Paul G., and Jean Vertut. *Journey through the Ice Age*. University of California Press, 1997.

Berresford Ellis, Peter. *The Celtic Empire*. Constable, 1990

————. *Dictionary of Celtic Mythology*. Constable, 1992. Very useful details.

————. *The Druids*. Constable, 1994. Good scholarly work.

Blamires, Steve. *Celtic Tree Mysteries, Secrets of the Ogham*. Llewellyn, 1997.

Bleakley, Alan. *Fruits of the Moon Tree*. Gateway Books, 1984. Highly imaginative.

Breatnach, Liam. "The Cauldron of Poesy," *Ériu* 32, 1981.

Brown, Norman O. *Love's Body*. Vintage, 1968.

Carr-Gomm, Philip, with Stephanie Carr-Gomm. *The Druid Animal Oracle*. Simon & Schuster, 1995.

————, ed. *The Druid Renaissance*. Thorsons, 1996.

————. *The Druid Way*. Element, 1993.

————. *The Elements of the Druid Tradition*. Element, 1991.

Chadwick, Nora. *The Celts*. Peguin, 1971. Scholarly, but outdated.

————. *The Druids*. University of Wales Press, 1966.

————. *Scottish Gaelic Studies*, vol.4, part 2, Oxford University, 1935.

Corkery, Daniel. *The Hidden Ireland*. Gill and Son, 1924.

Dames, Michael. *Mythic Ireland*. Thames and Hudson, 1992.

Darkstar, Erynn. *The Cauldron of Poesy: Lectures on Irish Magick, Cosmology and Poetry*. Preppie Biker Press, 1992. See also under Erynn Rowan Laurie.

Davidson, Hilda Ellis. *The Lost Beliefs of Northern Europe*. Routledge, 1993. Scholarly and emphasizes Scandinavia.

———. *Myths and Symbols in Pagan Europe: Early Scandinavian and Celtic Religions*. Syracuse University Press, 1988.

Dillon, Myles. and Nora Chadwick. *The Celtic Realms*. New American Library, 1967.

———.*The Cycles of the Kings*. Oxford University Press, 1946.

———. *Early Irish Literature*. University of Chicago Press, 1948.

Evans-Wentz, W. Y. *The Fairy-Faith in Celtic Countries*, 1911; reprint, Colin Smythe, 1977.

Forde-Johnston, J. *Hillforts of the Iron Age in England and Wales*. Liverpool University Press, 1976.

Graves, Robert. *The White Goddess*. Faber, 1952.

Green, Miranda J. *Celtic Goddesses*. British Museum, 1995.

———. *The Celtic World*. Routledge, 1995.

———. *Dictionary of Celtic Myth and Legend*. Thames & Hudson, 1992.

———.*The World of the Druids*. Thames & Hudson, 1997.

———. *The Gods of the Celts*. Alan Sutton, 1986.

Hancock, W. N. *Senchus Mór, The Ancient Laws of Ireland,* vol. 1. Wm. S. Hein Co., 1983.

Henry, P. L. "The Cauldron of Poesy," *Studia Celtica* 14/15, 1979/1980.

Hutton, Ronald. *The Pagan Religions of the Ancient British Isles: Their Nature and Legacy*. Basil Blackwell, 1991.

———. *The Stations of the Sun: A History of the Ritual Year in Britain*. Oxford University Press, 1996. Ronald tends to be critical in his scholarship, but enjoys a good pagan ritual.

Hyde, Douglas. *The Story of Early Gaelic Literature*. T. Fisher Unwin, 1894.

———. *A Literary History of Ireland*. 1899; reprint, London, 1967.

James, Simon. *The World of the Celts*. Thames & Hudson, 1993. Excellent History.

Jones, Prudence, and Nigel Pennick. *A History of Pagan Europe*. Routledge, 1995. A sound look at paganism and its revivals.

Keating, Geoffrey. *Foras Feasa ar Éirinn* (The History of Ireland, 4 vols.). Irish Texts Society, 1901, 1908, 1914.

King, John. *The Celtic Druids' Year: Seasonal Cycles of the Ancient Celts*. Blandford, 1994. Speculative.

Kurtz, Katharine: her Deryni series of novels treats many of the magical subjects discussed here in the context of an alternate universe. *Deryni Checkmate, Deryni Rising, High Deryni,* and *Deryni Magic* remain classics in the Fantasy genre.

Laurie, Erynn Rowan. *The Cauldron of Poesy: Lectures on Irish Magick, Cosmology and Poetry*. Preppie Biker Press, 1997. See also under Erynn Darkstar.

———. *A Circle of Stones: Journeys and Meditations for Modern Celts*. Eschaton, 1995.

Llywelyn, Morgan: all of her novels are highly recommended, especially *The Red Branch, Druid, Bard, Grania,* and *Finn Mac Cool*.

MacCana, Proinsias. *Celtic Mythology*. Hamlyn, 1970. Careful Irish scholarship, if chauvinistic.

MacCrossan, Tadhg. *The Sacred Cauldron: Secrets of the Druids*. Llewellyn, 1992.

———. *The Truth About the Druids* (pamphlet). Llewellyn, 1993.

Mann, Nicholas R. *The Dark God*. Llewellyn, 1996.

———. *His Story: Masculinity in the Post-Patriarchal World*. Llewellyn, 1995.

———. *The Isle of Avalon*. Llewellyn, 1996.

———. *The Keltic Power Symbols*. Glastonbury, 1987.

———. *The Silver Branch Cards: Divination Using Celtic Symbolism and Mythology*. Druidways, 2000.

Mann, Nicholas R., and Marcia Sutton. *Giants of Gaia*. Brotherhood of Life, 1995.

Markale, Jean. *Women of the Celts*. Editions Payot, 1972; reprint, Inner Traditions, 1986.

Matthews, Caitlín. *Arthur and the Sovereignty of Britain*. Arkana, 1989.

———. *The Elements of the Celtic Tradition*. Element Books, 1989. Fascinating and inspiring work.

———. *Mabon and the Mysteries of Britain*. Arkana, 1987.

Matthews, John. *The Druid Source Book*. Blandford, 1996. A full account of what has been written about Druidism, but, strangely, overlooks early Celtic sources of Druidism and is uncritical of recent fabrications.

———. *Taliesin: Shamanism and the Bardic Mysteries in Britain and Ireland*. The Aquarian Press, 1991.

Matthews, Caitlín and John. *The Encyclopaedia of Celtic Wisdom*. Element, 1994. Essential reading.

Metzner, Ralph. *The Well of Remembrance*. Shambhala, 1994. Norse/Germanic lore.

Michell, John. *The Dimensions of Paradise*, Thames & Hudson, 1988. Speculative, not Celtic.

———. *The New View Over Atlantis*. Thames & Hudson, 1983.

Miles, Dillwyn. *The Secret of the Bards of the Isle of Britain*. Gwasg Dinefwr Press, 1992. Contains no secrets, but has the history of the Welsh Eisteddfod.

Naddair, Kaledon. "Some Secrets from the Shamanistic Calendar." *Inner Keltia*, 8 (1985) and 9 (1987). Keltia Publications.

Nichols, Ross. *The Book of Druidry*. Aquarian Press, 1975; reprint, 1990.

O'Donohue, John. *Anam Cara*. HarperCollins, 1997.

Orloff, Judith, M.D. *Second Sight*. Warner Books, 1997.

Piggott, Stuart. *The Druids*. Thames and Hudson, 1968. An early and biased authority; not recommended.

Raftery, Barry. *Pagan Celtic Ireland: The Enigma of the Irish Iron Age*. Thames & Hudson, 1994. Excellent source for Irish Celtic archaeology.

Rees, Alwyn, and Brinley Rees. *Celtic Heritage: Ancient Tradition in Ireland and Wales*. Grove Press, 1961.

Rinpoche, Sogyal. *The Tibetan Book of Living and Dying*. HarperCollins, 1995.

Roads, Michael J. *Talking with Nature*. H J Kramer, 1987.

Ross, Anne. *Pagan Celtic Britain*. Routledge & Kegan Paul, 1967. A mine of information.

Rutherford, Ward. *Celtic Mythology*. Sterling Publishing, 1990.

Senches, Mór. *The Ancient Laws of Ireland*, vol.1, edited by W.N. Hancock. Wm. S. Hein Co., 1983.

Shallcrass, Philip. *A Druid Directory*. British Druid Order, St Leonards-on-Sea, 1995.

Sjoestedt, M. L. *Gods and Heroes of the Celts* (trans. M. Dillon). UC Press, 1982.

Skene, W. F. *The Four Ancient Books of Wales*. AMS Press, 1984-5.

Smith, Cam. *Notes from the Mountain*. (Self-published), 1971.

Spence, Lewis. *The History and Origins of Druidism*. Rider & Co, 1947. We include this citation only to warn our readers away from this work: this and *The Mysteries of Britain* are books to AVOID!

Squire, Charles. *Celtic Myth and Legend*. Gresham, 1905. Dated but useful.

Starhawk. *The Spiral Dance*. Harper San Francisco, 1989.

———. *Truth or Dare*. Harper & Row, 1990.

Stewart, R. J. *Celtic Gods, Goddesses*. Blandford Press, 1990.

Stewart, R. J., and Robin Williamson. *Celtic Bards, Celtic Druids*. Blandford, 1996.

Thom, Alexander. *Megalithic Sites in Britain*. Oxford, 1967.

Thorsson, Edred. *The Book of Ogham: The Celtic Tree Oracle*. Llewellyn, 1992.

Walton, Evangeline: her novels retell the Welsh legends of the *Mabinogion*: *Prince of Annwn*, *The Children of Llyr*, *The Song of Rhiannon*, and *The Island of the Mighty*. Collier Books.

Webster, Graham. *The British Celts and Their Gods Under Rome*. B. T. Batsford, 1986.

Whitefield, Patrick. *How to Make a Forest Garden*. Permanent Publications, 1996.

Young, Ella. *Celtic Wonder Tales*. 1910; reprint, Dover, 1995.

Index

C

H

I

J

K

L

M

N

V

W

☾ REACH FOR THE MOON

Llewellyn publishes hundreds of books on your favorite subjects! To get these exciting books, including the ones on the following pages, check your local bookstore or order them directly from Llewellyn.

ORDER BY PHONE

- Call toll-free within the U.S. and Canada, 1-877-NEW WRLD
- In Minnesota, call (651) 291-1970
- We accept VISA, MasterCard, and American Express

ORDER BY MAIL

- Send the full price of your order (MN residents add 7% sales tax) in U.S. funds, plus postage & handling to:

  Llewellyn Worldwide
  P.O. Box 64383, Dept. 1-56718-481-2
  St. Paul, MN 55164–0383, U.S.A.

POSTAGE & HANDLING

- **Standard** (U.S., Mexico, & Canada)
  If your order is:

  $20.00 or under, add $5.00
  $20.01–$100.00, add $6.00
  Over $100, shipping is free

  (Continental U.S. orders ship UPS. AK, HI, PR, & P.O. Boxes ship USPS 1st class. Mex. & Can. ship PMB.)
- **Second Day Air** (Continental U.S. only): $10.00 for one book + $1.00 per each additional book
- **Express** (AK, HI, & PR only) [Not available for P.O. Box delivery. For strect address delivery only.]: $15.00 for one book + $1.00 per each additional book
- **International Surface Mail**: Add $1.00 per item
- **International Airmail**: Books—Add the retail price of each item; Non-book items—Add $5.00 per item

Please allow 4-6 weeks for delivery on all orders.
Postage and handling rates subject to change.

DISCOUNTS

We offer a 20% discount to group leaders or agents. You must order a minimum of 5 copies of the same book to get our special quantity price.

FREE CATALOG

Get a free copy of our color catalog, *New Worlds of Mind and Spirit*. Subscribe for just $10.00 in the United States and Canada ($30.00 overseas, airmail). Call 1-877-NEW WRLD today!

Visit our web site at www.llewellyn.com for more information.

GLAMOURY
Magic of the Celtic Green World
Steve Blamires

Glamoury refers to an Irish Celtic magical tradition that is truly holistic, satisfying the needs of the practitioner on the physical, mental, and spiritual levels. This guidebook offers practical exercises and modern versions of time-honored philosophies that will expand your potential into areas previously closed to you.

We have moved so far away from our ancestors' closeness to the Earth—the Green World—that we have nearly forgotten some very important truths about human nature that are still valid. *Glamoury* brings these truths to light so you can take your rightful place in the Green World. View and experience the world in a more balanced, meaningful way. Meet helpers and guides from the Otherworld who will become your valued friends. Live in tune with the seasons and gauge your inner growth in relation to the Green World around you.

The ancient Celts couched their wisdom in stories and legends. Today, intuitive people can learn much from these tales. *Glamoury* presents a system based on Irish Celtic mythology to guide you back to the harmony with life's cycles that our ancestors knew.

1-56718-069-8, 352 pp., 6 x 9, illus.   **$16.95**

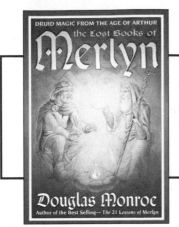

THE LOST BOOKS OF MERLYN
Druid Magic from the Age of Arthur
Douglas Monroe

Initiation and apprenticeship. Since the publication of *The 21 Lessons of Merlyn* five years ago, author Douglas Monroe has received more than 20,000 letters requesting help in how to touch these two ancient elements in our modern world.

The Lost Books of Merlyn is now that guide, and you are the apprentice. Become an active participant in three mythological stories, restored for today's reader from the famous and rare sixteenth-century Druid text entitled the *Book of Pheryllt*.

A grimoire follows each story that explains the magical elements in the story and provides instructions on how to reenact the lessons and replicate the rituals. These grimoires are the next best thing to viewing a magician's personal Book of Shadows, which contains knowledge specially reserved for a chosen apprentice.

1-56718-471-5, 480 pp., 6 x 9, illus. $14.95

To order, call 1-800-THE MOON
Prices subject to change without notice

CELTIC TREE MYSTERIES
Practical Druid Magic & Divination
Steve Blamires

Trees are living, developing aspects of the Green World. So too is the magic associated with them. It could be said that they are the only thing that has remained constant since the days of the ancient Irish druids. Now, *Celtic Tree Mysteries* revives the ancient knowledge and lore of the trees with a practical system of magical ritual and divination.

You will create your own set of Ogham sticks by working on three levels: physically, you will learn to locate and identify each of the twenty trees . . . magically, you will perform Otherworld journeys and rituals to prepare yourself and your Ogham sticks for use . . . spiritually, you will align yourself with the forces of the Green World in your area.

You will also learn to open the deeper, hidden meanings contained within the beautiful, ancient Celtic legends, especially the apparently superficial nature poetry, which contains very precise and detailed magical instructions.

1-56718-070-1, 312 pp., 6 x 9, illus.   **$14.95**

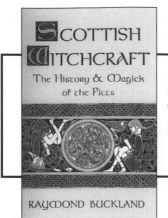

SCOTTISH WITCHCRAFT
The History & Magick of the Picts
Raymond Buckland

From the ancient misty Highlands of Scotland to modern-day America come the secrets of solitary Witchcraft practice. *Scottish Witchcraft* explores "PectiWita," or the craft of the Picts, the mysterious early Keltic people. The Scottish PectiWita tradition differs in many ways from the Wicca of England—there is little emphasis on the worship of the gods (though it is there), but more on the living and blending of magick into everyday life.

Many people attracted to modern-day Wicca are unable to contact or join a coven. PectiWita is a path for the solitary Witch; and here, for the first time, are full details of this solitary branch of the Old Ways. Learn the history of the Picts, their origins and beliefs. Learn how to make simple tools and use them to work magic. Through step-by-step instructions you are brought into touch and then into complete harmony with all of nature. Explore their celebrations, talismans, song and dance, herbal lore, runes and glyphs, and recipes. Learn how to practice the religion in the city and with groups. Ray Buckland's contact with the late Aidan Breac, a descendent of the Picts, led to his interest in *Scottish Witchcraft* and to writing this present volume.

0-87542-057-5, 256 pp., 5¼ x 8, illus., photos   **$9.95**

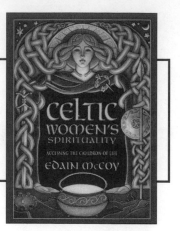

CELTIC WOMEN'S SPIRITUALITY
Accessing the Cauldron of Life
Edain McCoy

Every year, more and more women turn away from orthodox religions, searching for an image of the divine that is more like themselves—feminine, strong, and compelling. Likewise, each year the ranks of the Pagan religions swell, with a great many of these newcomers attracted to Celtic traditions.

The Celts provide some of the strongest, most archetypally accessible images of strong women onto which you can focus your spiritual impulses. Warriors and queens, mothers and crones, sovereigns and shapeshifters, all have important lessons to teach us about ourselves and the universe.

This book shows how you can successfully create a personalized pathway linking two important aspects of the self—the feminine and the hereditary (or adopted) Celtic—and as a result become a whole, powerful woman, awake to the new realities previously untapped by your subconscious mind.

1-56718-672-6, 352 pp., 7 x 10, illus.   **$16.95**

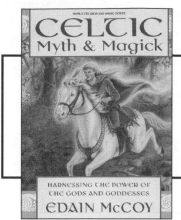

CELTIC MYTH & MAGIC
Harness the Power of the Gods & Goddesses
Edain McCoy

Tap into the mythic power of the Celtic goddesses, gods, heroes, and heroines to aid your spiritual quests and magickal goals. *Celtic Myth & Magic* explains how to use creative ritual and pathworking to align yourself with the energy of these archetypes, whose potent images live deep within your psyche.

Celtic Myth & Magic begins with an overview of forty-nine different types of Celtic Paganism followed today, then gives specific instructions for evoking and invoking the energy of the Celtic pantheon to channel it toward magickal and spiritual goals and into esbat, sabbat, and life transition rituals. Three detailed pathworking texts will take you on an inner journey where you'll join forces with the archetypal images of Cuchulain, Queen Maeve, and Merlin the Magician to bring their energies directly into your life. The last half of the book clearly details the energies of over 300 Celtic deities and mythic figures so you can evoke or invoke the appropriate deity to attain a specific goal.

This inspiring, well-researched book will help solitary Pagans who seek to expand the boundaries of their practice to form working partnerships with the divine.

1-56718-661-0, 464 pp., 7 x 10 $19.95

A BARD'S BOOK OF PAGAN SONGS
Stories and Music from the Celtic World
Now with music CD inside!
Hugin the Bard

Enchant the ears and imaginations of all who hear you play the fifty original songs in this book. Plus, you can now hear Hugin the Bard perform selections from the book on the CD that has just been added!

Everything you need to perform the songs is provided: complete lyrics, chord charts, and lead sheets with the key signature, chords, and melody lines. Each song is accompanied by a story, tale, or bit of Pagan lore all set down in Hugin's own calligraphy.

The new CD features Hugin's enthusiastic rendition of "Bardic Tales from the Mabinogion." The *Mabinogion* is a collection of ancient Welsh tales, put down in the old Welsh language in the sixth century. Hugin brings them to life through song, guitar, and storytelling in the 60 minute CD.

• Celebrate the Goddess, magic, love, and adventure through songs, chants, and stories

• Immerse yourself in the beautiful tales from the Mabinogion

• Journey through the Wheel of the Year with eleven songs that honor the Sabbats

• Raise energy for your Circles, feasts, and gatherings with Hugin's unique chants and invocations

• Make your rituals more rewarding and fun

1-56718-658-0, 272 pp., 8¼ x 10   **$19.95**

To order, call 1-800-THE MOON
Prices subject to change without notice

SHAPESHIFTER TAROT
D. J. Conway and Sirona Knight
Illustrated by Lisa Hunt

Like the ancient Celts, you can now practice the shamanic art of shapeshifting and access the knowledge of the eagle, the oak tree or the ocean: wisdom that is inherently yours and resides within your very being. The *Shapeshifter Tarot* kit is your bridge between humans, animals and nature. The cards in this deck act as merging tools, allowing you to tap into the many different animal energies, together with the elemental qualities of air, fire, water and earth.

The accompanying book gives detailed explanations on how to use the cards, along with their full esoteric meanings, and mythological and magical roots. Exercises in shapeshifting, moving through gateways, doubling out, meditation and guided imagery give you the opportunity to enhance your levels of perception and awareness, allowing you to hone and accentuate your magical understanding and skill.

1-56718-384-0, Boxed kit: 81 full-color cards, instruction book   **$29.95**

OMENS, OGHAMS & ORACLES
Divination in the Druidic Tradition
Richard Webster

Although hundreds of books have been written about the Celts and the druids, no book has focused exclusively on Celtic divination—until now. *Omens, Oghams & Oracles* covers the most important and practical methods of divination in the Celtic and druidic traditions, two of which have never before been published: an original system of divining using the druidic Ogham characters, and "Arthurian divination," which employs a geomantic oracle called druid sticks.

Even if you have no knowledge or experience with any form of divination, this book will show you how to create and use the 25 Ogham *fews* and the druid sticks immediately to gain accurate and helpful insights into your life. This book covers divination through sky stones, touchstones, bodhran drums and other means, with details on how to make these objects and sample readings to supplement the text. Beautiful illustrations of cards made from the Oghams, geomantic figures and more enhance this clear and informative book, which also includes chapters on the history, lives and philosophy of the Celts and druids.

Many Celtic divinatory methods are as useful today as they were 2,000 years ago—make modern forms of these ancient oracles work for you!

1–56718–800–1, 7 x 10, 224 pp.   **$12.95**

BY OAK, ASH & THORN
Modern Celtic Shamanism
D. J. Conway

Many spiritual seekers are interested in shamanism because it is a spiritual path that can be followed in conjunction with any religion or other spiritual belief without conflict. Shamanism has not only been practiced by Native American and African cultures—for centuries, it was practiced by the Europeans, including the Celts.

By Oak, Ash & Thorn presents a workable, modern form of Celtic shamanism that will help anyone raise his or her spiritual awareness. Here, in simple, practical terms, you will learn to follow specific exercises and apply techniques that will develop your spiritual awareness and ties with the natural world: shape-shifting, divination by the Celtic Ogham alphabet, Celtic shamanic tools, traveling to and using magick in the three realms of the Celtic otherworlds, empowering the self, journeying through meditation, and more.

Shamanism begins as a personal revelation and inner healing, then evolves into a striving to bring balance and healing into the Earth itself. This book will ensure that Celtic shamanism will take its place among the spiritual practices that help us lead fuller lives.

1–56718–166-X, 320 pp., 6 x 9, illus.   **$14.95**

To order, call 1-800-THE MOON
Prices subject to change without notice

CELTIC FOLKLORE COOKING
Joanne Asala

Celtic cooking is simple and tasty, reflecting the quality of its ingredients: fresh meat and seafood, rich milk and cream, fruit, vegetables, and wholesome bread. Much of the folklore, proverbs, songs, and legends of the Celtic nations revolve around this wonderful variety of food and drink. Now you can feast upon these delectable stories as you sample more than 200 tempting dishes with *Celtic Folklore Cooking*.

In her travels to Ireland, Wales, and Scotland, Joanne Asala found that many people still cook in the traditional manner, passing recipes from generation to generation. Now you can serve the same dishes discovered in hotels, bed and breakfasts, restaurants, and family kitchens. At the same time, you can relish in the colorful proverbs, songs, and stories that are still heard at pubs and local festivals and that complement each recipe.

1-56718-044-2, 264 pp., 7 x 10, illus.   **$17.95**

ENCHANTMENT OF THE FAERIE REALM
Communicate with Nature Spirits & Elementals
Ted Andrews

Nothing fires the imagination more than the idea of faeries and elves. Folklore research reveals that people from all over the world believe in rare creatures and magickal realms. Unfortunately, in our search for the modern life we have grown insensitive to the nuances of nature. Yet those ancient realms do still exist, though the doorways to them are more obscure. Now, for the first time, here is a book with practical, in-depth methods for recognizing, contacting, and working with the faerie world.

Enchantment of the Faerie Realm will help you to remember and realize that faeries and elves still dance in nature and in your heart. With just a little patience, persistence, and instruction, you will learn how to recognize the presence of faeries, nature spirits, devas, elves, and elementals. You will learn which you can connect with most easily. You will discover the best times and places for faerie approach. And you will develop a new respect and perception of the natural world. By opening to the hidden realms of life and their resources, you open your innate ability to work with energy and life at all levels.

0-87542-002-8, 240 pp., 6 x 9, illus.   **$10.00**

CELTIC DRAGON TAROT

D.J. Conway & Lisa Hunt

Are dragons real? Since they do not live on the physical plane, scientists cannot trap and dissect them. Yet magicians and psychics who have explored the astral realms know firsthand that dragons do indeed exist, and that they make very powerful co-magicians. Dragons tap into deeper currents of elemental energies than humans. Because of their ancient wisdom, dragons are valuable contacts to call upon when performing any type of divination, such as the laying out of tarot cards. Tarot decks and other divination tools seem to fascinate them. *The Celtic Dragon Tarot* is the first deck to use the potent energies of dragons for divination, magickal spell working, and meditation.

Ancient mapmakers noted every unknown territory with the phrase "Here be dragons." Both tarot and magick have many uncharted areas. Not only will you discover dragons waiting there, but you will also find them to be extremely helpful when you give them the chance.

1-56718-182-1
**Boxed set: 78 full-color cards
with 216 pp., 6 x 9 book**   **$29.95**